Katherine Mansfield and Periodical Culture

Katherine Mansfield and Periodical Culture

Chris Mourant

EDINBURGH
University Press

Edinburgh University Press is one of the leading university presses in the UK. We publish academic books and journals in our selected subject areas across the humanities and social sciences, combining cutting-edge scholarship with high editorial and production values to produce academic works of lasting importance. For more information visit our website: edinburghuniversitypress.com

Edinburgh University Press Ltd
The Tun – Holyrood Road, 12(2f) Jackson's Entry, Edinburgh EH8 8PJ

First published in hardback by Edinburgh University Press 2019

Typeset in Sabon and Futura
by R. J. Footring Ltd, Derby

A CIP record for this book is available from the British Library

ISBN 978 1 4744 3945 9 (hardback)
ISBN 978 1 4744 3946 6 (paperback)
ISBN 978 1 4744 3947 3 (webready PDF)
ISBN 978 1 4744 3948 0 (epub)

Contents

List of Figures

Acknowledgements

Many people have helped me bring this book to publication and I have accumulated many debts of gratitude. Firstly, I am extremely grateful to Nadia Lasserson, daughter of Miron Grindea, for opening her home to me so that I could examine archival material relating to *Adam International Review* and for kindly granting permission to reproduce some of this material here. Additionally, I would like to thank the following archives and institutions for granting permission to reproduce images or to quote from unpublished material: the Alexander Turnbull Library in Wellington; the Special Collections at the University of Edinburgh; the Fergusson Gallery in Perth; the Modernist Journals Project; the National Library of Australia; the King's College London Archives; and the Special Collections at the University of Leeds. Parts of the section '"Bites from the Apple"' in Chapter 1 will also be published in *Aphoristic Modernity* (ed. Kostas Boyiopoulos and Michael Shallcross, Rodopi/Brill, 2019). A version of the section 'The French debate' in Chapter 1 was originally published in *Katherine Mansfield's French Lives* (ed. Claire Davison and Gerri Kimber, Rodopi/Brill, 2016: 108–24). A version of the section 'Parodic translation' in Chapter 2 was originally published in *Katherine Mansfield Studies*, 7 (2015): 15–30. And a version of the section 'Between two worlds' in Chapter 3 was originally published in *Katherine Mansfield and the Bloomsbury Group* (ed. Todd Martin, Bloomsbury, 2017: 161–80). I am grateful to the publishers for permission to reprint this work here. Despite my efforts, some copyright holders remained untraced, or had not replied to correspondence at the time this book went to press. If you hold or administer rights for materials published here, please contact the publisher. I am also grateful to the King's College London Graduate School and the Leverhulme Trust for providing the funding that helped to support my research.

Most importantly, I would like to acknowledge the numerous professional and personal debts I have accumulated in writing this book. My ideas took shape in a doctoral thesis completed at King's College London under the kind and patient supervision of Anna Snaith. This book would not have been possible without Anna's guidance and expertise. The feedback of Max Saunders and Mark Turner in the early stages of this project also helped to shape its direction, while my examiners Rebecca Beasley and Janet Wilson provided useful suggestions on how the thesis might be developed into a monograph. Since 2013, I have been fortunate to work alongside a number of inspiring people on the executive committee of the British Association for Modernist Studies, and my research has benefited immeasurably from the activities of the Katherine Mansfield Society. Special thanks go to Gerri Kimber, who has done so much for Mansfield scholarship, and Claire Davison, for her remarkable generosity in encouraging my work. Since completing my doctorate, the friendship and support offered by a number of colleagues at Nottingham Trent University and the University of Birmingham have enabled me to finish this book. Thanks in particular go to Arin Keeble, Rachel Sykes and Toria Johnson, and to the members of the Centre for Modernist Cultures at Birmingham, including Andrzej Gąsiorek, Deborah Longworth, Dan Moore, Nathan Waddell and Emma West. I would also like to thank my students, for the stimulating discussions in seminars and supervisions that have helped me to develop and clarify ideas about the print cultures of modernism. My editors at Edinburgh University Press, Jackie Jones and Ersev Ersoy, have been supportive throughout the process from proposal to publication, for which I am very grateful, and the detailed, considered comments offered by my anonymous readers were invaluable in helping to make this a better book.

Finally, I am immensely grateful to my friends and family, who have lived patiently with Katherine Mansfield for several years now. Thank you to the Wain clan, for all the fun. Thank you to my sister Katy and my parents, Gill and Nick, whose love and support have made this possible. And last but by no means least, thank you to Jessica – for everything.

Introduction: 'The famous New Zealand Mag.-story writer'

> My literary career began with short-story writing in New Zealand. I was nine years old when my first attempt was published. I have been filling notebooks ever since. After I came to London I worked for some time for *The New Age*, and published *In a German Pension* in 1912 [*sic*]. It was a bad book, but the press was kind to it. Later, I worked with my present husband, Mr John Middleton Murry, editor of *The Athenaeum*, but at that time editor of *Rhythm* and *The Blue Review*. In the past two years I have reviewed novels for *The Athenaeum*, and I have written more short stories.[1]

Katherine Mansfield viewed her literary career through the prism of periodical publication. Written in the summer of 1921, the above draft of a letter composed in one of her notebooks provides a striking illustration of how Mansfield presented her credentials to others and assessed her reputation as a writer prior to the publication of her most successful short story collection, *The Garden Party and Other Stories*, in that *annus mirabilis* of literary modernism, 1922. Comprising satirical sketches first printed in the political weekly *The New Age*, Mansfield's first short story collection, *In a German Pension*, was published at the end of 1911. It was another nine years before she published another book, with *Bliss and Other Stories* appearing in December 1920. In the intervening years, however, Mansfield was prolific in her output, contributing work to 'little magazines' such as *Rhythm*, *The Blue Review* and *The Signature*, to established periodicals such as *The New Age* and *The Athenaeum*, as well as making brief appearances in diverse publications such as *T.P.'s Weekly*, *The Saturday Westminster Gazette*, *The Times Literary Supplement* and *The English Review*. Before the publication of *The Garden Party* in 1922, therefore, it was as a contributor to magazines and periodicals on which Mansfield's reputation hinged; indeed, even with *The Garden Party* in circulation, Wyndham Lewis could still describe her as 'the famous New

Zealand Mag.-story writer'.[2] Encompassing a dismissive attitude towards Mansfield's nationality as well as disdain for the kind of mass-market magazines for which she was beginning to write, Lewis's comment was certainly not meant as a compliment, but his pithy characterisation speaks volumes about how Mansfield was viewed by her contemporaries. In the decade spanning the years 1910 to 1920, it was as a colonial woman contributing to magazines and periodicals that Mansfield made a name for herself within the London literary establishment.

This book examines Mansfield's contributions to and interactions with early twentieth-century periodical culture as a means of defamiliarising and recontextualising her life and work. As Faye Hammill and Mark Hussey have recently observed, 'print culture scholarship is not only adding knowledge to our understanding of modernism, but also transforming what we thought we knew about canonical writers'.[3] It is the central claim of this book that situating Mansfield's work within the original print contexts of magazines and periodicals fundamentally changes how we understand and interpret her writings. In making this claim, I am responding to an explosion of scholarly interest over recent years in early twentieth-century print cultures. Major digitisation projects, such as the Modernist Journals Project, the Blue Mountain Project and the Modernist Magazines Project, have made a wealth of primary material readily accessible to scholars of the modernist period, leading to the emergence of 'modern periodical studies' as a distinct field of academic enquiry. Such initiatives have stimulated an astonishing breadth of research that is best represented by *The Oxford Critical and Cultural History of Modernist Magazines*, published in three volumes and containing chapters by hundreds of scholars examining the magazines and periodicals of Britain and Ireland, North America and mainland Europe. Such wide-ranging work has reshaped the contours of modernist studies.

Katherine Mansfield has gained an increasingly central position within this field of modern periodical scholarship. In tracing the development of her writing career, Mansfield's biographers have always recognised the importance of her association with magazines and periodicals. In particular, our understanding of Mansfield's life and work would be much poorer in this regard if it weren't for Antony Alpers's unsurpassed biography.[4] Until very recently, however, Mansfield's biographical narrative has dominated how we have understood her interactions with periodical culture. Rather than pay close attention to the magazines and periodicals themselves as texts worthy of study, it has been commonplace for scholars to explain Mansfield's association with various publications through biographical contexts, such as her romantic relationship with John Middleton Murry, editor of many of the magazines to which she contributed, or her volatile rivalry with Beatrice Hastings, co-editor of *The New Age*. Recent scholarship, however, has begun to look beyond the personal, reorienting focus on the publication contexts themselves and extending our understanding beyond the limitations of biographical analysis. Such work has made significant inroads in revealing the manifold ways in which Mansfield made full use of the opportunities afforded by magazines and periodicals as media. Entering these publication spaces, Mansfield engaged with various social, political and cultural debates, and developed her writing style by playing with different identities, genres and modes of address. As a result of this scholarship, it is no longer possible to explain away Mansfield's work for the periodical press through reference to her personal loyalties and rivalries, or the financial necessity of making money by her pen; frequently, the periodical press provided an enabling space that Mansfield approached with very specific political and literary preoccupations.

Whilst there exists no single study devoted to examining Mansfield's relation to periodical print culture, therefore, this book responds to a range of recent scholarship that has begun to position Mansfield as a prototypical 'magazine modernist'. By resituating her work in *The New Age*, for instance, Lee Garver has shown how Mansfield's early writings were influenced by contemporary political thought.[5] Likewise, Carey Snyder has examined how Mansfield's association with *The New Age* enabled her to experiment with satire and parody.[6] Snyder has also shown how Mansfield's contributions to *Rhythm* engaged with the ideas and aesthetics of modernist primitivism promoted across the magazine.[7] The latter article by Snyder is indicative of the increasing attention *Rhythm* has garnered in much recent work on Mansfield as a means of reassessing her status as a colonial woman writer working in London. Angela Smith, in particular, has been at the forefront of a critical reappraisal of Mansfield as a writer of non-belonging, a 'liminal' artist at home neither in England nor in New Zealand, constantly writing from a position 'in-between'. In order to advance this argument, Smith has written extensively about Mansfield's association with *Rhythm* and her interactions with the expatriate Fauvist contributors to the magazine.[8] Similarly, Anna Snaith has focused on Mansfield's contributions to *Rhythm* in order to situate her within a constellation of colonial women writers working in London in the early twentieth century who 'used periodicals to construct, reinvent and test out their otherness'.[9] Most importantly, Faith Binckes's study of *Rhythm* provides a thorough, fully contextualised analysis of the magazine that examines its visual components and interrogates the ways in which Mansfield repositioned her work following her break with *The New Age*.[10] Like Binckes, Sydney Janet Kaplan offers a detailed historicist account of Mansfield's periodical contributions, highlighting the circulation of ideas that took place between Mansfield, Murry and D. H. Lawrence after 1916.[11] Whilst Kaplan is at pains to demonstrate equivalences between the personal lives of all three writers and their work, grounding her analysis in a group biographical narrative, she also focuses on the inter-textual echoes that exist across their writings in *The Athenaeum* and, after Mansfield's death, in *The Adelphi*, examining the specific contexts of periodical publication, the mechanics of textual recirculation and the role played by literary networks.

As implied by Lewis's dismissal of Mansfield as 'the famous New Zealand Mag.-story writer', there was a time when Mansfield's self-proclaimed position as the 'little colonial' – suspiciously embroiled in the feminised mass market of 'popular' literature and the messy commercial world of writing for money – risked placing her beyond the parameters of literary modernism; or, more specifically, a version of 'high modernism' institutionalised in the mid-twentieth century that centred around the so-called 'men of 1914' such as Lewis, Ezra Pound, T. S. Eliot and James Joyce.[12] Since the 1980s, those parameters have been decisively challenged and reconfigured by feminist scholars such as Bonnie Kime Scott, whose work has revealed that the 'gender of modernism' was anything but exclusively male, as well as critics influenced by postcolonial theory, who have extended the borders of the modernist canon to include writers such as Mansfield, Mulk Raj Anand, Claude McKay, Una Marson and Jean Rhys.[13] Responding to the work of Andreas Huyssen, moreover, recent scholarship has contested the notion of a 'great divide' between 'high modernism' and mass culture, examining the role played by economics, advertising and marketing techniques in promoting modernist art and literature.[14] Foundational work in the field of periodical scholarship has been at the forefront of this reappraisal, with studies such as Lawrence Rainey's *Institutions of Modernism: Literary Elites and Public Culture* (1999) and Mark Morrison's *The Public Face of Modernism: Little Magazines, Audiences and Reception, 1905–1920* (2001) highlighting connections between literary production and the marketplace of mass culture and self-promotion. Influenced by these studies as well as the 'material turn' inaugurated by the work of George Bornstein and Jerome McGann, Jenny McDonnell's *Katherine Mansfield and the Modernist Marketplace: At the Mercy of the Public* (2010) has examined how Mansfield forged a position for herself across various sites of publication, negotiating the 'popular' and 'literary' markets.

McDonnell's study is an important intervention in Mansfield scholarship and a significant antecedent to this book; it builds on the work of biographers such as Alpers and scholars such as Smith to outline a compelling narrative of Mansfield's life and work as a professional writer. The present book, however, is distinguished from *Katherine Mansfield and the Modernist Marketplace* in several important ways. Firstly, McDonnell's focus is the publishing 'marketplace' widely conceived, and she draws little distinction between the limitations and liberties presented to Mansfield through book publication, on the one hand, and periodical publication, on the other. Developments in periodical scholarship over recent years highlight the importance of remaining critically attuned to these differences. In particular, the present book responds to work in the field of periodical studies that has theorised magazines and periodicals as multi-vocal texts. In an article subtitled 'The Rise of Periodical Studies' published in 2006, for example, Sean Latham and Robert Scholes argued that periodicals are 'rich, dialogic texts' that present many voices and multiple perspectives, and that reveal the complex networks of modernism.[15] Paying particular attention to *The New Age*, likewise, Ann Ardis has also emphasised that periodicals can reveal cultural conflicts and 'Bakhtinian dialogics in the public sphere'.[16] In line with this idea of dialogic exchange, Suzanne Churchill and Adam McKible have proposed 'a conversational model for modernism' when analysing periodicals and magazines; these publications, they write, 'provide loci of identification and difference, allowing us to recover lines of connection, influence, conflict, and resistance that entangle the many strands of modernism'.[17] Similarly, in their general introduction to *The Oxford Critical and Cultural History of Modernist Magazines*, Peter Brooker and Andrew Thacker observe that examining periodicals and magazines helps to expose 'the dialogic matrix of modernism'.[18] McDonnell's narrative of authorship allows little room for this kind of analysis. Notably, McDonnell provides only the most cursory contextualisation of each magazine and periodical that she considers, giving little sense of the various political, aesthetic or social contexts that shaped each publication and Mansfield's interactions with it. Similarly, the writings of key contemporaries of Mansfield are not examined in any depth. The work of Beatrice Hastings, for example, which this book demonstrates must be examined in detail if Mansfield's writings for *The New Age* are to be understood fully, receives no analysis by McDonnell; instead, she offers only a narrative description of the personal relationship between the two women. Indeed, McDonnell states that her focus is on describing 'the editorial relationships that Mansfield forged at these papers'.[19] McDonnell's book is therefore positioned within a tradition of Mansfield scholarship that emphasises the personal, explaining Mansfield's writings through recourse to a biographical narrative. Instead, *Katherine Mansfield and Periodical Culture* looks to capture the rich, multi-vocal and complex nature of magazines and periodicals; it situates Mansfield's writings in dialogue with the work of others and examines the ways in which these writings were intrinsically conditioned by the specific contexts of their first publication. Rather than considering Mansfield's career in isolation, therefore, this book attempts to highlight the ways in which her work was composed and circulated within networks of conversation and conflict, or identification and difference.

Whereas McDonnell's study is invested in ideas of the 'material turn', moreover, this book responds to the 'transnational turn' that has taken place across modernist studies. In 2008, Douglas Mao and Rebecca Walkowitz identified what they termed the 'new modernist studies' of the previous decade, revisionist work that had sought to provide a richer, thicker historical contextualisation of modernism.[20] Modern periodical studies has been integral to this development, revealing previously marginalised voices in the history of modernism and demonstrating how the boundaries between 'high' art and popular forms of mass culture, previously viewed by critics as entrenched, were in fact highly entangled. As well as this 'vertical' expansion of modernist studies, Mao and Walkowitz also divided the new modernist studies into the categories of 'temporal' and 'spatial' expansions. Whilst scholarship belonging to the former category has extended the chronological boundaries of modernism beyond the first half of the twentieth century, scholarship of the latter has widened the field of modernist studies to include alternative writers and traditions; it has extended the canon beyond the metropolitan centres of Britain, America and continental Europe to consider the cultural legacy of anti-colonial movements and postcolonial peoples, and highlighted the connections between modernism and imperialism, nationhood and race. Moreover, this scholarship has emphasised the importance of both linguistic and geographical border crossings and transgressions, examining the role of translational and transnational mobility, circulation and exchange in the development of modernist literature. As a result, what Mao and Walkowitz have identified as the 'transnational turn' in modernist studies has challenged and dissolved previously rigid binaries between centre and periphery, revealing a far more complex picture. As a colonial woman from New Zealand who travelled to England to become a writer, acutely aware in her fiction of the politics and history of exile, race, nationhood and empire, Mansfield has occupied a prominent position within much of this scholarship. In addition to the invaluable work conducted in this area by Smith, Snaith and Snyder referred to above, critics such as Saikat Majumdar and Mark Williams have focused on the cultural legacy of Mansfield's New Zealand heritage,[21] Elleke Boehmer and Urmila Seshagiri have examined the centrality of race in her work,[22] Janet Wilson and Mary Ann Gillies have positioned Mansfield as a 'liminal' artist of non-belonging, situated between both metropolitan centre and colonial periphery,[23] and Claire Davison has examined the significance of Mansfield's collaborative translations with S. S. Koteliansky in shaping the development of her writing practice.[24] Such work has placed Mansfield at the centre of a modernist canon reconfigured by the transnational turn.

What has not been examined in any depth, however, is how periodical culture provided opportunities for Mansfield throughout her career to negotiate many of the issues and concerns discussed above. Whilst my analysis of Mansfield's contributions to magazines and periodicals remains highly attentive to the interpretative strategies promoted by the material turn, focusing on the 'bibliographic codes' of editorial design, page layout and the interaction between textual and visual elements, for example, I also look to scholarship of the transnational turn as offering analytical and theoretical models for approaching and evaluating these engagements with the periodical press. In doing so, this book meets the challenge posed by Patrick Collier, that we must look to establish 'substantive connections between two currently separate and non-communicative – not to say hostile – enterprises in contemporary modernist criticism: on one hand work that focuses on global modernisms, transnational exchange, and modernism's imbrication with empire'; on the other, work that analyses 'print culture and new media rhetorics'.[25] Until recent years, as the tripartite divisions in Mao and Walkowitz's 2008 article suggest, modern periodical studies has remained largely segregated from developments and formulations of the transnational turn. However, there have been some notable attempts to integrate spatial analysis into modern periodical scholarship. Paul Peppis, for example, has highlighted the relation between modernism and empire in the British periodical press, analysing the virulent, recrudescent forms of nationalism and imperialism that found expression in magazines such as *The English Review*, *The New Age* and *BLAST*.[26] Adam McKible's *The Space and Place of Modernism* (2002) focuses on American magazines such as *The Dial* and *The Little Review*, using the concept of 'space' to indicate how each magazine looked to create 'a landscape or geography of the imagination'.[27] As such, McKible examines the ways in which early twentieth-century magazines facilitated imagined transnational and transcultural interactions between America and Russia. The collection of essays edited by Ardis and Collier titled *Transatlantic Print Culture, 1880–1940: Emerging Media, Emerging Modernisms* (2008) emphasises networks of exchange between the print cultures of Britain and North America and maps the ways in which the periodical press in this period enabled the transnational circulation and reception of texts and ideas. Likewise, in *Modernism and the New Spain: Britain, Cosmopolitan Europe, and Literary History* (2012), Gayle Rogers outlines a history of transnational periodical networks in the inter-war period, examining intellectual and translational collaborations between José Ortega y Gasset's *Revista de Occidente* and T. S. Eliot's *The Criterion*, as well as Virginia Woolf's correspondence with Victoria Ocampo, editor of the Argentinian magazine *Sur*. As Peter Kalliney has observed, Rogers's 'scholarship shows a form of cosmopolitanism that was not merely imagined by modernist writers, but also actually practiced through translation and specific cultural institutions'.[28] In *Transatlantic Avant-Gardes: Little Magazines and Localist Modernism* (2013), likewise, Eric White focuses on the periodical networks that connected 'localist' forms of American modernism with European avant-gardes. As such, White looks to establish intersections between the 'physical loci of geographic places, the temporal flux of cultural spaces and the textual locus of the printed page'.[29] And in *Little Magazine, World Form* (2016), Eric Bulson analyses how the form of early twentieth-century Anglo-American and European 'little magazines' travelled and translated into postcolonial national contexts in the second half of the twentieth century, becoming a 'world form'.[30] The attention paid by each of these scholars to the specificities and complexities of transnational periodical networks has helped to challenge simple divisions between the 'transnational' and 'local', the 'international' and 'national', or the 'cosmopolitan' and 'regional'. As Brooker and Thacker have observed, whereas 'an earlier generation of critics tended to talk about the international nature of the "little magazine" spawned by modernism, as if one type fitted all manifestations of the genre', recent scholarship has highlighted the ways in which the inherently dialogic, conflict-riven nature of modernist magazines and periodicals complicates simple binary oppositions.[31] Peppis, for example, demonstrates how 'the cosmopolitan intelligentsia's doctrine of cultural internationalism' in this period was, at base, 'patriotic and imperialist' in its intentions.[32] Rather than impeding or obscuring scholarly interest in the different national and sometimes nationalist traditions of modernist print culture, therefore, the 'transnational turn' has in fact renewed critical attention on these; examples include Sascha Bru's research on Dutch avant-garde periodicals, David Carter's work on the modernity of Australian print cultures and Dean Irvine's study of the women editors of Canadian little magazines.[33]

As well as building on some of this recent work in modern periodical studies, this book also responds to a longer tradition of scholarship in Victorian print studies, a field that has extensively theorised the intersections between periodical space and geographical space. Whilst modern periodical studies has come to prominence only in the last fifteen years, the analysis of print culture has flourished in Victorian studies for decades; the Research Society for Victorian Periodicals, for instance, was established in 1968. As such, the spatial imaginaries of nineteenth-century periodicals have received significant attention. In one of the foundational texts of Victorian periodical studies, for example, Joanne Shattock and Michael Wolff observed that the periodical press provided the context within which people derived their 'sense of the outside world'.[34] This led others to examine the ways in which the material, textual space of the periodical structured perceptions of geographical real-world space, becoming a major site for the production and re-production of national identities and ideologies of empire.[35] As Julie Codell has argued, for example, periodicals 'reshaped the imagined, the virtual, the geopolitical, and perhaps even the physical geographies between Britain and the colonies'.[36] In his examination of *The Illustrated London News*, likewise, Collier has focused on how Victorian periodical culture replicated the imperialist gaze by presenting a commanding view of other lands and subject peoples; the Victorian periodical press, Collier argues, placed 'the reader imaginatively at the centre of a set of overlapping spatial arrays of power' and provided 'the reader with "imaginary mobility" through these spaces'.[37] Collier suggests that the logic of nineteenth-century periodicals was therefore 'metonymic and microcosmic: they shrink the world, on a daily or weekly basis'.[38] A representative example of this metonymic logic is W. T. Stead's *The Review of Reviews*, established in 1890 and published across three continents. Including a prominent image of the globe on every issue as well as a regular opening column titled 'The Progress of the World', *The Review of Reviews* metonymically made the 'world' legible, containable and knowable for its readers.

This metonymic logic can also be seen in the pages of *The New Age*, which is the focus of Chapter 1 of this book. A literary supplement to the issue of the periodical containing Mansfield's second contribution, published in March 1910, includes a map highlighting the journal's international distribution, titled 'The "New Age" World' (Figure I.1). In the first instance, this illustration highlights the periodical networks that *The New Age* forged around the world, announcing the transnational reach of the periodical to cities including Beirut, Shanghai, Buenos Ayres,

Figure I.1 'The "New Age" World'

New Mexico, Penang, Calcutta, Yokohama, Cairo, Mombasa, as well as Mansfield's Wellington. The image therefore highlights what Ardis has identified as 'the *external dialogics* of magazines': 'the mappings of geographical (and temporal) space that they perform as they claim the territories they report on, distribute copies to, take advertisements from'.[39] An international readership was also complemented by a contributor list that included Mansfield as a New Zealander, Hastings from South Africa and writers such as the Irish nationalist Francis Sheehy-Skeffington, the Indian B. K. Das and the Sudanese-Egyptian Duse Mohamed Ali. The periodical therefore served as an international meeting point, connecting people and places across vast geographical distances. Despite the apparently benign gesture of internationalism motivating the publication of 'The "New Age" World', however, the image also implies a politics of imperialist control. Metonymically linking the textual space of the periodical and global space, the illustration promotes the idea that *The New Age* shrinks the world on a weekly basis, making it legible and instantly knowable. In turning the pages of the periodical, therefore, readers are placed in a position of observational power, the 'world' opening out in front of them: by mapping the world, as Ardis suggests, the periodical is able to 'claim' it. As such, the illustration highlights how the spatial imaginary promoted by *The New Age* was integrated into larger projects of nation- and empire-building. This is emphasised by the visual tropes of imperialist mapping in the image, such as the prominent female figure of Britannia, the larger black dot around the United Kingdom and the emphasis on naval domination, which all connect the 'world' of the periodical to the world of the British Empire.

Originally founded as a Christian weekly in 1894, *The New Age* was relaunched under the editorship of A. R. Orage in 1907 to promote socialism. In his first editorial, Orage advocated the foundation of 'a Socialist Federation – a Socialist Empire' and argued that 'the task implicitly before us all, is nothing less than the creation of a British Empire'.[40] Gestures of internationalism in the periodical, such as a 'Socialist Federation', therefore, were almost always formulated with Britain, or more specifically England, positioned at the centre. In the same issue of the periodical containing 'The "New Age" World', for instance, Orage writes in his opening 'Notes of the Week' that 'England has always led the constitutional way [and this] entitles her to ignore the belated and, as it were, consequential experience of other countries' that 'may be inclined to follow'.[41] Affirming a spatial-temporal logic that posits England, the centre of empire, as the crucible of progress, Orage reasons that 'we are English nationalists of an even bigoted order'.[42] This use of the editorial 'we' prompts two questions. To what extent was a writer such as Mansfield excluded from the identity politics promoted by the periodical? And how did a writer from one of those 'other countries' at the peripheries of 'The "New Age" World' map negotiate the competing demands of transnational colonial affiliation and a 'bigoted' form of English nationalism or British imperialism?

In August 1910, Mansfield wrote a letter to the correspondence pages of *The New Age* posing as 'a respectable citizeness [*sic*] of pagan England'.[43] In this short piece, Mansfield disowns her national identity in order to dismiss a recent novel by another colonial writer, glibly observing that if Elinor Glyn is 'the prophetic woman's voice crying out of the wilderness of Canadian literature, let her European sister novelists lift shekelled [*sic*] hands in prayer that the "great gulf" may ever yawn more widely'.[44] Mansfield can be seen here affecting the superior tone of the English metropolitan writer. Whilst this letter is shot through with irony and playfulness, at its heart is a serious anxiety about 'voice' and who has the authority to speak. As a colonial woman just beginning her career as a professional writer, it is significant that Mansfield felt the need to mimic a 'respectable' English critic if she was to come out of the 'wilderness' herself and bridge the 'great gulf' between England and New Zealand. With the colonial peripheries seen as backward and 'wild' in contrast to the civilising centres of Europe, therefore, this letter reaffirms the spatial-temporal logic advanced by Orage. And yet, throughout her other contributions to *The New Age*, as Chapter 1 of this book examines, Mansfield looked to unsettle and challenge the politics of English nationalism and British imperialism; through satire and parody, her sketches offer an overt and radical critique of the very logic that her letter from 'a respectable citizeness of pagan England' appears to subscribe to. In the story 'Being a Truthful Adventure', contributed to *The New Age* in 1911, Mansfield's semi-autobiographical protagonist even identifies herself as an isolated New Zealander. Throughout her writing career, as this book demonstrates, Mansfield's engagements with the periodical press were characterised by exactly these kinds of conflicting allegiances and ambivalent self-identifications.

Mansfield always struggled with feelings of internal division. In a letter written in 1922, for example, she observed: 'I am a divided being: I am always conscious of this secret disruption in me'.[45] As Elleke Boehmer has argued, Mansfield occupied a dualistic position of 'modernist artist as outsider' when in Wellington and 'colonial outsider as modernist' when in London.[46] Returning to New Zealand at the age of seventeen after completing her schooling at Queen's College in London, where she had contributed to the school magazine, studied the cello, learned French and German, gone on brief trips to Europe, and discovered with exhilaration the writings of Oscar Wilde, Walter Pater and Henrik Ibsen, among others, Mansfield viewed Wellington, by contrast, as a dull backwater of bourgeois provinciality. Convinced that she could achieve her ambition of becoming a writer only by returning to London, Mansfield implored her family to let her make the journey back: 'I must get back because I know I shall be successful', she wrote.[47] In 1908, at the age of nineteen, Mansfield made this journey, destined never to see New Zealand again. This early enthusiasm for London as a place of opportunity, however, was quickly superseded by Mansfield's sense of alienation and displacement. Within weeks of her arrival, for example, she writes in a letter: 'I am physically sick – with no home – no place in which I can hang up my hat – & say here I belong – for there is no such place in the wide world for me'.[48] And in her journal, she records feeling that she is merely a trespasser in London: 'I am the little Colonial walking in the London garden patch – allowed to look, perhaps, but not to linger [. . .] a stranger – an alien'.[49] Mansfield has long been recognised as an emblematic figure of modernist exile, isolation and homelessness. As Janet Wilson has observed, however, there remains room 'for further development of a critical practice' that 'challenges the colonial/metropolitan binary in order to reposition Mansfield more decisively as a liminal artist, a colonial-metropolitan modernist who is located outside as well as within the international establishment'.[50] Highlighting the ways in which she was never fully integrated into the communities of print to which she sought access, the examination of Mansfield's periodical contributions allows for a reassessment such as this.

Mansfield's position within the metropolitan periodicals market was doubly precarious, with both her gender and colonial status continually threatening to place her at the margins of cultural authority. As her interactions with *The New Age* highlight, Mansfield's integration into the London literary establishment was often predicated on her performing different authorial identities and negotiating different editorial expectations that required her either to erase her national identity or to adopt different masks that unsettled any sense of a stable, integrated 'self'. The authorial anxiety and uncertainty that this produced, however, frequently manifested themselves in deliberately disruptive interventions that reveal the extent to which early twentieth-century magazines and periodicals accommodated cultural difference and dialogic exchange, rather than consistently imposing hegemonic consensus. In particular, this book is interested in the ways in which Mansfield at times conformed to and at other times critiqued the spatial imaginaries promoted by the magazines and periodicals to which she contributed, and how an examination of these conflicting attitudes of affiliation and resistance allows us to reposition her more decisively as a liminal writer and colonial-metropolitan modernist, located both within and outside the institutional centres figured by the London periodical press.

In analysing these aspects of early twentieth-century periodical culture, this book extends the postcolonial critique of Benedict Anderson's famous formulation of the 'imagined communities' fostered by print.[51] In his seminal study, first published in 1983, Anderson argued that the proliferation of print media after the Reformation, such as daily newspapers and journals, created a temporality of periodicity which conferred a sociological solidity upon the imagined world of the nation; print media linked together members of a national community who may not necessarily have known one another but nevertheless became aware of their experiential synchronicity, day by day or week by week. According to Anderson, the 'imagined community' of a national culture therefore develops through the 'homogeneous empty time' of modernity and the serial progress signified by print. The spatial-temporal logic promoted by Orage in *The New Age* would support this thesis: the periodical provides a voice for the imagined, collective 'we' of the English nation, the modernity of which is constituted in opposition to the 'belated and, as it were, consequential experience of other countries'. Whilst Anderson's concept of the 'imagined community' has provided the starting point for many expositions of print culture, however, it has also been thoroughly disputed. Arjun Appadurai, for instance, has argued that the idea of the 'imagined community' becomes unsustainable in the increasingly globalised world of the twentieth century. Extending Anderson's concept to postulate the existence of 'imagined worlds' that can overlap and come into conflict, Appadurai instead highlights global 'disjuncture' and 'difference', pointing to those who 'are able to contest and sometimes even subvert the "imagined worlds" of the official mind'.[52] Likewise, Homi Bhabha emphasises the 'borderline engagements of cultural difference' and the disruptive, discontinuous presences that reinscribe 'the social imaginary of both metropolis and modernity'.[53] Employing Mikhail Bakhtin's concept of 'the enunciative subject of heteroglossia and dialogism', Bhabha argues that 'the structure of meaning and reference [is always] an ambivalent process' that produces moments of 'hybridity' and conflict.[54] In contrast to Anderson's notion of bounded consensus, therefore, Bhabha's focus is instead on the dialogic '[c]ounter-narratives of the nation' that 'disturb those ideological manoeuvres through which "imagined communities" are given essentialist identities'.[55] In this book, I want to bring these ideas of dialogism, disjuncture and difference together with theorisations in modern periodical studies of the inherently multi-vocal, conflicted and dialogic nature of print. Employing the concept of 'dialogism' used across both postcolonial and modern periodical studies, this book considers how early twentieth-century magazines and periodicals provided mediating, multi-vocal spaces of contest and negotiation in which it was possible for writers from 'outside' to articulate alternative and potentially disruptive positions of difference that challenged hegemonic ideas of 'community' and dominant imaginaries of metropolis and modernity, nation and empire. As such, *Katherine Mansfield and Periodical Culture* contributes to the on-going critique of rigid centre/periphery binaries across contemporary literary studies, focusing on the ways in which peripheral, marginal, exilic and emergent voices found expression from within the institutions of metropolitan literary culture.

To highlight the ways in which early twentieth-century magazines and periodicals provided spaces of mediation, in which writers could negotiate conflicting positions and translate their experiences in one country into a new cultural context, I now turn to some of Mansfield's earliest engagements with periodical culture. At the turn of the new century, on the day before her twelfth birthday, Mansfield made her first appearance in a national publication with a short story titled 'His Little Friend', printed on the 'Children's Page' of *The New Zealand Graphic and Ladies' Journal*. As Redmer Yska, who discovered the story, has observed, *The New Zealand Graphic* 'flourished between 1890 and 1908. Its swirl of elite gossip, royal bulletins and moody pictorials of Māori maidens was an irresistible confection for local rumps of colonial society fixated on rank, wealth and fashion.'[56] On the pages of the journal immediately preceding Mansfield's story was the regular section 'As Seen Through Woman's Eyes' and an article titled 'Wild Women I Have Met', describing the threat of the 'Advanced Woman' to conventional gender roles.[57] This indicates the kind of social world in which Mansfield was raised, one in which topics relating to women's emancipation, such as dress reform and bicycling, were discussed politely, but preference was always given to advising 'Young Wives', for instance, about 'Kitchen Necessities'.[58] The memory of being published in this periodical evidently stayed with Mansfield. A cartoon printed directly alongside her story in the journal titled 'The Biter Bit' comically depicts a man hurling a cat into the ocean, only for the cat to be caught by the wind, knocking the 'Cat Murderer' into the water as well. Mansfield picks up on this image in one of the stories set in New Zealand that she later published in the London-based magazine *Rhythm*, 'Ole Underwood': 'He tucked the little cat in his coat and stole out of the wood-yard, and slouched down towards the wharves [. . .] He tore the little cat out of his coat and swung it by its tail and flung it out to the sewer opening.'[59] This contribution to a metropolitan magazine, therefore, is layered with a veiled allusion to Mansfield's first appearance in print when in New Zealand.

Another formative experience reading periodicals took place when Mansfield left New Zealand to study at Queen's College, London. In 1906, as Alpers has observed, Mansfield's school friend Vere Bartrick-Baker lent her the July 1890 issue of *Lippincott's* magazine in which Oscar Wilde's *The Picture of Dorian Gray* had been published in its entirety.[60] Reading this periodical promised access to the scandal and controversy still attached to Wilde's name following his trial for indecency in 1895; passed between the girls like contraband, the periodical clearly figured a rebellious act of transgression. Following this foundational reading experience, Mansfield began to fill her notebooks with epigrammatic quotations from Wilde, which she then interspersed with her own aphorisms. From Wilde's cult of the artificial, moreover, Mansfield also developed ideas about New Zealand. Writing in her journal in early 1907, for example, she observed: 'When New Zealand is more artificial, she will give birth to an artist who can treat her natural beauties adequately. This sounds paradoxical, but is true.'[61] And to her sister, she wrote in 1908:

> I am ashamed of young New Zealand, but what is to be done. [. . .] They want a purifying influence – a mad wave of pre-Raphaelitism, of super-aestheticism, should intoxicate the country. They must go to excess in the direction of culture, become almost decadent in their tendencies for a year or two and then find balance and proportion.[62]

When Mansfield arrived back in Wellington after finishing her schooling, the 'super-aestheticism' of Wilde, first encountered in London, served as a symbol for the urbane, metropolitan culture that she had left behind. It was to this 'purifying influence' that Mansfield looked when she began writing her first professional magazine contributions, made to the Australian journal *The Native Companion* in the autumn of 1907.

In total, eleven issues of *The Native Companion* were published between January and December 1907, with the first volume edited by Bertram Stevens and the second by E. J. Brady. This short life span, coupled with the distinctive, modern aesthetic foregrounded on covers of the second volume (Figure I.2), indicates that *The Native Companion* was a typical 'little magazine'. Published in Melbourne, the magazine was one among a constellation of new literary journals founded in the decade following the Federation of Australia in 1901 as alternatives to the established weekly periodical *The Bulletin*, which had begun publication

Figure I.2 *The Native Companion*. National Library of Australia

in 1880. These magazines included the Sydney-based *Lone Hand*, which Mansfield contributed to in October 1909, as well as titles such as *Gadfly*, *Trident* and *Heart of the Rose*. These magazines, as Ken Gelder and Rachel Weaver argue, created 'alternative literary spaces not only for *Bulletin* contributors themselves, but also for a newer generation of aspiring writers (and editors) who had come to regard the *Bulletin* as limited in its range'.[63] *The Native Companion* was therefore the perfect venue for a young, aspiring writer like Mansfield. It is also not surprising that Mansfield began her publishing career by contributing to an Australian magazine. As Jane Stafford and Mark Williams have observed, 'Australia and New Zealand were virtually one market for New Zealand writers in the early 1900s, a reflection not only of the difficulties of publishing in New Zealand but also of the close ties between the two countries that developed in the 1890s'.[64] When Tom L. Mills, a journalist on the New Zealand *Evening Post*, was asked by Mansfield's father to read some of her verses and sketches, therefore, he suggested that she send these to *The Native Companion*. Not only did contributing to this magazine make Mansfield a paid writer, it also gave her a new identity.[65] Born Kathleen Beauchamp, Mansfield adopted her pseudonym for the first time in print, writing to the editor: 'please do not use the name K. M. Beauchamp. I am anxious to be read only as K. Mansfield or K.M.'[66]

Carol Mills describes Brady, the editor of the second volume of *The Native Companion*, as 'clamorously nationalistic'.[67] The title of the magazine referred not only to the popular name given to the brolga, the bird depicted on the cover, therefore, but also to an implicit nationalist politics. However, Mills also states that Brady looked to distinguish his magazine from the 'popular herd' and to foster new, exclusive bohemian networks.[68] In line with this, as Gelder and Weaver note, Brady's magazine promoted 'a feminine aesthetic more attuned to emergent forms of literary modernism' than other magazines, and the 'vignette' became an important genre in contributions to *The Native Companion* made by women writers, such as Mabel Forrest, Sumner Locke, Beatrix Tracy, B. Cecil Doyle and Sydney Partridge; these stories 'provide brief glimpses into a character's consciousness, rendering intensely-felt emotions and embedding themselves in the particularity of their setting'.[69] Positioning herself within this 'emergent' modernism, Mansfield's first contribution to the magazine was pointedly titled 'Vignettes'. This collection of sketches opens with the narrator imagining the twilight hour, when 'London stretches out eager hands towards me, and in her eyes is the light of knowledge': this is the hour when 'Convention has long since sought her bed' and when 'nothing [shall] remain hidden'.[70] Both in style and thematic focus, the 'Vignettes' clearly resemble Wilde's prose poems and the psychological sketches popular among the Decadents and Aesthetes of the 1890s. Like Wilde, Mansfield distinguishes between the 'inner life' of imagination or emotion and the 'outer life' of convention or custom; for instance, a 'hidden' 'knowledge' is revealed when the narrator recalls how '[a] year ago we sat by the fire, she and I, hand in hand, cheek to cheek [. . .] The long night dragged coldly through, while I watched her, and thought, and longed.'[71] The story articulates this transgressive homosexual desire, recalled across a distance of time. More than this, however, 'Vignettes' also performs a spatial, geographical transgression, with the penultimate line revealing that each of the sketches has been written from 'at the other end of the world': 'To-day, at the other end of the world, I have suffered, and she, doubtless, has bought herself a new hat at the February sales'.[72] Whilst the story is firmly located in the imaginative realm of London, therefore, the narrator reveals that the 'Vignettes' have been composed in Wellington, with the rain from the wharves lashing against her window to the sound of 'a foghorn far out at sea'.[73] The story pivots on this sense of the narrator being dislocated from her own narrative, positioned 'miles away' from a city that is the site of illicit desire and where all stultifying conventions are quashed.[74] In this way, Mansfield translates her experience in England back to the place of publication, highlighting by contrast what she considered to be the 'monotonous' and 'dull, steady, hopeless' aspects of life in New Zealand.[75] Unlike other vignettes published in *The Native Companion*, therefore, Mansfield's 'Vignettes' were not embedded 'in the particularity of their setting'. Instead, the action of her narrative takes place in the ambivalent, liminal space between London and Wellington, privileging the 'elsewhere' and imagining mobility across global space. This focus on the 'world' is also highlighted in the very last line of 'Vignettes': '*Sic transit gloria mundi*', which translates as 'thus passes the glory of the world'.[76] Whilst 'Vignettes' contributed to the development of the new modernist aesthetic promoted across *The Native Companion*, therefore, in these sketches Mansfield also looked to undermine the magazine's focus on the local, native landscape as the space in which this modernism would be formulated.

Most significantly, perhaps, Mansfield's emulation of metropolitan English culture and Wilde's aestheticism put her directly at odds with the periodical against which many other writers of the newer generation in New Zealand and Australia were also positioning themselves, *The Bulletin*. In his study of the modernity of Australian print cultures, David Carter observes that the 'reference points' for *The Bulletin* in the last decades of the nineteenth century and the first decades of the twentieth were 'not English but the weird or unconventional American and Continental. Precisely because of the colonial relation no English modernity can be visible: modernity was anti-English.'[77] Quoting the research of D. R. Jarvis, Carter notes that 'the development of the *Bulletin*'s "egalitarian poetics" occurred between a negative account of Oscar Wilde and aestheticism and a positive account of Emile Zola and realism'.[78] Clearly, Mansfield's 'Vignettes' presented a very different vision of modernity. In December 1907, moreover, Mansfield again imitated Wilde with a contribution to *The Native Companion* titled 'In a Café', in which a young man and woman talk through the 'witty remarks' of *fin-de-siècle* epigram, about 'Art, Art, Art, and youth, scarlet youth, and mortality, and life, and the Ten Deadly Conventions'.[79] In the same issue of the magazine, a story by Mansfield appears under the male pseudonym 'Julian Mark' titled 'In the Botanical Gardens'. In this story, the narrator walks to the edge of the cultivated, colonial gardens, encountering the wild 'bush' landscape beyond:

> I turn from the smooth swept paths, and climb up a steep track, where the knotted tree roots have seared a rude pattern in the yellow clay. And, suddenly, it disappears – all the pretty, carefully-tended surface of gravel and sward and blossom, and there is bush, silent and splendid. On the green moss, on the brown earth, a wide splashing of yellow sunlight. And, everywhere that strange, indefinable scent. As I breathe it, it seems to absorb, to become part of me – and I am old with the age of centuries, strong with the strength of savagery.[80]

Mansfield was certainly acquainted with *The Bulletin*. As Jenny McDonnell was the first to suggest, her story 'The Woman at the Store', published in *Rhythm* in 1912, is clearly indebted to Henry Lawson's 'The Drover's Wife', published in *The Bulletin* in 1892.[81] Lawson was the most prominent among a group of writers who popularised the 'outback genre' and horse-and-saddle school of colonial writing in *The Bulletin*; as Mark Williams has observed, these stories place male pioneers, bravely taming the wild landscape of the bush, in opposition to vulnerable women, confined to domestic space.[82] Such writing advanced a hyper-masculine narrative of the nation and colonial settlement. As Gelder and Weaver note, *The Bulletin* was also integrated into 'larger, nationally representative projects, an obvious example of which [was its] slogan "Australia for the Australians" – which became "Australia for the White Man" under James Edmond's post-Federation editorship in 1903'.[83] The explicit nationalism of *The Bulletin*, as Carter suggests, served as 'a statement of its modernity, a way of placing Australia in the contemporary world'.[84] The horse-and-saddle stories by writers such as Lawson, firmly rooted in a particular local setting and advancing the hegemonic narrative of white male nationalism, contributed to this feeling that a 'national school of literature' was beginning to emerge; as Carter notes, 'Australian literature could be seen to have its own time and place, no longer merely as a "supplement" to English literature'.[85]

If the focus on transgressive female desire in 'Vignettes' presented an alternative to the hyper-masculine, hetero-normative narratives of *The Bulletin*, then 'In the Botanical Gardens' also unsettled ideas promoted in the periodical about the national modernity of Australia, and by extension New Zealand. The story replicates the spatial-temporal logic of empire, not by looking to London as a site of progress and modernity but by casting the native bush as eternally 'old with the age of centuries, strong with the strength of savagery'. At the same moment when European modernists were beginning to look to the past of 'primitive' cultures as a way of reinvigorating their own modernity, Mansfield makes a similar gesture. This does not equate to support for empire, however. Unlike the frontier stories popularised in *The Bulletin*, which celebrate the lone male pioneer who retains the country for the 'White Man' by taming the wild landscape, Mansfield's story instead reveals the suppressed history of racial violence behind colonial settlement:

> Bending down, I drink a little of the water. Oh is it magic? Shall I, looking intently, see vague forms lurking in the shadow staring at me malevolently, wildly, the thief of their birthright? Shall I, down the hillside, through the bush, ever in the shadow, see a great company moving towards me, their faces averted, wreathed with green garlands, passing, passing, following the little stream in silence until it is sucked into the wide sea. . . .[86]

From mid-November to mid-December 1907, at the time when this story was published in *The Native Companion*, Mansfield undertook a caravan expedition through the central territories of New Zealand's North Island. The journal that she kept during this expedition records her impressions, in which she sees hostile, ghostly presences emanating from the natural landscape: for example, 'now and again the silver tree-trunks, like a skeleton army, invade the hills' and '[v]isions of long dead Maoris, of forgotten battles and vanished feuds, stirred in me'.[87] 'In the Botanical Gardens' evokes these suppressed presences: felt in the liminal space between the cultivated gardens and the wild bush, as Angela Smith has observed, this 'great company' is a manifestation of a repressed colonial guilt regarding the theft of the Māori 'birthright'.[88] Whilst this sketch employs racial stereotypes linking the native population with 'savagery', its recognition of a suppressed otherness and a violent past behind the cultivated, 'carefully-tended' façade of the modern nation offers a radical critique of the history of settlement. The use of a male pseudonym for this story invites the reader to falsely position it in a tradition of the hyper-masculine 'outback' stories popularised by *The Bulletin*. The content of the story, however, invites a very different reading: the story disrupts the 'imagined community' of the nation, revealing the presence of a suppressed otherness, and thereby critiques the hegemonic narrative of colonial settlement.

From the very beginning of her literary career, therefore, Mansfield used the magazine form as a space of subversion in which to translate her writing across cultures and articulate fantasies of global movement, unsettling established ideas about modernity, nation and empire. Revealing her desire for metropolitan assimilation 'at the other end of the world', these stories also point to the essential 'homelessness' of Mansfield's writing, in which the place of identity is always located elsewhere, in 'other' places across the globe. When in Wellington, as her contributions to *The Native Companion* demonstrate, Mansfield looked to transpose London into the publication spaces of Australia and New Zealand as a way of articulating her 'outsider' status and critiquing hegemonic narratives of the colonial nation. In an inversion of this, when she began contributing to periodicals and magazines published in London, Mansfield now looked back with nostalgia to the country of her birth, as well as 'other' places across Europe and the imagined world of an 'undiscovered country'. An example of this inversion can be seen in *Rhythm*, where Mansfield now parodied the tropes of modernist primitivism as a way of holding a mirror up to her metropolitan reader. This book examines the ambivalent negotiations performed by Mansfield throughout her contributions to London magazines and periodicals in the decade spanning 1910 to 1920; interrogating the ways in which her writings variously conform to and resist the dominant spatial imaginaries promoted in these publications, I argue, enables us to reposition Mansfield more decisively as a colonial-metropolitan modernist and liminal artist.

Chapter 1 focuses on *The New Age*, examining the ways in which Mansfield's interactions with contemporary feminist politics in the periodical enabled her to unsettle established ideas about nationhood and empire. After Mansfield travelled to England from New Zealand at the end of August 1908, she started a love affair with the musician Garnet Trowell, which resulted in an unwanted pregnancy and a short-lived marriage to another man designed to give legitimacy to her unborn child. Hearing of this scandal, Mansfield's mother sailed from New Zealand and shuttled her daughter away to a pension in Bavaria, Germany, where Mansfield underwent the trauma of either a miscarriage or giving birth to a stillborn child on her own. Returning to London at the beginning of 1910, Mansfield was introduced by her husband, George Bowden, to A. R. Orage. The contributions that Mansfield made to Orage's periodical from February 1910 were her first published stories in England, and these viciously satirical sketches, caricaturing German coarseness, comprised her first book publication, *In a German Pension*. In these stories, Mansfield translates her experience as an 'outsider' in Germany into the pages of a British periodical as a way of articulating a critique of British nationalism and imperialism. Scholars have often interpreted the 'Pension Sketches' either as autobiographical fiction, produced in response to the isolation Mansfield felt whilst in Bavaria, or as scare-narratives about possible invasion or international war. Citing the consistent focus on foreign affairs and prevailing anxieties about the increasing military dominance of Germany expressed throughout *The New Age*, critics have frequently interpreted these stories as deliberately positioned in a periodical that stoked anti-German sentiment and British nationalism in the years immediately prior to the conflagration of the First World War. Rather than focusing on biographical contexts, however, Chapter 1 instead traces textual convergences between Mansfield's stories and the writings produced for the periodical by Orage's notoriously vituperative editorial assistant, Beatrice Hastings; and instead of arguing that the 'Pension Sketches' fuelled British nationalism, I examine the ways in which Mansfield's interactions with Hastings's feminist writings in fact helped to unsettle and challenge established ideas in the periodical about 'community', nationhood and the British Empire.

Like Mansfield, Hastings was an 'outsider' in London; born in South Africa, her writings demonstrate a sustained engagement with the politics of empire and offer a radical critique of metropolitan consensus regarding questions of gender and female suffrage. The first section of

Chapter 1 examines how the radical version of individualist feminism advanced by Hastings in *The New Age* responded to a contemporary cultural discourse linking gender and empire. It was in the context of this public discourse that both Hastings and Mansfield formulated remarkably similar, coterminous ideas about female suffrage, marriage and maternity. This section of the chapter focuses on Hastings's pamphlet *Woman's Worst Enemy: Woman* and the serialised novella *Whited Sepulchres*, both published in 1909, reading these texts alongside a newly discovered short story by Mansfield titled 'A Little Episode' (1909). The second section of the chapter examines the ways in which Mansfield's contributions to *The New Age* between 1910 and 1911 deployed Hastings's feminist politics in order to subvert and critique dominant ideas about national health, racial stability and imperial power advanced elsewhere in the periodical, exposing connections between the early twentieth-century politics of gender and race, motherhood and imperialism. Finally, in the last two sections of the chapter, I examine how both writers employed fragment forms in their later contributions to *The New Age*, such as aphorism and ellipsis, in order to disrupt linear, systematised discourse and thereby challenge notions of male superiority or English national, cultural and linguistic integrity; in this way, both writers used periodical publication to unsettle dominant belief systems and formulate alternative modes of identification. These sections of the chapter, as such, highlight another aspect of this book, which looks to recover and interrogate the many different literary forms that Mansfield used throughout her career, in order to reposition her as a writer who was not restricted exclusively to the short story form, as is commonly assumed. The chapter also examines original archival findings, including Mansfield's 'A Little Episode' and her collection of fifty aphorisms titled 'Bites from the Apple' (1911), as well as typescript fragments by Hastings, which are the only known documents to have survived her systematic attempt to destroy all her papers before her suicide in 1943.

At the beginning of 1912, Mansfield began to consider alternative outlets for her work and started publishing in a self-consciously 'modernist' little magazine titled *Rhythm*, edited by John Middleton Murry. Published quarterly and then monthly, *Rhythm* was a short-lived, avowedly experimental coterie magazine that was very different to *The New Age*, a political weekly with a broad readership and long publication run. As such, contributing to *Rhythm* presented Mansfield with new opportunities and possibilities for her writing; she quickly established herself as an assistant editor to Murry and began publishing stories clearly influenced by her colonial upbringing. Furthermore, Mansfield began exploring different authorial signatures in *Rhythm*. As Chapter 2 examines, Mansfield used *Rhythm* as a performative space in which to develop multiple authorial identities and cultivate different national registers in her work, employing parody, satire and mimicry as modes of critique. Firstly, this chapter argues that Mansfield reframed some of her poems as 'parodic translations' in order to open up a liminal space between centre and periphery in her contributions to the magazine. The chapter then examines the ways in which Mansfield's short story contributions to *Rhythm* parody the outback genre of colonial writing typified by stories in *The Bulletin* in order to unsettle both the masculine gaze and the colonial quest narrative that permeates visual illustrations and other written contributions to *Rhythm*, in which the female body is universally equated with verdant landscapes and virgin territories. Whilst identifying with the metropolitan modernism advanced by the magazine, I argue in this chapter, Mansfield sought to introduce aspects of cultural difference into *Rhythm* that challenged the spatial imaginaries upon which its discourse of communal affiliation had been constituted. This ambivalent negotiation of the colonial/metropolitan binary clearly structures Mansfield's satire 'Sunday Lunch', which is examined in the third section of the chapter.

After *Rhythm* folded in March 1913, Murry and Mansfield established a similar little magazine, *The Blue Review*, publishing three issues between May and July 1913. A notable contributor to *The Blue Review* was D. H. Lawrence. In the autumn of 1915, Lawrence worked with Murry and Mansfield to found another little magazine, titled *The Signature*, in response to the 'corruption' and 'disintegration' of the First World War. Again, only three issues were forthcoming. Over the next three and a half years, Mansfield published little and inconsistently, returning to the pages of *The New Age* with several contributions in 1917 and publishing the stories 'Bliss' and 'Carnation' the following year in *The English Review* and *The Nation* respectively. When Murry was appointed editor of the established periodical *The Athenaeum* at the beginning of 1919, tasked with rejuvenating it as a modern literary review, however, Mansfield finally found a publication venue in which she was free to contribute liberally. Between April 1919 and December 1920, Mansfield published over a hundred reviews under the initials 'K.M.' in *The Athenaeum*, finding her voice as a literary critic; she also contributed a series of translations of Anton Chekhov's letters and diaries, produced in collaboration with the Ukrainian émigré S. S. Koteliansky, poems written under the pseudonym 'Elizabeth Stanley', three leading articles and a number of short stories. Mansfield's time working for *The Athenaeum* figures her clearest integration into the London literary establishment. Associating with the likes of Virginia Woolf, E. M. Forster, T. S. Eliot and Bertrand Russell, Mansfield was also writing with newfound critical authority in this period. Excepting brief surveys by Clare Hanson, Kaplan and McDonnell, however, Mansfield's reviews have received almost no sustained scholarly attention.[89]

Chapter 3 examines Mansfield's reviews in *The Athenaeum* against a critical discourse first articulated in *The Signature*. The first section of the chapter interrogates the ways in which Mansfield linked the 'new word' of modernist formal experimentation with the spatial imaginary of an 'undiscovered country' or 'new world'. This critical vocabulary was first formulated in *The Signature* by Lawrence and Murry, who had postulated the idea of a 'new word' that would counteract the 'spiritual crisis' of the war and thus inaugurate a 'new world' of possibility. The chapter examines how this idea of being 'between two worlds' shaped the editorial philosophy of *The Athenaeum* after the war and influenced Mansfield's language of liminality and geographical discovery in her reviews. Employing metaphors equating the writing process with 'sailing' across the world, Mansfield in this late stage of her career now looked back fondly to the colonial 'new world' as a source of cultural rejuvenation. In her reviews, moreover, Mansfield consistently looked with admiration to other national literatures from across the world, such as those in Russia and Japan, and her co-translations with Koteliansky also helped to privilege transnational exchange as the basis for a revivifying form of global modernism in the immediate post-war years. As this chapter examines, concepts such as the 'new world' and 'undiscovered country' of literature provided a geographical imaginary through which Mansfield could distinguish literary realism from an emergent modernism. In the second section of the chapter, I examine how this idea of the 'two worlds' also shaped the language of 'spirit', 'emotion', 'love' and 'feeling' employed throughout the critical writings produced by both Mansfield and Virginia Woolf at this time. This section traces a dialogue between Mansfield and Woolf in the years 1919–20, highlighting the ways in which both writers privileged deep 'emotion' as the basis for a modernist 'new word'. Finally, the conclusion to the chapter demonstrates how the language of Mansfield's reviews conditioned the contemporary response to her own short stories.

After Mansfield resigned as a reviewer on *The Athenaeum* in December 1920, she negotiated a position for her writing across 'popular' and 'literary' markets by contributing short stories to diverse publications such as *The London Mercury*, *The Sphere*, *The Saturday Westminster Gazette* and *The Nation and the Athenaeum*, a title which was the result of a merger between the two periodicals after Murry resigned as editor of *The Athenaeum* at the start of 1921. This negotiation of the 'popular' and 'literary' in Mansfield's late magazine contributions has been examined in depth by McDonnell, and I do not intend to repeat such analysis in the present book. Instead, Chapter 4 analyses the ways in which Mansfield's reputation was moulded and mediated in Murry's magazine *The Adelphi* after her death in January 1923. The chapter interrogates the ways in which Murry now sought to elide those disruptive and disjunctive aspects of Mansfield's work examined in the first three chapters of the book: of Mansfield the feminist, who eschewed gender stereotypes of feminine 'purity' and 'saintliness' in *The New Age*; of Mansfield the (post)colonial writer, who negotiated a deliberately ambiguous position for her work between England and New Zealand in *Rhythm*; and of Mansfield the modernist, whose critical writings in *The Athenaeum* indubitably helped to shape the literary innovations of the early 1920s.

This book offers a new perspective on Mansfield's life and work by analysing the original print contexts in which she produced the majority of her writings. Tracing a chronological narrative, *Katherine Mansfield and Periodical Culture* inevitably provides another iteration of Mansfield's biography; however, I seek to reorient scholarly focus away from personal contexts and instead towards the contexts of publication. This is not to say that we should overlook important biographical reasons for Mansfield's association with certain magazines and periodicals, especially as such involvement was often predicated upon her romantic involvement with Murry. However, rather than reading Mansfield's biography onto her work, this study instead focuses on the textual record, to the greatest degree possible reading each periodical as 'an autonomous object of study'.[90] In this way, this book looks to position Mansfield's work within networks of production, uncovering the manifold ways in which she engaged with the writings of others and responded to the particular political, aesthetic and social contexts of early twentieth-century periodical culture.

Notes

1. Katherine Mansfield, *Journal of Katherine Mansfield: Definitive Edition*, ed. John Middleton Murry (London: Constable, 1954), p. 252.
2. Wyndham Lewis (c. 20 September 1922), quoted in Antony Alpers, *The Life of Katherine Mansfield*, rev. edn (Harmondsworth: Penguin, 1982), p. 372.
3. Faye Hammill and Mark Hussey, *Modernism's Print Cultures* (London: Bloomsbury, 2016), p. 174.
4. Alpers, *The Life of Katherine Mansfield*.
5. Lee Garver, 'The Political Katherine Mansfield', *Modernism/Modernity*, 8.2 (April 2001), pp. 225–43.
6. Carey Snyder, 'Katherine Mansfield and the *New Age* School of Satire', *Journal of Modern Periodical Studies*, 1.2 (2010), pp. 125–58.
7. Carey Snyder, 'Katherine Mansfield, *Rhythm*, and Metropolitan Primitivism', *Journal of Modern Periodical Studies*, 5.2 (2014), pp. 139–60.
8. Angela Smith, *Katherine Mansfield: A Literary Life* (Basingstoke: Palgrave, 2000); 'Fauvism and Cultural Nationalism', *Interventions: International Journal of Post-colonial Studies*, 4.1 (June 2002), pp. 35–52; 'Katherine Mansfield and *Rhythm*', *Journal of New Zealand Literature*, 21 (2003), pp. 102–21; 'J. D. Fergusson's Painting *Rhythm*', *Katherine Mansfield Studies*, 2 (2010), pp. 184–7; '"As fastidious as though I wrote with acid": Katherine Mansfield, J. D. Fergusson and the *Rhythm* Group in Paris', *Katherine Mansfield Studies*, 3 (2011), pp. 4–20.
9. Anna Snaith, *Modernist Voyages: Colonial Women Writers in London, 1890–1945* (Cambridge: Cambridge University Press, 2014), p. 132.
10. Faith Binckes, *Modernism, Magazines, and the British Avant-Garde: Reading* Rhythm, *1910–1914* (Oxford: Oxford University Press, 2010).
11. Sydney Janet Kaplan, *Circulating Genius: John Middleton Murry, Katherine Mansfield and D. H. Lawrence* (Edinburgh: Edinburgh University Press, 2010)
12. Mansfield, *Journal of Katherine Mansfield*, p. 157.
13. Bonnie Kime Scott (ed.), *Gender in Modernism: New Geographies, Complex Intersections* (Urbana: University of Illinois Press, 2007).
14. Andreas Huyssen, *After the Great Divide: Modernism, Mass Culture, Postmodernism* (Bloomington: Indiana University Press, 1986).
15. Sean Latham and Robert Scholes, 'The Changing Profession: The Rise of Periodical Studies', *PMLA*, 121.2 (March 2006), p. 528.
16. Ann L. Ardis, 'The Dialogics of Modernism(s) in *The New Age*', *Modernism/Modernity*, 14.3 (September 2007), p. 409.
17. Suzanne W. Churchill and Adam McKible, 'Introduction', in Suzanne W. Churchill and Adam McKible (eds), *Little Magazines and Modernism: New Approaches* (Aldershot: Ashgate, 2007), pp. 12, 4.
18. Peter Brooker and Andrew Thacker, 'General Introduction', in Peter Brooker and Andrew Thacker (eds), *The Oxford Critical and Cultural History of Modernist Magazines, Volume I: Britain and Ireland, 1880–1955* (Oxford: Oxford University Press, 2009), p. 3.
19. Jenny McDonnell, *Katherine Mansfield and the Modernist Marketplace: At the Mercy of the Public* (Basingstoke: Palgrave Macmillan, 2010), p. 6.
20. Douglas Mao and Rebecca L. Walkowitz, 'The New Modernist Studies', *PMLA*, 123.3 (May 2008), pp. 737–48.
21. Saikat Majumdar, 'Katherine Mansfield and the Fragility of Pākehā Boredom', in *Prose of the World: Modernism and the Banality of Empire* (New York: Columbia

University Press, 2013), pp. 71–100; Mark Williams, 'Mansfield in Maoriland: Biculturalism, Agency and Misreading', in Howard J. Booth and Nigel Rigby (eds), *Modernism and Empire* (Manchester: Manchester University Press, 2000), pp. 249–74; Jane Stafford and Mark Williams, 'Katherine Mansfield: A Modernist in Maoriland', in *Maoriland: New Zealand Literature 1872–1914* (Wellington: Victoria University Press, 2007), pp. 142–70.

22. Elleke Boehmer, 'Mansfield as Colonial Modernist: Difference Within', in Gerri Kimber and Janet Wilson (eds), *Celebrating Katherine Mansfield* (Basingstoke: Palgrave Macmillan, 2011), pp. 57–71; Urmila Seshagiri, *Race and the Modernist Imagination* (Ithaca: Cornell University Press, 2010).
23. Janet Wilson, '"Where is Katherine?" Longing and (Un)belonging in the Works of Katherine Mansfield', in Gerri Kimber and Janet Wilson (eds), *Celebrating Katherine Mansfield* (Basingstoke: Palgrave Macmillan, 2011), pp. 175–88; 'Mansfield as (Post)colonial-Modernist: Rewriting the Contract with Death', in Janet Wilson, Gerri Kimber and Delia da Sousa Correa (eds), *Katherine Mansfield and the (Post)colonial* (Edinburgh: Edinburgh University Press, 2013), pp. 29–44; Mary Ann Gillies, 'Oceans Apart? Emily Carr and Katherine Mansfield's Encounters With Modernism', in Mary Ann Gillies, Helen Sword and Steven Yao (eds), *Pacific Rim Modernisms* (Toronto: University of Toronto Press, 2009), pp. 233–60.
24. Claire Davison, *Translation as Collaboration: Virginia Woolf, Katherine Mansfield and S. S. Koteliansky* (Edinburgh: Edinburgh University Press, 2014); 'Introduction', in Claire Davison, Gerri Kimber and Todd Martin (eds), *Katherine Mansfield and Translation* (Edinburgh: Edinburgh University Press, 2015), pp. 1–11.
25. Patrick Collier, 'Imperial/Modernist Forms in the *Illustrated London News*', *Modernism/Modernity*, 19.3 (September 2012), pp. 487–8.
26. Paul Peppis, *Literature, Politics, and the English Avant-Garde: Nation and Empire, 1901–1918* (Cambridge: Cambridge University Press, 2000).
27. Adam McKible, *The Space and Place of Modernism: The Russian Revolution, Little Magazines, and New York* (London: Routledge, 2002), p. 8.
28. Peter Kalliney, *Modernism in a Global Context* (London: Bloomsbury, 2016), p. 71.
29. Eric B. White, *Transatlantic Avant-Gardes: Little Magazines and Localist Modernism* (Edinburgh: Edinburgh University Press, 2013), p. 2.
30. Eric Bulson, *Little Magazine, World Form* (New York: Columbia University Press, 2016).
31. Brooker and Thacker, 'General Introduction', pp. 1–2.
32. Peppis, *Literature, Politics*, p. 55.
33. Sascha Bru, '"The Will to Style": The Dutch Contribution to the Avant-Garde. Leiden: *De Stijl* (1917–32), *Mécano* (1922–3); Amsterdam: *Wendingen* (1918–32), *i10* (1927–9); and Groningen: *The Next Call* (1923–6)', in Peter Brooker, Sascha Bru, Andrew Thacker and Christian Weikop (eds), *The Oxford Critical and Cultural History of Modernist Magazines, Volume III: Europa 1880–1940* (Oxford: Oxford University Press, 2013), pp. 293–312; David Carter, *Almost Always Modern: Australian Print Cultures and Modernity* (Melbourne: Australian Scholarly Publishing, 2013); Dean Irvine, *Editing Modernity: Women and Little-Magazine Cultures in Canada, 1916–1956* (Toronto: University of Toronto Press, 2008).
34. Joanne Shattock and Michael Wolff, 'Introduction', in Joanne Shattock and Michael Wolff (eds), *The Victorian Periodical Press: Samplings and Soundings* (Leicester: Leicester University Press, 1982), p. xv.
35. See Peter Sinnema, *Dynamics of the Pictured Page: Representing the Nation in the* Illustrated London News (Aldershot: Ashgate, 1998); Paula Krebs, *Gender, Race,*

and the Writing of Empire: Public Discourse and the Boer War (Cambridge: Cambridge University Press, 1999); Julie F. Codell (ed.), *Imperial Co-Histories: National Identities and the British Colonial Press* (London: Associated University Presses, 2003); Simon J. Potter, *News and the British World: The Emergence of an Imperial Press System* (Oxford: Oxford University Press, 2003); Linda E. Connors and Mary Lou MacDonald, *National Identity in Great Britain and British North America, 1815–1851: The Role of Nineteenth-Century Periodicals* (Farnham: Ashgate, 2011).

36. Julie F. Codell, 'Introduction', in Julie F. Codell (ed.), *Imperial Co-Histories: National Identities and the British Colonial Press* (London: Associated University Presses, 2003), p. 18.
37. Collier, 'Imperial/Modernist Forms in the *Illustrated London News*', pp. 493–4.
38. Ibid., p. 492.
39. Ann L. Ardis, 'Staging the Public Sphere: Magazine Dialogism and the Prosthetics of Authorship at the Turn of the Twentieth Century', in Ann L. Ardis and Patrick Collier (eds), *Transatlantic Print Culture, 1880–1940: Emerging Media, Emerging Modernisms* (Basingstoke: Palgrave Macmillan, 2008), p. 38.
40. Anon. [A. R. Orage], 'The Outlook', *New Age*, 1.1 (2 May 1907), p. 1.
41. Anon. [A. R. Orage], 'Notes of the Week', *New Age*, 6.18 (3 March 1910), p. 411.
42. Ibid.
43. Katherine Mansfield, 'North American Chiefs', *New Age*, 7.17 (25 August 1910), p. 407.
44. Ibid.
45. Katherine Mansfield, *The Collected Letters of Katherine Mansfield, Volume V: 1922–1923*, ed. Vincent O'Sullivan and Margaret Scott (Oxford: Clarendon Press, 2008), p. 304.
46. Elleke Boehmer, *Colonial and Postcolonial Literature: Migrant Metaphors*, 2nd edn (Oxford: Oxford University Press, 2005), p. 127.
47. Katherine Mansfield, *The Collected Letters of Katherine Mansfield, Volume I: 1903–1917*, ed. Vincent O'Sullivan and Margaret Scott (Oxford: Clarendon Press, 1984), p. 41.
48. Ibid., p. 91.
49. Mansfield, *Journal of Katherine Mansfield*, p. 157.
50. Wilson, '"Where is Katherine?"', pp. 185–6.
51. Benedict Anderson, *Imagined Communities: Reflections on the Origin and Spread of Nationalism*, rev. edn (London Verso, 2006).
52. Arjun Appadurai, 'Disjuncture and Difference in the Global Cultural Economy', *Theory and Society*, 7 (1990), pp. 296–7.
53. Homi K. Bhabha, *The Location of Culture*, rev. edn (London: Routledge, 2004), pp. 3, 9.
54. Ibid., pp. 269, 53–5.
55. Ibid., p. 213.
56. Redmer Yska, *A Strange Beautiful Excitement: Katherine Mansfield's Wellington, 1888–1903* (Dunedin: Otago University Press, 2017), p. 215.
57. Anon., 'Wild Women I Have Met', *New Zealand Graphic and Ladies' Journal*, 25.15 (13 October 1900), p. 704.
58. Anon., 'As Seen Through Women's Eyes', *New Zealand Graphic and Ladies' Journal*, 25.15 (13 October 1900), pp. 705–6.
59. Katherine Mansfield, 'Ole Underwood', *Rhythm*, 12 (January 1913), p. 336.
60. Alpers, *The Life of Katherine Mansfield*, p. 35.
61. Mansfield, *Journal of Katherine Mansfield*, p. 10.

62. Mansfield, *The Collected Letters of Katherine Mansfield, Volume I*, p. 44.
63. Ken Gelder and Rachel Weaver, 'Literary Journals and Literary Aesthetics in Early Post-Federation Australia', *JASAL: Journal of the Association for the Study of Australian Literature*, 14.5 (2014), p. 1.
64. Stafford and Williams, 'Katherine Mansfield', p. 148.
65. Mansfield received £2 for 'Vignettes' and £2.7.6 for 'In a Café' and 'In the Botanical Gardens', according to the Thomas Lothian Papers in the State Library of Victoria, quoted in Jean E. Stone, *Katherine Mansfield: Publications in Australia, 1907–09* (Sydney: Wentworth Books, 1977), p. 13.
66. Mansfield, *The Collected Letters of Katherine Mansfield, Volume I*, p. 27.
67. Carol Mills, *The Native Companion: Complete Indexes to Text, Illustrators, Book Notices and Subjects and Brief Bibliographies and an Introduction* (Canberra: Mulini Press, 1999), p. 4.
68. Ibid.
69. Gelder and Weaver, 'Literary Journals and Literary Aesthetics', p. 4.
70. K. [Katherine] Mansfield, 'Vignettes', *Native Companion*, 2.3 (1 October 1907), pp. 129–30.
71. Ibid., pp. 129–30, 132.
72. Ibid., p. 132.
73. Ibid., p. 131.
74. Ibid.
75. Ibid.
76. Ibid., p. 132.
77. Carter, *Almost Always Modern*, p. 5.
78. Ibid.
79. K. [Katherine] Mansfield, 'In a Café', *Native Companion*, 2.5 (2 December 1907), p. 265.
80. 'Julian Mark' [Katherine Mansfield], 'In the Botanical Gardens', *Native Companion*, 2.5 (2 December 1907), p. 286.
81. McDonnell, *Katherine Mansfield*, pp. 48–9. Mark Williams also connects Mansfield's story to 'the outback genre identified with Henry Lawson' – Williams, 'Mansfield in Maoriland', p. 259. Henry Lawson, 'The Drover's Wife', *Bulletin* (23 July 1892), pp. 21–2.
82. Williams, 'Mansfield in Maoriland', pp. 258–9.
83. Gelder and Weaver, 'Literary Journals and Literary Aesthetics', pp. 1–2.
84. Carter, *Almost Always Modern*, p. 18.
85. Ibid.
86. Mansfield, 'In the Botanical Gardens', p. 286.
87. Mansfield, *Journal of Katherine Mansfield*, pp. 23–4.
88. Smith, *Katherine Mansfield*, p. 25.
89. Clare Hanson (ed.), *The Critical Writings of Katherine Mansfield* (London: Macmillan, 1987); Kaplan, *Circulating Genius*; Jenny McDonnell, '"Wanted, a New Word": Katherine Mansfield and the *Athenaeum*', *Modernism/Modernity*, 16.4 (November 2009), pp. 727–42.
90. Latham and Scholes, 'The Changing Profession', p. 518.

THE

NEW AGE

A WEEKLY REVIEW OF POLITICS, LITERATURE AND ART.

NEW SERIES. Vol. VI. No. 12. THURSDAY, JAN. 20, 1910. [Registered at G.P.O. as a Newspaper.] THREEPENCE.

INDIGESTION.

Figure 1.1 *The New Age*

Chapter 1

The New Age: Gender, Nation and Empire

Within a month of her return to London in 1908, keen to embrace the opportunities that the city had to offer, Katherine Mansfield attended her first suffrage meeting, on which she intended to write a newspaper report. Recounting the experience, she wrote in a letter:

> Immediately I entered the hall two women who looked like very badly upholstered chairs pounced upon me, and begged me to become a voluntary worker. There were two hundred present – all strange looking, in deadly earnest – all looking, especially the older ones, particularly 'run to seed'. And they got up and talked and argued until they were hoarse, and thumped on the floor and applauded – The room grew hot and in the air some spirit of agitation of revolt, stirred & grew. It was over at 10.30. I ran into the street – cool air and starlight [. . .] & decided I could not be a suffragette – the world was too full of laughter.[1]

Critics have long interpreted this antipathy towards the suffrage movement as evidence of Mansfield's political naivety or lack of political engagement. Antony Alpers, for instance, argues that 'Kass Beauchamp was never an incipient feminist' and suggests that none of her early writings 'would have bestirred an Edwardian reader to "sit down and write a cheque"' in support of women's causes.[2] Andrew Bennett, likewise, asserts that 'Mansfield's feminism is largely invisible', whilst Sydney Janet Kaplan contends that Mansfield 'did not articulate her social critique of human suffering in recognizably political terms' or connect this critique to 'feminist political analysis'.[3] I argue in this chapter, however, that it was precisely Mansfield's aversion to the suffrage movement that connects her to the feminist movement. Situating her contributions to *The New Age* within the original historical contexts of publication enables us to trace the ways in which Mansfield helped to foster an emergent, radical version of individualist feminism constituted in clear opposition to the suffrage movement and shaped by contemporary discourses about nationhood and empire.

In particular, this chapter examines the ways in which Mansfield's contributions to *The New Age* augmented the intellectual critique of liberal feminism spearheaded within the periodical by Beatrice Hastings, a South African-born writer whose given name was Emily Alice Haigh. Hastings was the self-proclaimed shadow 'co-editor' of *The New Age* between 1907 and 1914, as well as the partner of its editor, A. R. Orage. In one of the most temperate assessments of Hastings's position on the periodical, fellow contributor Philip Mairet observed: 'She was the one woman who held her place for years amongst the regular writers of the paper and she did it by sheer force of character and volume of production'.[4] Astonishingly, Hastings made nearly 400 contributions to *The New Age*, regularly sparking controversy in the periodical with intentionally provocative articles penned under a dizzying array of pseudonyms.[5] The anonymity with which Hastings circulated her writings, however, has meant that her prominent position on the periodical has often gone unnoticed. When she is remembered, if at all, it is usually for her venomous memoir, published after Orage's death, in which she accused him and his circle of conducting 'a social cabale' (*sic*) against her, 'a literary boycott that does, or should, matter to every reading person'.[6] Having left London for Paris in 1914, Hastings returned to England in the early 1930s to find herself excluded from the literary circles in which she had once been so prominent. In her memoir, titled *The Old 'New Age': Orage and Others* (1936), Hastings claimed that it was she who had 'had entire charge of, and responsibility for, the literary direction of the paper, from reading and selection of MSS. to the last detail of spacing and position' and that it was she who had discovered and then championed both Mansfield and Ezra Pound, rather than Orage.[7] The actual position that Hastings occupied on the periodical is difficult to ascertain with any certainty, however, as all archival records for *The New Age* were lost to posterity when the Cursitor Street offices were bombed in the Second World War; moreover, Hastings systematically destroyed her personal papers before committing suicide in 1943, putting them to the fire after they were rejected by the British Museum.[8] Inevitably, her reputation has suffered in the face of this lacuna. By adopting so many masks throughout her writings, moreover, Hastings effectively wrote herself out of literary history; subsequently, her claims against Orage have largely been dismissed as the vindictive ravings of a bitter ex-lover.

Figure 1.2 Beatrice Hastings, photographed by Man Ray (November 1921).

Similarly, Mansfield scholars have often overlooked Hastings's writings due to the particularly spiteful, acrimonious rivalry that existed between the two women after Mansfield left *The New Age* for *Rhythm*. As such, Hastings's influence over Mansfield's development as a writer has often been elided.

This chapter seeks to recuperate Hastings's centrality as an important figure in the emergence of early twentieth-century literary modernism, crediting her with a crucial role in the formation and development of Mansfield's first published writings in London. Whilst their literary careers ultimately took very different trajectories, there are striking similarities in the biographies of Mansfield and Hastings. Significantly, both

Figure 1.3 Beatrice Hastings (unknown date)

were born in outposts of the British Empire. This has led biographers to associate both writers with a 'wild' factor attributed to their 'colonial' status: for example, Claire Tomalin describes Mansfield as a 'wild Colonial girl', an epithet that Jeffrey Meyers then uses for the title of a chapter on Hastings in his biography of Amedeo Modigliani.[9] Both were the daughters of prosperous self-made colonial merchants, and both enjoyed rebelling against the bourgeois conventions of their parents. Both were sent to finish their schooling in England, before courting scandal with brief marriages and unwanted pregnancies. And both made being 'colonial' or '*déracinée*' sound exotic and fashionable, until it suited them to play the sophisticated metropolitan. As well as being acutely aware of their 'outsider' status, therefore, both women were also prone to a profound sense of a divided or dual identity, cultivating multiple personae and employing various pseudonyms within their work. In Hastings's case, this divided identity can be seen in the portraits

BEATRICE HASTINGS.
Cartoon by TOM TIT.

Figure 1.4 Tom Titt (Jan Junosza de Rosciszewski), 'Beatrice Hastings'

of her created by Tom Titt, the cartoonist on *The New Age* (Figure 1.4), and Modigliani (Figure 1.5): the first was sketched for publication in the periodical, depicting Hastings as both genteel Edwardian and raging gorgon; and the drawing by Modigliani, in which Hastings is both reading a periodical and modelling as artist's muse, clearly associates her immersion within periodical culture as a precondition for her multi-faceted personalities. Fiercely intelligent, caustic and quick-witted, both Mansfield and Hastings possessed a mordant sense of humour that found

BEATRICE HASTINGS
by
MODIGLIANI.

Figure 1.5 Amedeo Modigliani, 'Beatrice Hastings'

expression in the repeated publication of satires and parodies. Quick to launch into an argument, however, both women were also highly strung and subject to violent tempers. The poet Ruth Pitter, for instance, recalled entering the offices of *The New Age* on one occasion to find the floor scattered with beads after Mansfield and Hastings had come to blows with their necklaces.[10] It was this shared temperamental volatility that ultimately led to their estrangement, with each expressing violent dislike for the other from 1915 onwards.

Despite these evident similarities, however, the creative and intellectual reciprocity between the two writers has received almost no critical attention. Scholars have failed to interrogate Mansfield's association with Hastings on *The New Age* in any real depth, often taking the bitter pronouncements made about Hastings in Mansfield's later correspondence and journals as gospel. This is in stark contrast to Mansfield's literary relationship with Virginia Woolf, which has been the focus of several comprehensive analyses. This imbalance is largely attributable to the fact that Hastings consistently has been presented derogatively in one-sided biographies of her more famous contemporaries and has often been dismissed as merely the 'fiery mistress' to various male protagonists of modernism, such as Orage, Wyndham Lewis and Modigliani.[11] Meyers, for example, dismisses Hastings as a 'rabid feminist', responsible only for fulfilling male sexual appetites and (possibly) arranging an illegal abortion for Mansfield.[12] In their introduction to the first volume of Mansfield's collected letters, likewise, Vincent O'Sullivan and Margaret Scott credit Hastings with instructing Mansfield only in 'swank and bitchiness'.[13] Similarly, Mansfield's most authoritative biographer, Alpers, reflects the critical consensus about Hastings when he states that she was 'raging' and 'fanatically jealous' of Mansfield.[14] There have been some significant recent attempts at revision, however. In 2004, Stephen Gray published a monumental, meticulously researched biography of Hastings that is indispensable for the dedicated reader of her works but sadly now available only through specialist booksellers.[15] In articles and book chapters, moreover, Ann Ardis has argued for Hastings's centrality on *The New Age*, Lucy Delap has shown how she was an important figure within the feminist avant-garde and Robert Scholes has examined the contributions she made to *The New Age* from 1914 whilst living in Paris.[16] A selection of Hastings's writings was included in the ground-breaking anthology edited by Bonnie Kime Scott, *Gender in Modernism* (2007), and a book published in 2016 for 'The Unsung Masters Series' of the Pleiades Press reproduced selections of her writings across multiple genres alongside six critical essays examining her work.[17] Despite these advances, however, more in-depth examination is clearly required of Hastings's literary and intellectual connections to Mansfield. Lee Garver makes passing reference to the influence Hastings's feminism may have exerted in the development of Mansfield's early work, and Carey Snyder has examined how Hastings's satirical writings for *The New Age* shaped Mansfield's own, but this influence patently demands closer analysis.[18]

As John Carswell has observed, Mansfield and Hastings 'represent a centripetal tendency in British culture': they both moved 'from the circumference' of global space to the imperial centre of London in order 'to criticise not commend what they found. Literary passion, which consumed them both, was in them a combative one, a desire to acquire, elaborate, and employ language to etch the folly and scotch the institutions of the metropolis.'[19] In particular, I argue in this chapter, both writers responded to the ideologies of nation and empire in order to challenge and unsettle the political assumptions of mainstream feminism. In the first section of the chapter, I examine how the radical version of individualist feminism advanced by Hastings in *The New Age* responded to a contemporary cultural discourse linking motherhood and imperialism, gender and nationhood. It was in the context of this public discourse that both Hastings and Mansfield formulated remarkably similar, coterminous ideas about female suffrage, marriage and maternity. Whereas Hastings subscribed to the eugenicist beliefs of her day, promoting notions of national health and racial stability, however, Mansfield's feminist politics helped her to advance a piercing critique of nationalism and empire. The second section of the chapter examines the ways in which the so-called 'Pension Sketches' that Mansfield contributed to *The New Age* between 1910 and 1911 subvert dominant national and imperial imaginaries. Finally, in the last two sections of the chapter, I examine how both writers employed fragment forms in their later contributions to *The New Age*, such as aphorism and ellipsis, in order to disrupt linear, systematised discourse and thereby challenge ideas of male superiority or English national, cultural and linguistic integrity; in this way, both writers used periodical publication to unsettle dominant belief systems and formulate alternative modes of identification.

Renegade feminism

In early twentieth-century British public discourse, as Jane Garrity has argued, 'the categories of *gender* and *national identity* are inseparable'.[20] Economic and political competition from recently industrialised nations such as Germany, the United States and Japan, a disastrous military campaign in the Boer War (in which a third of volunteers had been rejected as physically unfit for service), increased infant mortality among the poor and a birth rate that had been steadily declining since the turn of the century were all factors that exacerbated fears that Britain was about to be eclipsed as an imperial power and that the population was becoming degenerate and racially inferior. As Anna Davin suggests, the 'result was a surge of concern about the bearing and rearing of children – the next generation of soldiers and workers, the Imperial race'.[21] In the first decade of the twentieth century, the number of voluntary organisations promoting public health, hygiene and motherhood expanded year on year: the Institute of Hygiene (1903), the Infants' Health Society (1904), the National League of Health, Maternity and Child Welfare (1905), the Eugenics Education Society (1908) and the Women's League of Service for Motherhood (1910) being prime examples.[22] With the population viewed as a national resource that guaranteed the power of the empire, it was argued that if Britain was to continue to compete on the international stage then the country must rear healthy, virile children. In the context of this public discourse, as Garrity has argued, the 'white, middle-class, procreative female body was regarded as integral to the well-being of the nation and central to empire-building, key to conceptions of racial fitness and national stability'; as Garrity clarifies, 'the word "race," when applied to women in early twentieth-century Britain, invariably had imperial connotations and functioned as a synonym for "nation"'.[23] The body of the white, middle-class Englishwoman, therefore, was valued as a national asset that 'would both stabilize the imaginary borders of the nation and contribute to the expansion of its empire': the female body was the guarantor of 'British racial stability' and national identity.[24]

These ideas reaffirmed the belief that a woman's 'natural' role was in the home. As Major-General Sir Frederick Maurice declared in 1903, quoting the Emperor of Germany and thereby drawing an explicit comparison between Britain and its principal international rival, 'for the raising of a virile race, either of soldiers or of citizens, it is essential that the attention of the mothers of the land should be mainly devoted to the three K's – Kinder, Kuche, Kirche' (Children, Kitchen, Church).[25] In this context, 'new women' who challenged the 'natural' division of the sexes were viewed with increasing hostility. A doctor writing in the *Eugenics Review* in 1911, for example, declared that whilst 'the new woman is a more interesting companion than her predecessors', 'womanliness' finds its best 'expression in the domestic sphere and more particularly in the roles of wife and mother': the 'new women' may be intelligent and capable in the arts and sciences, trades and professions, he argued, but they were not fit 'to become the mothers of a stronger and more virile race, able to keep Britain in its present proud position among the nations of the world'.[26] This view shaped the backlash to the increasing demands for female suffrage in the first years of the twentieth century. Writing in the *Anti-Suffrage Review* in 1910, for instance, Lord Cromer declared: 'can we hope to compete with such a nation as this [Germany] if we war against nature, and endeavour to invert the natural roles of the sexes?

We cannot do so.'[27] The 'natural' division of the sexes into the different spheres of the 'public' and 'domestic', it was argued, would secure the power of the British Empire and produce a stronger, 'more virile race'.

One of the striking features of the suffrage movement in the early twentieth century, however, was the ready acceptance of this 'natural' domestic and maternal role for women. A leader of the Women's Social and Political Union (WSPU), Emmeline Pethick-Lawrence, for instance, confirmed that a woman's 'most sacred duty' and 'greatest privilege' was 'the nurture and care of little children': writing in the periodical *Votes for Women*, she declared that the suffrage movement 'means the coming into the world of new and noble race ideals' and that this would help women 'rear a healthy race'.[28] With many in the WSPU becoming disenchanted by this rhetoric, as well as by the growing autocracy of Pethick-Lawrence and Christabel and Emmeline Pankhurst, the Women's Freedom League (WFL) split from the Union in 1906. Following this development, the WSPU began to disentangle itself from its previous affiliation with the Independent Labour Party and increasingly moved away from its socialist origins. For many, such as Teresa Billington-Greig, the leader of the WFL, the WSPU came to represent a conformist and avowedly middle-class movement that was focused exclusively on attaining the vote at the expense of identifying and attempting to alleviate the economic basis for gender inequality. For these critics, the underlying acceptance within the WSPU of the existing political, economic and social system was further exposed by the outbreak of the First World War: WSPU members were among some of the first to hand out white feathers to men who did not enlist and the first to call for national conscription; making an agreement with Lloyd George to put the campaign for the vote on hold until after the war, the WSPU also changed the title of its periodical from *The Suffragette* to *The Britannia* in October 1915, signalling that it was now the national interest and the protection of empire that mattered more than the attainment of the vote.

The WSPU and the 'suffragettes' have been afforded a prominent place in histories of early twentieth-century feminism, largely due to the highly public tactics of militancy employed before the war, such as window-smashing and painting-slashing. As a result, as Helen McNeil has observed, the diversity of *avant-guerre* feminisms has often been overlooked, obscuring the history of other individuals and political movements that were positioned in direct opposition to the WSPU.[29] In *Revolutionary Socialism and the Woman's Movement* (1910), for instance, Lily Gair Wilkinson attacked the suffrage movement as merely reformist, arguing that female suffrage would benefit only those 'who belong to the privileged or propertied class in society'.[30] The following year, Billington-Greig wrote a denunciatory treatise titled *The Militant Suffrage Movement – Emancipation in a Hurry*, in which she argued that WSPU militancy was 'determinedly conventional' and simply a publicity stunt, attacking 'soft' targets rather than large Liberal-owned factories, and that the Pankhurst autocracy prevented independent thought.[31] Similarly, the majority of contributors to the radical magazine *The Freewoman*, founded by Dora Marsden after she split from the WSPU in 1911, argued that the suffrage movement merely reaffirmed stereotypical gender roles which perpetuated the oppression of women and that the struggle for a single reform, the vote, served only to divert energies away from wider feminist debate. These alternatives to the WSPU-dominated narrative of early twentieth-century feminism, as Les Garner has observed, reveal a constellation of 'revolutionary perspectives on sexuality, reproduction and the domestic and maternal ideology'.[32]

The writings of Beatrice Hastings belong to this other history. From 1907, as Delap has examined, Hastings was instrumental in orchestrating debate within *The New Age* about the 'Woman Question' and brought the periodical into contact with other journals devoted to feminism and the suffrage movement, creating a 'periodical community' that included *Votes for Women* and *The Englishwoman*.[33] This ensured that *The New Age* continued to be read by feminists and suffragists despite the journal's strong anti-suffrage tendencies. Indeed, in the pre-war years, *The New Age* was an important platform for widely divergent opinion on the 'Woman Question', from the staunch anti-feminism of Ernest Belfort Bax, for example, to the feminist rallying cries of Billington-Greig. Hastings used her many pseudonyms and various personae in *The New Age* to reflect and satirise this wide range of opinion: she played with the identities of 'feminist' and 'anti-feminist', often using one pseudonym to comment upon work penned under a different name, thereby simulating debate and fabricating controversy. As such, Hastings's views do not necessarily represent a unified system of thought: very quickly, for example, she moves from equivocal support for the suffrage movement to an uncompromising, radical eschewal of all collectivist politics. Through her many contributions to *The New Age* and her many shifts in viewpoint, however, Hastings arrived at what we might term a 'feminist anti-suffragist' position. Inspired by Nietzsche's philosophy, she advocated the importance of individual female agency, personality and strength of will as the necessary preliminaries to social change. In this sense, Hastings anticipated by almost two years the 'individualist feminism' more commonly associated with Marsden and *The Freewoman*. Whilst Hastings's views were often contradictory and intentionally ambiguous, therefore, her political philosophy can be categorised by its consistent emphasis on the free and dissenting individual: what I term here 'renegade feminism'.

In her first contribution to *The New Age* in 1907, a short sketch titled 'A Modern Bacchante', Hastings suggests that 'modern' women, if they are really free, should *flaunt* their freedom.[34] Following this, she quickly became a regular voice within the periodical, enlarging controversies surrounding feminism and the suffrage movement. Writing as Beatrice Tina, in direct response to Belfort Bax's article 'Feminism and Female Suffrage', for example, Hastings argued that 'women alone know what women need', that women love 'liberty of mind and body' just as much as men, and that women will never achieve greater equality so long as it is dictated to them by an all-male establishment.[35] Belfort Bax had argued that men suffered under a number of legal disabilities that more than outweighed women's lack of the vote; Hastings responded that the 'return made for women's disability in bearing children is meanly inadequate', arguing that trivial legal rights could not compensate for women's contribution to society through the horror of repeated childbirth.[36] This argument echoed that made by the eugenicist M. D. Eder in *The Endowment of Motherhood*, a pamphlet published by the New Age Press in 1908. The call for 'endowment' was a demand for the financial recognition by the state that motherhood contributed to the good of society; Eder argued that mothers should receive a weekly wage, plus free housing, food and fuel. As well as echoing this demand, Hastings's article, titled 'Woman as State Creditor', generated notoriety in *The New Age* for its suggestion that women did not universally seek motherhood. The author Edith Nesbit, for instance, wrote to the letters page of the periodical to suggest that Hastings was an 'abnormal female' in her dislike of maternity, concluding: 'Why scream and kick and bite and scratch and make faces at the Life-force?'[37] This article launched Hastings's career and provided the kernel for a pamphlet written under the Beatrice Tina pseudonym and published by the New Age Press, *Woman's Worst Enemy: Woman* (1909).

In this pamphlet, Hastings used her personal experience of marriage and unwanted maternity to denounce both: she links repeated childbirth to the industrialisation of labour; argues that training women as obstetricians would minimise the danger of child delivery (having seen her younger sister die in childbirth); demands greater availability of contraception, so that sexual pleasure may be separated from procreation; and, most forcefully of all, argues for less obfuscation surrounding marriage, so that young women may be educated about sex. *Woman's Worst Enemy: Woman* opens with the line: 'This book is written for the pleasure of denouncing the sort of female whose modesty howls for silence on such important matters as sex and maternity'.[38] The paradox of the pamphlet's title, therefore, is addressed to a particular 'sort of female' that Hastings elsewhere terms the 'Other Woman', those who perpetuate a cycle of enforced innocence among the young. This designation is very similar to Marsden's later concept of the slavish 'Bondwoman' who is opposed by the independent 'Freewoman'.[39] Writing in 1908, for instance, Hastings defined the 'Other Woman' thus:

> It is the Other Woman who [. . .] intensifies the fury of competition by her covetous demands, and exasperates class distinctions by her insolent exclusiveness. It is the Other Woman [. . .] who preaches content and resignation to the poor that her own may have the fairer field and more favour. [. . .] It is the Other Woman (for the most part) who has the children, and therefore gets full opportunity of instilling her gospel, such as it is, into the receptive ears of young England. The Other Woman's power is thus already enormous, and out of all proportion to the influence wielded by the thinking few. [. . .] When the young girl begins to think, and wants to be Woman and not Other Woman, who is it helps her? [. . .] The Other Woman is the real formative influence in society.[40]

By employing the concept of the Other Woman, therefore, Hastings sought to reintroduce a socialist critique of class and capitalist economics into feminist political analysis. Writing as 'A Reluctant Suffragette', she concludes this article by stating that the Other Woman 'reigns in any case, and at present very badly. She must be taught the uses of her power, and if nothing but a vote can teach her, in Heaven's name give her a vote.'[41] This is indicative of the way in which Hastings's early support for the suffrage movement was always equivocal and conditional. In other articles written in 1908, for example, Hastings endorsed suffrage militancy, but not as a means of achieving the vote; militancy was the only way to counter an oppressive British social system, Hastings argued, and she drew particular attention to the degradations suffered by imprisoned suffragettes and an incident at a suffrage meeting at the Albert Hall at which several women had been raped by Liberal stewards.[42] As she wrote at the end of 'Woman as State Creditor' and retained in the version republished as

Woman's Worst Enemy: Woman: 'The militant suffragettes have saved us from the last ignominy of the slave – the obligation to give thanks for enfranchisement'.[43]

It was Hastings's concept of the Other Woman that ultimately made it impossible for her to support the suffrage movement, however. When she wrote that the logic of anti-feminists such as Belfort Bax 'presents itself to my mind as being so deeply and rationally irrefutable' it was because she loathed what she perceived to be the female 'parasites' who campaigned for the vote, not for greater 'sex freedom', but in order to gain material advantages within marriage, to 'grab after' their 'husband's earnings'.[44] Like Lily Gair Wilkinson, Hastings argued that female suffrage would enfranchise only the Other Woman, who would use the vote to protect her own self-interests and those of the moneyed classes. For Hastings, therefore, female suffrage did not equate to female freedom: far better to be a woman 'with the spirit to be free' than to be a parasite with the vote.[45] There is a clear strain of misogyny in these writings, as when Hastings quips: 'The world is not hard upon women; women are'.[46] However, she always had a particular 'sort of female' in mind, such as Nesbit, who upholds sexual difference and celebrates maternity and marriage in the sacralised language of 'God' and 'Life-force'. In this way, Hastings consistently positioned herself within *The New Age* as a champion of the 'thinking few', versus the mass of what she perceived to be the unthinking, conventional, class-bound and parasitic 'Other Women'.

These ideas shaped the editorial philosophy of *The New Age*. In an article titled 'The Superman', published in December 1910 as part of a regular series of Socratic dialogues on modern themes written by Orage, for example, one of the interlocutors – who is a mouthpiece for Orage's own editorial opinions – distinguishes between the 'intelligent woman' who is averse to 'procreation' and 'ideals of motherhood' and the woman who submits to the 'overwhelming force of ignorance': 'the race is kept going by the stupid', he states.[47] Discussing this idea in relation to 'the modern woman's movement', he concludes:

> I am prepared to maintain not only that feminism is a revolt against feminism, but that the most intelligent feminists are aware of it. Just when, in fact, the value of motherhood is seen to be declining in the world-market, women who have no other commodity begin to cry up its value. Of such women there are, I admit, many in the feminist movement. But from the same cause other women, with other commodities than motherhood for sale, desire an amplified scope for themselves. These are the real feminists and, as I say, they are averse from procreation.[48]

Orage here singles out the 'real feminists' as the 'thinking few' who revolt against mainstream feminism. Whereas the majority celebrate 'the dignity of motherhood and the solemn duty of women to maintain the purity and vigour of the race', Orage writes, the 'real feminists' insist on 'an amplified scope for themselves'.[49]

Throughout her writings, Hastings develops this distinction between the 'ignorant' and the 'intelligent woman'. In *Woman's Worst Enemy: Woman*, for instance, she denounces motherhood as mentally debilitating: 'To a highly-developed, imaginative woman maternity means months of odious ignominy, and finally a struggle with death as through waves of flame', she writes, whereas to 'the perfect mother the whole process of maternity should be from beginning to end a sensuous and a spiritual enjoyment'.[50] In drawing this distinction, Hastings clearly subscribed to the eugenicist ideals of her day. Arguing that the population was a national resource that should be controlled and managed by the state, for instance, she writes that: 'Good breeding is a communal matter, and the ideal State would be one wherein every person born was really welcomed, and every person dead one really missed'.[51] Only good mothers give birth to good children, Hastings argues, and 'a community will demand quality rather than quantity': 'numbers count less than intelligence'.[52]

It was for the good of the nation, therefore, that motherhood should be a choice. Hastings argued that this choice could be facilitated only by women's financial independence from men, or 'economic freedom – that is, the control of her sex instincts independently of man's control of the means to live'.[53] Again echoing the idea of 'endowment', she writes that women 'must be freed from the terror of starvation in case they become mothers': 'If at such a period all classes of women were economically freed, it would be possible to predict the immediate birth of happily and freely born children, and perhaps an even constantly renewable source of energy for the nation'.[54] As such, Hastings's ideas were clearly formulated within the public discourse outlined above, linking motherhood and childbirth with racial stability and national power. So long as women remained financially dependent upon men, Hastings argued, 'the birth-rate steadily declines' and 'numberless women continue to bear unwanted children, to whom they bequeath a failing generative energy, which finally weakens the whole nation into sterility and ignominious decay'.[55] Hastings's ideas were therefore formulated in response to prevailing anxieties about racial degeneracy:

> A decadent nation, in attempting to restore its energy by forcing women into becoming mothers, merely burns the candle at both ends. There is only one possible way in which such a State may recuperate its strength, and that way is to imitate the instinct of young nations in neglecting marriage bonds and giving its women sex-liberty, so that those with the strongest maternal instinct may freely direct the genius of motherhood.[56]

Hastings argued that 'the offspring of unhappy women could not be but poor stuff' and that the continued need for reform in attitudes to motherhood and childbirth 'is decimating the population-rate'.[57] In this, her concern was with preserving the strength of the nation. Adopting the apocalyptic language of the Old Testament, for instance, she admonishes the 'English Adam': ''Tis thine own fault that thou shalt die the slow death of past nations' and 'Thou deserves well thy quiver full of dolts and cripples': 'Behold the ruins of all the world before us. There under, lowest down, lie the women who should never have been mothers.'[58]

These ideas were given imaginative expression in a novella by Hastings titled *Whited Sepulchres*, serialised in *The New Age* under the 'Beatrice Tina' pseudonym from April 1909. The protagonist of this story is Nan Pearson. In the first scene of the novella, we see Nan in her bedroom sat 'in the novelistic fashion' reading Rossetti's 'The Blessed Damozel' and surrounded by a 'demi-romantic arrangement' of art needlework, pink ribbons and religious watercolours.[59] Nan's knowledge about sex is limited to the biblical phrase of 'one flesh' and she is described as 'the merest child in her conception of the secrets of marriage'.[60] On the night before Nan's wedding, her mother equips her with only a few words of useless advice:

> 'Now listen, my dearest Nan. You really need a little plain commonsense [*sic*]. Love and marriage are not at all the nonsense you seem to imagine they are. Men are but men, and before the honeymoon is over you will discover what I mean. [. . .] Marriage is not romantic at all in actual fact. There is a good deal of – er – disagreeableness to be encountered, and probably much pain, but you must put up with it. It is natural and ordained by Providence. It is the lot of all women [. . .]'[61]

On the honeymoon, a violation occurs: naivety is swept away by this traumatic sexual initiation and romantic expectation is replaced with realistic dismay. Nan reflects, fatalistically: 'So that is marriage'.[62] When she tries to leave, her husband forces her to stay, holding her by the neck and throwing her down onto the bed. *Whited Sepulchres* is about the hypocrisy of the institution of marriage: that which is outwardly pure, beautiful and 'ordained by Providence' conceals violence, pain and unhappiness.

The next chapter advances eight years, close to the time of the work's publication, and is prefaced by a quotation from Hastings's 1908 article on the Other Woman written under the 'Reluctant Suffragette' pseudonym: 'What bars Woman's progress now is not so much Man as the Other Woman'.[63] This is an example of Hastings using multiple personae in order to generate the illusion of a conversation and identification between contributors to *The New Age*. The chapter prefaced by this quotation depicts the social world of the Other Woman. Nan – now 'Mrs Tom Heck' – holds 'at home' afternoons, in which the women discuss topical issues, such as the suffrage movement, but conclude: 'Of course, it's a shame that we should suffer and men get off free, but God arranged it like that, and we have to put up with it'.[64] In this social circle, 'intellectual things' (that which might interest the 'thinking few') are quickly dismissed; instead, the women prefer to talk exclusively about their children and the upcoming church bazaar.[65]

When Nan meets the young, cosmopolitan and artistically inclined Raymond Cattle, the novella builds towards the possible transgression occasioned by a society ball. However, Nan's romantic expectations are again misplaced. After a short kiss outside the ball, Raymond asks Nan: 'You love me? [. . .] You are mine?' but he quickly betrays her, thinking to himself:

> Fair and foolish, and a little faded, was his summary. He hated fair women, really – of course he did. And this one, with all her monstrous airs of puritanry [*sic*], was easy as a lazy demi-mondaine; and far more stupid. [. . .] He determined to keep a certain promise he had made to reappear in Paris on Sunday evening. There was chic in Paris, the real chic, and real gay love – and no scandal.[66]

In the correspondence pages of *The New Age*, Hastings described *Whited Sepulchres* as a depiction of 'the common stagnant life': 'The fact is that such stories have been written hundreds of times, but always in the vocabulary of romance'.[67] Nan hopes to find release from 'the common stagnant life' in a love affair with Raymond, but this romantic expectation is replaced by the dismal reality of her marriage and motherhood. In particular, Hastings set out to subvert the tropes of romantic fiction by depicting the 'drudgeries of the nursery'.[68] Nan's son is a spoilt, screaming, unmanageable child who makes the house uninhabitable for

Mr Heck, who finds his respite in the brothels of the West End, fathering other children by other women. Hastings not only highlights the double standards of sexual morality in early twentieth-century Britain, but also depicts the 'failing generative energy' of the nation in the body of the unwanted tyrant child, a child who is the product of Nan's youthful ignorance about sex and the institutionalised male violence practised by her husband; a child who literally cries himself to death, choking in convulsions. With *Whited Sepulchres* illuminating the social hypocrisy surrounding marriage and maternity, Nan's son figures the racial degeneracy and national decay that Hastings believed were perpetuated by this hypocrisy, and the novella closes with Nan tired, haggard and old before her years.

Whited Sepulchres ignited heated discussion within the correspondence pages of *The New Age* over the following months, correspondence that covered the topic of rape within marriage and the advantage taken by men over women's ignorance about sex. Hastings's ideas would have been familiar to anyone reading *The New Age* over the summer of 1909, therefore. We know that Mansfield left England for Germany at some point in the week preceding 4 June, the date on which she arrived in Bavaria with her mother, who had sailed from New Zealand to cover up the scandal of Mansfield's hasty marriage to George Bowden. The last instalment of *Whited Sepulchres* was published on 10 June, so it would have been impossible for Mansfield to have read this or the previous instalment from the week before at the time of publication; however, she may well have followed the first five instalments of the novella. Indeed, Mansfield had first met Bowden in December 1908 at the St John's Wood home of Dr Caleb Saleeby, a well known science writer and regular contributor to *The New Age* with articles on race, eugenics and motherhood. In 1909, for instance, Saleeby published a book titled *Parenthood and Race Culture*, in which he wrote: 'The history of nations is determined not on the battlefield but in the nursery, and the battalions which give lasting victory are the battalions of babies'.[69] As a member of Saleeby's social circle, therefore, Mansfield would have been immersed in the public discourse of motherhood and imperialism outlined above. It is also highly likely that she would have been closely following debates within *The New Age* on this topic. At the end of 1908, *The New Age* was enjoying an all-time high circulation of 22,000 copies (and many single copies would have been passed between several readers). Whilst there exists no concrete evidence that Mansfield read *The New Age* before she began contributing to the periodical at the beginning of 1910, as an aspiring writer within Saleeby's social circle at a time when *The New Age* was widely distributed, it is not just possible but highly probable that Mansfield was a regular reader of the periodical when she was in London between August 1908 and June 1909; therefore, it is likely that Mansfield read the first five instalments of Hastings's novella, in which Nan has become trapped by marriage and hopes to find release in a love affair with the cosmopolitan and artistic Raymond Cattle, who writes to her from 'gay' Paris.[70]

A previously unknown short story by Mansfield that I discovered in a London archive, titled 'A Little Episode' and printed as Appendix II to this book, is based upon exactly this kind of love triangle: the young protagonist, Yvonne, is trapped in a loveless marriage to Geoffrey Mandeville; after reigniting a love affair with the Parisian pianist Jacques Saint Pierre, she hopes to find release from the stifling conventions of society; however, the story ends with Jacques betraying Yvonne, as he writes a letter in his hotel room to another lover in which he reveals that he sees Yvonne as 'quite a little Society lady' with 'the inevitable feminine passion for trying to relight fires that have long since been ashes'.[71] 'A Little Episode' ends with Yvonne 'instinctively with a little childish gesture' covering her face with one arm as she waits in bed for her husband, who walks up the stairs with 'heavy, ponderous footsteps'. This tableau, with its suggestion of rape within marriage, prefigures a similar scene in Mansfield's later story 'Frau Brechenmacher Attends a Wedding'. As already noted, it would have been impossible for Mansfield to have read the last two instalments of Hastings's novella at the time of publication, which makes it all the more remarkable that both writers independently arrived at the same narrative twist, ending their stories with the young female protagonist being betrayed by the cosmopolitan would-be lover and left to the institutionalised violence of a domineering husband.

The notable similarity between 'A Little Episode' and *Whited Sepulchres* highlights what Oliver Tearle has recently theorised in his examination of T. E. Hulme's writings as 'parafluence; that is, a convergent evolution of ideas' and modes of expression 'among contemporary like-minded thinkers and artists, which acknowledges the possibility of direct influence while at the same time remaining sceptical of any linear progression from one thinker to another'.[72] Like Nan, for example, Yvonne's life is mediated by 'Other Women': elder society ladies, Mrs Mason and Mrs Wood, who are portrayed as the cynical arbiters of English morality. The reader learns about Yvonne through the public dialogue of these two women, their voices 'full of withering contempt': after her father died in Paris, leaving her penniless at the age of seventeen, Yvonne was 'rescued' by her aunt and uncle, who took her to live with them in Manchester. This detail is then echoed at the end of the story, when we see Jacques 'in his rooms at the Hotel Manchester'. With these two references to Manchester, Mansfield alludes to her own biography, which helps us to date the composition of 'A Little Episode'. When Mrs Beauchamp arrived in England on 27 May 1909 (the day on which the fifth instalment of *Whited Sepulchres* was published), she took her daughter to the hotel in Manchester Street, London, before they travelled on to Germany. In a story in which the character structure clearly parallels Mansfield's own biography (Yvonne/Mansfield, Geoffrey Mandeville/George Bowden, Jacques Saint Pierre/Garnet Trowell), Mansfield associates her mother with the unwelcome bourgeois relatives who 'rescue' the protagonist from her unconventional life of love and art. As such, we can confidently date the composition of 'A Little Episode' to the summer of 1909. Composed at roughly the same moment, *Whited Sepulchres* and 'A Little Episode' highlight a striking 'parafluence' between the writings of Hastings and Mansfield, who both responded to contemporary debates about the 'Woman Question' with stories based upon the same character structure, the same narrative twist, and the same thematic focus on female independence versus social convention, the entrapment of naive girls within marriage, and the advantage taken by men.

Mansfield began contributing to *The New Age* at the end of February 1910. From the beginning of that year, Hastings had been writing under a new pseudonym, 'D. Triformis', which allowed her to shift position considerably. 'D. Triformis' is far more critical of the suffragettes than 'Beatrice Tina', especially of the 'Liberal' women associated with the WSPU and its journal *Votes for Women*.[73] Whereas 'Beatrice Tina' had observed that if 'woman is the apostle of liberty she must also be the devotee of equality', 'D. Triformis' argues that 'it is not sufficient that a woman should claim mere equality with men. She must proclaim herself superior.'[74] Whereas 'Beatrice Tina' had voiced conditional support for suffrage militancy, 'D. Triformis' writes:

> We have the unusual spectacle, in the battle between the Suffragettes and the Government, of beholding each side attempting to coerce the other. It is time, in face of the inhumane aspect which the situation begins to bear, for the most reasonable and truly progressive section to cease, or at least

> to abandon, the use of force in favour of some line of action safer for the nation as a whole. Will that reasonable and progressive section prove to be the women?[75]

Writing as 'D. Triformis' also enabled Hastings to promote her earlier work. In the issue of *The New Age* containing Mansfield's second contribution to the periodical, for instance, an article by 'D. Triformis' made pointed reference to *Woman's Worst Enemy: Woman*, 'a much earlier pronouncement by the feminist, Beatrice Tina, protesting merely against the abuse of marriage, [that has] been officially boycotted and privately denounced'.[76] This highlights Hastings's self-identification – or, rather, her identification of an earlier self – as 'feminist', and it also shows her changing positions. The Triformis/Tina exchange not only allowed Hastings to keep her earlier writings at the forefront of debate, reminding readers of its existence, but also enabled her to amend, revise and retract earlier statements and to clarify her current ideas. For instance, 'D. Triformis' observes:

> When Miss Beatrice Tina wrote: 'The militant suffragettes have saved us from the last ignominy of the slave – the obligation to give thanks for enfranchisement,' she penned, though in a spirited style, one of the most foolish fancies of the average thoughtless woman. [. . .] if we set our minds upon becoming free from within, we shall see that such epigrams, though fascinating, are untrue.[77]

This allowed for a response the following week from 'Beatrice (Tina) Hastings':

> I have no defence to make for my unlucky epigram. I admit that it is not true as it stands, and that the idea (unexpressed) in my mind at the time was certainly of 'mental' freedom, and then I am bound to agree with D. Triformis that mental freedom must be gained by thought. I have learned a good deal from D. Triformis and I hope that I may learn more.[78]

Hastings reminds readers of her earlier work by suggesting that it has been systematically boycotted, complaining of the 'mercenary spirit among [the] so-called advanced women' whom she has opposed: 'I have been killed out of the "advanced" movement. I now devote myself in the shades to art and humanitarianism.'[79] With this letter, Hastings revealed herself from behind the mask of 'Beatrice Tina' and subsequently used her own name to write articles promoting the 'humanitarian' campaign against capital punishment, whilst 'D. Triformis' continued to write about feminism and the suffrage movement. The shape-shifting between these three personae is suggested in the pseudonym chosen by Hastings, 'tri-formis'.

In an article titled 'To Your Posts, Feminists', mocking the rhetoric of suffrage militancy, 'D. Triformis' writes: 'The vote will make no woman free who is not individually free before she gets it. In the direction of cherishing individual freedom lies the work of true feminists.'[80] This is the consistent theme to Hastings's contributions to *The New Age* at this time. In an article titled 'Women and Freedom', for example, Hastings begins by quoting a contribution to *The Englishwoman* by the feminist and classical scholar Jane Harrison:

> We are humane so far as we are conscious or sensitive to the individual life. Patriotism is collective herd instinct, it is repression of individuality. You feel strongly because you feel alike, you are reinforced by the other homogeneous units, you sing the same song, you wave the same flag. Humanity is sympathy with infinite differences, with utter individualism, with complete differentiation, and it is only possible through the mystery of organic spiritual union.[81]

By quoting this passage to support her argument, Hastings claims that both the suffrage movement and patriotism suppress under homogeneity 'free personal choice in act and in thought'.[82] Like other critics of the WSPU, Hastings is here attacking the tactics and autocratic structure of the Union, emphasising instead the importance of wider feminist debate and individual opinion. At this time, Hastings loathed the WSPU for its quantitative logic – the way in which success was invariably measured by numbers of people or amounts of money. This logic, she claimed, suppressed individuality under the 'collective herd instinct': 'Mobs do not believe in the way of reason; they believe in noise and banners and the power of money'.[83] In contrast, Hastings believed that '[i]ndividuals, people who know themselves, are neither content to be herded nor to be the leaders of herds'.[84] I quote the following passage at length because it neatly encapsulates Hastings's individualist, renegade feminism:

> Physical freedom may well march around and wave a flag, dancing for very joy of unchained limbs. Released convicts and slaves fittingly breathe deep and set off somewhere at a run. But mental freedom is a different thing and has different attributes, inward and invisible, corresponding to the outward and visible matter of its advent. Physical freedom may be given from without. Mental freedom must be begotten from within. Thought begets it; and its only outward evidence is personal choice – a happy, but never a noisy, thing. The woman who is mentally free, knowing

> how imperceptible is the evolution of this freedom, knows, also, that to try and impart the free mind to a person who wants still to be shouting and waving a flag would be of as much use as to fasten a wing upon a lizard and bid it be a bird and fly.[85]

Hastings writes: 'all the slavery we endure we endure because our minds are not free. When we think freely we shall choose freely, we shall act freely.'[86] Moreover, by quoting Harrison, Hastings clearly equates the flag-waving patriot and the marching suffragette. This suggests a revision to the earlier rhetoric of communal, state-led, national eugenics promoted in *Woman's Worst Enemy: Woman*: now, Hastings implies that patriotism and nationalism exemplify the same 'repression of individuality' as the suffrage movement.

Writing in her journal in May 1908, Mansfield also expressed the belief that women were 'firmly held with the self-fashioned chains of slavery': chains that 'must be self-removed' through 'happiness and freedom'.[87] New Zealand had been the first country to extend the vote to women, but Mansfield writes that talk of 'our emancipated country' is 'pure nonsense!'[88] She observes: 'It is the hopelessly insipid doctrine that love is the only thing in the world, taught, hammered into women, from generation to generation, which hampers us so cruelly'.[89] To 'get rid of that bogey', she writes, women must embrace '[i]ndependence, resolve, firm purpose, and the gift of discrimination, *mental cleverness*' and 'individuality'.[90] These ideas are strikingly similar to those advanced by Hastings: both writers stress that women are responsible for their own emancipation, which is to be gained not with the vote but through mental freedom, individuality and a disregard for generational doctrine. This journal entry by Mansfield, as such, reveals a remarkable 'parafluence' between her ideas and the individualist feminism promoted by Hastings in *The New Age*.

Whilst acknowledging the possibility of direct influence from Hastings to Mansfield, I want to stress the convergence between the work of these two writers in the next section of this chapter, and the way in which the work of each illuminates that of the other. Clare Hanson and Andrew Gurr have suggested that Hastings exercised a direct influence upon Mansfield's work, helping to edit and shape her stories: 'It seems likely that many of the stories were first sketched out in Bavaria, and some even completed, but that most underwent considerable revision under the guiding hand of Beatrice Hastings before they were published'.[91] This seems entirely likely. On occasions, for example, Mansfield's stories directly and self-consciously echo Hastings's writings, as when the narrator of 'Frau Fischer' boldly declares 'I consider child-bearing the most ignominious of professions', a direct echo of the passage from *Woman's Worst Enemy: Woman* in which Hastings writes that '[t]o a highly-developed, imaginative woman maternity means months of odious ignominy'.[92] Whilst moments of direct influence are certainly possible, however, Mansfield independently arrived at very similar notions to Hastings before her arrival in London, as the extracts from the 1908 journal highlight. Examining the intersections between the writings of these two women therefore allows us to trace a convergent evolution of ideas and modes of expression, in which 'mental freedom' is privileged above 'physical freedom', and female 'individuality' is placed in opposition to the 'collective herd instinct'. Situating Mansfield's early writings within the original historical contexts of publication, as such, enables us to recognise the political resonance these stories would have had to her contemporary readers.

The 'Pension Sketches'

Mansfield's first contribution to *The New Age*, published on 24 February 1910 and titled 'Bavarian Babies: The Child-Who-Was-Tired', was a free transposition of a story by Anton Chekhov titled 'Spat Khochetsia' that had been published in English translation as 'Sleepyhead' in 1903. This first contribution immediately announced affinities between the writings of Mansfield and Hastings: like *Whited Sepulchres*, Mansfield's story is resolutely anti-maternal, focusing on the terror surrounding a screaming, unmanageable child. The 'Frau' of the story, for instance, complains that her 'insides are all twisted up from having children too quickly' and her servant girl has her own misgivings on learning of another baby on the way:

> 'Another baby! Hasn't she finished having them *yet*?' thought the Child. 'Two babies getting eye teeth – two babies to get up for in the night – two babies to carry about and wash their little piggy clothes!' She looked with horror at the one in her arms, who, seeming to understand the contemptuous loathing of her tired glance, doubled his fists, stiffened his body, and began violently screaming.[93]

The story ends melodramatically with the servant girl, desperate for sleep, smothering the baby to death as she tries to stifle its violent screaming.

Subsequently, between March 1910 and June 1911, Mansfield contributed a series of short stories to *The New Age* that can be divided into two kinds of narrative. First, there was a series of stories sometimes designated within the periodical as 'Pension Sketches', narrated in either the first or the third person but always focusing on the same semi-autobiographical protagonist, a young woman travelling alone and 'taking the cure' in a Bavarian spa town. These stories include 'Germans at Meat', 'The Baron', 'The Luft Bad', 'The Sister of the Baroness', 'Frau Fischer' and 'The Modern Soul'. These travel sketches found a welcome place in *The New Age*, a periodical which regularly featured travelogues, such as Bart Kennedy's 'A Continental Trip', which appeared weekly from October 1909, the 'American Notes' by the pseudonymous 'Juvenal' serialised in 1910, and the 'Letters from Abroad' by Huntly Carter, published in 1911.

The other stories by Mansfield are all narrated in the third person, do not have a shared protagonist, and instead depict the communal life of the Bavarian town. These include 'At "Lehmann's"', 'Frau Brechenmacher Attends a Wedding' and 'A Birthday'. These three communal stories all develop the critique of marriage and maternity first outlined in 'Bavarian Babies'. In 'At "Lehmann's"', for instance, youthful innocence is exposed as dangerous ignorance: 'She knew practically nothing except that the Frau had a baby inside her, which had to come out – very painful indeed. [. . .] Birth – what was it? wondered Sabina.'[94] In this story, Mansfield critiques the way in which society perpetuates ignorance about sex and childbirth among girls, establishing a stark juxtaposition at the story's climax between romantic naivety and the harsh, physical reality of maternity. Leading a 'Young Man' into the 'ladies' cloak room' at the back of the café, a 'warm place' filled with a burning fire, Sabina's first romantic encounter is interrupted by 'a frightful, tearing shriek' as the Frau gives birth in the room above.[95] Unable to connect her current situation with the Frau's physical condition, Sabina herself shrieks in frustration. Similarly, 'Frau Brechenmacher Attends a Wedding' highlights the perpetuation of ignorance about sex among young women, with the eponymous character fatalistically reflecting 'Girls have a lot to learn'.[96] The story depicts marriage as a coercive social convention: a priest is called to calm the bride Theresa's 'hysterics' before the wedding, and she is presented with the gift of a 'baby's bottle and two little cradles holding china dolls' that are 'dandled' before her by the bridegroom, tauntingly.[97] As the Brechenmachers arrive home after the wedding, Frau

Brechenmacher suddenly remembers 'how they had come home together the first night'.[98] Herr Brechenmacher has the same thought and, grinning, recalls how his wife had been 'an innocent one' who had resisted his advances and had to be 'taught'.[99] The violence of sexual initiation is echoed at the end of the story with an allusion to rape within marriage: 'She lay down on the bed and put her arm across her face like a child who expected to be hurt as Herr Brechenmacher lurched in'.[100] Lastly, 'A Birthday' depicts the threatened masculinity of a bourgeois man as he waits for the birth of his first son. Narcissistic and self-involved, Andreas Binzer can only think of his own 'helpless' suffering and 'sensitiveness' as the 'wailing cry' of his wife Anna is caught by the wind and echoes around the house.[101] Looking at a photograph of Anna as a young woman, taken before their marriage, her image suddenly becomes uncanny to Andreas: unable to think of Anna as anything other than wife or mother, she 'looked like a stranger – abnormal, a freak'.[102] 'A Birthday' satirises the male viewpoint on marriage and maternity, with Andreas Binzer failing to fully comprehend his wife's current pain or past agency.

The 'Pension Sketches' are distinguished from these rather bleak stories by their witty and irreverent central protagonist. In contrast to the other pension guests, who are 'dressed like upholstered chairs' (an echo of Mansfield's description of the 'women who looked like very badly upholstered chairs' at the suffrage meeting she attended in September 1908) and live out an institutionalised parasitism of enforced inactivity, the female narrator embraces the liberties of solitary travel and consistently asserts her own freedom and intellectual independence, refusing to be defined either by her body or by the predetermined gender roles of marriage or motherhood.[103] In these sketches, the procreative, female body is shown to be a symbolic site used within public discourse to guarantee the health and security of the nation. As Anne Fernihough has argued, '[t]he "I" of the *Pension* sketches is threatening because it is precisely that: a self, as opposed to a vehicle for racial progress or an appendage to the bourgeois male'.[104] In particular, the narrator's status as a national alien marks her out as eccentric, living outside national imaginaries and independently from existing social structures; for instance, she is described by her fellow pension guests as 'the stranger in our midst' and elsewhere reflects: 'I felt a little crushed [. . .] at the tone – placing one outside the pale – branding me as a foreigner'.[105] This status as 'outsider', 'foreigner' and 'stranger' is fundamentally empowering, however, enabling the protagonist to occupy an uncomfortable yet subversive, disruptive position from which to quietly critique the public discourse linking gender and race, motherhood and imperialism.

In particular, the narrator's evasive and ironic asides consistently articulate this quiet critique. In the story 'Germans at Meat', for instance, the protagonist repeatedly interrupts the explicit descriptions about consumption, excretion and pregnancy made by her fellow diners, who pick their teeth with hairpins, blow on their soup and eat around large potatoes as they talk. In this story, the excessive corporeality of the protagonist's fellow diners is connected to an aggressive expansionism of both the bourgeois family and the German Empire: excessive eating guarantees the birth rate of the nation and its military strength. This connection is made explicit by the 'Widow' character when she tells the vegetarian protagonist: 'Who ever heard of having children upon vegetables? It is not possible.'[106] When the 'Widow' asks the protagonist what her husband's favourite meat is, her ignorance elicits this response:

> 'But you cannot be in earnest! You would not have kept house as his wife for a week without knowing that fact. [. . .] No wonder there is a repetition in England of that dreadful state of things in Paris,' said the Widow, folding her dinner napkin, 'how can a woman expect to keep her husband if she does not know his favourite food after three years!'[107]

In this story, eating meat and giving birth guarantee the health of the nation as a family unit, and it is the woman's role to ensure this as wife and mother. With pride, for example, the 'Widow' tells of how she has had nine '[f]ine, healthy babies' and recounts an anecdote:

> 'A friend of mine had four at the same time. Her husband was so pleased he gave a supper party and had them placed on the table. Of course she was very proud.'
>
> 'Germany,' boomed the Traveller, biting round a potato which he had speared with his knife, 'is the home of the Family.'[108]

This image of four babies placed on the family dining table of Germany suggests national cannibalism. Mansfield is here satirising the utilitarianism of the eugenic theories espoused in *The New Age* by the likes of H. G. Wells and George Bernard Shaw, in which citizens were viewed as mere resources to be consumed by the nation. Moreover, the character Herr Rat describes the British army as 'a few little boys with their veins full of nicotine poisoning', an allusion to the high level of rejection of British recruits to the Boer War on the grounds of ill-health, a recurring subject for much anxiety in *The New Age* about Britain's ability to fight an impending European conflict.[109] These anxieties about the vulnerability of Britain in the face of the increasing industrial and military might of Germany are highlighted on the cover of the issue of *The New Age* published on 20 January 1910 (Figure 1.1). Titled 'Indigestion', this image depicts Germany as an overtly masculine figure, a phantom presence mercilessly gorging on the lifeblood of a supine, enervated John Bull. For the regular reader of the periodical, Mansfield's story about excessive German consumption would have registered as an inter-textual echo of this image, published only six weeks before.

Against these contexts of nervousness about national strength, the protagonist's position as a foreign, vegetarian and childless woman travelling alone all mark her as an 'outsider' in Germany and target for national competition. At the beginning of the story, for instance, Herr Rat, who boasts that he has 'had all I wanted from women without marriage' as he tucks 'his napkin into his collar', fixes his eyes on the protagonist with a look that suggests both the threat of military invasion and the threat of rape, a look that contains his voracious appetite for both women and land: 'He fixed his cold blue eyes upon Kathleen with an expression which suggested a thousand premeditated invasions'.[110] As such, the protagonist's body becomes a symbolic site for national contest and conquest, as when Mansfield makes the subtle but pointed transitions from 'England' to 'her' to 'you': '"Don't be afraid," Herr Hoffmann said. "We don't want England. If we did we would have had her long ago. We really do not want you."'[111] 'Germans at Meat' highlights how the white, middle-class, procreative female body serves to stabilise the imaginary borders of the nation and facilitate the expansion of empire: the pregnant body of the wife and mother guarantees national strength, whereas the body of the independent, childless woman is seen as a target in the competition between militaristic nations. The protagonist's consistent refusal to conform to the expectations of her fellow diners, therefore, positions her as a vulnerable target at the same time as it highlights her robust refusal to be co-opted into the logic of a public discourse connecting maternity and nationhood, motherhood and imperialism.

This connection between the body and nation, physicality and imperialist expansion, is a recurring theme throughout the 'Pension Sketches'. In 'The Modern Soul', for example, the German characters describe England as 'merely an island of beef swimming in a warm gulf sea of gravy': the nation is merely something to be consumed by the German Empire.[112] In 'Frau Fischer', likewise, the title character lets it be known how much she 'enjoy[s] discussing the functions of the body' and, in patriotic devotion, sleeps under a picture of the Kaiser.[113] Frau Fischer delights in the idea that marriages 'make the happy family bigger' and extols the virtues of having '[h]andfuls of babies', telling the childless narrator that 'that is what you are really in need of'.[114] The narrator responds by declaring that she regards 'child-bearing the most ignominious of all professions' and that she in fact likes 'empty beds', contrary to Frau Fischer's notion that an empty bed 'is like widowhood'.[115] Predominantly, however, the narrator rebuffs Frau Fischer by being evasive or simply lying: when the Frau squeezes her hand at the end of the story, the narrator doesn't squeeze back; and, after telling Frau Fischer the improbable fiction that her husband is 'a sea-captain on a long and perilous voyage' and subsequently enduring the Frau's unwelcome advice, the narrator finally resolves to 'wreck my virgin conception and send him down somewhere off Cape Horn'.[116] Mansfield's protagonist stages a silent rebellion against Frau Fischer, retaining her independence through her freedom of thought. In this sense, the narrator embodies the 'thinking' woman celebrated by Hastings, opposed to the unthinking, conventional 'Other Woman': like Hastings, Mansfield suggests that the only outward evidence of this 'mental freedom' is 'personal choice – a happy, but never a noisy, thing'.

Similarly, the protagonist in 'The Luft Bad' refuses to yield to the strong social pressure to define herself in physical terms. A woman who performs the dance from *Salome* before excitedly telling everyone how she is 'perspiring so splendidly' and another who proudly announces how she lives 'entirely on raw vegetables and nuts' accost the protagonist, who evades questions about her national identity by climbing on to a swing and experiencing a brief but immediate, stimulating moment of physical and mental freedom:

> 'Are you an American?' said the Vegetable Lady, turning to me.
> 'No.'
> 'Then you are an Englishwoman?'
> 'Well, hardly – '
> 'You must be one of the two; you cannot help it. I have seen you walking alone several times. You wear your – '
> I got up and climbed on to the swing. The air was sweet and cool, rushing past my body. Above, white clouds trailed delicately through the blue sky. From the pine forests streamed a wild perfume, and the branches swayed together, rhythmically, sonorously. I felt so light and free and happy – so childish! I wanted to poke my tongue out at the circle on the grass, who, drawing close together, were whispering meaningly.[117]

Mansfield's protagonist refuses to be defined by her body or what she eats. Instead, her freedom of mind and 'organic union' with nature (to echo the quotation from Harrison used by Hastings) enable the protagonist quite literally to rise above the circle of socialisation, the homogeneous 'Other Women', defined entirely through their physicality. Significantly, this moment of 'mental freedom' follows the protagonist's refusal to state her nationality unequivocally: her freedom arises out of the tensions of this ambiguity, a national indeterminacy and non-place between 'England' and 'America'. In other words, the protagonist occupies a disruptive, liminal position that threatens the public discourse linking the procreative, female body to national identity and racial stability.

The deliberately ambiguous national identity of the protagonist highlights her position as an uncanny and ambivalent presence throughout the 'Pension Sketches'. As Andrew Harrison has observed, this ambivalence is enacted at the level of form in several instances of linguistic uncertainty and failed translation; by concentrating on 'the uncanny potential of mixed languages, erratic voices and ambiguous expressions', 'the discomforting effects created when languages coalesce', and the 'surreal quality' generated by transliteration, Harrison argues, Mansfield highlights 'the uncanny nature of written and spoken language'.[118] For instance, 'The Baron' closes with a satirical distortion of a Latin phrase from Thomas à Kempis ('O quam cito transit gloria mundi' becomes 'Sic transit Gloria German mundi') and 'The Sister of the Baroness' ends with a composite French-Italian phrase ('Tableau grandissimo!').[119] Similarly, the German version of a child's counting rhyme ('eena-deena-dina-do') is used in 'The Sister of the Baroness' instead of the familiar English equivalent ('eenie-meenie-minie-mo'), which creates a jarring effect for Mansfield's English readers.[120] Descriptions made by the other pension guests of their regular spa routines become ridiculous when translated literally into English, such as the 'over-body' washing made by Fräulein Stiegelauer in 'Germans at Meat'.[121] Similarly, in 'At "Lehmann's"', the archaic Bavarian euphemism used to describe a woman's confinement before childbirth, a euphemism that only perpetuates Sabrina's ignorance about such matters, is literalised into English ('Sie ist nach Rom gereist' becomes 'She is on a journey to Rome').[122] As Harrison notes, this technique of transliteration in the story serves to 'lift the romantic veil shrouding maternity'.[123] Exposing the process of societal euphemism in this way, transliteration in the stories serves to underscore Mansfield's feminist political critique. Harrison suggests that linguistic uncertainty throughout the 'Pension Sketches' also creates a sense of the *unheimlich*, or the uncanny. Etymologically, *unheimlich* is the opposite of *heimlich* (homely) and *heimisch* (native). In other words, the protagonist's status as 'outsider' and 'foreigner' is also enacted at the level of form, in the linguistic hybridity and uncertainty that runs throughout the 'Pension Sketches'. Linguistic differences expose how the production of meaning is necessarily heteroglossic and the act of interpretation is always founded upon an ambivalence and disjunction between speaker and receiver: as Homi Bhabha has argued, this ambivalence 'quite properly challenges our sense of the historical identity of culture as a homogenizing, unifying force' and challenges 'hierarchical claims to the inherent originality or "purity" of cultures'.[124] In other words, the *unheimlich* quality of the 'Pension Sketches' introduces elements of hybridity and heterogeneity into *The New Age* that serve to challenge the imaginary borders of nationalism and the eugenicist principles of cultural or racial 'purity' used in the contemporary public discourse linking motherhood and imperialism. Translating her experience as an 'outsider' in England into the identifiably 'foreign' setting of Germany, Mansfield's stories place the reader in the position of 'stranger' and encourage the reader to enter an 'other' space where 'the meaning and symbols of culture have no primordial unity or fixity'.[125] In this way, the stories not only caricature Germans, but also call into question the very idea of nationalism itself, thereby challenging English chauvinism.

As well as overtly critiquing the idea of a 'pure' national and racial identity in the 'Pension Sketches', Mansfield, like Hastings, also sought to expose apparently 'advanced' or 'modern' women as in fact highly retrograde and conformist throughout her contributions to *The New Age*. In this sense, these early stories anticipate Mansfield's later, more celebrated critiques of 'advanced' social groups, as in the stories 'Bliss' (August 1918) and 'Marriage à la Mode' (December 1921). In 'The Modern Soul', for example, Sonia Godowska likes to think of herself as 'curiously sapphic' and incredibly modern, but then reveals how she 'think[s] the only solution lies in marriage'.[126] Similarly, in 'At the Club' (a sketch that bears a striking resemblance to Hastings's 'A Modern Bacchante'), Mansfield depicts a club ironically named the 'Advanced', in which copies of *Votes for Women* are strewn across tables and the women gossip and discuss the 'Woman Question', talk which is shown to be anathema to real action. In particular, Mansfield parodies the rhetoric of suffrage militancy in this sketch: 'sex is the only weapon we've got' one woman says, and then: 'Men can choose to realise it nor not, but we're on the battlefield as surely as they are'.[127] In the same issue of the periodical, a story by Mansfield titled 'A Marriage of Passion' satirises the social conventions of marriage: the name of the central married couple, Mr and Mrs 'De Voted', not only mocks the idea of romantic love but also explicitly connects this to support for suffrage, for the 'vote'.[128] Likewise, 'The Mating of Gwendolyn' (a story of disputed authorship that is often attributed to Mansfield) mocks the institution of marriage as a financial transaction driven by necessity.[129] In this way, Mansfield's contributions to *The New Age* served to augment Hastings's feminist critique, exposing apparently 'modern' and 'advanced' women to be conventional, traditional or simply misguided in their approaches to issues of gender.

In her contributions to *The New Age*, Mansfield also looked to expose how the suffrage movement repressed female individuality. In the summer of 1911, after the 'Pension Sketches', set in Bavaria, had all been published, Mansfield travelled to Bruges and Geneva, escaping the stifling heat of London in order to recover from a serious attack of pleurisy. The two stories she sent back to London to be printed in *The New Age* were based upon this experience of travel, 'The Journey to Bruges' and 'Being a Truthful Adventure'.[130] In the same issue of the periodical in which 'The Luft Bad' had been published in March 1910, Francis Grierson had observed:

> The bane of the modern travelling world is to be found in the tendency to see people, climate, countries, and art through someone's tinted spectacles, and, above all, by the aid of someone's guide-book. Italy has suffered more than any other country from the guide-book pest. Few sightseers are able to give you a vivid personal impression of people and things in this country.[131]

This contrast between the 'guide-book pest' and 'vivid personal impression' provides the oppositional thrust to 'Being a Truthful Adventure'. After quickly realising that the descriptions of her guidebook will never match the intensity of her own perception of things, the narrator of the story meets an old school friend, Betty, who gushes enthusiastically about 'the Suffrage' and the 'future of woman' as ardently as she describes 'the quaint streets and the Continental smells' of Bruges, a litany of the city's delights attained second-hand from the 'familiar guide book' that her husband carries in his pocket.[132] As Lee Garver has argued, Mansfield here connects the delegation of individual perception to the 'tinted spectacles' of the guidebook with the devolution of female agency to the organised politics of the suffrage movement.[133] In contrast to Betty, who is married with a child and fails to see how her independence is undermined by her continual use of the first person plural, the protagonist of the story expresses her feminism through individual acts of defiance, refusing to be bound either by a husband or by collectivist politics. After having her perception of the city mediated by a boatman who insists on pointing out bridges and house fronts, for instance, the protagonist abandons the boat at the first opportunity, by crawling under a fence into a meadow, as she prefers to sit alone under a tree watching a group of artists painting and 'the swifts wheel and dip in the bright air'.[134] As in 'The Luft Bad', therefore, the protagonist of 'Being a Truthful Adventure' transcends the 'collective herd' by asserting her intellectual independence and embracing the 'organic union' with nature. Like Hastings, Mansfield here emphasises the importance of perceptual immediacy, of that which is 'inward and invisible' and 'must be begotten from within', of that which is inexplicable to those who want 'still to be shouting and waving a flag'. As such, Mansfield's protagonist does not feel the need to explain her own beliefs to Betty and her husband, and instead evades their questions by shaking her head, sighing and biting her lip. In this story, therefore, Mansfield suggests that the suffrage movement represents a 'collective herd instinct' that suppresses female individuality, independent resolve and mental freedom.

In an article written as 'D. Triformis' titled 'Women and Literature', Hastings argued: 'Ideas form style'.[135] Whilst Mansfield openly challenged the eugenicist ideas of national health often advanced by Hastings, the political emphasis on the free and dissenting individual that I have termed here 'renegade feminism' helped Mansfield to form a recognisably 'modernist' style of literary impressionism in her fiction: in particular, the feminist emphasis on the 'inward and invisible' and on 'mental freedom' generated a related shift in her literary aesthetic towards perceptual immediacy and spiritual liberation. This is evident in such stories as 'The Luft Bad', in which the protagonist experiences a spiritually liberating moment on the swing, and 'The Journey to Bruges', a story that opens *in medias res* and refuses to cohere to the conventions of linear narrative, instead presenting the reader with a flux of sensory experience, a disorienting assemblage of various characters and snippets of overheard conversation. As Garver suggests, Mansfield here 'exhibits a close affinity' with 'modernist compatriots' in *The New Age*, such as T. E. Hulme and Ezra Pound, 'who argued that reality lay in the immediate flux of sensory appearance and not in a rational, conceptual order beyond it'.[136] More specifically, however, we can see how the emphasis within contemporary feminist political analysis on 'the free mind' generated a related shift from the aesthetics of realism, with its focus on the material, objective, exterior world, to a modernist aesthetics of impressionism and internal, lived experience.

This shift informed the piece Mansfield and Hastings co-authored together for *The New Age* in 1911, a collection of seven short parodies of famous Edwardian writers titled 'A P.S.A.' (initials standing for 'A Pleasant Sunday Afternoon').[137] The first is a parody of Bart Kennedy's many travelogues in *The New Age*, highlighting that Mansfield was aware of this series and suggesting that Kennedy's writings probably shaped Mansfield's own use of the travelogue genre. The last is a parody of H. G. Wells. When Wells published his novel about the 'New Woman', *Ann Veronica*, Hastings reviewed it for *The New Age*, writing that the novel was 'proof that men can only write of women from the outside'.[138] Hastings and Mansfield, by contrast, both looked to write of women from the 'inside'. 'A P.S.A.' ridicules Wells for the conventional and thoroughly male perspective that underpins his purportedly radical focus on biology and sex. Mansfield and Hastings also parody Arnold Bennett's many novels about the Potteries, satirising his lengthy, realist descriptions and his focus on minute material detail. Almost a decade before Virginia Woolf would take these Edwardian writers to task in her famous essays 'Modern Novels' and 'Mr Bennett and Mrs Brown', therefore, Mansfield and Hastings were making a claim for a new type of fiction, questioning the nature of 'reality' and the ways in which writing should best represent it.

In 'Women and Literature', Hastings argued that 'women have no tradition worth calling intellectual' and 'if we wish to create works of imagination we must first have knowledge of life to preserve us from sentimentalism and false ideals'.[139] This ambition to create a new 'tradition' of women's writing is reflected in Hastings's novel, *The Maids' Comedy: A Chivalric Romance in Thirteen Chapters*, an imaginative rewriting of *Don Quixote* from the female perspective that was serialised in *The New Age* from October 1910 before it was published in book form in 1911 by Stephen Swift, who also published Mansfield's *In a German Pension* and financed Dora Marsden's journal *The Freewoman* in the same year. Hastings's picaresque novel follows two 'Damsels errant', characters that her biographer, Stephen Gray, has suggested are 'obviously' based on

Mansfield and Hastings, being 'free women, independent-minded and mannered'.[140] The co-authored parodies in 'A P.S.A.' likewise encourage us to read the work of Mansfield and Hastings side by side, as part of a new tradition of women's writing. In particular, situating Mansfield's first published writings in England against the political ideas advanced by Hastings in *The New Age* counters the assumption that her early work was in some way politically naive or disengaged: the striking convergence or 'parafluence' between the work of these two writers at this time reveals an identifiable set of political beliefs constituted in opposition to the suffrage movement and the contemporary cult of motherhood. Both writers believed that women were responsible for their own freedom, which was to be gained through knowledge of life, strength of will, personal resolve, cleverness and individuality. In Mansfield's case, in particular, this 'renegade feminism' served to disrupt a public discourse connecting gender and race, motherhood and imperialism.

The 'Pension Sketches' are often pigeonholed as juvenile stories deliberately positioned by Mansfield in response to 'British anti-invasion literature': for instance, Isobel Maddison has argued that these stories caricatured Germans, stoked 'national paranoia' about the military threat to Britain and thereby anticipated the national prejudices that proliferated during the First World War.[141] Anti-German feeling certainly became prominent within the pages of *The New Age* from mid-1910, as evidenced by J. M. Kennedy's serialised reports on 'Foreign Affairs' that appeared from May onwards under the pseudonym S. Verdad, and Mansfield must have been aware that her stories would have found a ready readership. As Diane Milburn has shown, however, articles in *The New Age* were broadly sympathetic to the language and culture of Germany, and introduced a British audience to the work of Nietzsche, for example.[142] In the issue published on 6 January 1910, C. H. Norman illustrated the war-mongering taking place in the press in both England and Germany by citing extracts from English chauvinists alongside translations from their German counterparts. There is no evidence that Mansfield endorsed such anti-German sentiments. In 1914, for instance, she refused £500 to republish *In a German Pension* because she did not wish to be seen 'to be increasing the odium against Germany'.[143] At the height of anti-German feeling in Britain, in 1915, moreover, Mansfield wrote: 'there's no difference between England and Germany when the mob gets a hand in things – No difference between any nation on earth – They are all equally loathsome'.[144] And herein lies the key to understanding the 'Pension Sketches'. In satirising her German characters, Mansfield did not necessarily intend for her stories to be read as nationalistic in tone and message. Instead, these stories unsettle the very concept of nationalism itself and challenge a public discourse linking the female body with imperial power. As travel narratives, in particular, the 'Pension Sketches' foreground the protagonist's freedom to transgress borders and defy the 'domestic' and 'natural' roles of wife and mother that secure the imagined borders of the nation: refusing to yield to social pressures to define herself through her physicality, for instance, she instead asserts her 'mental freedom'. The silent protests of the protagonist continually disrupt the 'mob' narrative of the bourgeois, militaristic nation. As such, Mansfield's first contributions to *The New Age* both evoke and erase the contemporary idea of the procreative female body as a site that guarantees racial stability and national strength. These sketches were not prescient war stories of British nationalism, then, but directly responded to and destabilised a contemporary public discourse linking gender and race, motherhood and imperialism; these early contributions to *The New Age* did not seek to stoke national competition, in other words, but rather served to satirise and subvert the gender politics upon which such competition was premised.

'Bites from the Apple'

My interest in Hastings and the potential influence that she exercised in the development of Mansfield's writing began when I started exploring the history of a mid-twentieth-century magazine titled *Adam International Review*, in which the editor, Miron Grindea, had conducted extensive research throughout the 1960s into the lives of both writers. It was whilst examining the archive collection for *Adam International Review* that I found a file of previously unknown and unpublished writings by Mansfield, all in typescript, including several works of juvenilia, 'A Little Episode', and a collection of fifty aphorisms also reproduced as an appendix to this book titled 'Bites from the Apple'. The University of Texas holds an incomplete, three-page typescript of 'Bites from the Apple' that is signed by Mansfield and dated 1911. A letter sent to Grindea from Ida Baker, Mansfield's lifelong friend whom she called 'L.M.', appears to corroborate this date of composition. Responding to a request from Grindea for information about Hastings,

Baker wrote, rather ungenerously and not without personal bias: 'Don't be influenced by anything she [Hastings] says or rather said. She was connected with "Bites from an apple" [*sic*] and the "German Pension" period'.[145] Together with the typescript held in Texas dated 1911, this letter from L.M. not only corroborates the date of composition of 'Bites from the Apple' but also allows us to infer that these aphorisms were composed under the guiding hand of Hastings and were first intended for publication in *The New Age*.

Towards the beginning of 'Bites from the Apple', Mansfield observes: 'People are charmingly conservative. The story of the Garden of Eden is practically the only plot to fill and refill out West End theatres and the pages of our magazines'.[146] In the first instance, Mansfield's thematic focus on Original Sin and the Garden of Eden can be contextualised against the recurring debates about the 'Fall of Man' that raged across the pages of *The New Age* in its first years. Throughout 1907, for example, G. K. Chesterton and Hilaire Belloc initiated a long-running discussion of 'the Fall' in *The New Age* by attacking the utopian socialist idea of human perfectibility advanced by the likes of Orage, who consistently appealed for a recoverable 'Golden Age' or Garden of Eden in the early years of editing the periodical. In an article titled 'Towards Socialism', for instance, Orage writes:

> Men must redeem themselves, and they must redeem the world. The most daring enterprises are opening before the eyes of men – the conquest of irrational forces of nature, the subjection and transformation of all the devils and titans of earth and water, air and sky, the re-creation of Eden, and the return of man to the primeval garden. That, at least, is the aim that Socialists have. And we are intolerant of anything less.[147]

Like Chesterton and Belloc, another vigorous proponent of the Fall-myth in *The New Age* was T. E. Hulme. In his essay 'Romanticism and Classicism', written in 1911 but not published until 1924, Hulme adopts what he termed 'the sane classical dogma of original sin'.[148] Challenging the concept of man as a *tabula rasa* advanced by Rousseau and the romantics of the nineteenth century, Hulme instead argued that 'Man is an extraordinary fixed and limited animal whose nature is absolutely constant'.[149] And in an essay on the French philosopher Georges Sorel, Hulme affirms 'the conviction that man is by nature bad or limited, and can consequently only accomplish anything of value by disciplines, ethical, heroic, or political'.[150] Whereas the classicist 'believes in Original Sin', Hulme writes, romantics are those 'who do not believe in the

Fall of Man'.[151] In 'Romanticism and Classicism', he summarises this opposition thus:

> Put shortly, these are the two views, then. One, that man is intrinsically good, spoilt by circumstance; and the other that he is intrinsically limited, but disciplined by order and tradition to something fairly decent. To the one party man's nature is like a well, to the other like a bucket. The view which regards man as a well, a reservoir full of possibilities, I call the romantic; the one which regards him as a very finite and fixed creature, I call the classical.[152]

As a regular contributor to the periodical, Hulme's ideas would have been in wide circulation amongst those associated with *The New Age*, many of whom attended his weekly salon in Frith Street, and his influence can be traced across the periodical. In the same year as Hulme penned 'Romanticism and Classicism', for instance, Orage wrote in *The New Age* that 'man is a fixed species'.[153] Similarly, in articles that were serialised in the periodical throughout the summer of 1911 directly alongside contributions by Mansfield, J. M. Kennedy outlines a condensed history of Western political thought, denouncing the traditions of Protestantism and liberalism in favour of a conception of 'man in his fixed and permanent state'.[154]

Mansfield's 'Bites from the Apple' highlights her affinity with these 'classicist' ideas. In 'Romanticism and Classicism', for example, Hulme suggests that 'the whole of the romantic attitude seems to crystallise in verse round metaphors of flight', which becomes a symbol for the 'infinite' and limitless possibilities of man; in 'classical' writing, by contrast, 'there is always a holding back, a reservation'.[155] Similarly, Mansfield observes: 'Life's little flutter inevitably ends in "broken wings"'. This metaphor of painful non-flight registers a pessimism about human nature remarkably similar to that advanced by Hulme. In 'Bites from the Apple', man is characterised as a fixed, fallen and limited species without hope of redemption: for instance, repentance is described as the 'duster with which we sop up the spilt milk'; life is 'a game of cards – which mainly consists of shuffling'; and reality is only 'bearable for the dreams it brings'. For Mansfield, in short: 'We are all of us in a gigantic maze – running round and round'. This affinity with the 'classicism' of other contributors to *The New Age* has often gone unnoticed in critical accounts of her work, largely due to her later association with Murry and his canonisation of her as a 'romantic' writer. As Fernihough has observed, however, there is a 'strong anti-romantic impulse' in Mansfield's early writings.[156]

Throughout the 'Pension Sketches', for example, Mansfield focuses on the concrete and particular, such as the description in 'Bavarian Babies' of 'potatoes banked in one corner, beetroot in an old candle box, two tubs of sauerkraut and a twisted mass of dahlia roots'.[157] Like Hulme's poetry, Mansfield's story avoids abstractions, focusing instead on the earthy and everyday. Like Hulme, too, Mansfield satirises 'romantic' aspirations by rendering them in terms of rarefied flight. The young poet from Munich in 'The Sister of the Baroness', for example, is described as 'unyoking Pegasus' at the prospect of a baroness staying at the pension.[158] Likewise, Sonia Godowska in 'The Modern Soul' is enraptured at the sight of swallows in flight, which she describes as 'like a little flock of Japanese thoughts'.[159] In contrast, the semi-autobiographical narrator of the 'Pension Sketches' is detached and unwilling to reveal too much about herself to the other characters: in other words, 'there is always a holding back, a reservation'.

Whilst she adopted the same pessimistic, fatalistic tone about human limitation, however, Mansfield clearly diverged from Hulme's 'classicism' by using the Fall and story of Eden to articulate progressive feminist political commitments. Hulme was a proudly reactionary figure who despised the optimistic cult of Progress and described intellectual women as 'just misplaced whores'.[160] Like his contemporaries Ezra Pound and Wyndham Lewis, Hulme consistently associated masculinity with the hard, disciplined, concrete aspects of 'classicism', whereas the female body was invariably imagined in terms of the amorphous, fluid and threateningly uncontainable. In adopting the story of Eden to challenge this reactionary politics, Mansfield was responding to an alternative set of writers in *The New Age*, who used the story of Eden to discuss feminism and the contemporary 'Woman Question'. In 1907, for instance, Charlotte E. Holmes observed:

> Ever since an unfortunate episode in the Garden of Eden the greater half of the race has remained under a cloud. [. . .] but it is some consolation to a woman's vanity to think that the first woman was beguiled by the most 'subtil' of created things; which cannot quite be said of the first man.[161]

In both the title and content of Mansfield's aphorisms, the focus on the Garden of Eden tied 'Bites from the Apple' to a contemporary debate about feminism. In particular, Mansfield can be seen responding to the biblical rhetoric of *Woman's Worst Enemy: Woman*, which includes a section titled 'The Two Curses' in which Hastings writes: 'Hapless Eve!

Out of thy torment Adam adds to his glory. How shalt thou ever be rid of thy curse?' and 'Almighty Curse! That Adam, the builder and rebuilder of civilizations, must fall and fall again, defeated by the quailing womb of the woman who bears him.'[162] The thematic focus on the Genesis myth, therefore, linked Mansfield's aphorisms with Hastings's feminist politics.

In composing 'Bites from the Apple', Mansfield was also emulating Hastings's aphoristic writing style. Indeed, Hastings contributed a set of aphorisms to *The New Age* in September 1910, in which she clearly articulated her philosophy of individualist feminism: she writes that 'The same woman who cannot be dragged one step may lead over a precipice with equanimity'; and, 'No woman should have the vote until she is able to end a quarrel by going out and giving herself a treat'.[163] In the article that she wrote as 'D. Triformis' refuting the earlier statements of 'Beatrice Tina', Hastings also refers to a single sentence from *Woman's Worst Enemy: Woman* as an 'epigram'.[164] Indeed, archival evidence suggests that Hastings composed her articles for *The New Age* and later periodicals she edited by first writing pithy, aphoristic statements that she then integrated into longer prose. Many of these fragments echo the tonal register and thematic focus of Mansfield's aphorisms, discussing God, the Devil and 'man' with his 'hitherto impeccable wife' (Figure 1.6(a)). Mansfield was not only emulating the biblical rhetoric of Hastings's pamphlet, therefore, but also her aphoristic, epigrammatic writing style, deployed to articulate the ideas of individualist feminism.

Throughout 'Bites from the Apple', for example, Mansfield consistently alludes to a 'Fall' into knowledge and experience as a metaphor for contemporary female liberation:

> 29. The sooner Eve meets the serpent the better – then she leaves the Garden of Eden and has the whole world before her.
> 32. To be completely lost is to take the first step towards finding yourself.

For Mansfield, Eve's banishment from the confines of the Garden of Eden figures liberation rather than a curse, a transgression that enables her to realise self-knowledge, assert individual female agency and thereby have 'the whole world before her'. These moments of optimism, however, are always counterbalanced with an acute and bitter awareness of how carnal knowledge and sexual experience are often coupled with pain and sacrifice for women. For example: 'Those who eat greatly of the fruit of the Tree of Knowledge must expect to find themselves crucified on the bare branches'. Throughout 'Bites from the Apple', sexual experience is linked with a dubious and concealed past: 'There is the gift that we can do very well without – it is the Present that the Past persists in thrusting upon us'. It must be remembered that Mansfield wrote 'Bites from the Apple' after she had contracted gonorrhoea and undergone the trauma of a stillbirth or miscarriage in 1909, as well as a possible abortion arranged by Hastings in the spring of 1911: by yielding to 'temptation', Mansfield had suffered greatly. In writing these aphorisms, then, Mansfield evidently heeded Nietzsche's advice in *Human, All Too Human* that 'from the thorniest and unhappiest phases of one's own life one can pluck maxims'.[165]

After reading a biography of Nietzsche in 1915, Mansfield reflected in her journal: 'I read *The Lonely Nietzsche*; but I felt a bit ashamed of my feelings for this man in the past. He is, if you like, "human, all too human".'[166] Whilst Oscar Wilde's writings have long been recognised as shaping the aphorisms that Mansfield composed in her notebooks as a teenager in 1906 and 1907, 'Bites from the Apple' highlights another literary influence: written in 1911, these aphorisms are more obviously composed in emulation of the epigrammatic in-house style of *The New Age* and the predilection among its contributors for Nietzsche's work. In particular, the three short books that Orage penned immediately before becoming editor of *The New Age* would have exerted significant influence: *Friedrich Nietzsche, the Dionysian Spirit of the Age* (1906), *Consciousness: Animal, Human and Superman* (1907) and *Nietzsche in Outline and Aphorism* (1907). The first book provides an introductory survey to the life and ideas of Nietzsche, with each section of the book prefaced by a selection of his aphorisms. About these, Orage writes:

> Out of the oppressive thunder-cloud of his thought come shooting at every moment splendidly bright aphorisms like forked lightening; they are his thunderbolts carefully forged and shaped and sharpened. It is as an aphorist that he will live in literature even should an emancipated Europe forget her moral warriors.[167]

In the third book, each section of explanatory notes by Orage is supplemented with a selection of Nietzsche's aphorisms, grouped thematically under titles such as 'Life' or 'Man and Woman'. In this book, Orage quotes Nietzsche's observation that aphorism and sentence 'are the forms of eternity'.[168] In both books, therefore, Orage emphasises the formal qualities of the aphorism, 'carefully forged and shaped and sharpened'. Orage's engagement with the writings of Nietzsche provided an intellectual direction for *The New Age* when he became editor in 1907. Indeed, as David Thatcher has observed, for the first five years under Orage's editorship, 'Nietzsche's name is hardly absent' from the pages of the periodical.[169] One contributor to *The New Age* who was fundamental in introducing Nietzsche's philosophy to a British audience was Oscar Levy, whom Orage invited to become a contributor to the periodical after reading his book *The Revival of Aristocracy* (1906). Levy was then embarking upon the complete translation of Nietzsche's work into English, published between 1909 and 1913, and he brought with him to *The New Age* other translators on the project, including J. M. Kennedy, who became a regular contributor to the 'Foreign Affairs' column, and Anthony Ludovici, who made his name in *The New Age* as a controversial art critic in the years 1913–14. The immediate impact of this influence can be registered in a poem by Frederick Richardson contributed to the fifth issue (30 May 1907) and titled 'The New Dionysos', which begins with this Nietzschean prophecy of modernist rejuvenation:

> Soon will dawn the day of wonder,
> When, with many-footed thunder,
> Comes the fresh god, trampling under
> All the dead and outworn things.[170]

With such writers dominant across the periodical, Nietzsche's philosophical ideas permeate the pages of *The New Age*; and so too does his epigrammatic writing style. As Antony Alpers notes in his biography of Mansfield, Orage 'had a turn for epigram, and a taste for the balanced phrase'.[171] Articles in the periodical were punctuated by aphoristic observations, many of which were then published in the 'Memorandum' section of the next issue summarising an author's main argument and ideas. Additionally, *The New Age* frequently published collections of aphorisms. Kennedy, for instance, contributed translations of Nietzsche's aphorisms to the periodical in December 1909, before serialising translations of aphorisms by Niccolò Machiavelli and Albert Guinon between March and April 1911.

Hastings's example, however, would have highlighted to Mansfield that the aphoristic form of Nietzsche's philosophy could be divorced from his reactionary gender politics. In *Woman's Worst Enemy: Woman*, Hastings writes:

> A German artist who ruined his poetry by interpolating philosophical misinformation, wrote: 'Man wants to live! woman only wants to be the means to his life.' The history of all civilisation gives the lie to this

> bumptious masculinism. Civilised woman wants something more than to be the means to man's life: she wants to live herself.[172]

Hastings distinguishes the 'poetry' of Nietzsche's aphorisms from the politics of his 'bumptious masculinism'. The aphorism form relies upon witty turns of phrase and the evocation of multiple, dialogic strands of meaning. As Eric Johannesson notes, for example, it is 'a ludic form whose aesthetic delight is engendered by the verbal texture itself, by wit, allusion, and paradox'.[173] Likewise, writing about the aphorisms of Georg Christoph Lichtenberg, J. P. Stern argues that the 'charm' of an aphorism 'hides in an antithesis, perfectly integrated, issuing from a double look at a word or an idea'.[174] Not only are Mansfield's aphorisms textured by allusions to Hastings's writings, therefore, but Hastings's example would have shown to Mansfield that the aphorism form, playing with paradox and antithesis, could be deployed to challenge the 'bumptious masculinism' of Nietzsche and contemporaries such as Hulme, Pound and Lewis. Like Hastings, Mansfield uses the aphorism to articulate her politics of renegade individualist feminism.

In particular, the version of woman-hating feminism propagated by Hastings permeates 'Bites from the Apple'. For instance, Mansfield consistently echoes Hastings's idea that women are responsible either for their own subjugation or for their individual freedom, contrasting the gossiping, thoroughly conventional 'majority' with the 'progressive' woman who is radical because she is on the fringes of society and is 'wild':

> 43. Of course most people keep a skeleton in the cupboard. The trouble with the majority of women is that they will persist in shutting themselves up in that cupboard with that skeleton. . . .
> 44. Small wonder that a pillar box is such a channel for gossip – like a woman, it never shuts its mouth.
> 48. Progressive women can never be popular – why Eve gave Adam the pip – what can you expect. However, generous soul! he did not keep it, but gave it her for seed – And wasn't she wild! She just raised Cain as far as she was Able (Abel.)

Composed for *The New Age*, 'Bites from the Apple' augments Hastings's feminist critique, and places a similar emphasis on the freedom of the individual to transcend social conventions and constraints. For instance, Mansfield's aphorisms highlight the sexual double standard of Edwardian England and, like Hastings's writings, exhibit a clear disdain for the idea of 'equality' between the sexes as well as the social conventions of marriage:

4. If a man bore in mind the fact that when he chose his wife his wife also chose him, there would be less talk of the equality of the sexes and more realisation.
41. Love is the Wine of Life – Marriage the non-alcoholic beverage.

Like Hastings in 'A Modern Bacchante', therefore, Mansfield suggests that 'modern' women, drinking 'the Wine of Life', should flaunt their freedom.

'Bites from the Apple' ends with an aphorism that considers the relation between the 'modern' text and literary posterity: 'The classic is that which is eternally modern – the modern that which can never be classic'. Never published within her own lifetime and long hidden within the archives, 'Bites from the Apple' exemplifies this idea of modern ephemerality. Indeed, the collection is clearly of its time: we can fully understand Mansfield's aphorisms only if we read them against the print contexts for which they were composed. When positioned alongside Hastings's writings in *The New Age*, 'Bites from the Apple' highlights how Mansfield used the aphorism form to challenge the politics of 'bumptious masculinism' and articulate ideas of female independence and individual freedom. Moreover, the collection now deserves to be recognised as a pivotal point in Mansfield's stylistic maturation, the brevity, wit and sharp impersonality of the aphorisms all becoming defining traits of her later work; with the use of aphorism representing a deliberate move towards formal fragmentation, in particular, 'Bites from the Apple' signifies an important stage in the development of Mansfield's 'modernist' style.

The French debate

Following the success of *In a German Pension*, published in December 1911, Mansfield began to consider other outlets for her work and started a correspondence with the editor of a new and self-consciously 'modernist' little magazine titled *Rhythm*. John Middleton Murry had founded *Rhythm* in order to promote French philosophy, art and literature in England; as will be seen in the next chapter, invigorated by the 'republic of art' that he had come into contact with on his first visit to Paris, Murry championed in *Rhythm* the philosophy of Henri Bergson, reproduced new Fauvist art, and printed work by the writers of the Fantaisiste literary movement in the original French.[175] After contributing two poems and a short story to *Rhythm* in the spring of 1912, Mansfield quickly established herself as an assistant editor to Murry and became a shaping influence in the production of the magazine before it ceased publication in early 1913. Mansfield's newfound authority evidently riled Orage, who denounced his past protégé for being 'wilfully defiant of the rules of art' in the stories contributed to *Rhythm*.[176] This criticism turned personal when Orage savagely caricatured Mansfield over several weeks in his regular series 'Tales for Men Only' as the ignorant, uncultured and sexually promiscuous 'Marcia Foisacre', a woman who displays all 'the characteristics of the mob'.[177] In light of this evident vitriol, scholars have long understood Mansfield's association with *Rhythm* as a concomitant defection from *The New Age*. Yet this ignores the fact that Mansfield continued to contribute to Orage's periodical throughout the spring and summer of 1912; moreover, after another appearance in November 1915, she contributed a series of dialogues, a translation and several short stories to *The New* Age in 1917. Rather than departing from *The New Age* entirely in 1912, Mansfield continued to feel the pull of the periodical throughout her writing career, and her later contributions therefore demand closer analysis. In this section of the chapter, I will examine the ways in which Mansfield associated these contributions to *The New Age* with the cultural life of France for which *Rhythm* had been a metonym.

The son of a lower-middle-class civil servant, Murry had had to work hard in order to gain entry first to Christ's Hospital school and then Oxford University, and he was constantly troubled by an acute awareness of his class origins and his position as an outsider to the upper echelons of the English intelligentsia. Representing an egalitarian 'republic' free from class distinctions and restrictions, Paris offered a liberating space in which Murry felt he could gain legitimate entry into the realms of literature and art. It was perhaps to this 'lower middle-class' upstart, then, that Orage directed these barbed comments in his regular column 'Readers and Writers' in August 1913:

> The notion that Paris is a sort of literary Mecca, a journey to which 'saves' an author's style, is one of the superstitions of lower middle-class Englishmen (these include Americans). There is really, my friends, no salvation in Geography. Paris, it is true, is the arbiter of European taste; but arbiters do not create! [. . .] [S]hun Paris and cease reading French. The best preparation for writing great English is living in England and reading, writing and, above all, talking, English.[178]

These protestations of cultural nationalism seem surprising coming from the same man who insisted at the outset of his literary career that his surname be pronounced to echo the French for 'storm' in order to suggest Huguenot ancestry and conceal his own 'lower middle-class' Yorkshire roots. Such protestations also appear inconsistent with the publication history of *The New Age*, which had been introducing its readers over the last several years to French philosophy in the writings of T. E. Hulme, to new artistic movements born in Paris (such as post-impressionism and cubism) through the criticism of Huntly Carter, and to the major writers of French literature through Arnold Bennett's incredibly popular review column, written under the pseudonym Jacob Tonson. Yet *The New Age* was a decidedly Janus-faced publication. The moment that Hulme explained Bergson's philosophy of intuition, for instance, Ernest Belfort Bax rubbished it. And in the same pages in which Carter celebrated Paris for the vitality of its new art, a quotation from G. K. Chesterton denigrated a cubist study reproduced in the periodical as 'a piece of paper on which Mr Picasso has had the misfortune to upset the ink and tried to dry it with his boots'.[179]

When *The New Age* published a series of essays by Ezra Pound in the autumn of 1913 titled 'The Approach to Paris', therefore, it ran another series in tandem, a parody by Hastings under the pseudonym T.K.L. In his essays, Pound arrived at his now recognisable tone of isolated superiority, lambasting London (as compared with Paris) as 'just an easy-chair, the most comfortable place in the world' and building his argument around lots of long, untranslated passages of contemporary French poetry, stating abrasively: 'If a man is incapable of hearing this litany I cannot help it'.[180] By contrast, Hastings makes previously opaque quotations readily accessible through translation and adopts a characteristically irreverent tone to make Pound appear ridiculous: 'What? The "Canterbury Tales"? I smile explosively – all pure French, my dear sir! Now sit down and let me talk.'[181] As Ann Ardis has argued, this rhetorical skirmish between Hastings and Pound can be understood as representative of the 'dialogism' characterising *The New Age* more widely.[182]

The 'French debate' – as we might call it – highlights the fact that 'cosmopolitanism' and 'internationalism' were always highly contested terms within *The New Age* and that there was a clear anxiety that the language and culture of England should be protected from foreign influence, an anxiety that only increased as political tensions mounted in the years before the outbreak of the First World War, as Paul Peppis has shown.[183] For many of the conservative and 'classicist' contributors to *The New Age*, moreover, the ideals of the French Republic represented pernicious political abstractions. After Hulme famously renounced Bergson's philosophy in 1911, for instance, he followed Pierre Lasserre and Charles Maurras's right-wing Action Française group by arguing that 'romanticism' was the product of a cultural and linguistic dissociation from the real and authentic, a dissociation initiated by the philosophy of Rousseau and the egalitarianism of the French Revolution. And, at about the same time, Orage writes:

> Down with the Tricolour; by which you understand that I mean the three headed dog of Liberty, Equality and Fraternity. [. . .] Of all the curses that abortion, the French Revolution, brought amongst men, the worship of its trinity is the worst. Let France that raised the flag be the first to haul it down.[184]

In line with Nietzsche's critique of democracy as the rule of 'the mob', with its herd-like mentality, the majority of contributors to *The New Age* looked to promote an 'aristocracy' of the arts based upon the supreme individuation of the *Übermensch*, a form of freedom based not upon the abstractions of the state, such as 'Liberty', but upon hyper-individualism. In *The Revival of Aristocracy* (1906), for instance, Oscar Levy argued that the French Revolution had resulted from a failure of nerve in the aristocracy, a failure that needed to be recuperated. This rhetoric was a variant upon the discourse of Original Sin analysed in the previous section of the chapter: abstraction and dissociation represent the 'Fall' from a healthy, rooted national and aristocratic culture into a deracinated and decadent democracy. As such, the 'French debate' in *The New Age* had clear political resonance.

What is particularly interesting for our purposes, though, is the way in which this political debate crystallised around questions of literary style. In 1913, as quoted above, Orage employs the rhetoric of the 'Fall' and 'Redemption' when he declares that Paris does not offer 'salvation' for an author's 'style'. And when he provides his own judgement on Pound's 'Approach to Paris' essays, Orage writes:

> [W]hat qualification, I may ask, has Mr Pound revealed for making a fair estimate of English writing as compared with French? His critical knowledge of French I will take for granted – it does not much concern me; but his critical knowledge of English we English-writers are entitled to demand evidence of. Where is that evidence? As 'T.K.L.' has shown in a series of critical parodies constituting a tour de force of amazing cleverness (where is Tailharde now?) Mr Pound's own English style is a pastiche of colloquy, slang, journalism and pedantry. Of culture in Nietzsche's sense of the word – a unity of style – it bears no sign.[185]

Apparently unaware of the irony of his using the phrase 'tour de force' in this passage, Orage employed the concept of 'unity of style' in order to link aesthetics with politics. As Thomas Leddy has observed, Nietzsche's concept of 'unity of style' provided an evaluative framework by which the philosopher looked to consider both individuals and cultures as 'organic wholes'.[186] Moreover, 'Nietzsche analyses unity of style in terms of its opposite: the style of the cultural philistine. Unity of style comes to be understood not simply as homogeneity of style but as a style which results from a refusal to be shallow.'[187] In other words, high culture must resist mass culture: it must insulate itself from the 'colloquy' and 'slang' of the herd-like *Untermensch*; only by doing so can individuals and cultures achieve the organic integrity of the aristocratic *Übermensch*. This articulation of the high/low binary, so common to modernist writing of the early twentieth century, was framed in *The New Age* around the geographical separation between England and France, and the linguistic dissociation between English and French. It is not often that Pound can be accused of subordinating his writings to the demands of mass culture; for Orage writing in *The New Age* in 1913, however, Pound's prose style, in which French mixes so readily with English, represents both cultural philistinism and national deracination. Likewise, when Orage caricatured Mansfield as displaying all 'the characteristics of the mob' he was associating her with a deplored cultural democratisation. How did Mansfield respond to this in her later contributions to *The New Age*? In particular, if literary style is seen as the marker of cultural and national integrity, in what ways did Mansfield's formal experiments in these contributions encode a political critique that participated in the 'French debate'?

Again, one answer to these questions can be found in the contributions made to the periodical by Hastings. Whilst Hastings was more than ready to cut Pound down to size in her articles for *The New Age*, this did not mean that she subscribed to Orage's 'unity of style' as an alternative. Indeed, recalling the passage by Orage quoted above in her memoir of 1936, Hastings characterised Orage's own style as being far from unified or effortless, but instead 'stilted' and 'plagiaristic':

> [W]hen I wrote, as 'T.K.L.', a series of parodies of certain poets introduced by Pound, who took the jousting with tolerable literary manner, Orage, *butt*[*ed*] *in* with his flat, ponderous pen (and what a flat, ponderous, stilted, maundering, when not coy, conceited and facetious, when not plagiaristic or outright thievish 'literary' pen he had [. . .]).[188]

In the contributions that she made to *The New Age* from 1914 onwards, Hastings arrived at a new way of writing that challenged the very idea of a 'unity of style' by employing the 'colloquy' and 'slang' denigrated by Orage and by demonstrating a clear debt to her interactions and engagements with the language and culture of France. It was this intervention in the 'French debate', I argue, that had a profound influence in shaping Mansfield's later and often overlooked contributions to *The New Age* in 1915 and 1917.

In May 1914, Hastings left London for Paris and, over the next eighteen months, contributed sixty-eight articles to *The New Age* under the title 'Impressions of Paris'. Published under the pseudonym of 'Alice Morning', these contributions relate the dislocations of travel, in which the writer is 'tossed from side to side of the Boulevard by excited persons all directing me wrongly', for example, and shouts at pedantic administrators: 'I prefer the scrunch of my French to the squeak of your English'.[189] Indeed, the contrast between English and French is consistently conducive to humour and serves to emphasise English parochialism throughout the 'Impressions of Paris': 'Two English have got rooms here on opposite sides of the court, and every night one comes out and says in a great important whisper – Walk-*er*! Then he says – Commong ally voo? I think he thinks it means Goodnight.'[190] For Hastings, the 'English in Paris as a rule are tortures to hear'.[191] In an extended passage, for example, she mimics the upper-class accent of the decadent *Daily Telegraph*-reading public:

> They all affect their language in a way to fascinate the Nu Spelers but to make anyone else afraid for the country. 'End weh set neah the fahoontehn in the Lucks-om-booarg . . . Ai wis muhst engry, reahlly . . . the braidsmed's brathar is on the 'Delly Tellygreph' . . . Yas, sh's reahlly well orf b't naoow sh' g'ts f'ts o' 'conomy . . . Fency, sh's dahoon t' guh tuh th' front, but sh's on'y duhn Farst Ed . . . Chorming w'm'n, b't sh'll nevah mek 'nangfairmiaire-nevah . . . Dr Hed'n Guest . . . yas, chorming, b't feahf'lly erretic 'n impahlsive . . . Yas, ai muhst goo . . . goo-bai!' A foreign friend of mine who rather fancies speaking English, always carefully says 'Goo-bai.' No wonder![192]

What is significant about this passage is the way in which Hastings highlights how the experience of travel and being abroad reveals the way in which people, both 'English' and 'foreign', '*affect* their language'. This focus on affectation and the malleability of language are of course typically 'modernist' and signal a stylistic freedom that is characteristic of Hastings's prose. Borrowing freely from 'the memoir, journalism, letters, guidebooks, confessional narrative, and, *most important*, fiction', as Michael Kowaleski has observed, the travelogue is a genre notoriously difficult to demarcate.[193] Hastings makes full use of this generic ambiguity, interweaving her reports about Paris under siege, for example, with descriptions about her own love affairs, or juxtaposing bits of gossip from her circle of new acquaintances among the artists of Montparnasse and Montmartre with letters back to *The New Age*, critiquing recent work by Pound or H. G. Wells. Like Mansfield in 'Being a Truthful Adventure', moreover, Hastings links the assertion of female agency with a refusal to conform to the guidebook or travelogue genre. She writes ironically, for instance:

> [L]et me guide. For a meal which won't completely starve you go to the Restaurant Boudet, two hundred something Boulevard Raspail. For rendez-vous comme il faut but where a word missed in the noise may change your whole career, there is Café Soufflet, 30, Boulevard St. Michel. For cigarettes – nowhere – smuggle in your own.[194]

There is also a clear note of defiance when Hastings observes: 'I haven't yet seen the uplifting things of Baedeker'.[195] Indeed, the first 'Impressions' in the series were categorised as 'Pastiche', signalling the fact that Hastings was parodying the travelogue genre. Instead, she develops a unique style of impressionistic journalism, discounting the major tourist attractions, such as the Louvre, in order to describe the chaos of a street scene or transcribe a fragment of a conversation overheard in a café. In this way, Hastings arrived at her own peculiar 'unity of style' throughout the 'Impressions of Paris' series, one based upon the disunity created by contrast and collage. As Hastings's biographer has observed, hers was 'the new female style: broken, adept at shifting tone', the 'kind of stylistic glossolalia' that dissolved rigid boundaries of genre and thereby challenged established cultural categories.[196]

This 'disunity of style' also became a fitting mode for depicting the fragmentation and disintegration caused by the war. After August 1914, the 'Impressions of Paris' series quickly became the diary of a city under siege, with narrative episodes frequently interrupted by the unexpected, such as Zeppelin raids and bombings:

> As I passed the Hotel de Ville I was glad that this fine and delicate building, spaced in every direction, was in small danger from bombardment. Then the crowd began to run. I had heard nothing, for the good reason that the two bombs which fell, one on Notre Dame and one in a square adjoining,

> did not burst. The French aviators soon rose in chase and the crowd became enormous. I am terrified of big crowds and got away, though into a little one where a discussion was going on. Some monsieur seemed to have been saying that we had no protection from bombs, which was obvious enough indeed. But the other persons resented such an idea. Up came a gendarme with the usual 'S'sh, s'sh, what's all this?' – and we were all breaking away when out started a young woman: 'Monsieur l'agent, arrest him. Yes! For a quarter of an hour he has worried me. Yes! He says we have no protection from bombs – and – and – and . . . ' all in the most whining tone which was utterly belied by a face and manner bold à la Caillaux.[197]

In the same article, Hastings lists '[s]craps of conversation overheard as you pass about the streets':

> A little girl: 'I never even said "monsieur," I said simply, "I excuse myself for saying Zut!"' Two monsieurs: – 'Everyone makes a rejection according to his own taste.' Three women at a door: 'In the arm, the foot and the leg!' A young soldier: 'Tell her . . . ' A very young man: 'I've cut her head off. I've done with her. Long live liberty!'[198]

Throughout the 'Impressions of Paris' series, reported speech is integral in creating this disjunction between the extraordinary and everyday, the violent and mundane, the life-threatening and quotidian. This style not only is a mode of parody, satirising home-front attitudes and anxieties, but also serves to reflect the absurdity of wartime reality for civilians.

When Mansfield travelled to Paris in the spring of 1915 in order to work in the writer Francis Carco's empty apartment on the Quai aux Fleurs, she often visited Hastings, who was then living in Montmartre with Modigliani in a house located off one of the side streets beyond the recently completed Sacré Cœur. Mansfield wrote to Murry about her 'cold interest in noting the signs' of her older friend's drunkenness and about an explosive scene in which Hastings 'flared up in a *fury* & we parted for life again'.[199] After this, she writes to Murry saying 'I think Orage wants kicking' and 'I don't want *anything* about Paris to go to the New Age – I must not make daisy chains in Biggy B's meadows', by which she meant Hastings's field of impressionistic journalism.[200] Yet, in November 1915, Mansfield did contribute to *The New Age* again; and, what's more, with a piece that employed Hastings's style of reported speech and her mimicry of tone and accent. 'Stay-Laces' is a savage satire of home-front attitudes to the war. These fragments of conversation, presented as if overheard on a bus or in a department store, demonstrate Mansfield's talent for producing writing in which an authorial perspective isn't imposed, so that the women of the piece are left to reveal their own shallow outlook to the reader:

> Mrs Busk: [. . .] I thought the war had done away with the idea that there was anything you couldn't speak about. I mean the things one reads in the papers, and the wounded that one sees in the streets have made such a difference, haven't they? I *love* the wounded, don't you? Oh, I simply love them. And their sweet blue and red uniforms are so cheerful and awfully effective, aren't they? I can't *think* who thought of that bright red tie against that bright blue.[201]

The dialogue form that Mansfield employs here was a recurring feature of contributions to *The New Age*. Inspired by his early enthusiasm for the writings of Plato, Orage sought to foster a form of Socratic debate within the periodical; pursuing this ideal, his own extended series of 'Unedited Opinions' was based upon the dialogue format of question and answer, as was – to a certain extent – the distinctly misogynistic series 'Tales for Men Only'. Based upon this classical model, the dialogue form offered a structured platform from which Orage could methodically advance his own opinions. In 1911, Mansfield emulated this by composing a dialogue on the occasion of George V's coronation and, 'with apologies to Theocritus', transposing a text set in ancient Greece into working-class suburban London.[202] At first glance, then, 'Stay-Laces' would appear to be entirely of a piece with the in-house style of *The New Age*. However, Mansfield makes a noticeable change here: the dialogue between the two women in 'Stay-Laces' isn't reciprocal, with the talk of Mrs Bone reduced to ellipses followed by question or exclamation marks.

With this contribution, as Gerri Kimber has observed in *Katherine Mansfield: The View from France*, Mansfield was emulating the French writer Colette, who often employed the 'dialogue for one voice' in her writings, using ellipses to figure gaps in conversation within stories such as 'L'Accompagnatrice' and 'L'Habilleuse', both published in *L'Envers du Music-Hall* in 1913.[203] An article printed in *The New Age* in September 1910 had mentioned the writings of Colette, and *The Blue Review* had featured a review of *L'Envers du Music-Hall* in June 1913, but it was most likely through her association with Carco and Hastings that Mansfield first began reading Colette seriously.[204] Carco was a friend to Colette (he had even been a ghost-writer for her ex-husband, known as 'Willy') and he had praised her work in three separate articles published in *Rhythm* in 1912, which Mansfield – as assistant editor – would certainly have read. In these articles, Carco writes of Colette's 'dazzling impressionism' ('Colette Willy cherit l'impressionnisme le plus éclatant') and groups her together with Paul Adam, Henri Bergson and Romain Rolland as representative of the 'young' generation of writers shaping modern sensibility.[205] For Hastings, writing in *The New Age* in January 1918, Colette's writings revealed 'an alphabet of psychology' unlike anything produced in English.[206] And, in an unpublished note written whilst in hospital in Paris in 1920, she writes:

> Colette, too, has the Cross. Delicious person. But I know more than one English woman-writer – what a word! – who would have had nothing to concede to Colette had she – the said woman-writer – not been English.
>
> Dickens knew, and he was a Man, that one cannot write well for the British public. 'If I had not been an Englishman, I should have been a great writer,' said he.[207]

The clear influence of Colette's elliptical form on Hastings's own work can be seen in the parody of 'the Nu Spelers' quoted above. For Hastings, Colette comes to represent an alternative female literary tradition based in Paris: this is a tradition that is by implication both aesthetically innovative and sexually transgressive (Colette 'has the Cross'), and it is a tradition that can be appropriated by the 'woman-writer' writing in English.

Like Hastings, Mansfield would have identified with Colette's fiercely held independence and the focus in her work on modern female subjectivity. After re-reading Colette's novel *L'Entrave* in November 1914, for example, she writes in her journal: 'I don't care a fig for anyone I know except her'.[208] In a letter to Murry written in December 1915, Mansfield recounts a dream in which she is with Colette in a box at the circus:

> I should like to be at a large circus tonight, in a box – very luxurious, you know, very warm, very gay with a smell of sawdust & elephants. A superb clown called Pistachio – white poneys [*sic*], little blue monkeys drinking tea out of Chinese cups – I should like to be dressed beautifully, beautifully down [to] the last fragment of my chemise, & I should like Colette Willy to be dressed just exactly like me & to be in the same box. And during the entr'actes while the orchestra blared Pot Pourri from The Toreador we would eat tiny little jujubes out of a much too big bag & tell each other all about our childhood.[209]

Colette's work, which consistently depicts the backstage worlds of the music hall, the ballet and the theatre, comes to represent a version of female performativity rooted in the experience of childhood, an idea that would exercise significant influence in Mansfield's later work. In the same month of December 1915, Mansfield again writes to Murry from Paris: 'I am longing for my Colette books'.[210] Then, in early October 1916, she writes: 'For me she [Colette] is more real than anyone Ive [*sic*] ever known. London is sad and dull.'[211] The immediate comparison with London here is revealing: Colette represents the same alternative, invigorating literary tradition that it does for Hastings.

This triangular identification between Mansfield, Hastings and Colette is further illuminated in a letter sent by Murry to Mansfield in March 1915:

> You see Beatrice (tho' I never have seen her) seems to be a smaller specimen of your kind. Well, they don't turn up very often. They're absolutely different from women in general; and all women in general are against them. Its [*sic*] easy to see why. It's not because you criticise them or are clever; but because they see in you the ideal they never can attain. [. . .] They're negatives – in you they come up against a positive and they hate it. They put up right & wrong against you, whose greatness is that there is no right and wrong save what you feel to be you or not-you. Well with so much against you, it's a hard row to hoe, to be really *you*. (You is a type – the wonderful type from Aspasia to B.B. Colette Vagabonde, and you above all moderns)[212]

'Aspasia' is a reference to the famous courtesan of Ancient Greece, whose beauty, culture and wit so captivated Pericles; 'B.B.' is a reference to Hastings, whose nickname from childhood was 'Biggy B'; and 'Vagabonde' refers to Colette's novel about her music-hall life, published in 1910, *La Vagabonde*. In this letter, Murry tells Mansfield that Hastings represents 'something which was – perhaps only a little bit – in you, that used to terrify me and almost killed me dead – I mean the Cabaret bit'.[213] Again, therefore, the identification between the writers comes to signify something performative and transgressive; with both Hastings and Colette having had notorious reputations for same-sex relationships, the passage also implies Murry's half-acknowledged awareness ('almost' and 'perhaps only a little bit') of Mansfield's own sexual past with women. Predominantly, however, Hastings and Colette signify a 'type' of modernity that Mansfield embodies 'above all': they represent the 'ideal' of female agency and self-knowledge, the 'positive' of female independence constituted against the 'negative' of social convention and 'women in general'.

Published in a periodical permeated with nods, winks and coded in-jokes, the ellipses in 'Stay-Laces' therefore served as a silent signal to those in the know that Mansfield was associating her writing with this contemporary female tradition. Mansfield adopts Colette's disruptive literary technique in order to achieve the same kind of broken style as Hastings in the 'Impressions of Paris' series, one adept at abruptly shifting tone. At the level of form, then, Mansfield was clearly undercutting the ideal of an organic and integrated 'unity of style'. In terms of content, too, 'Stay-Laces' represents a clear riposte to Orage's 'Tales for Men Only'. The sketch is populated entirely by women. Men are seen within the crowd on the bus, or across the street ('Look at that enormous Indian creature in khaki . . . Do you think you could ever be attracted by a dark man?'), but this is the extent of their involvement within the narrative. At a time when many women became bus conductors to fill the vacancies made by the war, it is not even clear whether the conductor who shouts 'Selfridges! Sel-fridges' is male or female. Yet Mansfield is not uncritical of the women that she depicts. Mrs Busk talks aimlessly about the latest fashions, about hairstyles, corsets and earrings, tells her companion how she 'loathe[s] getting on 'buses' because of the pushing and shoving of the herd-like crowd, is scandalised (yet clearly intrigued) by an overheard conversation about an abortion, is openly racist and presumptuously mistakes a woman for a shop assistant: 'But, really, she had something of the shop assistant about her, hadn't she? The earrings – and that enormous coloured comb . . . '.[214] In short, Mrs Busk is a snob: she is representative of the 'negatives' identified by Murry, a stand-in for 'women in general' or what Hastings termed the 'Other Women'. In many ways, then, Mansfield is no less misogynistic or hostile towards cultural democratisation than Orage; however, she reformulates his idea of 'the mob' in order to position herself against it. In this sketch, women bound by social convention and prejudice constitute the unthinking 'mob'. Mansfield's silent opposition to such women is enacted at the level of form, with the ellipses in 'Stay-Laces' signalling her alternative identification with the 'positive' type of modern woman exemplified by Colette and Hastings. Whilst Mansfield's politics were remarkably similar to the anti-democratic rhetoric of other contributors to the periodical, therefore, it is class-bound England that is the object of her satire and the culture of France that offers redemption from 'the mob'.

Mansfield's next contribution to the periodical came well over a year later, with a collection of 'fragments' published in the 'Pastiche' section. In the longest of these fragments, Mansfield mimics those contributors to *The New Age* arguing for the protection of the English language from foreign influence, with the narrator ironically admonishing herself in the mirror with: 'Don't speak French if you're English; it's a vulgar habit'.[215] Indeed, the title of the first fragment, 'Alors, Je Pars', also alerts us to the fact that Mansfield is entering the 'French debate' here: a romanticised description of nature is interrupted with a banal line of overheard gossip in the style of 'Stay-Laces', the ellipses again signalling the potential of women's writing formed in the tradition of Colette to disrupt conventional narrative and systematised discourse. In the last fragment, for example, Mansfield alludes to the first book of Plato's *Republic*, written in Socratic dialogue, a discourse which she undercuts by transposing the story of Cephalus into the realm of personal and contemporary female experience.

After this, Mansfield returned to the 'dialogue for one voice' and monologue forms with a collection of six pieces published from May into early June 1917. The first, titled 'Two Tuppenny Ones, Please', again employs the elliptical form of 'Stay-Laces' in order to satirise female attitudes to the war and the crippling obsession with class in England. We suspect that the 'Lady' of the piece is struggling against a rapid slide down the social scale caused by the economic restrictions imposed by the war. She repeatedly tries to avoid paying the extra penny required for her bus journey, and explains the loss of her maid as a result of what she perceives to be the hysteria created by the war:

> Yes, isn't it annoying! Just when I got her more or less trained. But she went off her head, like they all do nowadays, and decided that she wanted to go into munitions. I told her when she gave notice that she would go on the strict understanding that if she got a job (which I think is highly improbable), she was not to come back and disturb the other servants.[216]

As in 'Stay-Laces', the use of the 'dialogue for one voice' here is not only conducive to comedy, but also creates a character portrait in the tradition of Robert Browning's dramatic monologues, in which an individual's conversation reveals something subliminal or elided about their personality and psyche. In the above passage, for example, the Lady's apparent refusal to understand the reasons for her maid leaving the household highlights her refusal to confront her own diminishing social position. It was therefore not such a radical departure from the 'dialogue for one voice' for Mansfield's next contribution to *The New Age* to be a monologue. In this sketch, 'Late at Night', Mansfield resurrects the character of Virginia first used in *Rhythm* in January 1913 in a parody of the male clique of *The New Age* titled 'Virginia's Journal'. The arrival of a letter from the front in 'Late at Night' leads Virginia to think about the conflict in France, which becomes distorted through her own fears and insecurities. In this piece, Mansfield emphasises misunderstanding between the sexes as heightened by miscommunication across the Channel. Similarly, 'The Black Cap' and 'A Pic-Nic' disrupt the dialogue form to expose failures of communication and thereby satirise the failed attempts by the characters of each story to conduct their illicit love affairs and elopements.

If Mansfield's engagement with the 'French debate' in these pieces is implicit and limited to her formal experimentation with Colette's disruptive literary technique, however, then 'In Confidence' explicitly parodies the debate. The dialogue opens with an argument between five men, beginning with the observation that the 'lack of prudery in France merely seems to me to prove that the French do believe that man is au fond a rational animal. You don't dispute that, do you? I mean – well – damn it all! their literature's based on it. Isn't it?'[217] Excluded from this all-male conversation, Marigold takes Isobel into the hall, saying: 'Aren't men extraordinary? Don't they ever grow out of that kind of thing? No; never. [. . .] What on earth makes them do it? Vanity, my dear, and the masculine delight in showing off.'[218] In the same manner as her earlier satire of *The New Age* published in *Rhythm*, Mansfield portrays the 'Tales for Men Only' aspect of the periodical as just a lot of pretentious prattle. Yet, following on from 'Stay-Laces' and 'Two Tuppenny Ones, Please', she also blocks the possibility of any meaningful conversation between the two women, with Isobel's responses to Marigold limited to smiles, wistful glances and shakes of the head made in parenthesis. Mansfield here employs the omissions of Colette in order to highlight the impossibility of language ever meeting with perfect comprehension, the impossibility of anyone ever being able to truly articulate what they mean. In this way, she reveals as ridiculous the attempts by the men of the story to articulate exactly 'the thing that great art's got to have', a project motivated by their belief that 'the English must of necessity beat the French at this art game'.[219] As such, Mansfield parodies the way in which aesthetic ideals were equated with notions of national superiority in *The New Age*. 'In Confidence' therefore represents Mansfield's clearest intervention in the 'French debate'. It also highlights how the 'dialogism' that Ardis understands as constitutive of *The New Age* was not above critique. In this contribution to the periodical, dialogue is less about voicing opinion and more about the silencing of others; far from being inclusive, the dialogue operates upon exclusion. In this way, Mansfield gestures towards the way in which the 'French debate' within *The New Age* served to designate 'culture' as an exclusively male domain.

Having now clearly entered the 'French debate' in *The New Age*, Mansfield further emphasised her identification with Colette by contributing a story in dialogue form, published the week after 'In Confidence'; as Kimber has observed, 'The Common Round' is clearly based upon Colette's vignette 'L'Enfant de Bastienne'.[220] Mansfield reworks Colette's story of an impoverished ballerina in order to depict Ada Moss, an out-of-work singer and film extra haunted by the same processional visions of food as Colette's protagonist. An early version of Mansfield's story 'Pictures', 'The Common Round' highlights how Mansfield's experimentation with the dialogue form in *The New Age* shaped her later, more accomplished stories, in which the expected balance between narration and speech is disrupted in order to achieve the kind of cinematic theatricality that is the focus of the story. Additionally, Mansfield further emphasised her affinity with France by contributing a short story set in Paris and with a protagonist pointedly named Ian French ('An Album Leaf', later given the French title 'Feuille d'Album') as well as her own translation of a story by Alphonse Daudet, 'M. Seguin's Goat'. Like almost all of Mansfield's contributions to the periodical at this time, the latter narrative is framed as a 'dialogue for one voice', in which an older man admonishes the young Gringoire for refusing a job as a journalist in order to pursue his sentimental ambition to become a poet by telling him the cautionary tale of M. Seguin's young female goat, a creature with a pure white coat who longs to be free from her master and roam across the mountains, only to be eaten by a wolf when she does so. The narrative is about the dangers of women exerting independence and travelling to strange places; it is a cautionary tale about renouncing the protection of the patriarch and losing one's virginity, a story that all young girls in France, right up until the mid-twentieth century, were made to read in school. By choosing to contribute this translation to *The New Age*, Mansfield was making an ironic comment about the way in which generic distinctions between 'journalism' and 'poetry', for example, replicate and perpetuate gender politics, and was thereby satirising Orage's attempts to distinguish 'culture' from 'colloquy, slang, journalism and pedantry'. Moreover, this contribution highlights how the choices Mansfield made in her own life, to embrace the independence of solitary travel, for instance, were intimately bound up with her refusal to conform to the dictates of a prescribed 'unity of style'.

As I have argued in this section of the chapter, Mansfield's experimentation with the dialogue form in her later period of association with *The New Age*, in 1915 and 1917, can be contextualised against recurring debates within the periodical about the significance of the language and culture of France. By adopting the elliptical, broken style of Colette and Hastings, Mansfield associated her writing with a contemporary female literary tradition based in Paris, a tradition that offered an alternative to the 'sad and dull' restrictions of London. This broken style was a fitting mode for depicting the disintegration caused by the war. Satirising narrow-minded and 'negative' social attitudes on the home front, these late contributions to *The New Age* highlight Mansfield's opposition to 'women in general' and the class structures of England. Instead, Mansfield identified her writing with the 'positive' ideal of female agency, an ideal exemplified by the 'moderns' Colette and Hastings and clearly associated with the cultural life of France. In this way, Mansfield's writings challenged the idea propagated within *The New Age* of English national, cultural and linguistic integrity.

Conclusion

In 1921, Mansfield sent a letter to Orage, calling him 'my master' and stating: 'you taught me to write, you taught me to think; you showed me what there was to be done and what *not* to do'.[221] A number of other writers also credited Orage with fostering literary talent in the 'old days' of *The New Age*. When Orage founded *The New English Weekly* in 1932, for example, he received numerous letters expressing a similar sentiment to Mansfield. Ashley Dukes observed: 'They were grand years from 1907 to 1914, when so many of us were doing our apprenticeship under your shrewd direction'.[222] About *The New Age*, E. H. Visiak recalled: 'How well one remembers the enthusiasm of the new writers it attracted! How many a name, now famous, it brought to light!'[223] Similarly, S. G. Hobson concluded: 'It is universally recognised that it was the most stimulating and formative influence of that period.'[224] After Orage's death in 1934, moreover, *The New English Weekly* published a memorial issue of tributes to its late editor from a range of writers and artists, including George Bernard Shaw, G. K. Chesterton, Ezra Pound, Augustus John, H. G. Wells, Richard Aldington, Herbert Read, Eric Gill, Storm Jameson, Edwin Muir and John Middleton Murry. In his contribution to this memorial issue,

T. S. Eliot notes that Orage's death 'is a public loss' and that he will be remembered 'as the best literary critic of that time in London' and 'as the benevolent editor who encouraged merit and (what is still rarer) tolerated genius'.[225] Such universal praise for Orage provoked Hastings into penning her own memoir, published in 1936, in which she tried to put the record straight. The weight of public opinion, however, was against her.

Orage, who was present in Fontainebleau, Paris, when Mansfield died there in January 1923, has invariably been seen as the 'master' editor who nurtured her talent from beginning to end. Counterbalancing Mansfield's praise of Orage in her note of thanks, however, are several letters in which she completely repudiated the 'Pension Sketches' that had been published in his periodical. When Murry wrote to Mansfield in 1920 to ask whether she would consider republishing *In a German Pension*, for example, she replied describing the collection as 'far too *immature*' and '*not good enough*': 'Its [*sic*] positively *juvenile*', she wrote, and 'it's a lie'.[226] Unsurprisingly, this has led some scholars to dismiss the 'Pension Sketches' as immature and crass. Andrew Bennett reflects the low critical esteem in which Mansfield's first collection is generally held when he writes: 'with its intrusive and opinionated author-narrator, its insistence on emphasising the coarse, hateful Bavarian bourgeoisie, its sarcasm and cutting, pointed irony, the book has, for many readers, a strictly limited interest'.[227] These pronouncements made by Mansfield in 1920–1, however, in which she both praises Orage as her 'master' and disowns her early writings as '*not good enough*', are impossible to disentangle from her violent feelings of personal animosity towards Hastings at this time. In March 1920, after Hastings contacted Murry (who was then editor of *The Athenaeum*) to ask whether she could contribute to his periodical, for instance, Mansfield also wrote to him, stating:

> Yes, it is true, I *did* love B.H. but have you utterly forgotten what I told you of her behaviour in Paris – of the last time I saw her and how because I refused to stay the night with her she bawled at me and called me a femme publique in front of those filthy Frenchmen? She is loathsome & corrupt [. . .] Be fastidious, HURT bad people – rather than be hurt by them. Remember that B.H. is bad, has insulted us – insults us worse by thinking she has only to write to you for you to wag your tail. [. . .] I solemnly warn you that if you stir B.H. you will discover such a nest of serpents that you will repent it. Dont [*sic*] forget *Our Pride*. Not that shes [*sic*] so important in herself; its [*sic*] what she stands for. Dont [*sic*] you see?[228]

In November 1920, Mansfield had a dream in which Hastings led a drunken procession of '[v]ile people' into her parents' living room and screamed '*Femme marqué*' at her from across a table.[229] In 1922, moreover, Mansfield records in her diary receiving a 'frightening' letter from Hastings, and states: 'I feared her at Chancery Lane [off which the offices of *The New Age* were located, on Cursitor Street]. There was a peculiar recklessness in her manner and in her tones which made me feel she would recognise no barriers at all. At the same time, of course, one is *fascinated*.'[230]

Indeed, it was precisely the disregard for social conventions and 'barriers', exemplified by the dreamed intrusion into the bourgeois living room of her parents, which so 'fascinated' and attracted Mansfield to Hastings in her period of association with *The New Age*. As I have examined in this chapter, Mansfield found in Hastings a writer who had arrived at very similar ideas to herself about female suffrage, marriage and maternity. The clear resemblances between the work both writers submitted to *The New Age* forces us to reassess Mansfield's later pronouncements about her contributions to the periodical. These were not immature or naive stories, and they did not necessarily owe a debt of influence to Orage; rather, Mansfield's writings in *The New Age* were considered, carefully developed contributions that served to augment the intellectual critique of liberal feminism spearheaded within the periodical by Hastings. These possible lines of influence also force us to reassess the position occupied by Hastings on the periodical, and give credence to many of the assertions made in her 1936 memoir. Given the spectacular fallout between the two after they met in Paris in 1915, 'flared up in a *fury*' and 'parted for life again', it is unsurprising that Mansfield would later disown the stories she had published under Hastings's guiding hand. In the last years of her life, as the letters and diary extracts quoted above indicate, Mansfield was haunted by Hastings, who was an unsettling and domineering remembered presence.

Mansfield records the dream of Hastings leading a drunken procession of '[v]ile people' in a letter to Murry sent on 1 November 1920. Shortly after this, on 18 November, she sends another letter to Murry with a new short story enclosed, 'Poison'. In their editorial footnotes to this story in *The Collected Fiction of Katherine Mansfield*, Gerri Kimber and Vincent O'Sullivan suggest that both 'the story itself' and Murry's 'choosing *not* to publish it in the *Athenaeum*, are enmeshed in the biographical details of [his] flirtation in London with Princess Elizabeth Bibesco, and [Mansfield's] bitterness and loneliness as she waited for mail to arrive at Menton'.[231] As Todd Martin has observed, however, 'the dates don't quite mesh': Murry didn't pursue Bibesco until 29 November 1920, when he first kissed her, and nothing was confirmed to Mansfield about the affair 'until Murry sent his confessional letter, composed on December 10, in which he details several of his transgressions'.[232] Mansfield's 'Poison' was written against very different biographical contexts, I want to suggest, which are implied in no small part by the name she chose to give the main character of the story, Beatrice. Written in the days following her dream about Hastings, 'Poison' reflects back on Mansfield's relationship with her erstwhile mentor and estranged friend, and includes a number of allusions to Hastings's writings published in *The New Age*.

As she waits for the post to arrive, in a town in southern France, Beatrice talks with her younger lover, the unidentified narrator of the story: 'when she wished to speak of food, or the climate, or, playfully, of her love for me, she always dropped into French'.[233] When it comes to love, Beatrice dismisses the idea of marriage, despite the narrator wishing 'privately, in the depths of my heart' to stand 'beside her in a large, yes, a large, fashionable church, crammed with people' singing the hymn 'The Voice that breathed o'er Eden'.[234] Beatrice clearly parallels Hastings here, with her predilection for the language and culture of France and her renunciation of marriage, a 'fashionable' social convention envisaged in terms of the 'mob' and with an allusion to Eden that registers the contexts that had informed Mansfield's 'Bites from the Apple'. Furthermore, the narrator is struck by a 'ghastly feeling of absolute freedom, *her* absolute freedom, of course' and asks: 'Who was she? She was – Woman'.[235] In her contributions to *The New Age*, Hastings had contrasted the 'Other Woman' with the independent individual possessing 'the spirit to be free'. In articles such as 'Women and Freedom', she had stated: 'When we think freely we shall choose freely, we shall act freely'. Likewise, Beatrice in 'Poison' is Woman, not Other Woman; she is an individual who exhibits an 'absolute freedom' that terrifies the narrator, in much the same way as Mansfield feared yet was fascinated by the 'peculiar recklessness' of Hastings.

As the narrator and Beatrice talk, she becomes more and more agitated by the failure of the post to arrive. The creak of the gate and crunch of the gravel outside bring momentary excitement, but it is only the arrival of the newspaper. Beatrice diverts herself by reading the paper: '"There's nothing in it," said she. "Nothing. There's only some poison trial. Either some man did or didn't murder his wife".'[236] Beatrice is struck by the 'morbid curiosity' of the public to read reports of a person's guilt:

> 'Guilt!' she cried. 'Guilt! [. . .] They're fascinated like sick people are fascinated by anything – any scrap of news about their own case. The man in the dock may be innocent enough, but the people in court are nearly all of them poisoners. Haven't you ever thought' – she was pale with excitement – 'of the amount of poisoning that goes on? It's the exception to find married people who don't poison each other – married people and lovers. Oh,' she cried, 'the number of cups of tea, glasses of wine, cups of coffee that are just tainted. [. . .] The only reason why so many couples' – she laughed – '*survive*, is because the one is frightened of giving the other the fatal dose. That dose takes nerve! But it's bound to come sooner or later.'[237]

The longer the couple wait for the post to arrive, the clearer it becomes that Beatrice is expecting a letter from another lover. As the aperitifs are brought in, Beatrice evades the narrator's assertion that she has 'never poisoned anybody' and the story ends with the narrator taking a sip from a glass that might just contain 'the fatal dose': 'Good God! Was it fancy? No, it wasn't fancy. The drink tasted chill, bitter, *queer*.'[238]

The focus on poisoning in this story not only highlights the 'tainted' relationship between Mansfield and Hastings after 1915, it also alludes to particular periodical contexts. From January 1910, when she began using the 'D. Triformis' pseudonym to write about feminism, Hastings started using her own name to sign letters and articles in *The New Age* on the humanitarian issue of capital punishment. In the first of these, she argues that it is against 'Nature' to 'wreck upon the living' the 'unbearable vindictiveness' of telling a person the time and method of his or her death.[239] Hastings comments on the appetite among the public to read of hangings in the newspaper press, noting that 'England still prints in its breakfast journals the boast of a deputy-sheriff to having witnessed "fifty executions"', and recalls an attempted double suicide from the previous year, 'when that poverty-worn old woman, whose husband succumbed to the poison of which both had drunk, was sentenced to be hanged by the neck until she was dead'.[240] In the next article, 'Judicial Murder', Hastings discusses three cases 'of men shortly to be brought to trial' who will likely be sentenced to death for murdering their wives.[241] Compassionate and humane, Hastings argues that the mental health of such men should be brought into consideration: 'the most terrible reflection is that we mostly kill sick men'.[242] Over subsequent months, Hastings contributed to the letters page of *The New Age* almost every week on the issue of capital punishment, commenting on the progress of the trials of John Dickman, who was hanged in August 1910 for shooting John

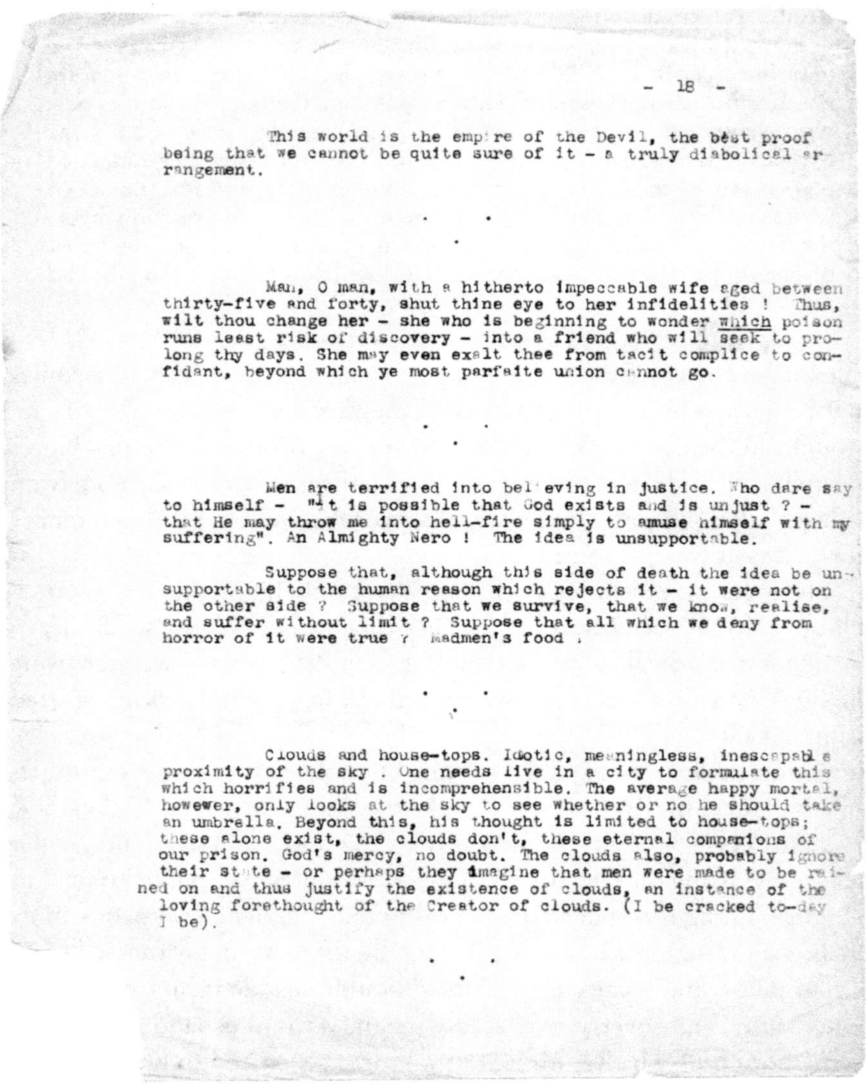

\- 18 -

This world is the empire of the Devil, the best proof being that we cannot be quite sure of it - a truly diabolical arrangement.

. . .

Man, O man, with a hitherto impeccable wife aged between thirty-five and forty, shut thine eye to her infidelities ! Thus, wilt thou change her - she who is beginning to wonder which poison runs least risk of discovery - into a friend who will seek to prolong thy days. She may even exalt thee from tacit complice to confidant, beyond which ye most parfaite union cannot go.

. . .

Men are terrified into believing in justice. Who dare say to himself - "It is possible that God exists and is unjust ? - that He may throw me into hell-fire simply to amuse himself with my suffering". An Almighty Nero ! The idea is unsupportable.

Suppose that, although this side of death the idea be unsupportable to the human reason which rejects it - it were not on the other side ? Suppose that we survive, that we know, realise, and suffer without limit ? Suppose that all which we deny from horror of it were true ? Madmen's food .

. . .

Clouds and house-tops. Idiotic, meaningless, inescapable proximity of the sky . One needs live in a city to formulate this which horrifies and is incomprehensible. The average happy mortal, however, only looks at the sky to see whether or no he should take an umbrella. Beyond this, his thought is limited to house-tops; these alone exist, the clouds don't, these eternal companions of our prison. God's mercy, no doubt. The clouds also, probably ignore their state - or perhaps they imagine that men were made to be rained on and thus justify the existence of clouds, an instance of the loving forethought of the Creator of clouds. (I be cracked to-day I be).

. . .

(a)

Figure 1.6 (a, b) Beatrice Hastings, typescript fragments (1920)

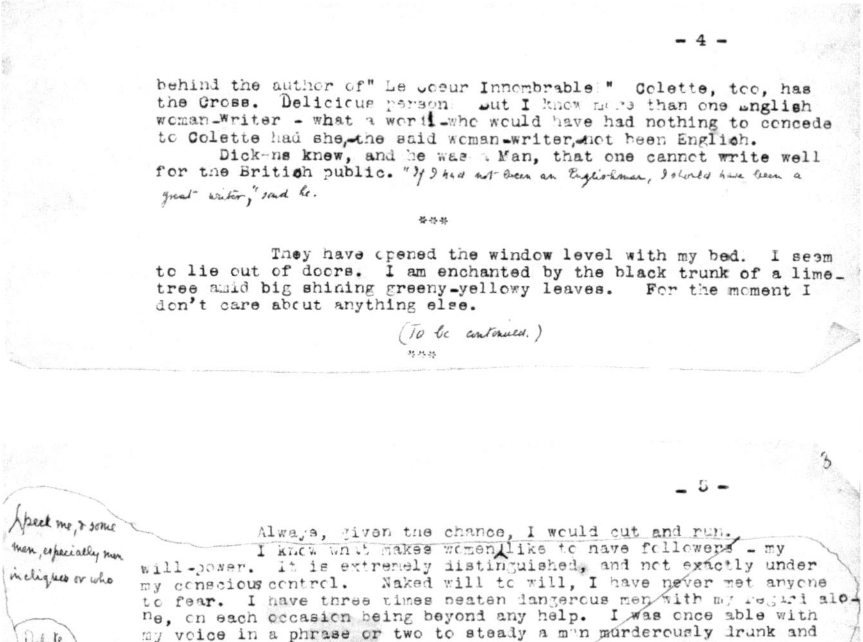

- 4 -

behind the author of" Le Coeur Innombrable " Colette, too, has the Cross. Delicious person. But I know more than one English woman-Writer - what a world - who would have had nothing to concede to Colette had she, the said woman-writer, not been English.

Dick-ns knew, and he was a Man, that one cannot write well for the British public. "If I had not been an Englishman, I should have been a great writer," said he.

***

They have opened the window level with my bed. I seem to lie out of doors. I am enchanted by the black trunk of a lime-tree amid big shining greeny-yellowy leaves. For the moment I don't care about anything else.

(To be continued.)

***

- 5 -

Speak me, & some men, especially men in cliques or who

Delete all This.

Always, given the chance, I would cut and run.

I know what makes women like to have followers - my will-power. It is extremely distinguished, and not exactly under my conscious control. Naked will to will, I have never met anyone to fear. I have three times beaten dangerous men with my regard alone, on each occasion being beyond any help. I was once able with my voice in a phrase or two to steady a man murderously drunk and blind with rage, whose victim kneeled behind me: this was on a public bridge and scores of people stood away, afraid to interfere. Yet, physically, I am not a hard'un. My force is purely moral. When I interview anyone, I gain what is essentiel, what I feel must be gained - must!

This will-power, which I have never abused or strained, is at my command only when I really need it. I cannot summon it without reason worthy of it.

On the other hand, I understand nothing of intrigue. I rage in the nets and pull them tighter. Wherefore, I fear women reasonably, and they fear me instinctively. Often, they explain their fear of me by accusing me of sex-rivalry. This makes me smile. I have never but once in my whole life - this long and so peopled life - taken another woman's man, and then at first I had not know of her existence, and anyway they were on the point of publicly separating. I am so stuck-up that the mere discovery that a man I want is interested in any other than me destroys my desire for him. A married man were as welcome in my arms as a frozen snake, less so! (But I touch wood. An aversion so starkly stated must be on the point of metamorphosis) Ha, and those women jealous of me whose husbands had beards. Could they have only known! Not Croesus, not Beethoven, not Napoleon, not Jupiter or Apollo - not any the greatest in any way ever recorded could make pleasing impression on me from behind a beard. (This, also, may be on the way to changing!, I get on well with bearded men because I treat them with most respectful and considerate young womanishness. But they are all to me as my Father, whatever their age. C'est plus fort que moi.

(b)

Nisbet, and the notorious Dr Crippen, who was hanged in November 1910 for the murder of his wife by poison. The trial of Dickman was the focus of the opening 'Notes of the Week' in the issue for 28 July 1910. Two weeks later, a letter on 'The Dickman Case' written by Hastings appeared directly alongside a letter on 'The Case of Crippen' by one R. Dismale Stocker as well as a letter written by Mansfield titled 'A Paper Chase', in which she observes that 'if we are to believe the Little Fathers of Fleet Street the whole world has been bursting its sides over Crippen':

> I believe that the English nation has the reputation of not being particular with regard to its food – quantity, never mind quality, being the axiom. Certainly the stomach for which the Press caters is a mighty affair indeed, and now the staple joint of the Crippen menu being 'off,' demands the scrapings of prison plates which the 'Daily Mail' so obligingly heats up for breakfast each morning.[243]

Crippen became infamous after allegedly poisoning his wife with the calming drug scopolamine before dismembering her body and hiding the remains under his basement floor. The British press avidly followed the details of this gruesome murder case, especially after Crippen attempted to evade arrest by fleeing to America with his lover. Mansfield's 'A Paper Chase' is another example of the influence exercised by Hastings, who contributed several letters on the Crippen case to *The New Age* as well as a parody of the trial set in heaven and adjudicated by St Peter and Rabelais.[244] In the 'Notes of the Week' for 10 November 1910, the editor again turns attention to the treatment in the national press of the Crippen case:

> It must be remembered that our newspapers, with all their faults, are practically the only schoolbooks yet devised for the political education of public opinion. While subjects of national interest are under the ban in them it therefore happens that the public lightly turns to the columns of murder, crime, and punishment. For instance, the Crippen case, with its sickening publicity, owes nine-tenths of its prominence to the absence from public attention of any worthier subject.[245]

Crippen continued to be referred to in articles published throughout 1911 and 1912 in *The New Age*. As late as 5 December 1912, for example, Hastings contributed a letter to the periodical in which she states that Crippen's 'temporary madness was not accompanied by anything resembling the dirty tricks worked against him by the lawyers'.[246]

Against these print contexts, the poison trial reported in the newspaper in 'Poison' clearly links Beatrice with Hastings. In a letter sent to

Murry on 23 November 1920, Mansfield writes that she intended the reader to see how Beatrice's '*commonness* peeps out – the newspaper touch of such a woman'.[247] Given the way in which the murder trials were used in *The New Age* to comment upon the dire state of newspaper journalism in Britain, the 'newspaper touch' of Beatrice in 'Poison' can be interpreted as a damning attack on Hastings's character as well as her abilities as a writer. There was certainly no love lost between Mansfield and Hastings after 1915. Hastings is particularly bitter in her memoir, writing that, in the last years of her life, 'Katherine began to play saint, prate about God and [. . .] "twittered" her way out of a world she had fouled wherever she went'.[248]

Despite this animosity, however, there remained a remarkable 'parafluence' and simultaneous convergence of ideas between the writings of both women, unbeknownst to each. In one of her typescript fragments, composed when she was confined to a hospital bed in Paris for six weeks in October and November 1920, Hastings writes:

> Man, O man, with a hitherto impeccable wife aged between thirty-five and forty, shut thine eye to her infidelities! Thus, wilt thou change her – she who is beginning to wonder *which* poison runs least risk of discovery – into a friend who will seek to prolong thy days. She may even exalt thee from tacit complice to confidant, beyond which ye most parfaite union cannot go.[249]

The parallels between this and Mansfield's 'Poison', a story written in the same month as Hastings's typescript fragment but not published until several years later in the posthumous collection *Something Childish and Other Stories* (1924), are striking. Whilst their own relationship became distinctly poisonous, therefore, the two writers remained eerily in tune, far more similar than each cared to admit.

Notes

1. Katherine Mansfield, *The Collected Letters of Katherine Mansfield, Volume I: 1903–1917*, ed. Vincent O'Sullivan and Margaret Scott (Oxford: Clarendon Press, 1984), p. 60.
2. Antony Alpers, *The Life of Katherine Mansfield*, rev. edn (Harmondsworth: Penguin, 1982), p. 328.
3. Andrew Bennett, *Katherine Mansfield* (Tavistock: Northcote House, 2004), p. 46; Sydney Janet Kaplan, *Katherine Mansfield and the Origins of Modernist Fiction* (New York: Cornell University Press, 1991), pp. 16–17.
4. Philip Mairet, *A. R. Orage: A Memoir* (London: Dent, 1936), pp. 46–7.

5. Hastings's many pseudonyms included: 'Pagan', 'Annette Doorly', 'Beatrice Tina', 'Robert á Field', 'A Reluctant Suffragette', 'Hastings Lloyd', 'Mrs Beatrice T. Hastings' ('B.H.'), 'D. Triformis', 'Alice Morning' ('A.M.'), 'Mrs Malaprop', 'T.K.L.', 'E. Agnes R. Haigh', 'Edward Stafford', 'Sydney Robert West', 'H.M.', 'G. Whiz', 'J. Wilson', 'T.W.', 'A.M.A.' and 'Cynicus'. In her memoir, *The Old 'New Age': Orage and Others* (London: Blue Moon Press, 1936), p. 43, Hastings also claimed to have written over sixty articles for the column 'Present-Day Criticism' as 'R.H.C.', a pseudonym usually attributed to Orage.
6. Hastings, *The Old 'New Age'*, p. 3.
7. Ibid.
8. I have discovered scraps of typescript that survived this attempted self-erasure in the private archives of Nadia Lasserson, daughter of Miron Grindea, editor of *Adam International Review*. Three of these fragments are reproduced as images here, in Figure 1.6(a, b).
9. Claire Tomalin, *Katherine Mansfield: A Secret Life* (London: Viking, 1987), p. 2; Jeffrey Meyers, *Modigliani: A Life* (London: Duckworth Overlook, 2008), p. 130.
10. John Carswell, *Lives and Letters: A. R. Orage, Beatrice Hastings, Katherine Mansfield, John Middleton Murry, S. S. Koteliansky, 1906–1957* (London: Faber, 1978), p. 74.
11. Jeffrey Meyers, *Katherine Mansfield: A Darker View* (New York: Cooper Square Press, 2002), p. 55.
12. Ibid., p. 58.
13. Vincent O'Sullivan and Margaret Scott, 'Introduction', in Vincent O'Sullivan and Margaret Scott (eds), *The Collected Letters of Katherine Mansfield, Volume I: 1903–1917* (Oxford: Clarendon Press, 1984), p. xi.
14. Alpers, *The Life of Katherine Mansfield*, p. 114.
15. Stephen Gray, *Beatrice Hastings: A Literary Life* (London: Viking, 2004).
16. Ann L. Ardis, 'Debating Feminism, Modernism, and Socialism: Beatrice Hastings' Voices in *The New Age*', in Bonnie Kime Scott (ed.), *Gender in Modernism: New Geographies, Complex Intersections* (Urbana: University of Illinois Press, 2007), pp. 160–85; 'The Dialogics of Modernism(s) in *The New Age*', *Modernism/Modernity*, 14.3 (September 2007), pp. 407–34; Lucy Delap, 'Feminist and Anti-Feminist Encounters in Edwardian Britain', *Historical Research*, 78.201 (August 2005), pp. 377–99; Robert Scholes, 'Model Artists in Paris', in *Paradoxy of Modernism* (New Haven: Yale University Press, 2006), pp. 221–56.
17. Bonnie Kime Scott (ed.), *Gender in Modernism: New Geographies, Complex Intersections* (Urbana: University of Illinois Press, 2007); Benjamin Johnson and Erika Jo Brown (eds), *Beatrice Hastings: On the Life and Work of a Lost Modern Master* (Warrensburg: Pleiades Press, 2016).
18. Lee Garver, 'The Political Katherine Mansfield', *Modernism/Modernity*, 8.2 (April 2001), pp. 225–43; Carey Snyder, 'Katherine Mansfield and the *New Age* School of Satire', *Journal of Modern Periodical Studies*, 1.2 (2010), pp. 125–58.
19. Carswell, *Lives and Letters*, p. 273.
20. Jane Garrity, *Step-Daughters of England: British Women Modernists and the National Imaginary* (Manchester: Manchester University Press, 2003), p. 5.
21. Anna Davin, 'Imperialism and Motherhood', *History Workshop*, 5 (spring 1978), p. 12.
22. Ibid.
23. Garrity, *Step-Daughters of England*, pp. 2, 23.
24. Ibid., p. 1.

25. Quoted in Davin, 'Imperialism and Motherhood', p. 16.
26. R. Murray Leslie, 'Woman's Progress in Relation to Eugenics', *Eugenics Review* (January 1911), p. 283. Quoted in Davin, 'Imperialism and Motherhood', pp. 20–1.
27. Quoted in Les Garner, *Stepping Stones to Women's Liberty: Feminist Ideas in the Women's Suffrage Movement 1900–1918* (London: Heinemann, 1984), p. 9.
28. Ibid., p. 50.
29. Helen McNeil, 'Vortex Marsden: A Little Magazine and the Making of Modernity', in Kate Campbell (ed.), *Journalism, Literature and Modernity: From Hazlitt to Modernism* (Edinburgh: Edinburgh University Press, 2000), p. 158.
30. Garner, *Stepping Stones to Women's Liberty*, p. 4.
31. Ibid., pp. 59–60.
32. Ibid., p. 72.
33. Delap, 'Feminist and Anti-Feminist Encounters', p. 393.
34. Pagan [Beatrice Hastings], 'A Modern Bacchante', *New Age*, 1.18 (29 August 1907), p. 279.
35. Beatrice Tina [Beatrice Hastings], 'Woman as State Creditor', *New Age*, 3.9 (27 June 1908), p. 169.
36. Ibid.
37. E. [Edith] Nesbit, 'Beatrice Tina and the Almighty', *New Age*, 3.10 (4 July 1907), pp. 197–8.
38. Beatrice Tina [Beatrice Hastings], *Woman's Worst Enemy: Woman* (London: New Age Press, 1909), p. 2.
39. Anon. [Dora Marsden], 'Bondwomen', *Freewoman*, 1.1 (23 November 1911), pp. 1–2.
40. A Reluctant Suffragette [Beatrice Hastings], 'The Other Women', *New Age*, 3.10 (4 July 1908), p. 187.
41. Ibid.
42. Beatrice Tina [Beatrice Hastings], 'Suffragettes in the Making', *New Age*, 4.6 (3 December 1908), p. 109; 'On Guard', *New Age*, 4.7 (10 December 1908), p. 123.
43. Tina [Hastings], *Woman's Worst Enemy*, p. 55.
44. Beatrice Tina [Beatrice Hastings], 'The Case of the Anti-Feminists', *New Age*, 3.18 (29 August 1908), p. 349; 'Mary Wollstonecraft', *New Age*, 5.5 (15 July 1909), p. 106.
45. D. Triformis [Beatrice Hastings], 'Lady McLaren's Charter', *New Age*, 6.23 (7 April 1910), p. 533.
46. Ibid.
47. Anon. [A. R. Orage], 'Unedited Opinions. The Superman', *New Age*, 8.5 (1 December 1910), p. 107.
48. Ibid.
49. Ibid.
50. Tina [Hastings], *Woman's Worst Enemy*, pp. 53, 9.
51. Ibid., p. 48.
52. Ibid., p. 47.
53. Ibid., p. 46.
54. Ibid., pp. 46–7.
55. Ibid., pp. 32, 6.
56. Ibid., pp. 6–7.
57. Ibid., p. 34.
58. Ibid., pp. 14, 18, 20.
59. Beatrice Tina [Beatrice Hastings], 'Whited Sepulchres', *New Age*, 5.1 (29 April 1909), p. 13.

60. Ibid.
61. Beatrice Tina [Beatrice Hastings], 'Whited Sepulchres', *New Age*, 5.2 (6 May 1909), pp. 35–6.
62. Beatrice Tina [Beatrice Hastings], 'Whited Sepulchres', *New Age*, 5.3 (13 May 1909), p. 55.
63. A Reluctant Suffragette [Beatrice Hastings], 'The Other Women', p. 187.
64. Beatrice Tina [Beatrice Hastings], 'Whited Sepulchres', *New Age*, 5.4 (20 May 1909), p. 77.
65. Ibid.
66. Beatrice Tina [Beatrice Hastings], 'Whited Sepulchres', *New Age*, 5.6 (3 June 1909), p. 119.
67. Beatrice Tina [Beatrice Hastings], 'A Reply to My Critics', *New Age*, 5.12 (15 July 1909), p. 243.
68. Hastings, 'Whited Sepulchres', *New Age*, 5.1 (29 April 1909), p. 13.
69. Quoted in Davin, 'Imperialism and Motherhood', p. 29.
70. Beatrice Tina [Beatrice Hastings], 'Whited Sepulchres', *New Age*, 5.5 (27 May 1909), p. 100.
71. For a further discussion of the discovery of this story, see Chris Mourant, '"A Little Episode": The Forgotten Typescripts of Katherine Mansfield, 1908–11', in Janet Wilson, Gerri Kimber and Delia da Sousa Correa (eds), *Katherine Mansfield and the (Post)colonial* (Edinburgh: Edinburgh University Press, 2013), pp. 154–66.
72. Oliver Tearle, *T. E. Hulme and Modernism* (London: Bloomsbury, 2013), p. 11.
73. D. Triformis [Beatrice Hastings], 'A Fallacy Behind the Militant Theory', *New Age*, 6.14 (3 February 1910), p. 322.
74. Beatrice Tina [Beatrice Hastings], 'Are Women Anarchists?', *New Age*, 4.20 (11 March 1909), p. 398; D. Triformis [Beatrice Hastings], 'Women and Literature', *New Age*, 6.24 (14 April 1910), p. 558.
75. D. Triformis [Beatrice Hastings], 'Militancy and Humanity', *New Age*, 6.10 (6 January 1910), p. 225.
76. D. Triformis [Beatrice Hastings], 'Feminism and the Franchise', *New Age*, 6.18 (3 March 1910), p. 415.
77. D. Triformis [Beatrice Hastings], 'Women and Freedom', *New Age*, 7.2 (12 May 1910), pp. 29–30.
78. Beatrice (Tina) Hastings [Beatrice Hastings], 'Women and Freedom', *New Age*, 7.3 (19 May 1910), p. 69.
79. Ibid.
80. D. Triformis [Beatrice Hastings], 'To Your Posts, Feminists', *New Age*, 8.16 (16 February 1911), p. 368.
81. Jane Harrison, quoted in Beatrice (Tina) Hastings [Beatrice Hastings], 'Women and Freedom', *New Age*, 7.2 (12 May 1910), p. 29.
82. Ibid.
83. Hastings, 'Women and Freedom', *New Age*, 7.2 (12 May 1910), p. 29.
84. Ibid., p. 30.
85. Ibid., p. 29.
86. Ibid.
87. Katherine Mansfield, *Journal of Katherine Mansfield: Definitive Edition*, ed. John Middleton Murry (London: Constable, 1954), p. 37.
88. Ibid., pp. 36–7.
89. Ibid., p. 37.
90. Ibid.

91. Clare Hanson and Andrew Gurr, *Katherine Mansfield* (Basingstoke: Macmillan, 1981), p. 31.
92. Katherine Mansfield, 'Frau Fischer', *New Age*, 7.16 (18 August 1910), p. 368; Hastings, *Woman's Worst Enemy*, p. 53.
93. Katharine [Katherine] Mansfield, 'Bavarian Babies: The Child-Who-Was-Tired', *New Age*, 6.17 (24 February 1910), pp. 396–7.
94. Katharine [Katherine] Mansfield, 'At "Lehmann's"', *New Age*, 7.10 (7 July 1910), p. 225.
95. Ibid., pp. 226–7.
96. Katherine Mansfield, 'Frau Brechenmacher Attends a Wedding', *New Age*, 7.12 (21 July 1910), p. 274.
97. Ibid.
98. Ibid.
99. Ibid., p. 275.
100. Ibid.
101. Katherine Mansfield, 'A Birthday', *New Age*, 9.3 (18 May 1911), pp. 62–3.
102. Ibid., p. 63.
103. Katherine Mansfield, 'The Modern Soul', *New Age*, 9.8 (22 June 1911), p. 184.
104. Anne Fernihough, 'Introduction', in Katherine Mansfield, *In a German Pension*, ed. Anne Fernihough (London: Penguin, 1999), p. xix.
105. Mansfield, 'The Modern Soul', p. 184; Katherine Mansfield, 'The Sister of the Baroness', *New Age*, 7.14 (4 August 1910), p. 323.
106. Katharine [Katherine] Mansfield, 'Germans at Meat', *New Age*, 6.18 (3 March 1910), p. 419.
107. Ibid., p. 420.
108. Ibid., p. 419.
109. Ibid.
110. Ibid.
111. Ibid.
112. Mansfield, 'The Modern Soul', p. 184.
113. Mansfield, 'Frau Fischer', p. 367.
114. Ibid., pp. 367–8.
115. Ibid., p. 368.
116. Ibid.
117. Katharine [Katherine] Mansfield, 'The Luft Bad', *New Age*, 6.21 (24 March 1910), p. 493.
118. Andrew Harrison, 'Ambivalence, Language and the Uncanny in Katherine Mansfield's *In a German Pension*', in Delia da Sousa Correa, Gerri Kimber, Susan Reid and Gina Wisker (eds), *Katherine Mansfield and the Fantastic* (Edinburgh: Edinburgh University Press, 2012), pp. 52, 57.
119. Katharine [Katherine] Mansfield, 'The Baron', *New Age*, 6.19 (10 March 1910), p. 444; Mansfield, 'The Sister of the Baroness', p. 324.
120. Mansfield, 'The Sister of the Baroness', p. 324.
121. Mansfield, 'Germans at Meat', p. 419.
122. Mansfield, 'At "Lehmann's"', p. 225.
123. Harrison, 'Ambivalence, Language and the Uncanny', p. 57.
124. Homi K. Bhabha, *The Location of Culture*, rev. edn (London: Routledge, 2004), pp. 54–5.
125. Ibid., p. 55.
126. Mansfield, 'The Modern Soul', p. 185.

127. Katherine Mansfield, 'Pastiche: At the Club', *New Age*, 10.19 (7 March 1912), pp. 449–50.
128. Katherine Mansfield, 'A Marriage of Passion', *New Age*, 10.19 (7 March 1912), pp. 447–8.
129. Mouche [Katherine Mansfield?], 'The Mating of Gwendolyn', *New Age*, 10.1 (2 November 1911), pp. 14–15.
130. The three sketches published in *The Blue Review* ('Epilogue: Pension Seguin', 'Epilogue: II' and 'Epilogue: III Bains Turcs', May–July 1913) are also drawn from Mansfield's experience in Geneva.
131. Francis Grierson, 'Impressions of Italy', *New Age*, 6.21 (24 March 1910), p. 491.
132. Katherine Mansfield, 'Being a Truthful Adventure', *New Age*, 9.19 (7 September 1911), pp. 451–2.
133. Garver, 'The Political Katherine Mansfield', p. 237.
134. Mansfield, 'Being a Truthful Adventure', p. 451.
135. Hastings, 'Women and Literature', p. 558.
136. Garver, 'The Political Katherine Mansfield', p. 235.
137. K.M. and B.H. [Katherine Mansfield and Beatrice Hastings], 'A P.S.A.', *New Age*, 9.4 (25 May 1911), p. 95.
138. Anon. [Beatrice Hastings], 'Ann Veronica', *New Age*, 5.25 (14 October 1909), p. 447.
139. Hastings, 'Women and Literature', p. 558.
140. Anon. [Beatrice Hastings], 'The Maids' Comedy', *New Age*, 8.8 (22 December 1910), p. 181; Stephen Gray, 'Beatrice Hastings', in *Free-Lancers and Literary Biography in South Africa* (Amsterdam: Rodopi, 1999), p. 66.
141. Isobel Maddison, 'Mansfield's "Writing Game" and World War One', in Isobel Maddison and Alice Kelly (eds), *Katherine Mansfield and World War One* (Edinburgh: Edinburgh University Press, 2014), pp. 42, 51.
142. Diane Milburn, *The Deutschlandbild of A. R. Orage and the New Age Circle* (Frankfurt: Peter Lang, 1996).
143. John Middleton Murry, quoted ibid., p. 61.
144. Mansfield, *The Collected Letters of Katherine Mansfield, Volume I*, p. 190.
145. Ida Baker, letter to Miron Grindea, KC/ADAM/LET/161, *Adam International Review* Archive, King's College London Archive, London.
146. All quotations from 'Bites from the Apple' can be found in Appendix III.
147. A. R. Orage, 'Towards Socialism', *New Age*, 1.23 (3 October 1907), p. 361.
148. T. E. Hulme, 'Romanticism and Classicism', in *Speculations: Essays on Humanism and the Philosophy of Art*, ed. Herbert Read (New York: Harcourt, 1924), p. 117.
149. Ibid., p. 116.
150. T. E. Hulme, 'Reflections on Violence', in *Speculations: Essays on Humanism and the Philosophy of Art*, ed. Herbert Read (New York: Harcourt, 1924), p. 256.
151. Ibid.
152. Hulme, 'Romanticism and Classicism', p. 117.
153. Anon. [A. R. Orage], 'Unedited Opinions', *New Age*, 9.4 (25 May 1911), p. 84.
154. J. M. Kennedy, 'Tory Democracy', *New Age*, 9.9 (29 June 1911), p. 197.
155. Hulme, 'Romanticism and Classicism', p. 120.
156. Anne Fernihough, *Freewomen and Supermen: Edwardian Radicals and Literary Modernism* (Oxford: Oxford University Press, 2013), p. 158.
157. Mansfield, 'Bavarian Babies', p. 397.
158. Mansfield, 'The Sister of the Baroness', p. 324.
159. Mansfield, 'The Modern Soul', p. 184.

160. Quoted by Christopher Tayler, 'A Modernist and a Reactionary', *Telegraph* (17 November 2002), available at http://www.telegraph.co.uk/culture/4729260/A-modernist-and-a-reactionary.html (last accessed June 2018).
161. Charlotte E. Holmes, 'A Voice from the Ranks', *New Age*, 2.7 (14 December 1907), p. 130.
162. Hastings, *Woman's Worst Enemy*, pp. 11, 13.
163. Beatrice Hastings, 'Epigrammata', *New Age*, 7.18 (1 September 1910), p. 417.
164. Triformis, 'Women and Freedom', p. 30.
165. Friedrich Nietzsche, *Aphorisms on Love and Hate*, trans. Marion Faber and Stephen Lehmann ([1878] London: Penguin, 2015), p. 1.
166. Mansfield, *Journal of Katherine Mansfield*, p. 73.
167. A. R. Orage, *Friedrich Nietzsche, the Dionysian Spirit of the Age* (Edinburgh: T. N. Foulis, 1906), pp. 14–15.
168. Orage, *Nietzsche in Outline and Aphorism* (Edinburgh: T. N. Foulis, 1907), p. 5.
169. David Thatcher, *Nietzsche in England, 1890–1914: The Growth of a Reputation* (Toronto: University of Toronto Press, 1970), p. 235.
170. Frederick Richardson, 'The New Dionysos', *New Age*, 1.5 (30 May 1907), p. 74.
171. Alpers, *The Life of Katherine Mansfield*, p. 108.
172. Tina [Hastings], *Woman's Worst Enemy*, p. 7.
173. Eric O. Johannesson, 'Vilhelm Ekelund: Modernism and the Aesthetics of the Aphorism', *Scandinavian Studies*, 56 (1984), p. 225.
174. J. P. Stern, *Lichtenberg: A Doctrine of Shattered Occasions* (Bloomington: Indiana University Press, 1959), p. 216.
175. John Middleton Murry, 'Coming to London', in John Lehmann (ed.), *Coming to London* (London: Phoenic House, 1957), p. 100.
176. Anon. [A. R. Orage], 'Present-Day Criticism', *New Age*, 10.22 (28 March 1912), p. 519.
177. R. H. Congreve [A. R. Orage], 'A Fourth Tale for Men Only', *New Age*, 11.3 (16 May 1912), p. 61.
178. R.H.C. [A. R. Orage], 'Readers and Writers', *New Age*, 13.18 (28 August 1913), p. 513.
179. G. K. Chesterton, quoted in Anon. [A. R. Orage], 'Present-Day Criticism', *New Age*, 10.7 (14 December 1911), p. 158.
180. Ezra Pound, 'The Approach to Paris, I', *New Age*, 13.19 (4 September 1913), p. 552; 'The Approach to Paris, II', *New Age*, 13.20 (11 September 1913), p. 578.
181. T.K.L. [Beatrice Hastings], 'The Way Back to America', *New Age*, 13.21 (18 September 1913), p. 604.
182. Ardis, 'The Dialogics of Modernism(s) in *The New Age*'.
183. Paul Peppis, 'Narratives of Ambition and Anxiety: Confronting Europe in *The New Age*' in *Literature, Politics, and the English Avant-Garde: Nation and Empire, 1901–1918* (Cambridge: Cambridge University Press, 2000), pp. 53–75.
184. Anon. [A. R. Orage], 'Unedited Opinions. Down with the Tricolour', *New Age*, 9.21 (21 September 1911), pp. 489–90.
185. R.H.C. [A. R. Orage], 'Readers and Writers', *New Age*, 13.26 (23 October 1913), p. 761.
186. Thomas Leddy, 'Nietzsche on Unity of Style', *Historical Reflections/Réflexions Historiques*, 21.3 (fall 1995), p. 553.
187. Ibid., pp. 553–4.
188. Hastings, *The Old 'New Age'*, pp. 6–7.
189. Alice Morning [Beatrice Hastings], 'Pastiche. Impressions de Paris', *New Age*, 15.3 (21 May 1914), p. 68.

190. Alice Morning [Beatrice Hastings], 'Impressions de Paris – III', *New Age*, 15.6 (11 June 1914), p. 138.
191. Alice Morning [Beatrice Hastings], 'Impressions of Paris', *New Age*, 17.13 (29 July 1915), p. 307.
192. Ibid.
193. Michael Kowaleski, quoted in Tim Youngs, 'Introduction', in Tim Youngs (ed.), *The Cambridge Introduction to Travel Writing* (Cambridge: Cambridge University Press, 2013), p. 1.
194. Alice Morning [Beatrice Hastings], 'Pastiche. Impressions de Paris – II', *New Age*, 15.5 (4 June 1914), p. 115.
195. Morning [Hastings], 'Pastiche. Impressions de Paris – III', p. 139.
196. Gray, *Beatrice Hastings*, p. 182.
197. Alice Morning [Beatrice Hastings], 'Impressions of Paris', *New Age*, 15.25 (22 October 1914), p. 598.
198. Ibid., p. 599.
199. Mansfield, *The Collected Letters of Katherine Mansfield, Volume I*, pp. 159, 165.
200. Ibid., pp. 170, 166.
201. Katherine Mansfield, 'Stay-Laces', *New Age*, 18.1 (4 November 1915), p. 15.
202. Katherine Mansfield, 'The Festival of the Coronation (With Apologies to Theocritus)', *New Age*, 9.9 (29 June 1911), p. 196.
203. Gerri Kimber, *Katherine Mansfield: The View from France* (Oxford: Peter Lang, 2008), pp. 119–20.
204. Vincent O'Sullivan, 'Like Everybody Else?', *New Age*, 7.18 (1 September 1910), p. 424; X. Marcel Boulestin, 'Recent French Novels', *Blue Review* (June 1913), pp. 138–9.
205. Francis Carco, 'Lettre de France', *Rhythm*, 10 (November 1912), p. 275; 'Revue des Revues', *Rhythm*, 9 (October 1912), p. 236.
206. Beatrice Hastings, 'Notes from France', *New Age*, 22.14 (31 January 1918), p. 269.
207. See Figure 1.6(b).
208. Mansfield, *Journal of Katherine Mansfield*, p. 62.
209. Mansfield, *The Collected Letters of Katherine Mansfield, Volume I*, pp. 212–13.
210. Ibid., p. 231.
211. Ibid., p. 282.
212. John Middleton Murry, *The Letters of John Middleton Murry to Katherine Mansfield*, ed. Cherry A. Hankin (London: Constable, 1983), pp. 53–4.
213. Ibid., p. 53.
214. Mansfield, 'Stay-Laces', p. 15.
215. Katherine Mansfield, 'Pastiche: Beware of the Rain!', *New Age*, 20.25 (19 April 1917), p. 595.
216. Katherine Mansfield, 'Two Tuppenny Ones, Please', *New Age*, 21.1 (3 May 1917), p. 14.
217. Katherine Mansfield, 'In Confidence', *New Age*, 21.4 (24 May 1917), p. 88.
218. Ibid.
219. Ibid.
220. Kimber, *Katherine Mansfield*, pp. 118–19.
221. Katherine Mansfield, *The Collected Letters of Katherine Mansfield, Volume IV: 1920–1921*, ed. Vincent O'Sullivan and Margaret Scott (Oxford: Clarendon Press, 1996), p. 177.
222. Letters to A. R. Orage, File 22, BC MS 20c Orage, Alfred R. Orage Archive, Special Collections, University of Leeds, Leeds.

223. Ibid.
224. Ibid.
225. T. S. Eliot, 'Orage: Memories', *New English Weekly*, 6 (15 November 1934), p. 100.
226. Katherine Mansfield, *The Collected Letters of Katherine Mansfield, Volume III: 1919–1920*, ed. Vincent O'Sullivan and Margaret Scott (Oxford: Clarendon Press, 1993), p. 206.
227. Bennett, *Katherine Mansfield*, p. 72.
228. Mansfield, *The Collected Letters of Katherine Mansfield, Volume III*, pp. 257–9.
229. Mansfield, *The Collected Letters of Katherine Mansfield, Volume IV*, p. 94.
230. Mansfield, *Journal of Katherine Mansfield*, p. 285.
231. Gerri Kimber and Vincent O'Sullivan, in Katherine Mansfield, *The Collected Fiction of Katherine Mansfield, 1916–1922*, ed. Gerri Kimber and Vincent O'Sullivan (Edinburgh: Edinburgh University Press, 2012), p. 260.
232. Todd Martin, 'Constructing Jealousy, Exacting Revenge: Katherine Mansfield's "Poison" and Robert Browning's "My Last Duchess"', in *Re-forming World Literature: Katherine Mansfield and the Modernist Short Story*, ed. Gerri Kimber and Janet Wilson (Stuttgart: Ibidem Press, 2018), p. 188.
233. Katherine Mansfield, 'Poison', in *The Collected Fiction of Katherine Mansfield, 1916–1922*, ed. Gerri Kimber and Vincent O'Sullivan (Edinburgh: Edinburgh University Press, 2012), p. 256.
234. Ibid.
235. Ibid.
236. Ibid., p. 258.
237. Ibid., pp. 258–9.
238. Ibid., p. 260.
239. Beatrice T. Hastings, 'On Capital Punishment', *New Age*, 6.13 (27 January 1910), p. 297.
240. Ibid.
241. Beatrice Hastings, 'Judicial Murder', *New Age*, 7.5 (2 June 1910), p. 102.
242. Ibid.
243. Katherine Mansfield, 'A Paper Chase', *New Age*, 7.15 (11 August 1910), pp. 354–5.
244. T.K.L. [Beatrice Hastings], 'The Trial', *New Age*, 7.26 (27 October 1910), pp. 615–17.
245. Anon. [A. R. Orage], 'Notes of the Week', *New Age*, 8.2 (10 November 1910), p. 25.
246. Beatrice Hastings, 'The White Slave Traffic', *New Age*, 12.5 (5 December 1912), p. 117.
247. Mansfield, *The Collected Letters of Katherine Mansfield, Volume IV*, p. 119.
248. Hastings, *The Old 'New Age'*, p. 28.
249. See Figure 1.6(a).

Figure 2.1 *Rhythm*

Chapter 2

Rhythm: Parody and (Post)Colonial Modernism

In May 1911 the art and theatre critic Huntly Carter reported in *The New Age* that the 'intuitional philosophy of Bergson – a system of philosophy for elevating and making vision more penetratingly human – has so taken possession of Paris that the spirit of it seems to fill every place'.[1] Carter summarised Henri Bergson's philosophy as the 'modern principles of continuity and *rhythm*'[2] and praised the second wave of Fauvist artists then exhibiting at the Société des Artists Indépendants, and headed by the expatriates J. D. Fergusson, Anne Estelle Rice and Jessica Dismorr, for their 'lyrics in colour, lyrics in line, lyrics in light to the new deity, *rhythm*' (my emphasis).[3] Carter's articles elicited a response in the correspondence pages of *The New Age* from John Middleton Murry, who reaffirmed the celebration of Paris as 'the great cosmopolis' and 'the very cross-roads of Continental ideas' and 'advanced art'.[4] Praising the new post-impressionist artists named by Carter for having applied Bergson's philosophy with 'the most comprehensive and vital results', Murry delighted in the fact that the new movement had 'sufficed at once to enrage and confound its critics' in England.[5] This letter to *The New Age* announced Murry's arrival on the London literary scene, and in the same month of June 1911 he published the first issue of a magazine devoted to Bergson's philosophy and Fauvist art that derived its title from the 'new deity': *Rhythm*.

Murry had met the artists Fergusson and Rice by chance on his first visit to Paris in the winter of 1910 in the Café d'Harcourt. In his autobiography, he recalled the importance of the word 'rhythm' in his early conversations with Fergusson:

> One word was recurrent in all our strange discussions – the word 'rhythm'. We never made any attempt to define it; nor even took any precaution to discover whether it had the same significance for us both. All that

> mattered was that it had some meaning for each of us [. . .] and the real purpose of 'this modern movement' – a phrase frequent on F-'s lips – was to reassert the pre-eminence of rhythm.[6]

In the spring of 1911, Murry travelled to Paris with his Oxford friend Michael Sadler (later Sadleir) and convinced Fergusson to be art editor of the new magazine they were founding: with its quality reproductions of modern art in black and white, *Rhythm* 'would be *The Yellow Book* of the modern movement'.[7] On this trip, Murry wrote to another friend at Oxford, Phillip Landon, outlining what he understood by the term 'modernism':

> Modernism means, when I use it, Bergsonism in Philosophy – that is a really *Creative* Evolution with only in the end an Intuition to put the individual at its heart roots; an intuition which is the raising of Personality to the nth degree, a conscious concentration of vision. [. . .] Now Bergsonism stands for Post Impressionism [. . .] it stands for a certain symbolism in poetry on the one hand; and a certain definite rejection of suggestion on the other. It stands equally for Debussy and Maehler [*sic*] in music; for Fantaisisme in Modern French literature, and generally if you like for 'guts' and bloodiness.[8]

With Fergusson as art editor, *Rhythm* was striking for its visual content and could boast an impressive list of contributors, including Pablo Picasso and André Derain, as well as Rice and Dismorr. Employing bold massed lines and depicting daring subject matter, visual contributions to the magazine promoted a post-impressionist aesthetic that conformed to the notion that modern art should be fearless and evocative of '"guts" and bloodiness'. Outlining the 'Aims and Ideals' of the magazine in the first issue, Murry emphasised this idea when he argued that modern art should be 'brutal':

> 'Before art can be human it must learn to be brutal.' Our intention is to provide art, be it drawing, literature or criticism, which shall be vigorous, determined, which shall have its roots below the surface and be the rhythmical echo of the life with which it is in touch. Both in its pity and its brutality it shall be real.[9]

The use of an organic metaphor – the 'roots below the surface' – emphasised the magazine's focus on the evolutionary vitalism of Bergson's philosophy, which was also central to Murry's definition of 'modernism' as that which lives below the 'outward surface' in the extended essay he wrote for the first issue of *Rhythm*, titled 'Art and Philosophy':

> The artist attains to the pure form, refining and intensifying his visions till all that is unessential dissolves away [. . .] Modernism is not the capricious

> outburst of intellectual dipsomania. It penetrates beneath the outward surface of the world, and disengages the rhythms that lie at the heart of things, rhythms strange to the eye, unaccustomed to the ear, primitive harmonies of the world that is and lives.[10]

In *Rhythm*, therefore, 'modernism' was synonymous with the 'brutal' and 'primitive'. The quotation above is one of the first printed uses of the word 'modernism' in such a context, and *Rhythm* is significant for these early, concerted attempts to delineate and define the term. When the magazine was advertised on the back cover of *Poetry Review* in January 1912, for instance, it was as 'The UNIQUE MAGAZINE OF MODERNIST ART' and a brochure for the magazine in a later issue of *Poetry Review* promised that 'a unique attempt will be made to unite within one magazine all the parallel manifestations of modernism in every province of art, education and philosophy'.[11] This multidisciplinary focus was also foregrounded in the magazine's subtitle, 'Art, Literature, Music'.

As well as crossing disciplinary boundaries, 'modernism' was also conceptualised as a decidedly 'international' and 'cosmopolitan' movement in *Rhythm*. In particular, Murry hoped that the magazine would reflect the cosmopolitan 'republic of art' that he had come into contact with on his first visit to Paris.[12] In the spring of 1911, for instance, he excitedly stressed that *Rhythm* 'is to be kept absolutely cosmopolitan': 'We are arranging to have the paper distributed in Edinburgh, Glasgow, Manchester, London, Oxford, Cambridge, Paris, New York, and Munich and *all over the world* by subscription' (my emphasis).[13] Similarly, Fergusson became art editor on the condition that the magazine would be cheap enough so that 'any herd boy – in Auckland or the extreme north of Scotland could have the latest information about modern painting from Paris'.[14] As well as these aspirations for an international distribution, the idea of 'internationalism' also became central to explications of new art in *Rhythm*. In an article on Debussy, for instance, Rollo Myers writes: 'Of course it is true, not only theoretically, but historically, that nationality has an influence upon art; but it is also true that the art which is least obviously "national" may be of the greatest permanent value'.[15] To this end, Murry welcomed contributions to *Rhythm* from anyone agreeing with the magazine's aims, '[n]o matter what their nationality'.[16] This avowed cosmopolitanism and openness to different national traditions highlights the extent to which *Rhythm* presented a liberating publication venue to Mansfield, in which she was able to fully explore her cultural origins as well as play with different national registers in her writing. Having left New Zealand in order to pursue her ambition to become a writer, she quickly identified with the group of cosmopolitan artists associated with the magazine, especially Rice (from America) and Fergusson (from Scotland), who shared her experience of an exile that had been self-imposed in the interests of artistic development. Writing in *The New Age* between 1910 and 1911, Mansfield had encoded her critique of metropolitan consensus through the experience of a travelling semi-autobiographical protagonist of indeterminate nationality, eliding mention of her own New Zealand origins, which she referenced only once, in the story 'Being a Truthful Adventure'. In 1912, by contrast, Mansfield now began contributing stories to *Rhythm* that were clearly set in New Zealand, focusing on female colonial experience.

Three of the stories that Mansfield contributed to *Rhythm* and its successor, *The Blue Review*, are set in the unforgiving backblocks of New Zealand and depict or gesture towards a murder.[17] This has led critics such as Angela Smith to emphasise how Mansfield's contributions to *Rhythm* 'pivot on an obvious barbarism': these stories, it has long been argued, were written in response to *Rhythm*'s edict that art must be 'brutal' and 'primitive'.[18] As this chapter examines, however, Mansfield's contributions to *Rhythm* occupy a far more precarious and ambiguous relation to modernist primitivism than this interpretation suggests. Smith also reflects a critical consensus about *Rhythm* when she writes: 'though *Rhythm* had no specific political affiliations, its stance was by implication anti-colonial'.[19] Murry's recollection that he established *Rhythm* to reflect the egalitarian 'republic of art' that he had found on his first visit to Paris would seem to support this idea of the magazine as a democratic, apolitical space. To substantiate her claim, Smith quotes statements made by Fergusson about his Scottish cultural nationalism from the 1940s to the 1960s and analyses Mansfield's contributions to the magazine, made from the fourth issue, published in the spring of 1912. This argument, however, anachronistically ascribes intention to Fergusson's association with *Rhythm* from statements made decades later and reads Mansfield's intervention as a continuous development from earlier issues of the magazine. Assumptions that *Rhythm* embodied an egalitarian 'republic' or was 'by implication anti-colonial' simply will not stand analysis. The publication of articles in French and Italian, for instance, placed the magazine beyond the reach of the average 'herd boy' in New Zealand or Scotland, and the consistent focus on Paris as the pre-eminent centre of new art and ideas belied a metropolitan focus that undermined the idealistic vision of democratic access from 'all over the world'. Furthermore, as this chapter examines, contributors to *Rhythm* consistently employed discursive and visual tropes of geographical expansion and spatial conquest, which forces us to question the extent to which the magazine functioned as an egalitarian space free from either gendered constraints or the ideology of imperialism. In line with Murry's emphasis on the 'brutal' and 'primitive' in art, for example, contributors to the magazine frequently deployed the rhetoric of the colonial quest narrative to describe the modernist aesthetic project, depicting the roving gaze of the male pioneer as an empowering position from which to dominate both land and the female body. Troublingly, on occasions, Mansfield also clearly participated in this discourse. After becoming assistant editor of the magazine in June 1912, for instance, she co-authored an editorial essay with Murry in which they praised the 'artists [who] sail in stately golden ships over this familiar and adventurous ocean' in a 'courageous acceptance of the unexplored'.[20] This is evidence of the highly ambivalent position that Mansfield occupied within *Rhythm*. In one sense, as this chapter examines, Mansfield's integration within the 'imagined community' of the magazine was clearly contingent upon her adopting the pose of the centred, authoritative metropolitan artist; in another, though, Mansfield's contributions to the magazine served to complicate and disrupt its spatial imaginaries and primitivist aesthetics, providing an outsider's perspective. Far from responding to the editorial call for 'brutal' and 'primitive' art, I argue, Mansfield's contributions to the magazine looked to negotiate an ambiguous, liminal position between metropolitan centre and colonial periphery that served to unsettle established ideas about race and gender, as well as frustrate metropolitan expectations about the colonial 'other' and barbaric 'primitive'.

In particular, this chapter examines how Mansfield used parody and satire as modes of critique throughout her contributions to *Rhythm*, ironising the tropes of imperial discourse in order to encode anti-colonial, anti-imperialist political commitments. As Janet Wilson has argued, we must look to position 'Mansfield as a (post)colonial modernist writer whose anticipatory discourse demonstrates a consciousness about resistance that precedes the founding of the postcolonial state; that is, an already known postcolonial vision'.[21] By positioning poems that she had in fact written herself as translations from the work of the made-up author 'Boris Petrovsky', for instance, Mansfield was able to identify her writings with nationalist movements in eastern Europe of political and cultural resistance to imperial hegemony; these 'parodic translations' not only anticipate the founding of the postcolonial nation state in Europe, but also open up a liminal space between centre and periphery that Mansfield then employed in her other poetry contributions to *Rhythm* in order to negotiate the ambiguities of her own cultural nationalism. Significantly, Mansfield's critique of imperialism in these fraudulent translations shows her mapping her postcolonial vision onto the spaces of Europe; it shows her utilising her experience as a colonial writer in order to expose the power dynamics between coloniser and colonised that were internal to Europe. As such, these 'translations' help us to reposition Mansfield more decisively as both a colonial and European writer, translating her experience of colonialism into the metropolitan spaces of Europe. This conjunction of Mansfield as a colonial-metropolitan modernist is further illuminated by her short story contributions to *Rhythm*, several of which focus on life in New Zealand. In these stories, Mansfield parodies the colonial melodrama and horse-and-saddle genres synonymous with the Australian periodical *The Bulletin* in order to unsettle the masculine gaze and colonial quest narrative that permeated visual illustrations and other written contributions to *Rhythm*, in which the female body is universally equated with verdant landscapes and virgin territories. As is examined in the second section of this chapter, Mansfield's stories offer a radical critique of the spatial imaginary upon which *Rhythm* had been founded whilst also enacting an uneasy negotiation between her possible identification as either a 'colonial' or a 'metropolitan' writer. The third section of the chapter then examines the ways in which Mansfield appropriated and parodied stereotypes of the colonial 'other' in order to undercut the tropes of modernist primitivism and lampoon the cultural imperialism of the English metropolitan elite in her satire 'Sunday Lunch'. Finally, the fourth section analyses Mansfield's later story 'Je ne parle pas français' (1918) as a critique of the power dynamics that had structured ideas of communal affiliation in *Rhythm*.

Mansfield's contributions to *Rhythm* highlight how early twentieth-century periodical culture facilitated modes of parody and satire, providing a space for textual recirculation and authorial self-fashioning. In these parodic writings, Mansfield formulates alternative modes of imagined affiliation that transcend national borders and linguistic barriers, exposing the logic of empire and exploring postcolonial possibilities. As such, these writings highlight the extent to which Mansfield's work was motivated by intercultural contact and translational, transnational exchange. If *Rhythm* was 'by implication anti-colonial', this chapter argues, then this was predominantly due to the intervention made by Mansfield from the fourth issue, with contributions that dissolve rigid centre/periphery binaries and bring metropolitan Europe into contact with the colonial 'other'.

Parodic translation

When Mansfield first began publishing in *Rhythm* in the spring of 1912, she contributed a short story set in the backblocks of New Zealand, 'The Woman at the Store', together with two poems 'Translated from the Russian of Boris Petrovsky'. These were fake translations, written by Mansfield herself. 'Boris Petrovsky' was the first pseudonym Mansfield used in *Rhythm*, a *nom de plume* that she returned to on four other occasions in the magazine. And the mask continues to trick readers. As recently as 2009, in his chapter on *Rhythm* in the first volume of *The Oxford Critical and Cultural History of Modernist Magazines*, Peter Brooker inaccurately observed: 'translations, probably by Mansfield, of poems by Boris Petrovsky served, once more, to confirm the magazine's internationalism'.[22] The confusion most likely arises out of the fact that Mansfield's poetry, in comparison with her prose, has received very little critical attention; whereas the pseudonymous prose pieces she contributed to *Rhythm* have all been republished and examined extensively, the 'Boris Petrovsky' poems remain relatively obscure in Mansfield's oeuvre.

Mansfield scholars tend to agree with Gerri Kimber that the 'reason for the Russian-sounding pseudonym is unclear'.[23] In comparison, the other pseudonyms used by Mansfield in *Rhythm* can be identified easily, and the reasons for their use readily accounted for. The surname of 'Lili Heron' refers to the middle name of Mansfield's brother and the idealised family home of the 'Heron' that she later imagined after his death, with the connotations of innocence attached to the lily flower reflecting the content of the two stories in which Mansfield used the pseudonym, 'How Pearl Button Was Kidnapped' and 'The Little Girl'. Similarly, the nickname 'The Tiger' that Mansfield shared with Murry provided her with a ferocious persona that resonated with the magazine's focus on *les Fauves* (the wild beasts) and evoked the eat-or-be-eaten world of the London literati that she depicted in her satire 'Sunday Lunch'. This nickname had been bestowed on the couple by the novelist Gilbert Cannan in reference to a woodcut by Margaret Thompson that had been published in the first issue of *Rhythm* of a tiger predatorily stalking a monkey (Figure 2.12). We might ask, then, why did Mansfield choose the 'Russian-sounding' pseudonym of 'Boris Petrovsky'? What are the possible origins of this imagined name? And – most importantly – why did she decide to frame these poems as fraudulent translations?

In the first instance, the persona of 'Boris Petrovsky' enabled Mansfield to experiment with writing in a different national register and to practise a certain kind of self-fashioning. As Faith Binckes has argued, this serves as a reminder that the 'internationalism' that Brooker identifies as integral to *Rhythm* 'was also about image and performance'.[24] In May 1912, Mansfield exhibited her proclivity towards everyday performance when she travelled to Paris in order to meet the cosmopolitan writers and artists who made up the body of contributors to the magazine. Anne Estelle Rice later recalled that Mansfield presented herself as 'a compelling and vivid personality' by first cultivating the image of the 'stranger, the girl from New Zealand'.[25] On her second meeting with Mansfield, however, Rice was forced to make a readjustment to this initial impression of a settled national identity:

> We had a rendezvous at the 'Closerie des Lilas' and, at the appointed time, and after a brief search, I saw a woman in a black cloak, wearing a black turban with a white fez; only the yashmak was missing. A hasty adjustment to a new acquaintance had to be made, for this was Katherine Mansfield's fez day. [. . .] Dressing-up was a very important part of Katherine Mansfield's imaginative nature. She enjoyed being Katoushka in a peasant's costume of brilliant colour – yards and yards of it – convincingly using a few Russian words to give local colour; or a *femme fatale* with a sequin scarf around her head, and a long black dress, sinuously reclining on a sofa. Many were the changes.[26]

This penchant for 'dressing-up' is materially imprinted on the pages of *Rhythm* in the many masks and pseudonyms Mansfield used for her contributions. As the quotation above highlights, Mansfield readily identified with Russia, calling herself at various times 'Katoushka', 'Katerina', 'Yekaterina', 'Kissienka' and 'Katya'.[27] The 'Boris Petrovsky' pseudonym was part of this multiplication. In the first instance, therefore, Mansfield's use of the pseudonym was linked to the performance and projection of a shifting authorial identity that enabled her to experiment with a new mode of writing and to forge a position for herself within the international avant-garde promoted by *Rhythm*.

Russia occupied a central place within this vision of the avant-garde. In the same issue of *Rhythm* in which the first Petrovsky poems were printed, as Caroline Maclean has observed, an article on Kandinsky by Sadler 'positioned the magazine at the heart of a new spiritually-inflected Russian aesthetics'.[28] Likewise, in review articles and illustrative contributions, *Rhythm* consistently focused on the productions of the Ballets Russes, which offered a model of a cross-disciplinary and thoroughly international artistic community that the magazine sought to emulate. Also printed in *Rhythm* are lithographs by the Russian 'neo-primitives' Natalia Goncharova and Mikhail Larionov, as well as a translation of prose by the Russian writer Leonid Andreev. And, once she became assistant editor from the fifth issue of the magazine, Mansfield used her personal contacts to secure a correspondent for Russia, Michael Lykiardopoulos, who was secretary to the directors of the Moscow Art Theatre.[29] Against this context, Mansfield's translations 'from the Russian' were entirely apposite.

Among Mansfield's other contributions to *Rhythm* is a story that is highly evocative of Chekhov, titled 'Spring in a Dream', and a set of three stories under the collective title 'Tales of a Courtyard' that reflect the contemporary vogue for Dostoevsky, with one of the characters even named 'Feodor' in a clear allusion to the novelist. Similarly, Frank Harris contributed a short story to the magazine titled 'The Holy Man (After Tolstoi)', a version of Tolstoy's 'The Three Hermits'. Together, these contributions by Mansfield and Harris highlight the fact that the magazine's 'internationalism' was consistently based upon image and performance: excepting the translation from Andreev, 'Russian' prose contributions to *Rhythm* were all simulated versions of a perceived national style. Again, therefore, Mansfield's fake translations 'from the Russian' were fitting entries into *Rhythm*, projecting a constructed image of the magazine's internationalism. Rather problematically, perhaps, this also demonstrates Mansfield's complicity in the kind of cultural appropriation that structured modernist primitivism at this time.

There were other publication contexts that informed the Petrovsky poems, however. In an introduction to an expanded edition of Mansfield's poems that he published in 1930, for instance, Murry recalled:

> I remember her telling me when we first met that the beautiful pieces now gathered together as 'Poems, 1911–13' had been refused, because

> they were unrhymed, by the only editor who used to accept her work. He wanted her to write nothing but satirical prose. This treatment made her very reserved about her verses. Those she published in *Rhythm* appeared as translations from an imaginary Russian called Boris Petrovsky.[30]

Murry's attempt at subtlety here fails completely: it would have been immediately obvious to his contemporary readers that the 'editor' to which he refers was Orage. This would suggest that the poems by Mansfield later published under the 'Boris Petrovsky' pseudonym were originally intended for publication in *The New Age*, at the time of her initial association with the periodical in 1910–11. Gerri Kimber's discovery in 2015 in the Newberry Library in Chicago of a poem cycle titled *The Earth Child* sheds light on another relevant context and another failed attempt by Mansfield to publish her poems. Compiled in 1910, *The Earth Child* was sent by Mansfield to the London publisher Elkin Mathews in the second half of that year and demonstrates her concerted efforts at this time to be taken seriously as a poet. Of the ten poems by Mansfield that were eventually published in *Rhythm* in 1912–13, seven had been composed for inclusion in *The Earth Child*. Together, Murry's testimony and Kimber's archival discovery suggest that Mansfield first submitted her poems to Orage for consideration before attempting to secure a publisher for the poems in book form, in much the same way that she contributed her separate 'Pension Sketches' to *The New Age* before Stephen Swift published them as the short story collection *In a German Pension*.

Texts are not stable entities. As critics such as Jerome McGann and George Bornstein have shown, an author's intention at the point of composition cannot contain the meaning of a text once that text is transmitted through different publication contexts.[31] The way in which Mansfield repurposed the poems that had been included in *The Earth Child* manuscript when she began contributing to *Rhythm* therefore demands attention. Indeed, any attempt we might make to map a straightforward equivalence between the poems collated for book publication in 1910 and those that in fact saw publication two or three years later in the magazine are unsettled by the way in which Mansfield removes individual texts from the poem cycle. Of the seven poems published in *Rhythm* that had been composed for *The Earth Child*, five were printed under the 'Boris Petrovsky' pseudonym and two under Mansfield's own name.[32] Likewise, of the remaining three poems by Mansfield published in *Rhythm*, she used both her own name and the Petrovsky pseudonym to sign her contributions.[33] Furthermore, of the two poems that announced Mansfield's entry into the magazine in the fourth issue, published in spring 1912, both were positioned as translations from the work of Petrovsky, but the first, titled 'Very Early Spring', had been included in *The Earth Child* sequence, whereas the poem that accompanied this in *Rhythm*, titled 'The Awakening River', had not. In other words, it is impossible to align unambiguously the poems originally included in the manuscript for *The Earth Child* with those selected by Mansfield for publication in *Rhythm*.

Periodical scholarship over recent years has shown how the contexts of publication generate meanings and allusions that are not deducible when a text is removed from those contexts. As such, the poems that Mansfield contributed to *Rhythm* can be interpreted differently to those included in *The Earth Child* manuscript or, for that matter, published posthumously as 'Poems, 1911–13'. Printed as select poems, rather than an integrated poem cycle or collection, directed to a different envisioned readership, shaped by a different editorial agenda, positioned alongside and in dialogue with work by other writers and artists, and, most significantly, deliberately framed by their author as fraudulent translations, the texts that were published in *Rhythm* provoke a different interpretation to the poems included in *The Earth Child*. It is also worth remembering that Mansfield's contemporary readers would have first engaged with these poems as they appeared in the pages of *Rhythm*, given that *The Earth Child* was never published; as such, the interpretations we arrive at once we read these texts in the original material contexts of the magazine are interpretations that Mansfield's contemporaries were also encouraged to make. Without disputing the fact that the majority of the poems Mansfield contributed to *Rhythm* were composed before the magazine even existed, this section of the chapter examines Mansfield's poems as they were published in the magazine, analysing the highly particular ways in which she repurposed these texts for a publication context different to that of *The Earth Child*.

In particular, we must ask why Mansfield decided to frame some of her poems as 'translations' when they were published in *Rhythm*. From mid-1911, *The New Age* began printing translations of poetry from Russia and eastern Europe by a young linguist, Paul Selver. The first of these, a group of four poems, appeared in May 1911, in the same issue of the periodical that carried Mansfield's story 'A Birthday'. Printed under the collective title 'Poems from the Slavonic', these poems were all translations from the Czech verse of Petr Bezruč. Mansfield scholars have long suggested that Selver's translations served as a direct source of influence for her Petrovsky poems. In her biographical account *Katerina: The Russian World of Katherine Mansfield*, for example, Joanna Woods makes reference to this connection.[34] The discovery of *The Earth Child* manuscripts means that we can now accurately date the composition of many of these poems to 1910, before the publication of Selver's translations, so that it is no longer possible to claim that Mansfield was directly imitating Selver. However, when she came to publish her poems in *Rhythm*, Mansfield's use of the 'Boris Petrovsky' pseudonym served as a direct reference to Selver's translations in *The New Age*: she reverses the initials of Petr Bezruč, then uses the Christian name of 'Petr' for the surname 'Petrovsky', both of which derive from the Greek word 'Petros'. Moreover, 'Petrovsky' is a locational name specific to Poland.[35] As such, Mansfield's poems clearly referenced the many 'Polish Fragments' published in *The New Age* by Selver.[36] These coded allusions to Selver's translations suggest that when Mansfield recycled the poems originally included in *The Earth Child* she did so in such a way as to initiate a dialogue-in-print between *Rhythm* and *The New Age*, another example of the 'conversational model for modernism' that early twentieth-century periodicals often looked to enact.[37]

The translations by Selver first published in *The New Age* were later collected in a book he edited titled *An Anthology of Modern Bohemian Poetry* (1912), which Mansfield reviewed for *Rhythm*. To her contemporary audience, therefore, the first of Mansfield's Petrovsky poems, 'Very Early Spring', would have recalled the significant number of 'Bohemian' poems translated by Selver that focus on nature and the seasons, such as Karel Červinka's 'Yearning in Early Spring', Fr. Kvapil's 'Spring Song', Julius Zeyer's 'In Spring' and Jaroslav Vrchlický's 'Spring Song'.[38] Mansfield's accompanying poem, 'The Awakening River', depicts gulls 'mad-in-love with the river', '[w]heeling and flying' with 'shining wings' and '[c]rying the rapture of the boundless ocean'.[39] With its implicit evocation of sexual ecstasy, this poem also echoes translations by Selver, such as Eliška Krásnohorská's 'Song' ('ye boisterous flock of birds') and Otakar Březina's 'Dithyramb of the Worlds' ('On the shores of a river ecstatic,/That flies in the outstretched embrace/Of thine ocean!').[40] And 'The Earth-Child in the Grass', in which a young girl becomes one with the grass in death, achieving a kind of union with her 'lover' who lies with 'the green blades pressed against his body', clearly resembles Petr Bezruč's 'Who Will Take My Place?' ('Above me the grass, when my body decays').[41] As discussed below, the thematic and tonal parallels between Mansfield's poems and the 'Bohemian' translations are not coincidental, given that she was deeply engaged with Slavic literature and politics, particularly that of Poland, from 1909. After the publication of 'The Earth-Child in the Grass' in September 1912, Mansfield subsequently used the Petrovsky pseudonym for 'To God the Father' (discussed below) and for 'Jangling Memory' and 'There Was a Child Once', two poems obviously based upon her previous relationship with William Orton. Mansfield scholars have long recognised the odd disjunction in these poems between the female voice and the male signature of Boris Petrovsky.[42] Indeed, the unstable narrative persona in these poems forces us to question the borderlines between Mansfield's impulse towards autobiographical self-exposure and pseudonymous disguise. How are we to interpret this play with identities? In framing these poems as 'translations from the Russian', moreover, what is the significance of Mansfield referencing an eclectic set of translations, rather than any one original text?

To begin to answer these questions, David Lloyd's study of the emergence of Irish cultural nationalism in the work of James Clarence Mangan provides a useful framework for interpretation. Lloyd notes that a significant proportion of writings by Mangan can be classified as 'fraudulent translations': these include poems purporting to be translated from German that Mangan 'attributed to the pseudonymic poets "Selber" (self) and "Drechsler" (turner, or, more appropriately, elaborator)'.[43] These fake translations challenge the 'ideal that the translated text should in some sense or other be the "equivalent" of the source text':

> The notion of 'equivalence' is crucial to a theory of translation for which the central issue is the primacy of the original and the conservation of its authenticity in the secondary text which is its translation. [. . .] Such idealism, however, retains the trace of precisely what is at stake in translation generally speaking, that is, the fundamental opacity of one language to another, or their basic incommensurability. If two languages, let alone two cultures, are irreconcilably different, on what ground is one to measure the equivalence of translation to original?[44]

In contrast, what Lloyd terms the 'parodic translation' maintains the play of linguistic and cultural difference by foregrounding 'the persistence of a dependent relationship to an anterior text' and holding 'open the oscillation between likeness and strangeness that defines the peculiar aura of the parallel text'.[45] Unlike the translated text that aspires to 'achieve an equivalence with the original so perfect, indeed, as to efface it', the parodic translation is 'marked by its refusal ever to supplant entirely the text on which it depends, so that no complete supersession of the original text takes place such as would finally reconstitute the parody or translation as itself an original'.[46] Lloyd suggests that Mangan's 'distortive' and 'refractive' translations illuminate the intermediate, 'parodic' stage in the three 'epochs' of progression in Goethe's theory of translation, in which the translator attempts to assume the position of the foreigner, but merely ends up appropriating and reproducing the foreign in his or her own sense; in this intermediate stage of translation, the text continually displays its own failure to achieve a perfect equivalence with, and supersession of, an original.[47]

Mangan's parodic translations become political, Lloyd argues, precisely because they displace notions of originality and autonomy. The defining characteristic of any 'major literature' is that it 'should be in some manner directed toward the production of an autonomous ethical identity for the subject'.[48] This is exemplified by the *Bildungsroman*, whereby the individual achieves ethical autonomy through aesthetic education (*Bildung*). The motif of 'self-realisation' in the *Bildungsroman* becomes a reciprocal allegory for the realisation of a unified and rational political state, as examined in detail by critics such as Franco Moretti and Jed Esty.[49] In *Letters on the Aesthetic Education of Man*, for instance, Schiller argues that aesthetic education gives a finished form to both the modern subject and the modern state. Alongside this 'narrative representation of the attainment of autonomy', Lloyd also observes, 'emerges the requirement that the work itself be autonomous, both self-contained and original': 'formal development is seen as the measure of political maturity'.[50] It is this logic that underpins Matthew Arnold's pronouncements that the failure of 'the Celtic races' to reach a 'sound and satisfying' aesthetic marks their readiness to be subordinated to a 'more politically, formatively, directed' culture.[51] In other words, notions of the originality and autonomy of the self, society and text not only shape literary canons but also bolster the political imperatives of imperialism. Positioned outside or against the canon and imperial hegemony, the writers of 'minor literature' adopt literary strategies, such as parody, translation and citation, which are designed to challenge these notions of originality and autonomy. What is common to all these strategies, Lloyd suggests, is the 'perpetuation of non-identity', a 'refusal to ground the possibility of identity on the recovery of origins, a strategy that evokes a critique of that narrative paradigm of major literature, the reproduction of an original or essential identity at a higher and self-conscious level'.[52] In the case of parodic translation, for instance, the 'multiplication of ungrounded appearances becomes the stimulus to an assiduous cultivation of suspicion with regard to the formative (*bildend*) power of originality and authenticity'.[53] This is at the heart of the Irish cultural nationalism fostered by Mangan's writings, as Lloyd perceives it: detached from any notion of an original or stable identity, Mangan's parodic translations challenge both the ideal of equivalence and assumptions of imperial hegemony.

Mansfield's poetry contributions to *Rhythm* conform to this idea of the 'parodic translation' by appropriating the 'foreign' to the autobiographical and simultaneously defying the notion of a stable authorial identity. In the introduction to his anthology, for example, Selver observes that the name 'Petr Bezruč' was itself a pseudonym, 'adopted by a postal official of Brünn in Moravia', and that the poet's personality, as a result, is 'shrouded in a certain amount of mystery'.[54] Mansfield's pseudonym of 'Boris Petrovsky' was a variation upon a pseudonym, therefore: a multiplication of non-identity, in which the notion of an original and stable 'author' is continually deferred and displaced. In her review of Selver's anthology, moreover, Mansfield critiques the ideal of equivalence:

> 'It is a noble, highly cultivated language, of whose kinship Russia may well be proud. Its facility for representing the finest shades of thought renders it peculiarly adaptable to lyric poetry.' Thus Mr Selver, speaking of the Bohemian language in the introduction to his anthology; and it is just this facility that makes his task of translation so extremely difficult. A good translation is not unlike a good reproduction of a drawing. It is dependent for success upon many of the same qualities – simple and sure treatment, directness of purpose, very clear treatment of the subject, preferably on a broad scale.[55]

Mansfield here highlights the main problem of translation: that the 'finest shades of thought' revealed in one language or culture cannot be communicated in the same way in another. The translation can never take the place of the source text. Instead, a good translation is like a 'reproduction' and is 'dependent': it can never be self-contained, original or autonomous. In the introduction to his anthology, by contrast, Selver observes: 'As regards the translations themselves, *they have been made as literal as possible*, and the metres of the originals have been reproduced as far as the varying rhythms of the two languages permitted' (my emphasis).[56] Considering the poems of Vileslav Hálek, for instance, Selver laments that 'the contents of his verse are almost too fragile to endure the ordeal of transformation into another language. What in the original is tender and sentimental appears almost grotesque and ridiculous when translated.'[57] This attempt to force a 'literal' equivalence between different languages produces what Mansfield identifies as Selver's 'uneven labours'.[58]

Despite these uneven labours, Mansfield finds 'Bohemian poetry' on the whole 'so vivid, its life so intense and sincere': 'it is the spirit of them which, to me, goes to the heart like the music of the Bohemian people, with the same ultimate and melancholy appeal'.[59] Again, Mansfield uses the analogy of another artistic discipline to reflect her sense of what a 'good translation' should aspire towards: it should be like a reproduction of a drawing or the music of a people, the trans-medial similes underscoring her emphasis on translation as a creative practice that moves 'between' languages and 'across' different sites of cultural production. Rather than superseding the original text, Mansfield suggests, a good translation is the product of a refractory process that transforms both the source and target cultures; transformation is not an 'ordeal' for Mansfield, as it is for Selver, but rather the necessary process by which translation conveys the 'spirit' and 'life' of the source culture to a new audience in a new form, making an 'appeal' that 'goes to the heart'.

In her review of Selver's anthology, Mansfield also demonstrates her awareness of how translation practices constitute the literary canon, observing: 'the works of the more obscure writers – of men who have escaped the blessed tradition of the folk song, to express more consciously, perhaps, the "finest shades" – he [Selver] has failed to interpret'.[60] As outlined above, ideals of originality and equivalence in translation are narrative paradigms of canonical 'major literature' that serve to reproduce imperial hegemony at the political level. Employing the double cipher of a pseudonym within a 'translated' text, Mansfield's Petrovsky poems served to unsettle and undercut these ideals. Whilst these writings parody the tropes of 'Bohemian' poetry, for example, none of them faithfully reproduces a single original. Framed in this way, these poems revel in the multiplication of non-identity and the absence of originals, illuminating the refractive reproducibility of translation more widely. As such, Mansfield's fraudulent translations become spaces of subversion in which she positions her writing against the narrative paradigms of 'major literature' and the political paradigms of imperial hegemony. Moreover, this resistance to imperialism in Mansfield's parodic translations can be traced in her references to specific cultural and national traditions.

Despite the apparent naivety and the formal simplicity of these poems, with their almost exclusive focus on nature and childhood, Mansfield knowingly positioned these texts against very specific political-historical contexts when they were published in *Rhythm*. Meeting the Polish critic and translator Floryan Sobieniowski whilst in Bavaria in 1909, Mansfield had been introduced to the ideas and works of the poet, playwright, painter and designer Stanisław Wyspiański, who had spearheaded the Young Poland movement at the turn of the twentieth century before his death in 1907. A modernist movement in the visual arts, literature and music, Young Poland was formed as a response to the suppression of an uprising in January 1863 against the occupying army of Imperial Russia, with its members promoting the Polish language and producing patriotic art inspired by national folk traditions. The Young Poland movement was indicative of a wider trend of patriotism and anti-imperialism across eastern Europe. As Selver observes in the introduction to his book, the poets that he had translated, writing in western Slavonic languages such as Czech, Polish, Slovakian and Hungarian, aimed 'to kindle the spark of patriotism in the hearts of the people, and the nature of their poetry was in accordance with this plan'.[61] Invariably, therefore, the poets in Selver's collection, like Wyspiański, pursued an agenda of cultural nationalism in direct opposition to the imperial hegemonies of Prussia to the west and Russia to the east.

The impact of Mansfield's relationship with Floryan Sobieniowski and her introduction to the patriotism of Wyspiański is registered in two poems that she wrote in 1909, 'To Stanisław Wyspiański' and 'Floryan Nachdenklich' (German for 'Floryan – pensive'). The poem about Sobieniowski was published in 1913 in *The Saturday Westminster Gazette* and then the New Zealand periodical *Dominion*, and in both tone and theme it echoes the Petrovsky poems, describing 'the great brown boughs of [an] Indian tree' on which '[l]ittle birds sing and preen their wings'.[62] Through Mansfield, Sobieniowski became *Rhythm*'s correspondent for Poland in 1912, helping to secure agents for the magazine in Warsaw and Kraków. Sobieniowski's portrait was printed in *Rhythm* midway through Mansfield's 'Spring in a Dream', as if to underline the 'Slavic' inspiration for the story. And when Sobieniowski himself contributed to the magazine, it was with a biography of Wyspiański. As Kimber notes, Sobieniowski and Mansfield even planned to devote an entire issue of *Rhythm* to Wyspiański, but the magazine folded before this plan could be put into effect.[63] In the article on Wyspiański that did see publication, Sobieniowski describes the artist-poet as the 'creator of new values for the Polish consciousness': 'his literary creation had two "Leitmotiven" – one, the necessity for close connection with national tradition; the second, the awakening of independence'.[64] Wyspiański's innovations, Sobieniowski tells us, followed a 'period of hateful servility' when the 'younger generation were taught that they must not speak of love for their home' and when 'the oppression of the victorious enemy and the depressing consciousness of their own weakness carried Polish thought along mistaken paths'.[65] Wyspiański died in 1907 after a period of great civil unrest: following the failed revolution of 1905–6, as Michael J. Mikoś has observed, the Polish Socialist Party was founded and 'openly set forth a program of Polish independence, formed battle squads, and engaged in a massive armed struggle against the Russian administration, police, and their collaborators'.[66] Mansfield was well aware of this history. In 'To Stanisław Wyspiański', which has become her most famous poem, she declares: 'I sing your praises, Magnificent warrior; I proclaim your triumphant battle'.[67]

As a locational name specific to Poland, the Petrovsky pseudonym aligned Mansfield's fake translations with this Polish tradition of patriotic resistance to the imperial hegemonies of Prussia and Russia. This is further underlined by the fact that Mansfield used the Petrovsky pseudonym to sign a poem contributed to *Rhythm* titled 'To God the Father', which Kimber has identified as having been directly inspired by a stained glass window in Kraków designed by Wyspiański, titled 'God the Father – Let it Be'.[68] Whilst Mansfield probably saw this design in reproduction, as Kimber also notes, it is entirely possible that she travelled with Sobieniowski to Poland in late 1909: in November, for example, she writes to her younger sister Jeanne to thank her for birthday money with which she had bought 'a fat Polish dictionary with a green leather binding [which] goes about with me every day'.[69] Mansfield's attempts to learn Polish are corroborated by Sobieniowski in an introduction to a translation of 'To Stanisław Wyspiański' that he published in a Warsaw weekly in December 1910. Sobieniowski writes that Mansfield 'decided to learn the Polish language' after gaining 'a superficial knowledge of our history' and 'literature from a few French, English and German translations'.[70] This literary influence can be heard in the poems that Mansfield composed in 1910 and eventually published in *Rhythm* in 1912–13, with each given what she later termed in her 1912 review of Selver's anthology as the 'simple and sure' and 'very clear treatment of the subject' that generates a tonal resemblance to the parallel text of translation and approximates the 'spirit' and 'life' of Bohemian poetry. This sense of an affiliation that crosses linguistic barriers is affirmed in Sobieniowski's introduction to Mansfield's 'To Stanisław Wyspiański', which ends with the observation that the poem reveals that 'there is only one common language for all human beings, understood in every geographical longitude and latitude – the language of action'.[71]

Mansfield looked to situate the Petrovsky poems within this revolutionary tradition of 'action' stretching beyond national borders and linguistic barriers, which explains why her 'Polish' poems are positioned as translations 'from the Russian'. Many of the nationalist poets of eastern Europe in the late nineteenth and early twentieth centuries identified themselves first and foremost as Slavs, sharing a common culture with Russia that was integral to their own patriotism. As Selver observes of the Czech poet Eliška Krásnohorská, for instance: 'Patriotism is the key-note of her poetry. She has shown her sympathy with the Slavonic cause in a practical manner by learning Russian and Polish.'[72] Identification with the language and culture of Russia did not necessarily equate to support for its political regime, therefore. This was particularly the case following the quashed revolution of 1905, when many avant-garde artists, such as Sergei Diaghilev and Natalia Goncharova, left Russia to develop their art in more liberating environs, such as Paris. Through the Petrovsky poems, then, Mansfield identified her writing with a dissident tradition common to both Poland and Russia. It is quite possible, for example, that she intended the name Petrovsky to echo the revolutionary Petrashevsky Circle of which Dostoevsky had been a member and for which he had suffered exile in Siberia. Furthermore, when Mansfield contributed a parody of Nikolai Gogol ('Green Goggles') to *The New Age* in July 1912, briefly returning to the pages of the periodical, she centred the narrative on an enigmatic female stranger on the run from the Russian authorities named Olga Petrovska.[73] By using this name, giving a contrived feminine ending to the masculine surname Petrovsky, Mansfield clearly aligned her own writing with the Boris Petrovsky poems published in *Rhythm* only a matter of weeks before, establishing an inter-textual dialogue across the two periodicals that unmasked the writer behind the pseudonym. When contextualised against the Boris Petrovsky name used in *Rhythm*, therefore, the Olga Petrovska character in 'Green Goggles' is revealed as a distorted self-portrait of Mansfield, an enigmatic and radical female 'outsider' confronting an uncertain exile, the green goggles she wears symbolising her unique perspective on and perception of the world. Of the many masks used by Mansfield throughout her writing career, this is one that has gone entirely unnoticed by previous scholars.

Indeed, the inter-textual dialogue that Mansfield's Petrovsky poems established between *Rhythm* and *The New Age* is audible only to the attentive reader of both publications. Mansfield's use of this pseudonym was clearly designed to pique the interest of only a small group of readers, being directed in particular toward Orage and Hastings; and the poems certainly caught their attention. When Mansfield began publishing in Murry's magazine, *Rhythm* suddenly came under intense scrutiny in *The New Age*.[74] There 'is no single page', Orage wrote in his regular column, 'that is not stupid, or crazed, or vulgar – and most are all three'.[75] One page in particular became the focus for the apoplectic derision of Orage and Hastings, the page on which the two 'translations' by Mansfield were printed. Orage dismisses 'The Awakening River' for 'pampering pretty feelings until the very rivers seemed to lie in a sexual ecstasy'.[76] In the space of just two stanzas, he writes, Mansfield's poem lies like a wounded bird, 'flapping and wappering'.[77] Of course, such poetry is ripe for parody. A few weeks later, Hastings contributed a piece to the 'Pastiche' pages of *The New Age* prefaced with the sardonic line: 'With profuse apologies to *Rhythm*'.[78] This skit ends with Hastings satirising the Petrovsky poems. In a reference to Thomas Moult, whose poem 'Vision' had been published in *Rhythm* on the same page as the denouement to Mansfield's story 'The Woman at the Store', Hastings satirises the transparency of the Petrovsky pseudonym, framing her parody of Mansfield as 'Translated from the Phlegmish by Thomasine Molefield'.[79] This poem, 'Dawn at Daybreak', reads:

> Away the little night-clouds cuddle:
> Aurora rises in-the-west,
> With variegated-coloured breast
> Bright-gleaming through her tattered vest,
> Like a pink worm in-a-puddle.[80]

Evidently familiar with Mansfield's unpublished poem 'The Changeling' (which had been included in *The Earth Child* manuscript and, given Murry's testimony that Mansfield had shown her poems to 'the only editor who used to accept her work', may have been presented to Orage for publication in 1910), Hastings stepped up the attack against Mansfield at the beginning of 1913 with a satirical portrait also titled 'The Changeling'. In this piece, Mansfield is caricatured as promiscuous, sentimental and deluded in her 'tame-tigrish' devotion to Murry as the 'coming genius'.[81] Later that year, moreover, Paul Selver observed in the 'Readers and Writers' section of *The New Age* that the 'unaffected poet' is becoming a 'rarer and rarer' type 'in these days of sky-blue periodicals and general noisy pretentiousness' – a clear allusion to *Rhythm*, with its 'sky-blue' cover, and *The Blue Review* – when 'parody gets taken seriously (and *The New Age* writers can tell of such happenings)'.[82]

Conscious that her erstwhile mentors at *The New Age* were familiar with her verse, Mansfield must have anticipated the savagery with which Orage and Hastings would attack her when she began contributing poetry to *Rhythm*. Using the double cipher of a pseudonym within a 'translated' text serves to distance Mansfield from these poems. At the same time, however, she would have known that these distancing techniques would always prove inadequate when placed before the editors of *The New Age*. As such, the Boris Petrovsky pseudonym becomes a transparent alias. This mask-which-is-not-a-mask introduces a distinct ambivalence into Mansfield's poetry contributions to *Rhythm*. Is this Mansfield, or not? And is this a serious attempt at poetry, or not? Orage articulates this uneasiness when he writes:

> Aware that Miss Mansfield has, on occasions, a sense of humour, we wonder if it is all a joke; especially as the verse is solemnly asserted to be a translation from the Russian! If no jest is meant, the sickly versifiers whom Miss Mansfield once satirised in *The New Age* are avenged.[83]

The parodic relation of Mansfield's pseudonym to anterior texts by Selver first published in *The New Age* also serves to disarm the capacity of that periodical's editor to criticise her poems. Likewise, the curious textual recirculation that takes place when Hastings parodies a parody only serves to turn the satire back on to the venue for which she writes, *The New Age*. In this way, Mansfield's ineffectual, transparent mask paradoxically operates as a mechanism of defence against cultural authority and criticism. This recalls Homi Bhabha's theory of 'colonial mimicry': the '*menace* of mimicry', Bhabha writes, is contained within the '*double* vision' produced by an 'ambivalence' that 'does not merely "rupture" the discourse, but becomes transformed into an uncertainty which fixes the colonial subject as a "partial" presence'.[84] According to Bhabha, the mimic '*is almost the same, but not quite*'.[85] As the author of the Petrovsky poems, Mansfield is only ever a partial presence, hiding behind the double cipher of a pseudonym within a 'translated' text.

Mansfield's distancing techniques in the Petrovsky poems encode a politics of resistance to cultural authority that is also revealed in her identification with Wyspiański's anti-imperialism. In his introduction to Mansfield's 'To Stanisław Wyspiański', Sobieniowski writes: 'The young English poetess who writes under the pseudonym of K. Mansfield, of Irish origin and French name – considered New Zealand her fatherland'.[86] This description includes a telling biographical inaccuracy: though Mansfield's real name (Beauchamp) was indeed French, her 'origin' was not Irish. Whether this was a lie Mansfield fed to Sobieniowski or was his own creation, this account of Mansfield as Irish established her for a Polish readership as a writer motivated by the same cultural project as Wyspiański, one of resistance to imperial hegemony (Ireland–Britain, Poland–Russia).[87] This idea of resistance shapes the depiction of New Zealand in 'To Stanisław Wyspiański'. At the beginning of the poem, Mansfield writes:

> From the other side of the world,
> From a little island cradled in the giant sea bosom,
> From a little land with no history,
> (Making its own history, slowly and clumsily
> Piecing together this and that, finding the pattern, solving the problem,
> Like a child with a box of bricks),
> I, a woman, with the taint of the pioneer in my blood,
> Full of a youthful strength that wars with itself and is lawless,
> I sing your praises, Magnificent warrior; I proclaim your
> triumphant battle.[88]

The repetition of 'From' in the first three lines emphasises a relational concept of space in which the 'little island' on 'the other side of the world' is clearly the denigrated half of the binary opposition. Moreover, the conventional simile infantilising the colony associates it with underdevelopment: New Zealand is devoid of a grand narrative, Mansfield suggests, its history being a 'problem' to be solved and pieced together. These associations demonstrate Mansfield's readiness to appropriate imperialist tropes denigrating the colony. By describing herself as having the 'taint' of the pioneer in her blood, however, she both suggests personal culpability and subverts the received notion of imperial power as integrated. In singing the praises of the heroic Polish patriot, therefore, Mansfield highlights how her own cultural nationalism has been compromised by the 'taint' of settlement, a history that creates a divided identity that 'wars with itself and is lawless'. Playing with different identities and 'dressing-up' in Mansfield's writing was not simply a matter of frivolous parody and imitation, therefore; it was also about conveying this sense of an identity divided against itself, an anxious identity caught in the liminal space between the centre of imperialism and the colonial periphery. Like texts belonging to the genre of 'parodic translation', then, 'To Stanisław Wyspiański' oscillates between likeness and strangeness.

This ambivalence characterises almost all of the poetry contributions to *Rhythm* that Mansfield made under her own name. In the poem 'Sea Song', for example, 'Memory' is personified as an old woman searching 'for something' with her 'withered claw' along a shoreline across the globe: 'Memory dwells in my far away home, / She is nothing to do with me'.[89] Similarly, the sea becomes an anti-maternal figure and symbol of cruel exile in the poems 'The Sea Child' and 'Sea': 'Into the world you sent her, mother, / [. . .] And drove her away from home'; 'If I leave you, you will not be silent / But cry my name in the cities'.[90] The sea in these poems becomes emblematic for a liminal space between nations and between the metropolitan, urban centre of imperialism and the colonial periphery; the sea represents an in-between space, in which the oscillation between likeness and strangeness, home and exile, the familiar and foreign is perpetual and irreconcilable. Like Wyspiański, Mansfield registers in her *Rhythm* poems the 'hateful servility' of a younger generation taught by imperial discourse 'that they must not speak of love for their home'. Similarly, these poems about 'memory' and the distance from 'home' echo the same 'melancholy appeal' heard by Mansfield in her review of Selver's translations. In December 1912, moreover, poems published under Mansfield's own name were linked to the 'new spiritually-inflected Russian aesthetics' promoted in *Rhythm* when they were printed directly alongside two lithographs by Goncharova based upon the religious polyptych that she had produced the previous year, titled 'Picking Grapes'. Like the Russian 'neo-primitive' artists, Mansfield displays a fascination in these poems for rural traditions and pre-modern superstitions, focusing on the natural environment of 'plains and forests' as well as a 'fairy' seen in the delicacy of 'snowflakes', 'thistledown' and 'a mote in a sunbeam'.[91] If we can see 'Katherine Mansfield' behind the mask of 'Boris Petrovsky', therefore, the tropes of an eastern European and Russian aesthetic also clearly shaped the poems published in *Rhythm* under Mansfield's own name. This identification with the 'minor literatures' and dissident political and artistic movements of cultural nationalism in eastern Europe, Russia and Ireland, therefore, articulated Mansfield's political commitment as a New Zealander living in London: emphasising the liminal and ambivalent, her *Rhythm* poems served to disrupt the received idea of imperial power as integrated and hegemonic.

Employing the Boris Petrovsky pseudonym, Mansfield looked to associate her writing with Slavic literature and forge a position for herself within the international avant-garde promoted by *Rhythm*. As her review of Selver's anthology makes clear, Mansfield viewed translation as a refractory process that transforms both the source and target cultures, whereby the aura of the translated text resides in non-equivalence and the oscillation between likeness and strangeness. Repurposing poems originally composed for inclusion in *The Earth Child* as 'translations' when they were printed in *Rhythm* helped Mansfield to underscore these ideas, as well as to reveal her artistic debt to Slavic literature. Whilst these poems are of debatable artistic merit, they must be interpreted within their original publication contexts as deliberately positioned in a parodic relation to translations in *The New Age*. Understood as examples of 'parodic translation', the perpetuation of non-identity in these poems serves to displace notions of originality and autonomy and thereby challenge the narrative paradigms of 'major literature' and the political paradigms of imperial hegemony. In Bhabha's terms, the Petrovsky poems highlight 'the performativity of translation as the staging of cultural difference' and, as such, emphasise 'the irresolution, or liminality, of "translation", the *element of resistance* in the process of transformation'.[92] This concept of translation as necessarily liminal, ambivalent and resistant also clearly shaped the poetry contributions Mansfield made to *Rhythm* under her own name, poems that were motivated by her lived experience of a radical disjuncture between home and exile, or the familiar and foreign. In this way, Mansfield's *Rhythm* poems encode an already known postcolonial vision, providing a critique of imperial power and anticipating the founding of the postcolonial nation state in both eastern Europe and New Zealand.

The New Zealand stories

After Mansfield's first two 'Boris Petrovsky' poems were published in *Rhythm* in the spring of 1912, she quickly allied herself to the magazine, rescuing it from almost certain financial ruin by securing Stephen Swift as publisher and becoming 'Editorial Assistant' to Murry by the next issue, published in June 1912. With this issue, the cover of *Rhythm* was changed from grey to a bold Fauvist blue, and the magazine transitioned from being a quarterly to a monthly publication. Murry and Mansfield also decided to use this point of transition as an opportunity to outline their aims in further detail in two co-authored editorial essays. These essays reiterate many of the distinctions analysed in the previous chapter, between true art and debased journalism, the creative individual and uninspired public, the work of genius and mediocrity, aristocracy and democracy, minority and mass. In the first of the essays, titled 'The Meaning of Rhythm', Murry and Mansfield write of 'the mob' and 'the eternal protest of democracy against aristocracy'.[93] Ignoring these protests, the aristocratic artist cultivates a form of 'freedom' and 'individuality' attained through his or her 'consciousness of superiority'.[94] Like their fellow contributors to *The New Age* at this time, Murry and Mansfield were anxious to carve out a space for themselves in a crowded and increasingly commercialised literary marketplace, using these binary oppositions to distinguish their own avant-garde artistic project from forms of popular mass culture, such as journalism and 'machine-made realism'.[95] In their second co-authored essay, titled 'Seriousness in Art', for instance, they contrast the outwardly 'serious' writer who views literature as 'a somewhat disreputable means to a purely commercial end, means only to be justified by ultimate financial success', with the 'true' artist, who 'is concerned with the labour and not with the hire'.[96] In 'The Meaning of Rhythm', Murry and Mansfield had observed that 'individuality' is to be attained through 'conquest', describing art as 'the splendid adventure, the eternal quest for rhythm'.[97] The second essay develops this metaphor of conquest and exploration, concluding with a passage that has been attributed by many critics to Mansfield's pen:

> True seriousness is an assertion, a courageous acceptance of the unexplored; the false is a negation, a cowardly clinging to the outworn known. The mob treads over this patch of threadbare ground with mechanical regularity, so poverty-stricken in itself that it asks for nothing but the tokens of poverty and is only comfortable and at ease when it finds nothing further. The land whereon these people live is barren and desolate, lying parcelled and monotonous in the midst of an unknown sea. The artists sail in stately golden ships over this familiar and adventurous ocean. Their gay flags of greeting stream in the sunlight; and far-off winds blow in their great sails and in their hair, as they go sailing by.[98]

In this section of the chapter, I examine how the language and imagery of spatial conquest deployed by Murry and Mansfield here structured articulations of 'community' across the magazine, with the idea of the colonial 'quest' serving as a synonym for and corollary to the idea of artistic 'rhythm'. Arguably, Mansfield's integration into the 'imagined community' of the magazine depended upon her deploying this rhetoric in the editorial essays co-authored with Murry in June and July 1912. Throughout her short story contributions to *Rhythm*, however, Mansfield exercised authorial autonomy by challenging the idea of the modernist 'pioneer' who conquers new aesthetic terrain, unsettling the hierarchical relation between metropolitan centre and colonial periphery that otherwise structured the narrative of the artist's 'adventure'. In particular, in this section I examine how Mansfield's short story contributions sought to disrupt the discourse of 'barbarism' and 'primitivism' upon which ideas of 'community' in *Rhythm* had been formulated.

This discourse is highlighted in the opening essay to the first issue of *Rhythm*, which looked to identify the new artistic 'community' that the magazine would bring together. Frederick Goodyear's 'The New Thelema' begins with the observation that 'men have always been homesick for an ideal community':

> The golden age was relegated to the remote past; the isles of the blest were set among the unexplored ocean-stream that circled the confines of the habitable globe; the former was thrust out beyond the verge of human time, the latter beyond the verge of human space.[99]

As Angela Smith observes, the title of Goodyear's essay is derived from Rabelais's Abbey of Thélème, in which the one edict to be observed is 'Do what thou wilt'.[100] As such, Goodyear writes that 'Thelema [. . .] will be essentially a place of liberty'.[101] In contrast to the 'illusory hope' of a future 'Heaven and the Elysian Fields', he asserts that the new Thelema of liberty and freedom can exist on Earth, 'not the never-never land of the theologian, but the ordinary human future that is perpetually transmuting itself into the past'.[102] This notion of temporal regression or simultaneity was extrapolated from Bergson's philosophy of the *élan vital*.

Asserting the role of the spirit in an era dominated by materialism, Bergson offered a radical alternative to contemporary mechanistic science. In particular, Bergson's theory of 'creative evolution' was an attempt to reconcile the material, scientific facts of Darwinian evolution, which he broadly accepted, with his own theories about the 'spirit' and 'life': he postulated the existence of the *élan vital*, a central 'life force' or 'vital impetus' that exists at the heart of things and that directs the flow of all life and all time, the flow of past and present into future. Mark Antliff has described the élan vital as a 'pantheistic life force latent within artistic creativity'.[103] Suggesting that the aesthetic experience could startle people out of their daily lives and prompt them to look at the world differently, Bergson's philosophy unsurprisingly had a large following within the arts. In *Rhythm*, for instance, Michael Sadler echoed Bergson's anti-materialist philosophy of 'intuition' when he observed: 'An art intent on expressing the *inner* soul of persons and things will inevitably stray from the *outer* conventions of form and colour; that is to say, it will be definitely unnaturalistic, anti-materialist'.[104] Similarly, in a catalogue preface to a 1908 exhibition featuring the work of Matisse, Derain and Vlaminck, Apollinaire echoed the ideas of 'inner soul' and 'spirit' used in Bergson's *L'Évolution Créatrice*, published the previous year, to declare that the spectator should become 'aware of his own divinity' when looking at the new art: 'To do that, one must take in at a single glance the past, the present, and the future'.[105] As Richard Lehan has observed, this Bergsonian idea that aesthetic perception involved a spiritual immersion in the past, present, and future implied that there existed a 'creative power' and 'deep subjectivity within which the mythic, *the primitive*, and the intuitive could thrive' (my emphasis).[106] Just as the internal world of 'intuition' exists beneath the external world of 'intellect' in Bergson's schema, his theory of 'creative evolution' and temporal simultaneity suggested that the 'primitive' and the world of 'pre-history' could exist alongside or within the 'civilised' and the world of 'modernity'. In *Rhythm*, this idea is reflected in Murry's definition of 'modernism' as the artistic expression of the 'primitive harmonies of the world'. In the second issue of the magazine, moreover, the idea of 'pure form' articulated in Murry's essay 'Art and Philosophy' was echoed by Rollo Myers, who describes the music of Debussy as a liberation of 'pure sound' that represents a 'return to primitive conditions'.[107] In *Rhythm*, therefore, Bergson's philosophy provided the vocabulary by which contributors looked to postulate the 'primitive' as a source for creative renewal.

This notion of a primal 'return' shaped ideas of a collective artistic project in *Rhythm*. Sadler, for instance, writes that the techniques and styles of 'primitive and savage art' have opened the possibility for a 'renaissance' of 'similar ideals today with, consequently, similar expression'; in particular, he celebrates the work of Kandinsky and Derain, whom he designates as 'neo-primitives'.[108] This idea of the 'neo-primitives' had wide currency in 1911.[109] In Munich, for example, Kandinsky and Franz Marc had founded the magazine *Der Blaue Reiter* to express their 'sympathy' and 'spiritual relationship with the Primitives'.[110] And in London, artists such as Augustus John, Christopher Nevinson, Mark Gertler and Stanley Spencer were finding inspiration in the work of the Italian 'primitives' of the early to mid-Renaissance, such as Giotto, Piero della Francesca and Botticelli.[111] As such, the idea of the 'neo-primitive' was employed at this time to express the notion of a second Renaissance, a second artistic 'rebirth' or 'revival'. In *Rhythm*, for instance, Holbrook Jackson observed:

> The artist is an instrument adopted by nature to recall man to the use of his perceptions; he is the scattered forces of insight, imagination, vision, of a whole human group, concentrated in one point of light. That is why all really great art revivals impress by their *naiveté*. They are actually primitive, because evolution needs the forces of young and uncouth vigour for her purpose. In order to grow we must continually throw back to what is primal.[112]

Using the Bergsonian language of evolutionary vitalism, Jackson continues: 'the modernist movement with all its new vitality has recaptured for its purpose the vision and spirit, and something of the design, of remote ages'.[113] Within the pages of *Rhythm*, therefore, the term 'primitive' was used to designate the otherness of a 'remote' and 'primal' past at the same time as it referred to the 'vitality' and 'uncouth vigour' of the magazine's contributors, gesturing towards the imagined 'community' of a new 'modernist movement'.

If the 'primitive' in *Rhythm* was based upon this temporal duality, then the term also suggested spatial expansion from the centre to the 'remote' periphery. In 'The New Thelema', for instance, echoing the dichotomy in Bergson's philosophy between 'intuition' and 'intellect', Goodyear champions the 'internal' mode of liberty as opposed to the 'external', which he denigrates as 'the business of the politician' and the 'design' of the architect; in contrast, the 'true creators' are those who develop internal, 'spiritual freedom': 'They are artists and philosophers'.[114] Like Sadler's 'neo-primitives', these 'true creators' are described as outcasts and 'neo-barbarians': they are 'pioneers' who 'go out into the backwoods' and are 'roughened by their contact with the wild'; where others stay 'at home', they enlarge 'existing boundaries', 'conquering new realms abroad'.[115] Evoking a return to the primordial clay or 'mud', Goodyear describes the 'call of the wild, greensickness, *nostalgie de la boue*' as 'a true impulse towards conscious freedom' and asserts that 'it is the neo-barbarians, men and women who to the timid and unimaginative seem merely perverse and atavistic, that must familiarize us with our outcast selves'.[116] Just as Bergson's philosophy suggests that nothing is 'beyond the verge of human time', this idea of the 'neo-barbarians' – thrusting ever outwards from an imagined centre to the wild peripheries – figures the utopian belief that nothing is now 'beyond the verge of human space' either.

This idea of the 'neo-barbarians' was clearly constituted in opposition to an imagined notion of the 'barbaric'. For example, Goodyear describes how the new Thelema will be built upon the 'intuitive consensus of developed wills' opposed to the 'mind of barbaric man [which] is just a wilderness of nature, a jungle of competing tyrannies': 'Part of the jungle is cut down and cleared and in its place there rises an ordered community'.[117] This opposition between the 'developed' and 'ordered' community of the 'neo-barbarians' and the 'wilderness' of 'barbaric man' structures Goodyear's essay according to the spatial-temporal logic outlined by Johannes Fabian in his seminal study *Time and the Other*. Fabian argues that disciplines such as ethnography and anthropology provided intellectual justification for the colonial project by placing 'not only past cultures, but all living societies [. . .] on a temporal slope [of evolution], a stream of Time – some upstream, others downstream'.[118] Echoing this colonial discourse, the 'barbaric' becomes the projected 'other' against which Goodyear can position *Rhythm*'s avant-garde community of 'neo-barbarians': it is the primitive past to their progressive modernity, the wilderness to their order.

This language of geographical expansion and spatial conquest was part of a shared discourse across *Rhythm*. In an article on the Fantaisiste poets, for example, Francis Carco observed: 'Ils ont à leur tour une singulière délicatesse d'accent, de l'ironie, de la vigeur, du naturel, du movement, de la ferveur [. . .] Qu'il suffise de montrer chez eux un retour à la vie "vivante"' ('They have in their turn a singular delicacy of accent, irony, vigour, naturalness, movement, enthusiasm [. . .] That is enough to show amongst them a return to the "living" life').[119] In the first issue of the magazine, Murry also employed this rhetoric of 'vigour' and 'movement' when he wrote that the artist's 'individuality consists in consciously thrusting from the vantage ground that he inherits' and that art is 'movement, ferocity, tearing at what lies before. It takes nothing for granted; and thrusts mercilessly, pitilessly.'[120] In 'The Meaning of

Rhythm', likewise, Murry and Mansfield describe individuality as 'the triumphant weapon' of the aristocratic artist.[121] Murry here builds upon Goodyear's description of the 'pioneers' who become 'roughened by their contact with the wild' in order to envisage the artist as a conqueror of virgin jungle territory and as a figure of muscular vitality and, as Angela Smith has observed, 'masculinist dynamism'.[122] Such metaphors clearly evoke the rhetoric of colonialism. In the gendered language of the colonial travel narrative, for instance, the native landscape is invariably portrayed as a feminised 'virgin land' subjected to the patriarchal control of the West. In this shared discourse of metaphorical violence, therefore, culture is an implicitly masculine domain and nature is gendered as female, a dichotomy which, as Antliff has observed, also structured the visual imagery of *Rhythm*'s cover (Figure 2.1): by removing the woman on the cover from any social context and instead placing her in an abstract, mythological setting, Fergusson made the body of this Eve figure representative of both 'primeval woman' and 'natural fecundity', an association which 'divides the creative process along gender lines'.[123]

The gendered aspects to this discourse of geographical expansion are also revealed in Fergusson's first draft drawing for the cover of the magazine, which he initially conceptualised under the title *The Quest* (Figure 2.2). The title first given to the magazine highlights a synonymous link between 'rhythm' and the 'quest'. Depicting a disembodied and aggressive stare, Fergusson's draft image also reveals how this idea of

Figure 2.2 J. D. Fergusson, draft cover image for *The Quest/Rhythm* (1911)

the 'quest' was connected to the gaze. In the imperial paradigm, as Iris Marion Young explains, 'the knowing subject is a gazer, an observer who stands above, outside of, the object of knowledge'.[124] The link between this gaze and periodical culture has been examined by Patrick Collier, who argues that images published in *The Illustrated London News* replicated the commanding, all-seeing gaze of imperialism, placing 'the individual colonial officer (and, by proxy, the newspaper reader) in the position of ocular/epistemological power'.[125] In the imperial paradigm, moreover, the gaze is clearly gendered. Catherine Nash, for example, suggests that imperialism presents a single, stable perspective on both the 'mapping of subject lands' and the 'representation of women'.[126] Anne McClintock has also argued that the maps of imperialism masculinise exploration and conquest by feminising colonial space.[127] Similarly, Gillian Rose notes that, 'as the eye traverses both field and flesh', the colonial gaze sees both land and the female body as 'something to own, and something to give pleasure'.[128] Foregrounding the penetrating, aggressive gaze, Ferguson's draft drawing for the magazine's cover suggests the extent to which the aesthetics of *Rhythm* were shaped by the visual ideology of imperialism, linking the quest narrative promoted throughout written contributions to the magazine with the gaze of the 'thrusting' and 'merciless' pioneer.

Far from being an egalitarian 'republic of art', therefore, *Rhythm*'s new Thelema would be built upon distinct hierarchies: between the past and modernity, nature and culture, primeval woman and civilised man, the periphery and centre, disorder and order, the 'unexplored' and 'habitable', the 'barbaric' and 'neo-barbarians'. Contributors to *Rhythm* consistently responded to these structural dynamics. The repeated focus in the magazine on the 'joyous splendour of orientalism' witnessed in the productions of the Ballets Russes, for example, created a visible contrast in *Rhythm* between Orient and Occident, East and West: between the regressive past at the margins of modernity and the localised 'stage' of a progressive metropolitan avant-garde.[129] This dichotomy was reiterated in essay contributions to the magazine, as when Murry writes that the 'future lies in a West that is conscious of the East' and Laurence Binyon argues that the 'simplicity' of 'Oriental art' has released the world from the 'nightmare of a mechanical universe'.[130] In each case, the 'East' (the past) is a resource that serves to reinvigorate Western metropolitan art (the future).

This metropolitan focus is repeated throughout *Rhythm*, a magazine that framed its connections with the cultural centre of Paris as 'an effect of its modernity'.[131] In particular, the magazine regularly published work by the Paris-based Fantaisiste writers in the original French. The majority of these contributions focus on the allure of lower-class women and prostitutes for the male café-dwelling *flâneur*. Carco's story 'Aprés Minuit' is typical in this regard, depicting drunks, pimps and women forced into prostitution by poverty, something that is not condemned but becomes the focus of desire for the male protagonist.[132] Also representative of the Fantaisiste aesthetic is a prose poem by Claudien, which describes an imagined 'world' of male sexual fantasy and '*sadisme*':

> Un monde imaginaire et mal défini se constitue ainsi autour de lui, monde dont il est le centre et dont la racine est cet instinct trouble et mauvais qu'il porte en son âme, approuvé en silence par le feu obscur et fétide, son seul compagnon.[133]

> [An imaginary and ill-defined world is around him, the world of which he is the centre and whose root is the troubled and bad instinct which he carries in his soul, silently approved by the dark and fetid fire, his only companion.]

Examples such as this highlight how *Rhythm* provided imaginary mobility throughout the 'world' for the implicitly male author/reader, enabling fantasies of sexual and geographical domination from the 'centre'. This is consistently reflected in visual contributions to the magazine, particularly in Margaret Thompson's many drawings of exotic landscapes and the recurring focus on the female nude in illustrations by other artists. The image used on the cover of the magazine (Figure 2.1), for example, is representative of a wider trend within Fergusson's aesthetic development, in which the female nude became a central motif. In the majority of these paintings, such as *Torse de femme* (1911), the woman's eyes are placed in shadow through a downward gaze, which draws attention to her body and serves to emphasise physicality above any sense of psychological interiority. Furthermore, as Antliff has observed, Fergusson's often voyeuristic focus on café women 'not concerned about respectability' (echoing the work of the Fantaisiste poets) was a 'protest against bourgeois male–female relationships' that only resulted 'in the fabrication of a stereotyped Other. The [lower-class] café women and the Fauve palette in which they are depicted are signs for a bourgeois escape from the conventional into the realm of the "natural"'.[134] This voyeuristic focus on a 'stereotyped Other' is reiterated in Ferguson's illustrative contributions to *Rhythm*, which often depict café women surreptitiously viewed from behind or overtly sexualised nudes.[135] Likewise, in a rather unsubtle poem contributed to the third issue of the magazine, Murry fixes his gaze firmly on the objectified female body: 'She is fair, / Her breasts like towers, and her chestnut hair / Flowing and fragrant, and her dancing eyes / Will burst with passion'.[136]

In contrast, depictions of the female body in the magazine by artists such Anne Estelle Rice and Jessica Dismorr have been celebrated by critics such as Binckes for their autonomy and empowered female sexuality, for their 'frank appraising stares and their divergence from conventional standards of feminine beauty'.[137] Referring to Rice's 'Schéhérazade' (Figure 2.3), for example, Carol A. Nathanson describes 'the composed, smiling subject' who 'locks gazes with the viewer. Aware that she is

SCHÉHERAZADE. BY ANNE ESTELLE RICE

Figure 2.3 Anne Estelle Rice, 'Schéhérazade'. © Estate of Anne Estelle Rice. All rights reserved, DACS 2018

DRAWING ANNE ESTELLE RICE

Figure 2.4 Anne Estelle Rice, 'Drawing'. © Estate of Anne Estelle Rice. All rights reserved, DACS 2018

being scrutinized, she [. . .] escapes becoming the subject of a privileged voyeurism to assert a sense of self and of possession of her body'.[138] As Nathanson notes, the women depicted by Rice in *Rhythm* are 'strong, unidealised forms' that celebrate the energy, vitality and independence of the moving, sensual female body.[139] However, images of the female nude by women artists were also integrated into the wider discourse of primitivism that pervades the magazine. Rice's contributions to *Rhythm*, for instance, often conflate 'woman' with 'natural fecundity' (Figure 2.4) or the female body with racial otherness (Figures 2.3 and 2.5). The women in Rice's drawings often have closed or half-closed eyes, suggesting an eclipsed gaze which is in stark contrast to the aggressive stare of

Figure 2.5 Anne Estelle Rice, 'Drawing'. © Estate of Anne Estelle Rice. All rights reserved, DACS 2018

Figure 2.6 Anne Estelle Rice, 'Drawing'. © Estate of Anne Estelle Rice. All rights reserved, DACS 2018

Fergusson's *Quest* drawing. Furthermore, the way in which these illustrations were framed within the publication contexts of *Rhythm* served to reinforce the association between the female nude and a male-bourgeois escape into the 'natural' and 'primitive'. For instance, a drawing by Rice in the second issue of the magazine not only equates 'woman' with 'nature' by making the female body part of a geometric background of exotic palms and flowers (Figure 2.6), but the poem on the preceding page frames this representation within the context of 'Ammon in the tents of Thebes', 'the Nile', 'the desert's dust' and 'Delphi's mount', a biblical geography that reveals to the narrator the Western colonial 'right' to '[f]ame, fear, and worship, and the power to smite'.[140] Similarly, in the third issue of the magazine, a drawing by Rice (Figure 2.7) accompanies

Figure 2.7 Anne Estelle Rice, 'Drawing'. © Estate of Anne Estelle Rice. All rights reserved, DACS 2018

a poem by W. L. George titled 'The Negress' which employs worn and tired orientalist motifs of racial and sexual otherness, describing the 'shade of palmtree' and the 'jungle airs'.[141] George writes, for instance: 'Oh, maid with breasts as black as ebony,/Say, are for me the languors of your eyes?'[142] Placed on adjacent pages, we are encouraged to read Rice's drawing in conjunction with this appallingly poor poem, so that the flowers in the former become the jungle setting of the latter, the direct gaze of the sitter in the illustration becomes languorous and submissive, and the racial identity that is elided by the two-tone publication of Rice's drawing becomes explicit and objectified, a 'Negress' with breasts 'smooth and black as ebony'.[143] In George's poem, the female body is an empty signifier for otherness, comparable to the 'jungle' landscape brought under the control of the male artist-pioneer in Goodyear's essay. Placed in such a publication context, Rice's image of an empowered female sexuality becomes the mere repository for male colonial fantasy.

Smith suggests that the conflation of gender signifiers in Fergusson's cover image (Figure 2.1), of 'aggressively jutting breasts' and a pose which 'is muscular and commanding rather than yielding and passive', encourages us to view the magazine itself as a space of gender equality and 'freedom from gendered constraints'.[144] Indeed, contemporary exhibitions such as that at the Salon d'Automne offer parallels as 'highly inclusive' spaces that 'welcomed women artists' and were 'emphatically internationalist'.[145] Within *Rhythm*'s pages, for instance, female artists such as Rice, Dismorr, Dorothy 'Georges' Banks, Thompson and Goncharova all found an open space for publication. Yet to subscribe to Murry's notion that *Rhythm* was some sort of egalitarian 'republic', free from gendered constraints, is to wilfully ignore the way in which the magazine perpetuated cultural hierarchies of difference and otherness, whereby nature and the 'primitive' were gendered as female and modern cultural production became implicitly masculine by contrast. Furthermore, such a reading ignores the way in which visual representations of women, including by female artists such as Rice, responded to the nexus of racial and sexual otherness integral to orientalism and Western conceptions of the primitive. The female body in the magazine becomes the site for a male-bourgeois escape from the conventional into the natural, from moribund Western civilisation into the pre-history of foreign cultures. Moreover, it is significant that Mansfield is the only woman to have had more than one written contribution published during the entire run of both *Rhythm* and its successor, *The Blue Review*, other than occasional articles on the theatre by Rice and Banks. This is a stark inequality that critics have been too ready to overlook in discussions of the magazine.

Mansfield's short story contributions to *Rhythm* critique and unsettle the dichotomous dynamics structuring the magazine's pervading discourse of geographical expansion and spatial conquest. In particular, her first story contribution departs from the visual ideology that permeates the magazine, challenging the idea of a stable masculine gaze of both gender and geography. 'The Woman at the Store' depicts an unnamed narrator travelling across the interior of New Zealand with two companions. The story opens with the 'uncanny' silence generated by one of the men, Jo, failing to sing a song he has been singing almost continuously for the last month and the narrator 'half [falling] asleep' in 'a sort of uneasy dream'.[146] Framing the narrative in this way, Mansfield alerts the reader to the significance of inarticulacy and psychological repression, and the story derives impetus from what is elided and left unseen. The three travellers stop at a secluded store which Jo describes as owned by a man 'who'll give yer a bottle of whisky before 'e shakes hands with yer' and his wife, the woman of the title, 'with blue eyes and yellow hair, who'll promise you something else before she shakes hands with you'.[147] On arriving at the store, however, the travelling companions discover that the husband is away shearing, that the woman has been driven to near-hysteria by loneliness, and that her body has been made 'ugly' by multiple pregnancies and the hardships of domestic life in an unforgiving environment. The woman says:

> It's six years since I was married, and four miscarriages. I says to 'im, I says, what do you think I'm doin' up 'ere? If you was back at the coast, I'd 'ave you lynched for child murder. Over and over I tells 'im – you've broken my spirit and spoiled my looks, and wot for [. . .] sometimes I'll be cooking the spuds an' I lifts the lid off to give em a prong and I 'ears, quite suddin again, 'Wot for.'[148]

Once 'as pretty as a wax doll' who 'knew one hundred and twenty-five different ways of kissing', the sexual 'promise' of the woman is now gone: this contrast between expectation and reality leads the narrator to exclaim, 'Oh, go on, Hin! She isn't the same woman!'.[149] The woman is an uncanny double of herself, a grotesque distortion with 'her front teeth knocked out' and her body reduced to looking like 'there was nothing but sticks and wires under that pinafore', with the narrator thinking '*mad*, of course she's mad!'[150] When Jo and the woman manoeuvre events so that they can spend the night together, the narrator and Hin are left to look after the woman's child, a 'mean, undersized brat, with whitish hair, and weak eyes' and a 'protruding' stomach; this child creates 'extraordinary and repulsively vulgar' pictures that are described as the 'creations of a lunatic with a lunatic's cleverness'.[151] Like the song left unsung, these drawings are made 'uncanny' by being withheld, becoming the focus of a repressed act of violence: at the climax of the story, saying 'I done the one she told me she'd shoot me if I did', the child shows the narrator a picture revealing that the woman has murdered her husband with a 'rook rifle'.[152]

Critics have long recognised that 'The Woman at the Store', in the words of Mark Williams, is 'governed by a deliberately literary intelligence' in its debt to the horse-and-saddle genre popularised by writers in the Australian periodical *The Bulletin* and associated in particular with Henry Lawson.[153] Such stories looked to depict the terror and isolation of outback life for women, and 'The Woman at the Store' self-consciously exaggerates the gothic tropes of this genre; as such, the story can be categorised as 'parody'.[154] As Lydia Wevers has observed, the story also subverts the narrative model of colonial romance fiction by presenting the 'object of desire' as 'a form of dressing concealing something undesirable; the puppet-like sticks and wires of a woman shooting at a man with a rook rifle'.[155] Carey Snyder has examined how Mansfield's parody of various colonial literary genres here also served to undercut the expectations of her London-based metropolitan readership in *Rhythm*.[156] Snyder draws attention to the pervasive primitivism of the magazine, highlighting the ways in which Mansfield frustrated metropolitan expectations of the exotic or colonial 'savage'. However, whilst Snyder argues that Mansfield's contributions to *Rhythm* are ambivalent interventions in the magazine, as I do as well, she does not examine the ways in which modernist primitivism in *Rhythm* is also supported by a wider discourse of spatial expansion and conquest, in which both gender and race serve as signifiers of otherness.

In contrast to *Rhythm*'s celebration of the 'pioneers' who 'go out into the backwoods' and are 'roughened by their contact with the wild', 'The Woman at the Store' depicts what Mansfield terms in her poem 'To Stanisław Wyspiański' as the '*taint* of the pioneer' (my emphasis): that is, the taint of violence, sexual abuse, domestic hardship, isolation and madness. As such, the story figures a Freudian return of the repressed, as highlighted in the name given to the 'lunatic' child, Els, the same name Mansfield gives to one of the lower-class girls excluded from the schoolyard clique in a later story, 'The Doll's House' (1921).[157] Living at the frontier, the woman and her child figure something 'else', something 'other'. The line drawings that this 'lunatic' child creates satirise the contemporary idealisation of children's art: in *Der Blaue Reiter*, for instance, children's drawings, produced from the 'moral and spiritual atmosphere' of 'inner tendency', were celebrated as 'primitive' art revealing 'internal truths'.[158] The child's drawings in 'The Woman at the Store' subvert these expectations of moral and spiritual 'truth', instead revealing a violent and brutalising 'truth'. The woman and her child therefore figure a repressed 'otherness' behind the discourse of modernist primitivism. This 'other' is also personified in the spectral, haunting presence that stalks the New Zealand landscape:

> There is no twilight to our New Zealand days, but a curious half-hour when everything appears grotesque – it frightens – as though the savage spirit of the country walked abroad and sneered at what it saw.[159]

In this story, the 'savage' and barbaric 'other' is not something that can be tamed or conquered; rather, it threatens to walk 'abroad' and 'sneer' at what it finds. In other words, Mansfield's story reverses the direction of travel taken by Goodyear's 'pioneers': by publishing in *Rhythm*, she brings the peripheries to the centre, confronting her metropolitan readership with the primal and savage 'other' against which the magazine's discourse of modernist primitivism and 'neo-barbarian' communal affiliation had been constituted.

In particular, 'The Woman at the Store' subverts the gendered aspects of *Rhythm*'s discourse of geographical expansion. Whilst the narrator of 'The Woman at the Store' is gendered female in reissues of the story, in the original *Rhythm* publication the narrator's gender is not stated definitively.[160] In this way, Mansfield disrupts expectations of a settled, commanding and clearly gendered colonial gaze. As Pamela Dunbar has argued, this intentional ambiguity is indicative of the way in which Mansfield sought to disrupt and deconstruct established ideas about gender in the story.[161] In particular, Mansfield frustrates the metropolitan fascination with viewing the body of the exotic colonial 'other'. Instead, she presents her reader with the vacuous and undesirable body of the female white settler; as such, Mansfield inverts the idealised notion of the voluptuous and racially 'other' female body found throughout illustrative contributions to the magazine. Furthermore, the story unsettles the link between 'natural fecundity' and the female body in *Rhythm*. Instead,

Mansfield's story associates the woman at the store with the barren landscape of a 'white pumice dust' that is 'like a dry-skin itching for growth on our bodies'.[162] Surveying the land, the narrator does not view a fertile or fecund landscape, a resource to own and give pleasure, but an arid and desolate 'dust' that prefigures his/her encounter with the woman at the store, whose body is 'nothing but sticks and wires'. As such, Mansfield's story dismantles the metropolitan idealisation of the colonial frontier as a place of abundance, a 'virgin territory' to be penetrated.

This opposition to the magazine's foundational discourse is highlighted by the illustrations published alongside and in juxtaposition to the story. Appearing underneath Thompson's illustrative header of an Asiatic caravan, for instance, 'The Woman at the Store' is framed by the visual tropes of modernist primitivism; whilst Mansfield's opening description of the 'tussock grass [. . .] patched with purple orchids and manuka bushes' clearly locates the narrative in the Antipodes, this geographical specificity is subsumed within the generalised exoticism of water buffalo and veiled women (Figure 2.8).[163] Inserted into Mansfield's text, likewise, is a reproduction of a painting by Henri Manguin of a

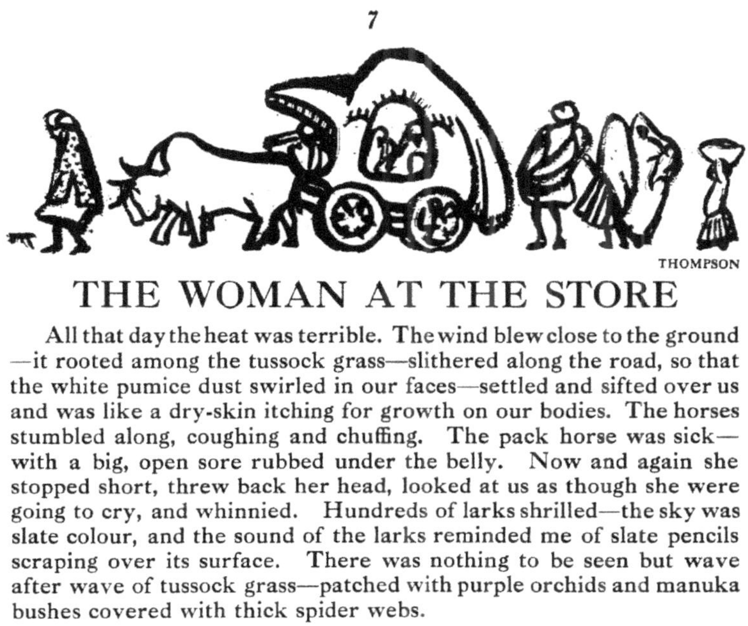
7

THOMPSON

THE WOMAN AT THE STORE

All that day the heat was terrible. The wind blew close to the ground—it rooted among the tussock grass—slithered along the road, so that the white pumice dust swirled in our faces—settled and sifted over us and was like a dry-skin itching for growth on our bodies. The horses stumbled along, coughing and chuffing. The pack horse was sick—with a big, open sore rubbed under the belly. Now and again she stopped short, threw back her head, looked at us as though she were going to cry, and whinnied. Hundreds of larks shrilled—the sky was slate colour, and the sound of the larks reminded me of slate pencils scraping over its surface. There was nothing to be seen but wave after wave of tussock grass—patched with purple orchids and manuka bushes covered with thick spider webs.

Figure 2.8 Margaret Thompson, 'Drawing'

LANDSCAPE HENRI MANGUIN

Figure 2.9 Henri Manguin, 'Landscape'. © ADAGP, Paris and DACS, London, 2018

cottage nestled in a verdant spring landscape of hills, bushes and trees in bloom (Figure 2.9). This image faces the narrator's description of his/her first view of the store: 'We were on the brow of the hill, and below us there was a whare roofed in with corrugated iron'.[164] As such, both Manguin's painting and Mansfield's prose place the reader of *Rhythm* in the position of 'the knowing subject [who] is a gazer' and therefore replicate or reaffirm the visual ideology of imperialism. Unlike the viewer of Manguin's painting, however, the narrator of 'The Woman at the Store' looks upon a poverty-stricken dwelling set within an unforgiving, barren landscape. As such, Mansfield's story unsettles the masculine colonial gaze, challenging the metropolitan idealisation of the peripheries of global space as places of fertility and fecundity.

Similarly, Mansfield's depiction of the woman at the store contrasts with a nude study by Lionel Halpert that is also inserted into the text of the story (Figure 2.10). In *Rhythm*, the female nude signifies both an ideal

Figure 2.10 Lionel Halpert, 'Study'

form of artistic education, as well as the objectified 'other' against which male cultural production is constituted. As Kate Krueger has argued, the image by Halpert reinforces 'the idea of Woman as sexual body and object to be viewed and captured in a traditionally male gaze'.[165] In Mansfield's story, Jo and Hin perceive the woman at the store as this objectified 'other': she is first the idealised 'wax doll' and is then reduced to simply 'female flesh' that Jo quickly sets about possessing.[166] Not only has the woman suffered four miscarriages, however, but her surviving child is born weak and malnourished, with the woman telling the men of the 'trouble' she had after birth: 'I 'adn't any milk till a month after she was born and she sickened like a cow'.[167] Whilst Halpert's corresponding artwork continues to reinforce the idea of 'woman' as an idealised, objectified 'other', therefore, the woman of the story is nothing like the imaginary ideal that the travellers formulate as they move towards the store, her biological 'trouble' and the sickness that she is associated with complicating the idealised link between the reproductive power of the female body and 'natural fecundity'.

In the nineteenth and early twentieth centuries, colonial settlement was supported by a hyper-masculine version of nationalism, a narrative of the nation in which the 'thrusting' and 'merciless' pioneer was responsible for taming the natural landscape alone; this was a narrative from which women were excluded and confined to domestic space. Mansfield's story highlights how such notions of domestic femininity become increasingly untenable in the harsh landscape of the colonial outback. When the woman apologises for the state of her dwelling ('I 'ven't 'ad time ter fix things to-day – been ironing'), for example, the narrator thinks: 'Good Lord, what a life! [. . .] Imagine bothering about ironing'.[168] Similarly, by taking up a gun to ward off potential intruders and to enact revenge upon her husband, the woman asserts her individual agency and disrupts codes of genteel femininity, unsettling the rigid gender binary structuring colonial settlement. This binary is reflected in the visual contributions to the fourth issue of *Rhythm*: in contrast to the idealised female form of Halpert's nude study, for example, André Dunoyer de Segonzac's 'Les Boxeurs' pivots on notions of muscular vitality and masculinist dynamism (Figure 2.11). The repeated lines of the boxers' legs and arms convey the same notion of vigorous movement that underpins the discourse of geographical expansion and spatial conquest in essay contributions to *Rhythm*. Whereas the female body is passively 'natural' and 'primitive' in these essays, de Segonzac's image of masculine movement is described elsewhere in *Rhythm* as 'a great primeval instinct satisfied'.[169] This quotation is from an article attributed to 'Arthur Crossthwaite' that was probably authored by Murry, who likely derived the pseudonym from the middle names of his younger brother, Richard Arthur Crossthwaite Murry. Depictions and discussions of de Segonzac's art in *Rhythm* indicate that masculine agency enables 'primeval instinct' to be resolved, whereas notions of feminine passivity cast the female body as eternally 'primitive' and 'other'. Mansfield's story clearly disrupts this gender binary, challenging representations of the

Figure 2.11 André Dunoyer de Segonzac, 'Les Boxeurs'. © ADAGP, Paris and DACS, London, 2018

female body as passive and thereby unsettling the discourse of the 'thrusting' and 'merciless' pioneer of colonial settlement and modernist art.

Significantly, 'The Woman at the Store' also includes a reference to metropolitan periodical culture. The narrator describes how the walls of the woman's dwelling are 'plastered with old pages of English periodicals' in which 'Queen Victoria's Jubilee appeared to be the most recent number'.[170] With this reference to metropolitan periodical culture and the British Empire, Mansfield appears to subscribe to the idea of the colonial periphery as a place of the pre-modern, outdated and underdeveloped: in comparison with the 'present' and 'progress' of the metropolitan centre, the periphery is seen as a place of stasis and regression. Mansfield thus emphasises a temporal, as well as spatial, disjunction between metropolitan centre and colonial periphery, maintaining an ironic distance between herself (publishing in a progressive 'modernist' metropolitan magazine) and her degenerate characters. By making the domestic space of the 'whare' a metonym for the publication space of the English periodical, however, she also suggests that the physical spaces of the story are a projection of the narrator's own imaginary mobility through periodical space. In this way, Mansfield forces her metropolitan readers to self-reflexively consider how the textual space of the magazine they are reading might serve to reinforce the structural dynamics of colonialism and the representational model constituting imagined ideas of 'savagery' and primal 'otherness'.

Just as 'The Woman at the Store' opens with the narrator riding towards the store in a kind of half-dream, it ends with the narrator waking up and riding away from the store, with the single line: 'A bend in the road, and the whole place disappeared'.[171] As such, the store comes to represent a liminal space, a psychological 'in-between' of the repressed through which the narrator is only ever passing. This is a space in which settled identities (of the 'pioneer' and 'settler', or the colonial 'other') not only become unfixed but are inverted: the 'settler' at the frontier of empire is *also* the savage and primal 'other'. For example, as the companions ride towards the store, the woman runs towards them with a gun, thinking that they are native Māori on the attack. Furthermore, the moment of revelation at the story's climax is also the moment at which the masculine colonial gaze of the quest narrative, dependent upon the stable perception of both women and land, finally becomes untenable; the woman at the store defies all settled expectations about the sexualised yet genteel, fertile and passive woman of colonial domesticity. As the narrator makes a turn in the road, he/she leaves behind a liminal dream world of repression and inversion. In the course of her narrative, therefore, Mansfield has renegotiated the power relations between centre and periphery upon which the magazine's discourse of artistic affiliation had been constituted.

Mansfield's story 'Ole Underwood' also pushes *Rhythm*'s discourse of metaphorical violence to its logical extreme, depicting an ex-convict who has served time in prison for murdering his wife. We learn of Ole Underwood's history through the conversation of a man talking about him in a pub: 'When he was a young fellow, thirty years ago, a man 'ere done in 'is woman, and 'e foun' out an' killed 'er. Got twenty years in quod up on the 'ill. Came out cracked.'[172] Mansfield's story depicts this 'cracked' psyche, conveyed through the repetition of single words that 'beat like a hammer', 'like some one beating on an iron in a prison, some one in a secret place – bang – bang – bang – trying to get free': 'Stop! Stop! Stop! Stop!'; 'Red – red – red – red!'; 'Kit! Kit! Kit!'; 'I will! I will! I will!'; 'Mine! Mine! Mine! beat the hammer'.[173] Ole Underwood struggles to contain these violent impulses towards self-assertion, described as the 'old, old lust', and moments of tenderness are fractured by his destructive energy.[174] When he finds a cat by the wharves on the seafront, for example, 'Ole Underwood sat up and took the kitten in his arms and rocked to and fro, crushing it against his face. It was warm and soft, and it mewed faintly. He buried his eyes in its fur'. Yet he quickly destroys these feelings of tenderness: 'He tore the little cat out of his coat and swung it by its tail and flung it out to the sewer opening. The hammer beat loud and strong.'[175] Ole Underwood has previously been described as being 'like a cat', 'sneak[ing] to one side' in the pub.[176] The senseless violence towards the kitten at the seafront, therefore, is also an attempt to realise his own self-destruction. As such, Ole Underwood is caught between this overwhelming desire for self-annihilation and the 'old, old lust' for self-assertion. As Dunbar has observed, Ole Underwood is 'a parody of the pioneer – rootless, piratical, at odds with all he meets': with 'his outward swagger and inner insecurities, his violence and vengeful puritanism', Ole Underwood 'offers an unflattering portrait of the pioneer – one which makes no concession at all to the glamorous remittance-man of received white New Zealand history'.[177] As such, 'Ole Underwood' challenges the celebration of the neo-barbarian 'pioneers' found elsewhere in *Rhythm*. In particular, the story is clearly set in Wellington, depicting the wharves at the foot of the 'windy hill' and the 'white manuka flower' that flies on the wind.[178] Therefore, Mansfield draws on her actual experience of colonial life in New Zealand in order to dismantle the abstract, glorified image of the lone 'pioneer' across both imperial discourse and the pages of *Rhythm*.

Unlike 'The Woman at the Store' and 'Ole Underwood', 'How Pearl Button Was Kidnapped' is often interpreted as an idealisation of the exotic colonial 'other' that is congruent with modernist primitivism: as Kate Fullbrook argues, for instance, the 'salient features of this story belong to the romantic tradition that glorifies the "naturalness" and "freedom" of the savage over the inhibitions and pleasure-denying aspects of mechanical civilization'.[179] I want to suggest, however, that the story is also based upon a clear and deliberate ambivalence that unsettles this binary between modern 'civilisation' and the noble 'savage'. Written in 1910, the story is told in the manner of fairy tale, and may well have been the 'satirical fairy tale' that Murry later recalled was Mansfield's first, rejected submission to *Rhythm*.[180] Indeed, 'How Pearl Button Was Kidnapped' alludes to darker themes behind its surface veneer of innocence and naivety, themes that allow us to categorise the story as 'satirical' or parodic; it is both a childhood escape into a new and magical 'other' world and also an escape from a very real, impending threat from the 'other'. Published directly alongside W. H. Davies's 'Smiles', a poem that fetishes racial difference, Mansfield's story employs the tropes of modernist primitivism in order to critique and unsettle such contemporary idealisations of the exotic colonial 'other'.

'How Pearl Button Was Kidnapped' is told through the eyes of a very young girl who is taken from her family home by 'dark women' dressed 'in red [. . .] yellow and green'.[181] Racial identity is never specified in the story beyond this detail of the women's 'dark' skin: however, Pearl's name clearly associates her with whiteness, and the 'green ornament' that hangs around the neck of one of the 'dark women' alludes to the 'tiki' symbol worn by the Māori people.[182] The women take Pearl from the regimented world of the bourgeois Pākehā community (those of European descent), symbolised in 'the House of Boxes' in which Pearl's mother is in 'the kitching, ironing-because-its Tuesday'.[183] In the Māori community, by contrast, Pearl is allowed to get her pinafore dirty, to spill the juice of a peach down her dress and to run to the sea, where she unbuttons her clothes and paddles in the water. In the standard interpretation of this story as exemplary of modernist primitivism, Pearl's 'kidnap' by the Māori women is in fact her liberation from the artificialities and limitations of European 'civilisation'. This accepted interpretation is apparently supported by the ending of the story, when the police find Pearl and she gives a 'frightful scream' as the 'little blue men [come] running, running towards her with shouts and whistlings'.[184]

There is an alternative reading of this story, however. As Anna Snaith has observed, the name 'Pearl Button' and 'the repeated references to unbuttoning and undressing in the story' generate 'associations of sexual threat, even rape': as such, the women's kissing of Pearl assumes a distinctly threatening quality.[185] 'How Pearl Button Was Kidnapped' thus prefigures Mansfield's later story, 'Je ne parle pas français', in which 'a racially-other, excessively maternal, figure' sexually abuses the narrator in childhood.[186] In particular, when this story is read against Mansfield's

Urewera notebooks, which repeatedly highlight an awareness of a suppressed history of violent settlement in New Zealand, Snaith argues, the body of the white child can be interpreted as Māori 'reparation for stolen land'.[187] As Janka Kascakova has also observed, when the women approach Pearl Button 'the text clearly indicates through their behavior that they are aware they are doing something wrong' ('The two women came up to her, keeping close to the hedge and looking in a frightened way towards the House of Boxes') and 'there can be no doubt that it is they, not the police officers, who do the wrong thing, no matter how the whole situation is (mis)understood by the child'.[188] As such, it is possible to interpret 'How Pearl Button Was Kidnapped' as a 'satirical fairy tale' in which Mansfield looks to unsettle the unquestioning idealisation within modernist primitivism of the exotic, sexualised and 'racially-other' female.

This story, therefore, cannot be viewed simply as an unambiguous celebration of the 'naturalness' and 'freedom' of a vibrant 'other'. Rather, 'How Pearl Button Was Kidnapped' is founded upon an intentional ambiguity: the 'kidnapping' of the title can refer to both the Māori women and the police officers as either abductors or liberators. In this way, the story collapses distinctions between the two cultures, emphasising instead the relativity of different cultural perspectives. Read in this way, the story is both a critique of imperial discourse (which serves to denigrate and dominate the indigenous population) *and also* of modernist primitivism (which looks to celebrate the exotic indigene without interrogating the history of unjust and violent colonial settlement). As examined in this chapter, Mansfield was clearly aware of how the modernist celebration of the 'primitive' echoed and reaffirmed the discourse of colonial expansion and spatial conquest. As a dual critique of imperialism and modernist primitivism, 'How Pearl Button Was Kidnapped' forces the reader of *Rhythm* to interrogate how the discourse of metaphorical violence advanced throughout the magazine paralleled the real historical violence of colonial settlement.

In conclusion, Mansfield's short story contributions to *Rhythm* did not unambiguously conform to the editorial call for 'brutal' and 'primitive' art; rather, these stories deserve to be understood as deliberately subversive interventions within an established periodical discourse. Mansfield's stories reveal the extent to which the 'imagined community' of the magazine, supposedly embodying an egalitarian 'republic of art', was in fact founded upon distinct spatial hierarchies of race and gender between metropolitan centre and colonial periphery. In particular, these stories disrupt visual representations of women and land in *Rhythm*, challenging and subverting the masculine colonial gaze of the quest narrative. Parodying *Rhythm*'s discourse of metaphorical violence and unsettling the magazine's celebration of the lone 'pioneer', Mansfield highlights how aesthetic theories of vigorous movement and spatial conquest in the magazine aligned with the imperial discourse of colonial settlement. As such, these short story contributions to *Rhythm*, emphasising a repressed violence behind the history of empire, counter the ideological assumptions of the magazine and encode an already known postcolonial vision.

'Sunday Lunch'

By the summer of 1912, Murry and Mansfield were not only the co-editors of *Rhythm* but they were also a couple, christened by Gilbert Cannan as 'the Two Tigers'.[189] In the ninth issue of the magazine, published in October, a satirical sketch titled 'Sunday Lunch' was printed under the pseudonym 'The Tiger', accompanied by a reproduction of the woodcut by Thompson that had originally appeared in the first issue, of a tiger stalking a monkey (Figure 2.12). This pseudonym provided Mansfield with a ferocious persona with which to attack the eat-or-be-eaten world of the London literati. The sketch opens: 'Sunday lunch is the last of the cannibal feasts. It is the wild, tremendous orgy of the upper classes, the hunting, killing, eating ground of all the George-the-Fifth-and-Mary English artists.'[190] Mansfield narrows the geographical focus of her attack further, from the 'English' to the cultural elite found in 'select squares' of London:

Figure 2.12 Margaret Thompson, tiger and monkey (untitled)

> The Society for the Cultivation of Cannibalism waxes most fat and kicks hardest (strictly under the table) in Chelsea, in St John's Wood, in certain select squares, and (God help them) gardens. Its members are legion, for there is no city in this narrow world which contains so vast a number of artists as London.[191]

The members of this 'select' world meet to carry out the ritual slaughter of literary criticism: 'with most deliberate lightness, a victim is seized by the cannibals' and is handed round before the knife comes down and they feast. 'This obvious slaughter of the absentees is only a preliminary to a finer, more keen and difficult doing to death of each other', Mansfield writes: 'With ever greater skill and daring the cannibals draw blood'.[192]

This satirical attack on the art-set found in the 'select squares' of London, written before she had met either Virginia Woolf or Ottoline Morrell, pre-empts Mansfield's later troubled relationship with 'the Bloomsberries'.[193] In 1918, Mansfield wrote to Morrell about her 'hatred of the Human Snigger' that she associated with 'the "Bloomsbury element" in life'.[194] Referring to Roger Fry and Clive Bell as 'the enemies of Art – of real true Art' the following year, she observed: 'The snigger is a very awful thing when one is young and the sneer can nearly kill'.[195] And, writing to S. S. Koteliansky in July 1919, Mansfield stated: 'the english [*sic*] literary world is given up to sniggerers, dishonesty, sneering, DULL DULL giggling'.[196] 'Sunday Lunch' depicts the back-stabbing, 'sneering' world of the London literati as Mansfield perceived it, with the murderous cannibal metaphor figuring the 'snigger' and 'sneer' that 'can nearly kill' a writer 'when one is young'.

As Aimee Gasston has observed, rather than deploying the stereotype of the cannibal 'savage' in order to denigrate a deplored cultural democratisation, as Woolf would later do in her description of a cinema audience as a group of 'savages', 'Mansfield's depiction of the cultural elite as barbarian is far more radical. It seeks to destabilise established anatomies of privilege and disrupt dominant metropolitan practices. In choosing the metaphorical modes that it does, it is also palpably anti-colonial.'[197] In particular, Mansfield appropriates the tropes of imperial discourse, of the wild and animalistic colonial 'other', in order to turn these stereotypes back on to the imperial centre. The Māori of New Zealand, for example, were consistently associated with cannibalism by colonialists, an association that served to underline the need for a civilising presence in the country. Inverting these associations in her depiction of the 'cannibals' of Chelsea, Mansfield unsettles this relation between centre and periphery, suggesting that savagery lurks beneath the staid surface of 'upper class' English decorum. This inversion serves to underline the same transgressive impulse that shapes the spatial imaginary of Mansfield's short story contributions to *Rhythm*. 'Sunday Lunch' satirises the metropolitan assurance that savagery dwells at the peripheries of global space: instead, Mansfield has the spirit of savagery walk among the 'select squares' of London, at the heart of the imperial centre.

Significantly, the cannibal-artists in 'Sunday Lunch' trade in the eclectic icons of modernist primitivism, with a French woman holding a 'Chinese fan' as she reclines on a 'leopard skin' and the hostess saying to one of her guests:

> 'Now I want to introduce you to Kaila Scarrotski. He's Hungarian. And he's been doing those naked backs for that café. And I know you know all about Hungary, and those extraordinary places. He's just read your "Pallors of Passion" and he swears you've Slav blood.' She presses the guest's hand thereby conveying: 'Prove you have. Remember I didn't ask you to my lunch to wait until the food was served and then eat it and go. Beat your tom-tom, dear.'[198]

The signifiers of colonial otherness (the leopard skin, the naked body, the tom-tom) and Orientalism (the Chinese fan) paradoxically become markers of cultural capital for the metropolitan 'cannibals'. Mansfield is parodying the way in which modernist primitivism exemplifies a form of cultural imperialism, of accumulation and appropriation of cultural artefacts taken from the peripheries to the centre of global space. This association between the cannibal-artists and Britain's imperialist class, in particular, is highlighted in the image of servants with 'foreign complexions' who circulate the room like 'marionettes'.[199]

The above passage, however, also suggests Mansfield's own potential complicity in this discourse of modernist primitivism. Indeed, the hostess's speech appears to be addressed to the narrator of the piece, an idea that is reinforced by the mention of the predilection for all things 'Slav' exhibited by this 'female cannibal'.[200] The publication of Mansfield's parodic translations would have firmly associated her with the Slavic among *Rhythm*'s readers. As such, Mansfield's satire is not only directed towards the contributors who show a penchant for the 'primitive' in the magazine, but is also directed towards herself: 'Sunday Lunch' self-reflexively parodies the way in which Mansfield bolstered her own writing in the magazine by appropriating the markers of other cultural and national traditions. This self-satire is underlined by the use of 'The Tiger' pseudonym, which suggests the very wildness and ferocity associated with the cannibal-artists. In 'Sunday Lunch', Mansfield not only seeks to reclaim the markers of colonial culture from appropriation by the metropolitan aesthetes of London, but she also attempts to out-savage these savages: in this eat-or-be-eaten world, Mansfield chooses to eat. As Gasston has observed, 'Mansfield hypocritically proves herself a most effective cannibal' by enacting 'the same savagery she seeks to deride, thus embroiling herself irrevocably with her own satire'.[201]

'Sunday Lunch' is therefore indicative of the highly ambivalent position that Mansfield forged for herself within *Rhythm*. In the first instance, she appropriates and parodies stereotypes of the colonial 'other' in order to undercut the tropes of modernist primitivism and position herself against the English metropolitan elite. Yet she also highlights her own complicity in the very thing she attacks. The anti-democratic, anti-commercial rhetoric satirised in 'Sunday Lunch', for example, echoes the editorials that Mansfield had co-authored for the magazine with Murry only months before. 'Sunday Lunch' therefore highlights how Mansfield's own cultural and editorial authority depended upon her incorporation into (or, perhaps, cannibalisation of) the very discourse that she sought to disrupt. Revealing the connections between modernist primitivism and cultural imperialism, however, 'Sunday Lunch' encodes an anti-colonial and anti-imperial critique, and thus maintains Mansfield's ironic, self-aware distance from this discourse. In particular, Mansfield 'others' the primitivists (including herself) and thus unsettles any pretensions towards essential binaries of race or class, or between centre and periphery. As such, Mansfield both identifies with *and* distances herself from both the 'savage' colonial 'other' *and* the 'sniggerers' of the 'english [*sic*] literary world': 'Sunday Lunch' positions Mansfield-as-Tiger in that liminal, ambivalent space between both possibilities. In this way, the sketch highlights Mansfield's knowing, self-aware position as an ex-centric writer, uncomfortable in identifying herself with either colonial New Zealand or the metropolitan centre of London.

'Je ne parle pas français'

Mansfield continued to parody *Rhythm* in her later writings. Widely interpreted by critics biographically as a story that parallels Mansfield's love triangle with Murry and Francis Carco in 1915, 'Je ne parle pas français', written in 1918, also constitutes one of her most developed critiques of the periodical culture that had brought all three writers together. The story focuses on the Parisian *petites revue* writer and self-serving gigolo Raoul Duquette, a stand-in for Carco, who serendipitously meets the spineless Englishman Dick Harmon 'at an evening party given by the editor of a new review', 'a very select, very fashionable affair' in which 'poetesses' 'in full evening dress' recline on 'cubist sofas'.[202] Duquette and Harmon are brought together by the print culture of a new modernist coterie, in much the same way as *Rhythm* had put Murry into contact with Carco by providing a publication venue for the Fantaisistes. Mansfield underscores this resemblance between *Rhythm* and the literary circles described in 'Je ne parle pas français' in Duquette's account of himself. Looking into the mirror, in a moment that highlights his shameless narcissism, Duquette tells his reader:

> I am going to write about things that have never been touched before. I am going to make a name for myself as a writer about the submerged world. But not as others have done before me. Oh, no! Very naively, with a sort of tender humour and from the inside, as though it were all quite simple, quite natural.[203]

This idea of touching the 'submerged world' can be understood in relation to Murry's definition of 'modernism' in the first issue of *Rhythm*, as that which 'penetrates beneath the outward surface of the world'; modernist art, 'be it drawing, literature or criticism', Murry tells us, 'shall have its roots below the surface and be the rhythmical echo of the life with which it is in touch'. Moreover, Duquette's references to the 'naivety' and 'naturalness' of the writing he hopes to produce clearly echo the many descriptions in *Rhythm* of a 'primal return' to simplicity among the modernists, as well as Carco's own account of how the Fantaisistes would 'return to the "living" life' by producing poetry characterised by 'a singular delicacy of accent, irony, vigour, *naturalness*, movement, enthusiasm' (my emphasis). As such, Duquette comes to personify the ideals upon which *Rhythm* had been founded. Indeed, Angela Smith has also argued that 'the story can be read through Fauvist painting': with its sharply delineated form, vivid colours and focus on the visual image, 'what the reader perceives is a Fauvist savagery in the story'.[204] Jenny McDonnell has also noted that Duquette's forename links him to the 'wild beasts' of Fauvism, suggesting a 'voracious appetite for prey, as Raoul is the French form of Ralph, meaning "wolf"'.[205] Moreover, the Fauvist impetus behind the story is shown in a letter that Mansfield wrote to Murry about its composition; recalling the 'Tiger' persona, she observes that she has 'gone for it, bitten deeper & deeper & deeper than ever I have before'.[206]

Importantly, however, Duquette is shown to be duplicitous, disingenuous and self-serving, abandoning Harmon's fiancée Mouse at the critical moment by failing to return to her, as promised, after Harmon has left for England. An indication of Duquette's character is given earlier in the narrative when he tells his reader that he is 'going in for serious literature' with a story serialised in the Parisian press titled 'Wrong Doors' and a book, *False Coins*, the titles of which alert us to the fact that his entry into the literary world is predicated on the dishonest, deceitful or morally corrupt.[207] With Duquette personifying the Parisian print culture that spawned *Rhythm*, Mansfield's story questions the authenticity of the ideals upon which the magazine had been founded. As McDonnell has observed, for instance, Duquette and Harmon are both described repeatedly as 'serious' writers, in a direct reference to the essay co-authored by Murry and Mansfield in *Rhythm* titled 'Seriousness in Art'; the story ironises such arrogant posturing, with both male characters figuring 'the isolated, "aristocratic" artist that had been held up as an ideal by Mansfield and Murry' in the pages of *Rhythm*.[208] Duquette's many references to 'Life', for instance, recall Murry's repeated capitalisation of the word in articles for the magazine, such as his assertion that by 'the creation of a new thing [. . .] Life proceeds and Art exists'.[209] Unlike Murry's idealisation of 'Life', however, Duquette envisages 'Life' as 'a rag-picker on the American cinema, shuffling along wrapped in a filthy shawl with her old claws crooked over a stick'.[210] As McDonnell has also argued, therefore, 'Je ne parle pas français' enacts Mansfield's 'rejection of the ideals embodied by *Rhythm*'.[211] In particular, I want to suggest, the story highlights Mansfield's awareness of how the magazine's ideals were entangled with projected notions of racial and sexual otherness.

'Je ne parle pas français' begins with Duquette sat in the corner of a café in Paris voyeuristically observing a succession of 'thin, dark girls' who have been made to look 'quite transparent' through long 'fatigue and hopelessness'.[212] Like the women sketched in Fergusson's art and Carco's writing, these women are denied any semblance of selfhood or individuality, with Duquette commenting: 'They are always the same, you know. The girls always have the same names.'[213] At the story's close, Duquette imagines 'some dirty old gallant' approaching him in the 'gloomy café', to whom he makes this proposition: 'But I've got the little girl for you, *mon vieux*. So little . . . so tiny. And a virgin'.[214] Duquette's predatory and exploitative character is earlier revealed in his observation that Paris is 'nothing but a great trap we had set to catch these sleepy innocents. Into the trap they walked and were snatched and taken off to be devoured. Where was my prey?' It is also revealed in his self-image throughout the story as a 'fox-terrier' pursuing the timid Mouse, an animal pairing that recalls Thompson's woodcut in *Rhythm* of a tiger predatorily stalking a monkey.[215] Duquette couches his everyday existence in the terms of sexual domination, imagining the moment when he might beat 'the old hag [. . .] Life' as 'the scene of my triumph, or the scene of the crime where I had the old bitch by the throat for once and did what I pleased with her'.[216] Duquette is not only a pimp and sexual predator, however, but also a male prostitute, renting himself out to 'kept women and elderly widows and shop girls and wives of respectable men, and even advanced modern literary ladies at the most select dinners and soirées'.[217] As well as voyeuristically observing the café women as an objectified 'other', therefore, Duquette also identifies with their position within the sexual economy of Paris, thinking of himself as being 'almost like a girl, with smooth shoulders' and observing:

> Isn't it strange I should have written all that about my body and so on? It's the result of my bad life, my submerged life. I am like a little woman in a café who has to introduce herself with a handful of photographs. 'Me in my chemise, coming out of an eggshell . . . Me upside down in a swing, with a frilly behind like a cauliflower . . . ' You know the things.[218]

In this story that describes a 'fattish old prostitute picking her way home through the slush', recalling Carco's 'Aprés Minuit', Duquette readily accepts his dual position as both exploiter and exploited.[219] Moreover, it is significant that Mansfield has Duquette link the 'submerged life' so venerated by Murry with the seedy and clichéd pornographic image. In what is perhaps an allusion by Mansfield to the print contexts of *Rhythm* and the prevalence of the female nude in visual contributions to the magazine, Duquette's apartment is also adorned with 'nude studies on the walls'.[220] As such, images of the female body may be representative of the vital 'submerged life' of a modernist art revival, Mansfield suggests, or they may indicate a darker, far more troubling 'bad life' of sexual exploitation and gendered power dynamics. When read in conjunction with *Rhythm*, therefore, 'Je ne parle pas français' gestures towards the politics of domination that underpinned otherwise idealistic conceptions of a modernist art revival in the magazine.

Intersections between the politics of gender and race are also revealed in Duquette's account of the 'one memory that stands out' from his past, a memory that he recalls 'vividly' and considers 'very significant as regards myself from the literary point of view':

> When I was about ten our laundress was an African woman, very big, very dark, with a check handkerchief over her frizzy hair. When she came to our house she always took particular notice of me [. . .] One day when I was standing at the door, watching her go, she turned round and beckoned to me, nodding and smiling in a strange secret way. I never thought of not following. She took me into a little outhouse at the end of the passage, caught me up in her arms and began kissing me. [. . .] And then with a soft growl she tore open her bodice and put me to her. When she set me down she took from a pocket a little round fried cake covered with sugar and I reeled along the passage back to our door.[221]

As Anna Snaith has observed, the sexual abuse of Duquette in childhood 'pav[es] the way for his own sexual exploitation of others', highlighting how the violence of the French colonial presence in Africa begets violence.[222] As Angela Smith has also noted, however, the African woman here 'is constructed as exotic, uninhibited and sexually challenging, comparable with the Tahitian women in Gauguin's paintings'.[223] Described in terms of excess, 'very big' and 'very dark', the African woman figures a racial and sexual threat that becomes the source of a 'primitive' desire; she is the objectified 'other' typical of modernist primitivism, her 'soft growl' linking her to the animalistic and her 'strange secret' promising access to a taboo desire censored by normative bourgeois European society. As Elleke Boehmer has observed, Duquette's recollection takes on significance because it 'introduces a hyper-disruptive moment into what is already a self-consciously perverse narrative'; it introduces 'an irruptive Africanness' that 'is not innocent of Lawrentian-type colonialist connotations' linking the black female body 'to visceral knowledge and intuition'.[224] Given that this memory is mediated through a suspect and duplicitous first-person narrative voice, however, Boehmer argues that we must 'read Duquette's story slant': 'quite separate from his portrait of [the African] as an abusive domestic, it is equally possible that the woman was a laundress who doubled as a paid wet-nurse'.[225] In this story in which the narrator readily accepts the dual position of exploiter and exploited, the African laundress can be viewed likewise 'as more used than using, more possessed than possessor, [so that] the apparently abusive and also colonialist situation of white child vis-à-vis its exotic molester is disrupted': as so often in Mansfield's work, Boehmer argues, 'the transgressive force of the stranger' reveals the extent to which 'margin and centre, victim and victimizer, the stranger without and the stranger within, are inextricably intertwined'.[226]

Duquette tells us that this memory of the African laundress is significant 'from the literary point of view' and we can see how it shapes his idea of himself as a would-be writer. Immediately before this recollection, Duquette states: 'About my family – it really doesn't matter. I have no family; I don't want any. I never think about my childhood. I've forgotten it.'[227] The memory of the African laundress is the exception to this willed erasure of the past. This illuminates Edward Said's definition of 'modernism' as a response to the 'crisis' of '*filiation* – linear, biologically grounded process, that which ties children to their parents – which produced the counter-crisis within modernism of *affiliation*, that is, those creeds, philosophies, and visions re-assembling the world in new non-familial ways'.[228] Duquette forgets his family in order to formulate a new creed of the 'submerged world', a world that he plans to access very 'naively', almost like a child. It is the vivid memory of the African woman standing bare-chested before the child that serves as the point of origin for this new vision of the world, and it is difficult not to think here of the many images that permeate *Rhythm* of powerful yet exoticised women in a state of undress, such as Rice's 'Schéhérazade' (Figure 2.3).

Indeed, 'Je ne parle pas français' highlights just how carefully Mansfield had thought about the politics of modernist affiliation in *Rhythm*. From the very first issue of the magazine, Frederick Goodyear's article on the 'neo-barbarians' outlined ideas of an 'ideal community' by positing the modernist artist as a 'pioneer' who reinvigorates moribund Western civilisation through his contact with the 'primitive', reconnecting the West with the vital 'life' associated with the global periphery. This is strikingly similar to how Duquette mythologises his self-conception as an artist, free from all familial ties and brought into the world by his contact with the African laundress. As 'Je ne parle pas français' makes clear, Mansfield was aware that this kind of creation myth of modernist affiliation was often predicated upon historical realities of exploitation and domination, with the contrast between progressive modernity and 'primitive' regression mapping onto a spatial relation between imperial centre and colonial periphery. Close analysis of Mansfield's contributions to *Rhythm* shows that she had thought in detail about this alignment between modernism and the ideology of imperialism in the years 1912–13.

Conclusion

To quote the prose poem by Claudien already cited in this chapter, the case study of *Rhythm* shows how early twentieth-century modernist magazines often figured an 'imaginary [. . .] world' placing the reader at the 'centre' of spatial arrays of power; examining Mansfield's writings illuminates the ways in which individuals could intervene within these spatial dynamics. Throughout her contributions to *Rhythm*, Mansfield unsettles rigid centre/periphery binaries, opening up liminal spaces that draw attention to her equivocal identification with the magazine's 'ideal community'. In particular, Mansfield's use of parody recalls Homi Bhabha's theory of 'colonial mimicry' as 'an *ironic* compromise' that creates instances of ambivalent '*double* vision'.[229] In her 'parodic translations', for example, Mansfield's use of a pseudonym turns the author into a 'partial' presence and emphasises a multiplication of authorial non-identity that challenges ideas of cultural and imperial hegemony. Parodying established literary genres in the stories set in New Zealand, likewise, Mansfield both depicts the colony as a space of regression to the 'primitive' and also disrupts dominant cultural hierarchies between centre and periphery by disturbing the discourse of communal affiliation advanced elsewhere across the magazine. Finally, 'Sunday Lunch' produces a satirical 'double vision' of identification and difference by turning the colonial 'other' and the metropolitan artist into interchangeable 'savages'. This ambivalent negotiation of centre/periphery binaries throughout Mansfield's contributions to *Rhythm* allows us to designate her more decisively as a colonial-metropolitan modernist.

Consistently founded upon ironic performance and the ambiguity of self-fashioning, Mansfield's contributions to *Rhythm* highlight how her identification with the 'neo-barbarian' community of the magazine was always founded upon the excess, uncertainty and slippage generated by imitation and parody. As her use of pseudonyms makes clear, she was highly aware of the performativity of identity in the magazine. This awareness is also shown in her later statements in letters in which she articulates her sense of identification with those who had contributed to the magazine by repeating the same discourse of communal affiliation that her writings had previously sought to challenge. Writing to Murry in 1915, she states: 'I feel sometimes very much like Fergusson'.[230] And after meeting the artist again in 1917, she describes their 'real understanding':

> We might have spoken a different language – returned from a far country. I just felt all was well, and we understood each other. Just that. And there was 'ease' between us. There is a division: people who are my people, people who are not my people. He is mine.[231]

Writing to Anne Estelle Rice in March 1920, likewise, Mansfield develops this opposition:

> I am lying here with 'relations' the dearest people *only* they are not artists. You know what that means? I love them and theyve [*sic*] just been too good & dear to me but they are not in the same world that we are & I pine for *my own people* my own 'wandering tribe'.[232]

This last example conforms to Edward Said's idea of modernist affiliation as produced by a crisis and renunciation of familial 'relations'. In these letters, moreover, it is the imaginaries of cultural otherness and global travel ('We might have spoken a different language – returned from a far country') and of the modern 'primitive' ('my own "wandering tribe"') that enable Mansfield to designate '*my own people*'. In other words, whilst her magazine contributions had challenged the discourse of geographical expansion and modernist primitivism advanced across *Rhythm*, it was precisely through this discourse that Mansfield later expressed her sense of identification with these artists. Whilst this may be indicative of Mansfield's greater integration into metropolitan culture after 1915, it is perhaps more representative of the fact that this was a discourse that she performed and negotiated self-consciously, and that she was aware that her assimilation into the imagined communities of metropolitan modernism was contingent upon deploying this rhetoric effectively.

As I have examined in this chapter, however, in her contributions to the magazine, Mansfield consistently maintained an ironic distance from the discourse of metaphorical violence and spatial conquest promoted in *Rhythm*. This distance from the metropolitan modernism figured by the magazine became more pronounced as it progressed towards the end of its short publication life. The high point for *Rhythm* and Mansfield's association with the magazine came with the publication of the ninth issue, in October 1912, which contained Mansfield's story 'New Dresses' as well as 'The Little Girl' (published under the 'Lili Heron' pseudonym), 'Sunday Lunch' (by 'The Tiger'), the review of Selver's *Anthology of Modern Bohemian Poetry* and a caricature of Mansfield by Dorothy 'Georges' Banks (Figure 2.13). After this issue appeared, however, the

Figure 2.13 Dorothy 'Georges' Banks, 'Caricature of Katherine Mansfield'

magazine's publisher (Stephen Swift, aka Charles Granville) absconded from London due to bankruptcy, leaving Murry to shoulder significant debts. Mansfield wrote to Edward Marsh, editor of the famous *Georgian Poetry* anthologies, imploring him to help the magazine. Marsh secured Martin Secker as an alternative publisher, and in his wake followed a flood of Georgian poets to the pages of *Rhythm*. Moreover, in December 1912, Fergusson brought his position as art editor to an end. As a result, the visual content of the magazine became decidedly less avant-garde, and Murry and Mansfield were forced to recycle illustrative contributions that had appeared in earlier issues. In the fourteenth and last issue of *Rhythm*, published in March 1913, the title of a contribution by D. H. Lawrence signalled the new direction Murry would take with his subsequent publishing venture, supported by Secker: the successor to *Rhythm*, *The Blue Review*, became an organ for 'The Georgian Renaissance'.

Mansfield was listed as 'Associate Editor' of *The Blue Review*, but her role in the production of the magazine, seemingly limited to correspondence, was greatly diminished from what it had been on *Rhythm*. This change is also signalled by Mansfield's contributions to the magazine: whilst 'Millie' is another parody of the colonial 'outback' genre that can be grouped together with 'The Woman at the Store' and 'Ole Underwood', this story is anomalous among Mansfield's contributions to *The Blue Review*. Tellingly, Mansfield instead returned to the fiction-travelogue genre first developed in *The New Age*, with stories narrated by a detached, young woman travelling alone through Europe. When Murry insisted that she cut one of these stories by half a page, Mansfield responded with what has become one of her best-known statements on the importance of form in her work:

> I've nursed the epilogue to no purpose. Every time I pick it up and hear 'youll [*sic*] keep it to six,' I *cant* [*sic*] cut it. To my knowledge there aren't any superfluous words: I mean every line of it. [. . .] Im [*sic*] a powerful stickler for form in this style of work. I hate the sort of licence that English people give themselves – to spread over and flop and roll about. I feel as fastidious as though I wrote with acid. [. . .] I'd rather it wasn't there at all than sitting in the Blue Review with a broken nose and one ear as though it had jumped into an editorial dog fight.[233]

The staff members of *The Blue Review* included Rupert Brooke, Walter de la Mare, J. D. Beresford and John Drinkwater, an English male clique of Georgian poets from which Mansfield was evidently excluded by both nationality and gender. Antony Alpers writes, for instance, that when Mansfield missed an editorial meeting, it was decided in her absence that she would write on 'dress'.[234] This exclusion evidently fuelled Mansfield's frustration with Murry in the letter quoted above: with the Georgian poets now dominant, there was certainly plenty of English 'flopping' and 'rolling about' going on in the magazine. Positioning herself against this 'sort of licence', Mansfield distinguished her writing by a 'fastidiousness' associated with her outsider status. Newly pronounced by the changes made in the transition from the internationalist and cosmopolitan *Rhythm* to *The Blue Review*, which was implicitly 'English', this felt status as a national 'outsider' perhaps explains Mansfield's return to the fiction-travelogue genre. As in *The New Age*, her exclusion from the imagined national community of *The Blue Review* resulted in Mansfield producing stories in which critique is limited to the silent protests of an ostracised, itinerant, semi-autobiographical protagonist.

As Murry tried to secure funds for *The Blue Review* before publication of the first issue in May 1913, Mansfield wrote to him, stating:

> I am beginning to 'pretend' that you are a sailor – trading with all sorts of savages from Monday to Friday – & that the *Blue Review* is your schooner & Secker the Fish Eyed Pilot. Couldn't you write a

Figure 2.14 Katherine Mansfield and John Middleton Murry, Chaucer Mansions, Kensington, London (1913). Ref: 1/2-028643-F. Alexander Turnbull L brary, Wellington, New Zealand

> long-complicated-extremely-insulting-symbolical-serial around that idea with minute, obscene descriptions of the savage tribes . . . ?[235]

The use of scare quotes around 'pretend' emphasises Mansfield's caustic tone and her ironic distance from the narrative that she sketches. Significantly, this was precisely the narrative upon which Murry had outlined the aims and ideals of *Rhythm* two years previously: of the aristocratic artist-pioneer, thrusting ever outwards to the imagined peripheries of global space in a domination of land, sea and the 'barbaric' or 'savage' other. As this chapter has examined, Mansfield's contributions to *Rhythm* enact an uneasy, ambivalent negotiation of this discourse: on the one hand, she clearly identified with the metropolitan modernism and cultural cosmopolitanism advanced within the magazine, co-authoring editorial essays that celebrate the 'splendid adventure' undertaken by the artist-pioneer; on the other, however, her contributions to *Rhythm* reverse the direction of travel taken by the artist-pioneer in order to locate 'savagery' at the heart of empire, in the white settler communities at the frontier and in the 'select squares' of London. The parodic contributions that Mansfield made to *Rhythm* foreground resistance to imperial power and disrupt the discourse of geographical expansion by which contributors to the magazine had previously articulated ideas of modernist affiliation, figuring an ironic and subversive intervention within the magazine.

Notes

1. Huntly Carter, 'The "Blue Bird" and Bergson in Paris', *New Age*, 9.2 (11 May 1911), p. 44.
2. Ibid.
3. Huntly Carter, 'The Independants and the New Intuition in Paris', *New Age*, 9.4 (25 May 1911), p. 83.
4. John Middleton Murry, 'Bergson in Paris', *New Age*, 9.5 (1 June 1911), pp. 115–16.
5. Ibid.
6. John Middleton Murry, *Between Two Worlds: An Autobiography* (London: Jonathan Cape, 1935), pp. 155–6.
7. Ibid., p. 157.
8. John Middleton Murry to Phillip Landon (April 1911), quoted in F. A. Lea, *The Life of John Middleton Murry* (London: Methuen, 1959), p. 24.
9. John Middleton Murry, 'Aims and Ideals', *Rhythm*, 1 (summer 1911), p. 36.
10. John Middleton Murry, 'Art and Philosophy', *Rhythm*, 1 (summer 1911), p. 12.
11. Quoted in Andrew Thacker, 'Modern Tastes in *Rhythm*: The Visual and Verbal Culture of Advertisements in Modernist Magazines', *Katherine Mansfield Studies*, 2 (2010), p. 11.
12. John Middleton Murry, 'Coming to London', in John Lehmann (ed.), *Coming to London* (London: Phoenix House, 1957), p. 105.
13. Quoted in Lea, *The Life of John Middleton Murry*, pp. 24–5.
14. Quoted in Angela Smith, '"As fastidious as though I wrote with acid": Katherine Mansfield, J. D. Fergusson and the *Rhythm* Group in Paris', *Katherine Mansfield Studies*, 3 (2011), p. 14.
15. Rollo H. Myers, 'The Art of Claude Debussy', *Rhythm*, 2 (autumn 1911), p. 29.
16. John Middleton Murry, 'What We Have Tried To Do', *Rhythm*, 3 (winter 1911), p. 36.
17. The three stories are 'The Woman at the Store', 'Ole Underwood' and 'Millie'.
18. Angela Smith, *Katherine Mansfield: A Literary Life* (Basingstoke: Palgrave, 2000), p. 95.
19. Angela Smith, 'Fauvism and Cultural Nationalism', *Interventions: International Journal of Postcolonial Studies*, 4.1 (June 2002), p. 49.
20. John Middleton Murry and Katherine Mansfield, 'Seriousness in Art', *Rhythm*, 6 (July 1912), p. 49.
21. Janet Wilson, 'Introduction', in Janet Wilson, Gerri Kimber and Delia da Sousa Correa (eds), *Katherine Mansfield and the (Post)colonial* (Edinburgh: Edinburgh University press, 2013), p. 1.
22. Peter Brooker, 'Harmony, Discord, and Difference: *Rhythm* (1911–13), *The Blue Review* (1913), and *The Signature* (1915)', in Peter Brooker and Andrew Thacker

(eds), *The Oxford Critical and Cultural History of Modernist Magazines, Volume I: Britain and Ireland, 1880–1955* (Oxford: Oxford University Press, 2009), p. 316.

23. Gerri Kimber, 'Mansfield, *Rhythm* and the Émigré Connection', in Janet Wilson, Gerri Kimber and Susan Reid (eds), *Katherine Mansfield and Literary Modernism* (London: Continuum, 2011), p. 17.
24. Faith Binckes, *Modernism, Magazines, and the British Avant-Garde: Reading* Rhythm, *1910–1914* (Oxford: Oxford University Press, 2010), p. 81.
25. Anne Estelle Rice, 'Memories of Katherine Mansfield', *Adam International Review*, 300 (1965), p. 76.
26. Ibid., p. 77.
27. See Gerri Kimber, 'Circles of Influence: Katherine Mansfield, S.S. Koteliansky and Russia', in Sarah Ailwood and Melinda Harvey (eds), *Katherine Mansfield and Literary Influence* (Edinburgh: Edinburgh University Press, 2015), pp. 78–90.
28. Caroline Maclean, 'Russian Aesthetics in Britain: Kandinsky, Sadleir, and *Rhythm*', in Rebecca Beasley and Philip Ross Bullock (eds), *Russia in Britain, 1880–1940: From Melodrama to Modernism* (Oxford: Oxford University Press, 2013), p. 147.
29. As Kimber notes, Mansfield probably met Lykiardopoulos through Aleister Crowley. Kimber, 'Mansfield, *Rhythm* and the Émigré Connection', p. 20.
30. John Middleton Murry, 'Introduction', in John Middleton Murry (ed.), *Poems by Katherine Mansfield* (London: Constable, 1930), pp. xii–xiii.
31. Jerome McGann, *The Textual Condition* (Princeton: Princeton University Press, 1991); George Bornstein, *Material Modernism: The Politics of the Page* (Cambridge: Cambridge University Press, 2001).
32. The poems that appeared under the Petrovsky pseudonym are 'Very Early Spring', 'The Earth-Child in the Grass', 'To God the Father', 'Jangling Memory' and 'There was a Child Once'. The poems that appeared under Mansfield's own name are 'The Opal Dream Cave' and 'Sea'.
33. The poem that appeared under the Petrovsky pseudonym is 'The Awakening River'. The poems that appeared under Mansfield's own name are 'The Sea Child' and 'Sea Song'.
34. Joanna Woods, *Katerina: The Russian World of Katherine Mansfield* (Auckland: Penguin, 2001), p. 95.
35. Available at <http://www.surnamedb.com/Surname/Petrovsky> (last accessed 2 January 2018).
36. See, for example, Kazimierz Przerwa-Tetmajer, 'Czardas. A Fragment', trans. P. [Paul] Selver, *New Age*, 9.7 (15 June 1911), p. 161.
37. Suzanne W. Churchill and Adam McKible, 'Introduction', in Suzanne W. Churchill and Adam McKible (eds), *Little Magazines and Modernism: New Approaches* (Aldershot: Ashgate, 2007), p. 12.
38. 'Boris Petrovsky' [Katherine Mansfield], 'Very Early Spring', *Rhythm*, 4 (spring 1912), p. 30.
39. 'Boris Petrovsky' [Katherine Mansfield], 'The Awakening River', *Rhythm*, 4 (spring 1912), p. 30.
40. Eliška Krásnohorská, 'Song', in Paul Selver (ed.), *An Anthology of Modern Bohemian Poetry* (London: Henry J. Drane, 1912), p. 91; Otakar Březina, 'Dithyramb of the Worlds', in Selver (ed.), *An Anthology of Modern Bohemian Poetry*, p. 50.
41. Boris Petrovsky [Katherine Mansfield], 'The Earth-Child in the Grass', *Rhythm*, 8 (September 1912), p. 125; Petr Bezruč, 'Who Will Take My Place?', in Selver (ed.), *An Anthology of Modern Bohemian Poetry*, p. 33.

42. As Gerri Kimber and Angela Smith observe in an editorial note to the poem 'Jangling Memory': 'An odd feature of the poems attributed to Boris Petrovsky, as here, is that they are often written from a female perspective'. Gerri Kimber and Angela Smith (eds), *The Poetry and Critical Writings of Katherine Mansfield* (Edinburgh: Edinburgh University Press, 2014), p. 84.
43. David Lloyd, *Nationalism and Minor Literature: James Clarence Mangan and the Emergence of Irish Cultural Nationalism* (London: University of California Press, 1987), p. 103.
44. Ibid., p. 104.
45. Ibid., p. 115.
46. Ibid., pp. 114–15.
47. Ibid., p. 113.
48. Ibid., p. 19.
49. Franco Moretti, *The Way of the World: The Bildungsroman in European Culture* (London: Verso, 1987); Jed Esty, *Unseasonable Youth: Modernism, Colonialism, and the Fiction of Development* (Oxford: Oxford University Press, 2012).
50. Lloyd, *Nationalism and Minor Literature*, pp. 19, 9.
51. Ibid.
52. Ibid. p. 22.
53. Ibid., p. 128.
54. Paul Selver, 'Modern Bohemian Poetry', in *An Anthology of Modern Bohemian Poetry*, p. 16.
55. 'K.M.' [Katherine Mansfield], '*An Anthology of Modern Bohemian Poetry* by P. Selver', *Rhythm*, 9 (October 1912), p. 235.
56. Selver, 'Modern Bohemian Poetry', p. 4.
57. Ibid., p. 11.
58. Mansfield, '*An Anthology of Modern Bohemian Poetry* by P. Selver', p. 235.
59. Ibid.
60. Ibid.
61. Selver, 'Modern Bohemian Poetry', p. 10.
62. Katherine Mansfield, 'Floryan Nachdenklich', *Saturday Westminster Gazette*, 41.6129 (18 January 1913), p. 7.
63. Gerri Kimber, '"That Pole outside our door": Floryan Sobieniowski and Katherine Mansfield', in Janka Kascakova and Gerri Kimber (eds), *Katherine Mansfield and Continental Europe* (Basingstoke: Palgrave Macmillan, 2015), p. 76.
64. Floryan Sobieniowski, 'Stanislaw Wyspianski – 1868–1907', *Rhythm*, 11 (December 1912), pp. 311, 316.
65. Ibid., pp. 315–16.
66. Michael J. Mikoś, *Polish Literature from 1864 to 1918: Realism and Young Poland* (Bloomington: Slavica, 2006), p. 237.
67. Katherine Mansfield, 'To Stanisław Wyspiański', in Gerri Kimber and Angela Smith (eds), *The Poetry and Critical Writings of Katherine Mansfield* (Edinburgh: Edinburgh University Press, 2014), p. 74.
68. Kimber, 'Mansfield, *Rhythm* and the Émigré Connection', p. 24.
69. Katherine Mansfield, *The Collected Letters of Katherine Mansfield, Volume I: 1903–1917*, ed. Vincent O'Sullivan and Margaret Scott (Oxford: Clarendon Press, 1984), p. 93.
70. Quoted in Jeffrey Meyers, 'Katherine Mansfield's "To Stanislaw Wyspianski"', *Modern Fiction Studies*, 24.3 (autumn 1978), p. 340.
71. Ibid.

72. Selver, 'Modern Bohemian Poetry', p. 20.
73. Katherine Mansfield, 'Pastiche: Green Goggles', *New Age*, 11.10 (4 July 1912), p. 237.
74. For further analysis of the rivalry and inter-textual exchanges between *The New Age* and *Rhythm*, see Faith Binckes, 'Lines of Engagement: *Rhythm*, Reproduction, and the Textual Dialogues of Early Modernism', in Suzanne W. Churchill and Adam McKible (eds), *Little Magazines and Modernism: New Approaches* (Aldershot: Ashgate, 2007), pp. 21–34.
75. Anon. [A. R. Orage], 'Present-Day Criticism', *New Age*, 10.22 (28 March 1912), p. 519.
76. Anon. [A. R. Orage], 'Present-Day Criticism', *New Age*, 10.25 (18 April 1912), p. 589.
77. Orage, 'Present-Day Criticism', *New Age*, 10.22 (28 March 1912), p. 519.
78. Anon. [Beatrice Hastings], 'The Model Boys-Will-Be-Boys Pseudo-Intellectual Magazine', *New Age*, 10.23 (4 April 1912), p. 548.
79. Ibid.
80. Ibid.
81. Alice Morning [Beatrice Hastings], 'The Changeling', *New Age*, 12.9 (2 January 1913), p. 212.
82. Paul Selver, 'Readers and Writers', *New Age*, 13.10 (3 July 1913), p. 265.
83. Orage, 'Present-Day Criticism', *New Age*, 10.22 (28 March 1912), p. 519.
84. Homi K. Bhabha, *The Location of Culture*, rev. edn (London: Routledge, 2004), pp. 126, 123.
85. Ibid., p. 122.
86. Quoted in Meyers, 'Katherine Mansfield's "To Stanislaw Wyspianski"', p. 340.
87. For Mansfield's identification with the political struggle for Irish independence, see Mansfield, *The Collected Letters of Katherine Mansfield, Volume I*, p. 265: 'It is still awfully difficult to credit what has happened and what is happening in Ireland. One cant [*sic*] get round it – This shooting, Beatrice, this incredible shooting of people! [. . .] I can understand how it must fill your thoughts – for if Ireland were New Zealand and such a thing had happened there . . . it would mean the same for me – It would really (as *un*fortunately George-Out-of-Wells would say) Matter Tremendously . . .'. See also p. 271: 'Heavens! What a sight it was but they all looked very happy and they all wore bunches of green ribbon or green badges – I very nearly joined them and I rather wish I had.'
88. Mansfield, 'To Stanisław Wyspiański', p. 74.
89. Katherine Mansfield, 'Sea Song', *Rhythm*, 14 (March 1913), p. 453.
90. Katherine Mansfield, 'The Sea Child', *Rhythm*, 5 (June 1912), p. 1; 'Sea', *Rhythm*, 11 (December 1912), p. 307.
91. Katherine Mansfield, 'The Opal Dream Cave', *Rhythm*, 11 (December 1912), p. 306; 'Sea', p. 307.
92. Bhabha, *The Location of Culture*, pp. 325, 321.
93. John Middleton Murry and Katherine Mansfield, 'The Meaning of Rhythm', *Rhythm*, 5 (June 1912), p. 18.
94. Ibid.
95. Ibid., p. 19.
96. Ibid.
97. Ibid., pp. 20, 18.
98. Murry and Mansfield, 'Seriousness in Art', p. 49.
99. Frederick Goodyear, 'The New Thelema', *Rhythm*, 1 (summer 1911), p. 1.
100. Smith, *Katherine Mansfield*, p. 82.

101. Goodyear, 'The New Thelema', p. 2.
102. Ibid., p. 1.
103. Mark Antliff, *Inventing Bergson: Cultural Politics and the Parisian Avant-Garde* (Princeton: Princeton University Press, 1993), p. 82.
104. Michael T. H. Sadler, 'After Gauguin', *Rhythm*, 4 (spring 1912), p. 24.
105. Quoted in Charles Harrison, Francis Frascina and Gill Perry (eds), *Primitivism, Cubism, Abstraction: The Early Twentieth Century* (London: Open University Press, 1994), p. 139.
106. Richard Lehan, 'Bergson and the Discourse of the Moderns', in Frederick Burwick and Paul Douglass (eds), *Crisis of Modernism* (Cambridge: Cambridge University Press, 1992), pp. 307–8.
107. Rollo Myers, 'The Art of Claude Debussy', *Rhythm*, 2 (autumn 1911), p. 33.
108. Sadler, 'After Gauguin', p. 23.
109. As examined in the previous section of the chapter, Mansfield clearly identified with the Russian 'neo-primitives' who were associated with *Der Blaue Reiter*, such as Natalia Goncharova. This section of the chapter suggests that this identification was complicated by Mansfield's short story contributions.
110. Wassily Kandinsky, *The Art of Spiritual Harmony*, trans. Michael T. H. Sadler (London: Constable, 1914), p. 6. Kandinsky and Sadler corresponded about *Der Blaue Reiter Almanach*, which suggests that the German magazine provided a model for the editors of *Rhythm*.
111. David Boyd Haycock, *A Crisis of Brilliance: Five Young British Artists and the Great War* (London: Old Street Publishing, 2009), p. 91.
112. Holbrook Jackson, 'A Plea for Revolt in Attitude', *Rhythm*, 3 (winter 1911), p. 9.
113. Ibid., p. 10.
114. Goodyear, 'The New Thelema', pp. 1–2.
115. Ibid., p. 3.
116. Ibid.
117. Ibid., pp. 2–3.
118. Johannes Fabian, *Time and the Other: How Anthropology Makes Its Object* (New York: Columbia University Press, 1983), p. 17.
119. Francis Carco, 'Lettre de Paris', *Rhythm*, 6 (July 1912), p. 66.
120. Murry, 'Art and Philosophy', p. 10.
121. Murry and Mansfield, 'The Meaning of Rhythm', p. 20.
122. Angela Smith, 'Katherine Mansfield and *Rhythm*', *Journal of New Zealand Literature*, 21 (2003), p. 104.
123. Antliff, *Inventing Bergson*, p. 85.
124. Iris Marion Young, 'The Scaling of Bodies and the Politics of Identity', in Linda McDowell and Joanne Sharp (eds), *Space, Gender, Knowledge: Feminist Readings* (London: Arnold, 1997), p. 221.
125. Patrick Collier, 'Imperial/Modernist Forms in the *Illustrated London News*', *Modernism/Modernity*, 19.3 (September 2012), p. 499.
126. Catherine Nash, 'Remapping the Body/Land: Cartographies of Identity, Gender, and Landscape in Ireland', in Alison Blunt and Gillian Rose (eds), *Writing Women and Space: Colonial and Postcolonial Geographies* (New York: Guildford Press, 1994), p. 234.
127. Anne McClintock, *Imperial Leather: Race, Gender and Sexuality in the Colonial Contest* (New York: Routledge, 1995).
128. Gillian Rose, *Feminism and Geography: The Limits of Geographical Knowledge* (Minneapolis: University of Minneapolis Press, 1993), pp. 97–9.

129. Anne Estelle Rice, 'Les Ballets Russes', *Rhythm*, 7 (August 1912), p. 108.
130. Murry, 'Art and Philosophy', p. 11; Laurence Binyon, 'The Return to Poetry', *Rhythm*, 4 (spring 1912), p. 2.
131. Binckes, *Modernism, Magazines, and the British Avant-Garde*, p. 79.
132. Francis Carco, 'Aprés Minuit', *Rhythm*, 3 (winter 1911), pp. 25–7.
133. Claudien, 'Une Vie', *Rhythm*, 4 (spring 1912), p. 33.
134. Antliff, *Inventing Bergson*, pp. 73–6.
135. See, for example, J. D. Fergusson, 'Drawing', *Rhythm*, 6 (July 1912), p. 42; 'Study', *Rhythm*, 7 (August 1912), p. 98.
136. John Middleton Murry, 'Life', *Rhythm*, 3 (winter 1911), p. 17.
137. Binckes, *Modernism, Magazines, and the British Avant-Garde*, p. 159.
138. Carol A. Nathanson, 'Anne Estelle Rice: Theodore Dreiser's "Ellen Adams Wrynn"', *Women's Art Journal*, 13.2 (autumn 1992–winter 1993), p. 5.
139. Ibid.
140. Julian Park, 'Priestcraft', *Rhythm*, 2 (autumn 1911), p. 21.
141. W. L. George, 'The Negress', *Rhythm*, 3 (winter 1911), p. 5.
142. Ibid.
143. Ibid.
144. Smith, *Katherine Mansfield*, pp. 78–80; Smith, '"As fastidious as though I wrote with acid"', p. 15.
145. Carol A. Nathanson, *The Expressive Fauvism of Anne Estelle Rice* (New York: Hollis Taggert Galleries, 1997), p. 9.
146. Katherine Mansfield, 'The Woman at the Store', *Rhythm*, 4 (spring 1912), p. 7.
147. Ibid. p. 8.
148. Ibid. pp. 11; 17–18.
149. Ibid., p. 16.
150. Ibid., pp. 11, 13.
151. Ibid., pp. 16, 19.
152. Ibid., p. 21.
153. Mark Williams, 'Mansfield in Maoriland: Biculturalism, Agency and Misreading', in Howard Booth and Nigel Rigby (eds), *Modernism and Empire* (Manchester: Manchester University Press, 2000), p. 258.
154. Mansfield's story 'Millie' (published in *The Blue Review* in June 1913) also parodies the tropes of this genre.
155. Lydia Wevers, 'The Short Story', in Terry Sturm (ed.), *The Oxford History of New Zealand Literature in English* (Oxford: Oxford University Press, 1991), pp. 217–18.
156. Carey Snyder, 'Katherine Mansfield, *Rhythm*, and Metropolitan Primitivism', *Journal of Modern Periodical Studies*, 5.2 (2014), pp. 139–60.
157. Mansfield, 'The Woman at the Store', pp. 19, 14.
158. Kandinsky, *The Art of Spiritual Harmony*, p. 6.
159. Mansfield, 'The Woman at the Store', p. 13.
160. Similarly, 'Jo' and 'Hin' become (the clearly male) 'Joe' and 'Jim' in later republications of the story by Murry.
161. Pamela Dunbar, *Radical Mansfield: Double Discourse in Katherine Mansfield's Short Stories* (London: Macmillan, 1997), p. 45.
162. Mansfield, 'The Woman at the Store', p. 7.
163. Ibid.
164. Ibid., p. 8.
165. Kate Krueger, *British Women Writers and the Short Story, 1850–1930: Reclaiming Social Space* (Basingstoke: Palgrave Macmillan, 2014), p. 14.

166. Mansfield, 'The Woman at the Store', pp. 16, 14.
167. Ibid., p. 14.
168. Ibid., pp. 12–13.
169. Arthur Crossthwaite, 'A Railway Vision', *Rhythm*, 3 (winter 1911), p. 34.
170. Mansfield, 'The Woman at the Store', p. 12.
171. Ibid., p. 21.
172. Mansfield, 'Ole Underwood', *Rhythm*, 12 (January 1913), p. 335.
173. Ibid., pp. 334–7.
174. Ibid., p. 336.
175. Ibid.
176. Ibid., p. 335.
177. Dunbar, *Radical Mansfield*, pp. 49–50.
178. Mansfield, 'Ole Underwood', p. 334.
179. Quoted in Saikat Majumdar, *Prose of the World: Modernism and the Banality of Empire* (New York: Columbia University Press, 2013), p. 95. See also Snyder, 'Katherine Mansfield, *Rhythm*, and Modernist Primitivism', pp. 146–50.
180. Murry, 'Coming to London', p. 100.
181. Lili Heron [Katherine Mansfield], 'How Pearl Button Was Kidnapped', *Rhythm*, 8 (September 1912), p. 136.
182. Ibid., p. 137.
183. Ibid., p. 136.
184. Ibid., p. 139.
185. Anna Snaith, *Modernist Voyages: Colonial Women Writers in London, 1890–1945* (Cambridge: Cambridge University Press, 2014), p. 124.
186. Ibid.
187. Ibid., pp. 127–8.
188. Janka Kascakova, 'Katherine Mansfield's "How Pearl Button Was Kidnapped"', *Explicator*, 72.2 (2014), p. 120; Mansfield, 'How Pearl Button Was Kidnapped', p. 136.
189. This nickname stuck, with both Mansfield and Murry continuing to refer to the other as 'Tig' and 'Wig'.
190. 'The Tiger' [Katherine Mansfield], 'Sunday Lunch', *Rhythm*, 9 (October 1912), p. 223.
191. Ibid.
192. Ibid., p. 225.
193. Katherine Mansfield, *The Collected Letters of Katherine Mansfield, Volume III: 1919–1920*, ed. Vincent O'Sullivan and Margaret Scott (Oxford: Clarendon Press, 1993), p. 42.
194. Katherine Mansfield, *The Collected Letters of Katherine Mansfield, Volume II: 1918–1919*, ed. Vincent O'Sullivan and Margaret Scott (Oxford: Clarendon Press, 1987), p. 168.
195. Ibid., p. 336.
196. Ibid., p. 341.
197. Aimee Gasston, 'Katherine Mansfield, Cannibal', in Janet Wilson, Gerri Kimber and Delia da Sousa Correa (eds), *Katherine Mansfield and the (Post)colonial* (Edinburgh: Edinburgh University Press, 2013), p. 20.
198. Mansfield, 'Sunday Lunch', p. 224.
199. Ibid.
200. Ibid.
201. Gasston, 'Katherine Mansfield, Cannibal', p. 21.

202. Katherine Mansfield, 'Je ne parle pas français', in *The Collected Fiction of Katherine Mansfield, 1916–1922*, ed. Gerri Kimber and Vincent O'Sullivan (Edinburgh: Edinburgh University Press, 2012), p. 119.
203. Ibid., p. 117.
204. Smith, *Katherine Mansfield*, pp. 15, 19.
205. Jenny McDonnell, *Katherine Mansfield and the Modernist Marketplace: At the Mercy of the Public* (Basingstoke: Palgrave Macmillan, 2010), p. 114.
206. Mansfield, *The Collected Letters of Katherine Mansfield, Volume II*, p. 52.
207. Mansfield, 'Je ne parle pas français', pp. 117, 122, 119.
208. McDonnell, *Katherine Mansfield and the Modernist Marketplace*, p. 113.
209. Murry, 'Art and Philosophy', p. 11.
210. Mansfield, 'Je ne parle pas français', p. 113.
211. McDonnell, *Katherine Mansfield and the Modernist Marketplace*, p. 112.
212. Mansfield, 'Je ne parle pas français', pp. 112–13.
213. Ibid., p. 114.
214. Ibid., p. 134.
215. Ibid., pp. 124, 121.
216. Ibid., p. 113.
217. Ibid., p. 117.
218. Ibid., p. 118.
219. Ibid., p. 133.
220. Ibid., p. 117.
221. Ibid., p. 116.
222. Snaith, *Modernist Voyages*, p. 124.
223. Smith, *Katherine Mansfield*, p. 20.
224. Elleke Boehmer, 'Mansfield as Colonial Modernist: Difference Within', in Gerri Kimber and Janet Wilson (eds), *Celebrating Katherine Mansfield* (Basingstoke: Palgrave Macmillan, 2011), pp. 68–9.
225. Ibid., p. 69.
226. Ibid.
227. Mansfield, 'Je ne parle pas français', p. 116.
228. Edward Said, *Beginnings: Intention and Method* (New York: Columbia University Press, 1975), p. xiii.
229. Bhabha, *The Location of Culture*, p. 122 (original emphasis).
230. Mansfield, *The Collected Letters of Katherine Mansfield, Volume I*, p. 225.
231. Katherine Mansfield, *Journal of Katherine Mansfield: Definitive Edition*, ed. John Middleton Murry (London: Constable, 1954), pp. 123–4.
232. Mansfield, *The Collected Letters of Katherine Mansfield, Volume III*, p. 250
233. Mansfield, *The Collected Letters of Katherine Mansfield, Volume I*, p. 124.
234. Antony Alpers, *The Life of Katherine Mansfield*, rev. edn (Harmondsworth: Penguin, 1982), p. 157.
235. Mansfield, *The Collected Letters of Katherine Mansfield, Volume I*, p. 120.

APRIL 11, 1919 No. 4641

THE ATHENÆUM

A JOURNAL OF LITERATURE, SCIENCE AND THE ARTS

THE NEW IMPERATIVE

WHETHER we will or not, the war has been the dividing line between one epoch of the spirit and another. Possibly to a remoter eye than ours what went before and what will come after will not appear to have a frontier more absolute than that which separates two phases of a single movement; it is also possible that the break will seem sudden and abrupt, like an old Roman road ending high in air on a cliff-edge. It may prove to have been of spiritual advantage that material civilization should again become, for the majority of men, rudimentary. The choice between material comfort and intellectual leisure may become a dilemma, so that plain living would be the necessary condition of high thinking instead of its fitful accompaniment. Unfortunately, this Stoic, yet not uninviting vista is not the only one we can discern. Material impoverishment may also degrade the spirit, at least for a season long enough to outlast the life of anyone now in the springtime of his intellectual powers. We may be so much the children of our age that nothing less than a century will suffice to wean us from our comfortable mother, and in the process we may grow to old men, and eventually die without having achieved immunity from infant maladies.

And if by the compulsion of material conditions we may be driven to make our choice between the life of the spirit and the life of ease, on the spiritual side the *decree nisi* has already been made absolute. The decision of the spirit is taken; it could fall only in one way. It accepts and realizes the truth that reason and imagination have no validity in the real world; it also knows that the only civilization that can rightly wear the name, and the only tradition that is not merely animal, are based upon reason and imagination. Civilization and the tradition are no more than the homage paid to reason and imagination by mankind at large. When the habit of homage has been lost--and who knows whether it may not have been lost for ever during this four years' moratorium?—civilization and the tradition are moribund. They are then nothing more than the secret language of a little band of old believers.

Perhaps they never were really anything more. But they believed they were; they were allowed and encouraged to believe they were. Possibly they will be encouraged still to believe in their own sovereignty. After all, they showed themselves gullible enough, and there is no obvious reason why the attempt to gull them should not be renewed. Nevertheless, we believe that they will not be deceived again, not, at least, for many years; and this new realism will be the quality which will distinguish the coming epocn from that which went before it. The spirit is now like a man who has learned that he is suffering from a mortal disease. His brain begins to work transparently clear. He has nothing but a polite and incredulous smile for the protesting friends who tell him he will live to be as old as Methuselah and as glorious as Solomon. They bore him. Moreover, they distract him from his work. To his new vision it is clear how much there is to do. He does not believe that there is anything to be gained by doing it; he knows that death may overtake him at any moment and all his achievements crumble into indistinguishable dust. Yet the desire that his work should be perfect and without flaw consumes him with a hundred times fiercer flame. He sees a new satisfaction, and is assailed by a new imperative.

And this new imperative is categorical, though not in the sense in which Kant persuaded himself that his was. It is a paradoxical imperative, deriving its strength and urgency from the very realization that it is not universal, and may even cease to be felt at all. We begin to see that the life of the spirit, because it must henceforward be lived in and for itself, may be triumphant as it never could have been while it was enthroned; and we begin to understand, translated into subtler loyalties, the impulse and the victory of those Roman senators who took their solemn seats in the Capitol and arranged their robes with the greater dignity because the republic over which they ruled had been overwhelmed by the barbarian onset.

CONTENTS

Figure 3.1 *The Athenaeum*

Chapter 3

The Athenaeum: 'Wanted, a New Word' (World)

In June 1920, Katherine Mansfield set down her most developed exposition of what she understood by modern short fiction in a review for *The Athenaeum* titled 'Wanted, a New Word'. Clare Hanson has described this as 'virtually the only "manifesto" KM produced for the kind of fiction she herself wrote'.[1] When Murry later collected this review in *Novels and Novelists* (1930), however, he erroneously gave it the title 'Wanted, a New World', which was then subsequently used in Hanson's edition of *The Critical Writings of Katherine Mansfield* (1987) and in B. J. Kirkpatrick's *A Bibliography of Katherine Mansfield* (1989). This slippage not only calls attention to the mutability of Mansfield's writing as it passed through different textual transmissions, encouraging us to return to the original sites of publication in periodicals and magazines, but also suggests a direct correlation between her ideas of modernist formal experimentation and a geographical imaginary of discovery.

Indeed, after the death of her brother in October 1915, when Mansfield travelled to the south of France, she made a series of famous notebook entries linking her commitment to finding a new 'form' with making the 'undiscovered country leap into the eyes of the old world'. The 'form that I would choose has changed utterly', she wrote, addressing her brother; 'I feel no longer concerned with the same appearance of things':

> Oh, I want for one moment to make our undiscovered country leap into the eyes of the old world. It must be mysterious, as though floating – it must take the breath. It must be 'one of those islands' [. . .] Then I want to write poetry. I feel always trembling on the brink of poetry. [. . .] But especially I want to write a kind of long elegy to you – perhaps not in poetry. No, perhaps in Prose – almost certainly in a kind of special *prose*.[2]

Mansfield instinctively reaches for a spatial vocabulary of empire when thinking about writing and language here, positioning herself as a New

Zealander narrating the colonial nation (the 'new world') within the context of the European 'old world'. Subsequently, metaphors of the 'undiscovered', 'unexplored' and 'hidden country' begin to recur with astonishing frequency in Mansfield's letters to describe her formal approach to fiction. Writing to J. D. Fergusson in September 1918, for example, she states that 'it is extraordinary how little people have done – at any rate – at my job – and how content they have been with the chance encounter or a matrimonial stodge. All that lies between is almost undiscovered and unexplored.'[3] In a letter written to Ottoline Morrell in July 1919, likewise, in which she notes the 'peculiar *male* arrogance' of writers such as Joyce and Pound, Mansfield observes:

> I *do* believe that the time has come for a 'new word' but I imagine the new word will not be spoken easily. People have never explored the lovely medium of prose. It is a hidden country still – I feel that so profoundly.[4]

Similarly, writing to the painter Dorothy Brett, Mansfield consistently employed the idea of the 'undiscovered' to describe their artistic endeavours. In 1920, for example, she asks what urges them as artists to 'feel that you *must* make *your* discovery and that I *must* make *mine*?'[5] On another occasion, with paradoxical playfulness, she tells Brett: 'Do come soon and tell me of your discovery if its undiscoverable'.[6] Then later: 'I always feel I am at sea – on a ship – anchored before a new, undiscovered country'.[7]

As Angela Smith notes, Mansfield derived the phrase 'undiscovered country' from Shakespeare's Hamlet, for whom it is death, the destination from which no traveller returns.[8] It is tempting, therefore, to interpret Mansfield's commitment to finding a new form after 1915 through the biographical contexts of her brother's death, and this is overwhelmingly the position that critics have adopted. Furthermore, it is regularly noted that the intensification and illumination of the everyday that Mansfield identified as the quality of 'special prose' ('all must be told with a sense of mystery, a radiance, an after glow') became the defining characteristic of her best-known stories, written in the last years of her life and set in the New Zealand of her youth, such as 'Prelude', 'At the Bay', 'The Doll's House' and 'The Garden Party'.[9] What has not been examined, however, are the ways in which Mansfield's interrelated ideas of a 'new word' and an undiscovered, unexplored 'new world' were also conditioned by the wider cultural contexts of periodical publication, rather than by feelings of personal loss and grief, and the extent to which these ideas shaped not just Mansfield's late short stories but also the critical vocabulary that she employed in her literary reviews.

This chapter examines the ways in which Mansfield linked the 'new word' of modernist formal experimentation with the spatial imaginary of a 'new world' throughout her contributions to *The Athenaeum*, a periodical edited by Murry from early 1919. Unlike the coterie magazines that Murry had previously edited, *The Athenaeum* was an established periodical with established credentials. First launched in 1828, it had gained a reputation as 'the mirror of Victorian culture'.[10] Under the editorship of the political journalist Arthur Greenwood during the First World War, however, *The Athenaeum* was reimagined as a 'Journal of Reconstruction'; the quality of the periodical's literary content diminished, with Greenwood instead focusing almost exclusively on the political, economic and social issues arising from the war. As Mansfield observed in a letter to Ottoline Morrell composed in February 1919, for example: 'The dreadful truth is, of course that for the last 2 years the A. has not been literary at all but a journal of reconstruction concerned especially with problems such as: Why should not every Working mans [*sic*] Cottage have its P.W.C?'[11] With the financial backing of the chocolatier Arnold Rowntree, Murry was tasked with returning the periodical to its pre-war character as a literary review, and was given three months to prepare his first issue, published on 4 April 1919.

As Michael Whitworth has observed, 'Murry had a sense of mission about the editorship: he wanted to make the journal a success again, "as a duty to literature & my country"; to fail would be "an act of treachery to English literature"'.[12] Whilst he retained the conservative typography and layout of *The Athenaeum* (Figure 3.1), Murry turned the periodical into a vital organ for an emerging 'modernist' literary culture in Britain, assembling a team of regular contributors culled from the artistic circles of Bloomsbury and Garsington. These included Leonard and Virginia Woolf, T. S. Eliot, Aldous Huxley, Bertrand Russell, Lytton Strachey and his brother James, Clive Bell, Roger Fry and E. M. Forster. Virginia Woolf identified Murry's periodical as having 'the most brilliant list of contributors on record'.[13] Similarly, after reading through the second issue of the periodical, Lytton Strachey wrote to Ottoline Morrell describing *The Athenaeum* as 'a great addition to existence'.[14] As David Goldie has observed, *The Athenaeum* was 'for a short time the pre-eminent literary journal in England'.[15] From April 1919 until February 1921, when Murry announced that he would be resigning as editor and that the periodical would be merged with *The Nation*, *The Athenaeum* succeeded in bringing together a set of contributors of whom the majority, in the words of Oscar Wellens, 'were soon to emerge as the shapers of a new literary and critical culture in Britain'.[16] On hearing of the periodical's demise, for example, H. G. Wells referred to *The Athenaeum* as having been 'the one hope of literary decency in England'.[17] Likewise, Eliot later described 'the brief and brilliant life of the *Athenaeum* under Mr Middleton Murry' as 'a high summer of literary journalism'.[18]

Katherine Mansfield was central to this success. Between April 1919 and December 1920, Mansfield put creative writing on hold as she worked overtime to meet the demands of reviewing for *The Athenaeum*, writing at least one literary review, and sometimes two or three, each week. After she travelled to the Italian Riviera due to worsening illness, Murry regularly wrote to Mansfield with letters obviously intended to raise her spirits but which nevertheless give a clear indication of how highly her reviews were held in esteem back in England:

> Tommy [H. M. Tomlinson] told me the other day that he was talking to a sub-editor of the *Weekly Dispatch*, just a hardened professional journalist, and he asked him what he thought of the *Athenaeum*. He said he thought it jolly good, but one thing especially. He would buy it for K.M.'s article alone, every week. [. . .] So keep it up my darling & send me an extra article when you can. You'll be making a terrific reputation for yourself before the winter's out.[19]

At dinner parties, guests would agree that Mansfield's 'novel-reviews were the finest in England' and Murry became convinced that 'there can't be a really bad number of the *Athenaeum*' so long as 'your novel page is there': 'It's quite unlike – in a different class to – anything that's being done in the way of reviewing anywhere to-day'.[20]

Given this almost ingratiating praise, it is perhaps surprising that Murry consistently gave Mansfield novels to critique that were, in the words of her first review, nothing more than 'little puppets, little make-believes, playthings on strings with the same stare and the same sawdust filling'.[21] When she wrote to Murry as the centenary of George Eliot's birth approached in late 1919, asking him to send a life of the author and some of the novels so that she could write the leader that would undoubtedly be published in *The Athenaeum*, for instance, Murry not only failed to send these books but also gave the leader to Mansfield's cousin, Sydney Waterlow. As Angela Smith has observed, Mansfield's letters to Murry at this time contain astute observations about Shakespeare, Chekhov, Dickens and Keats, 'all of which cry out for fuller treatment' in *The Athenaeum*.[22] In the face of this apparent refusal to entrust Mansfield with appraising illustrious, canonical writers, scholars have often adopted a rather indignant attitude towards Murry on Mansfield's behalf, inferring that he did not consider her to be sufficiently intellectual or well educated enough to handle such material.

This inference, however, fails to recognise the important and unique place that Mansfield's 'novel page' occupied within *The Athenaeum*. In one of her reviews, Mansfield writes that in 'seeking for pearls in such a prodigious number of new books':

> What is extremely impressive to the novel reviewer is the modesty of the writers – their diffidence in declaring themselves what they are – their almost painful belief that they must model themselves on somebody. [. . .] One would imagine that round the corner there was a little band of jeering, sneering, superior persons ready to leap up and laugh if the cut of the new-comer's jacket is not of the strangeness they consider admissible. In the name of the new novel, the new sketch, the new story, if they are really there, let us defy them.[23]

Challenging the contemporary writer to defy convention and tradition, Mansfield's reviews countered the seriousness of established literary criticism, and she adopted a writing voice that was by contrast disarmingly conversational and witty. In a letter to Murry, Mansfield echoes this idea of the 'little band of jeering, sneering, superior' critics when she writes:

> One must have an open mind. Its [*sic*] so difficult not to find a *sneerer*. Whats [*sic*] the good of sneering? Imagine what Strachey or V.W. would think of a man like Brett Young – but hes [*sic*] WORTH considering. One must keep a balance – i.e. one must be critical. Theres [*sic*] your mighty pull over your whole generation – and there's what's going to make the Athenaeum what it is in your imagination.[24]

Mansfield viewed the openness of her 'novel page' to all kinds of writing as integral to the success of *The Athenaeum*. In October 1919, likewise, Murry wrote to Mansfield: 'I want the *Athenaeum* to be judicial, to praise what is really good *wherever* it comes from'.[25] The following month, she writes: 'Thats [*sic*] what I like about the A. – the way it *steadies* opinion'.[26] What we would term today 'popular' or 'middlebrow' writers were 'worth considering' for Mansfield because their work provided 'balance' and steadied opinion, and it was only by being receptive to all writing that the critic might perceive the coming of the 'new word' in a novel, sketch or story.

As such, Mansfield considered her reviewing to be part of a vital post-war project of cultural rejuvenation that would pave the way for the arrival of a 'new word'. Whilst she ultimately finds Francis Brett Young's novel *The Young Physician* 'readable to a fault' and too focused on providing 'entertainment' for an 'impatient public', for instance, she also perceives in it 'a very honest sincere attempt to face the great difficulty which presents itself to the writers of to-day – which is to find their true expression and to make it adequate to the new fields of experience':

> [W]e live in an age of experiment, when the next novel may be unlike any novel that has been published before; when writers are seeking after new forms in which to express something more subtle, more complex, 'nearer' the truth; when a few of them feel that perhaps after all prose is an almost undiscovered medium and that there are extraordinary, thrilling possibilities. . . .[27]

This example highlights the way in which Mansfield used unpromising or unsuccessful material in her reviews for *The Athenaeum* in order to carve out her own ideas about the 'thrilling possibilities' of formal innovation. The 'middlebrow' writers were important for Mansfield in revealing this vacuum in post-war literature, an 'undiscovered' space that would be filled with 'new forms' able to adequately express the 'new fields of experience' created by the war. Mansfield's reviews therefore demand closer attention, not just for what they tell us about individual writers and works, but also for what they reveal about the development of Mansfield's own ideas about literature and modernist formal experimentation after the war.

Mansfield's light, conversational tone in her 'novel page', coupled with the fact that the majority of books that she reviewed have not stood the test of time, perhaps accounts for the fact that scholars have often underestimated or discounted the importance of her critical writings. Rather than thinking about the historical circumstances or print contexts underpinning her reviews, most commentators have emphasised biographical contexts to explain Mansfield's association with *The Athenaeum*. In particular, on the rare occasions that they have been discussed, Mansfield's critical writings have often been interpreted as motivated either by feelings of duty towards Murry or by feelings of resentment towards Virginia Woolf. Marysa Demoor, for example, implies that Mansfield's decision to work for the periodical was motivated by a desire to 'establish her husband's renommée as an editor'.[28] Similarly, Wellens interprets Mansfield's commitment to reviewing as a sign that she 'gave her active support to her husband's performance of his editorial obligations'.[29] Most significantly, Mansfield's review of Woolf's novel *Night and Day* in November 1919 has dominated discussions of her association with *The Athenaeum*. As Jenny McDonnell has observed, this has had the effect of 'reducing almost two years of her professional writing career to the composition of a solitary review'.[30] Invariably interpreted as an expression of Mansfield's feelings of resentment towards the older writer's burgeoning success, the review of *Night and Day* has led scholars such as David Dowling to argue that the entirety of Mansfield's critical writings were blinkered by feelings of jealousy towards contemporaries and feelings of inadequacy towards writers of the past, such as Chekhov.[31] Such biographical exaggerations and inaccuracies, as McDonnell has argued, give insufficient consideration to the material that Mansfield actually wrote and to the publishing environment of *The Athenaeum*, aspects that have garnered greater critical attention in McDonnell's own scholarship, as well as in work by Clare Hanson and Angela Smith.[32]

Far from being the dutiful appendage to her husband, Mansfield was incredibly active in the production of *The Athenaeum*. This is highlighted in the letters that she wrote to Murry whilst she was living abroad. Composing long letters critiquing individual issues of the periodical, Mansfield often states with emphasis: '*This one simply thrills me*'; or, 'that *PAPER. It simply fascinates me*. If only I were by your side, sharing the work more, discussing it more, seeing the people more, helping more.'[33] In one letter, she exclaims 'The Athenaeum for Ever!!!!!' and describes the periodical as 'our future'.[34] After all, *The Athenaeum* was not only increasing Murry's 'renommée as an editor' but was also securing what he described as Mansfield's 'terrific reputation' as a critic. Mansfield certainly viewed the periodical as a joint enterprise, describing it as 'our paper' and stating 'We are both *slaves* to the Athene'.[35] Mansfield tells Murry that she is 'always thinking of the paper & wondering about it' and asks practical editorial questions, such as: 'How is our circulation?'[36] This involvement in the running of the periodical is demonstrated further when Mansfield returned to London in the spring of 1920. She writes to Sydney and Violet Schiff, for instance, describing how she is 'buried alive under the Athenaeum': 'this week is covered under manuscripts to be read, poems, essays to choose "finally," novels to review, schemes to draft, [and] an article to write on *why we intend to publish short stories*'.[37] In these letters, Mansfield highlights just how enthusiastically she endorsed and stoked the youthful idealism of the periodical:

> We discussed all the way home, a new Athenaeum – the idea of throwing overboard all the learned societies and ancient men and reviews of Dull old Tomes, and opening the windows to the hurrying sounds outside, and throwing all the old gang into the river.[38]

Mansfield was therefore clearly devoted to the periodical, far beyond a marital commitment to Murry as editor-husband, and this is demonstrated in just how seriously she approached the task of reviewing. Writing from Italy, she tells Murry: 'Its [*sic*] a thousand times harder for me to write reviews here [. . .] I have to get into full divers [*sic*] clothes & rake the floor of the unprofitable sea. All the same *it is my life: it saves me.*'[39] Considering her 'work' for *The Athenaeum* in October 1920, she again emphasises: '*I could not live here without it*'.[40] Similarly, Mansfield's notebooks from this time evidence how seriously she took the practice of reviewing. They contain remorselessly self-critical assessments of her own criticism: 'Not good enough. Uneven, shallow, forced. Very thin, pocket muslin handkerchief vocabulary!'; 'I did not say what I set out to say. It is not close knit enough'; 'Shows traces of hurry, & at the end, is pompous!'[41] Likewise, she regularly writes to Murry imploring him to be harsh in his criticism of her reviews and to haul her 'over the very hottest coals'.[42] For Mansfield, reviewing was a craft that required unremitting hard work. As such, the reviews deserve to be positioned as an important genre within Mansfield's oeuvre; Mansfield devoted almost two years of her late career to reviewing for *The Athenaeum*, and her critical writings demand renewed academic attention.

This chapter examines the ways in which ideas advanced within Mansfield's reviews were conditioned by the contexts of periodical publication, existing in dialogue with the work of other writers. In particular, the title that Murry later gave his autobiography for these years, *Between Two Worlds* (1935), suggests a point of entry for this chapter. As a contemporary reviewer of the book noted, the 'two worlds' of Murry's title 'will commonly be regarded as the world of phenomena or objective presentation, and the world of the spirit or subjective interpretation [. . .] But there is another possible reading of these two worlds, suggested by Mr Murry's text from Matthew Arnold.'[43] In 'Stanzas from the Grande Chartreuse', Arnold had described himself as '[w]andering between two worlds, one dead/The other powerless to be born'.[44] As I examine in the first section of this chapter, this notion of the 'two worlds' shaped the intellectual response to the First World War in *The Signature* and then *The Athenaeum*, with contributors consistently contrasting the old, pre-war world with an emerging, unrealised 'new world'. Furthermore, the 'new world' was regularly posited as a 'world of the spirit or subjective interpretation' in *The Athenaeum*, so that there was in fact much overlap between the twin readings of the 'two worlds' identified by Murry's reviewer. The second section of the chapter examines how this concept of a 'new world' of 'subjective interpretation' shaped Mansfield's critical vocabulary. Envisaging language as a negotiation between the 'inner' and 'outer' life throughout her critical writings, Mansfield developed notions of the liminal 'moment' and epiphanic 'revelation' as concepts mediating between the objective, exterior world and inner, spiritual world. As is examined, these conceptual ideas and individual word choices reflect an on-going dialogue between Mansfield's reviews and critical essays by Virginia Woolf outlining the aesthetic principles of literary impressionism, a dialogue that exemplifies the 'conversational model for modernism' that Churchill and McKible have suggested early twentieth-century periodicals looked to enact.[45] Rather than being motivated by feelings of jealousy or resentment towards Woolf, as scholars have previously asserted, therefore, Mansfield's critical writings for *The Athenaeum* provide a detailed and extensive material record of her sustained engagement with Woolf's writings.

Turning our attention to Mansfield's reviews for *The Athenaeum*, a considerable yet much overlooked body of work, we can trace how she formulated ideas about literature and modernist formal innovation in response to specific cultural and historical contexts as well as particular intellectual exchanges with individual writers such as Murry and Woolf. In particular, the critical vocabulary that Mansfield developed in *The Athenaeum* to articulate her sense of a coming 'new word' was shaped not just by a spatial imaginary of empire, of the 'new world' and 'undiscovered country', but also by the contemporary intellectual response to the First World War and the cultural shift from objective realism to the 'inner life' of literary impressionism. As such, Mansfield's literary reviews help to reveal the deeply historicised and highly relational model of creation that early twentieth-century periodicals sustained.

The spiritual crisis

In the autumn of 1915, Mansfield and Murry joined D. H. Lawrence in establishing a little magazine titled *The Signature*. The project had been suggested by Lawrence, who was motivated to do something in the face of the 'disintegration' of the First World War: 'One must speak for life and growth amid all this mass of destruction and disintegration', he declared to Harriet Monroe, and one must 'hold up the other, living truth, of Right, and pure reality, the reality of the clear, eternal spirit [. . .] So I bring out this little paper.'[46]

The Signature certainly was 'little'. Produced on cheap brown paper, it was neither attractive nor ambitious in scope, containing work only by Lawrence, Murry and Mansfield. To Cynthia Asquith, Lawrence professed: 'I don't want the *Signature* to be a "success", I want it only to rally together just a few passionate, vital, constructive people'.[47] Lawrence proposed to publish six issues of the magazine, with each issue serialising a section of his own philosophical meditation on the war, titled 'The Crown'. There needed to be 250 subscribers to pay for the 250 copies of each of the six issues: by 22 September, two days before Lawrence sent the printer the manuscript of the first part of 'The Crown' for the first issue, there were about thirty subscribers; by 2 October, when he had prepared all six parts, there were still only about fifty-six subscribers.[48] These included George Bernard Shaw, Albert Rothenstein, Frank Swinnerton, Clifford Bax and Lytton Strachey, yet with just a fifth of the total number of subscribers needed, *The Signature* could not continue; in the end, only three issues were published. The venture was patently not a success, and critics have subsequently tended to discount the significance of *The Signature* in Mansfield's career. Saralyn Daly, for example, dismisses the magazine as 'a short-lived fiasco'.[49] When it is considered, if at all, *The Signature* is often positioned as a brief coda to the publication history of *Rhythm* and *The Blue Review*, the venues in which Lawrence first came into contact with Murry and Mansfield. Peter Brooker, for example, writes that '*The Signature* brought the uneven, sometimes utopian, sometimes catastrophic adventures of three magazines and three publishers, heavy debts, and bankruptcies in a period of less than six years to an end'.[50] This narrative is mistaken, I believe. *The Signature* was important in Murry's progression as an editor and in Mansfield's development as a writer, not as a sorry endnote, but as the beginning of a trajectory that culminated, less than four years later, in Murry's resounding success at the helm of *The Athenaeum* and in the extensive body of critical writings that Mansfield produced for the latter periodical.

The main reason that Mansfield scholars have not examined *The Signature* in any depth is that she was clearly peripheral to the project.

Lawrence summarised the division of labour on the magazine in the same way across several letters, trying to secure subscriptions: 'I am going to do the preaching – sort of philosophy – the beliefs by which one can reconstruct the world: Murry will do his ideas on [. . .] freedom for the individual soul, Katharine [*sic*] Mansfield will do her little satirical sketches'.[51] Under the pseudonym Matilda Berry, Mansfield contributed to the magazine two short stories under the title 'Autumns' (the second story was later rewritten as 'The Wind Blows') as well as 'The Little Governess', which was published in the magazine in two parts. None of the stories had a direct connection to the war, which was the central subject of the essays by both Lawrence and Murry, and 'The Little Governess' had in fact first been intended for publication in an entirely different magazine, the New York-based 'magazine of cleverness' *The Smart Set*. As such, Mansfield's short stories in *The Signature* seem out of place, with each having little connection to the 'preaching' that flanked it. When Murry wrote to Mansfield asking her for more contributions, for example, she responded: 'Ill [*sic*] send you something for the Signature but don't flatter me – Im [*sic*] only the jam in the golden pill – and I know my place, Betsey'.[52]

The magazine, however, was important in introducing Mansfield to a certain vocabulary and mode of writing formulated in direct response to the 'disintegration' and 'destruction' of the war. Attempting to articulate 'the beliefs by which one can reconstruct the world' in *The Signature*, for instance, the phrase a 'new world' permeates Lawrence's writings at this time. At the end of December 1915, for example, he writes to Mansfield, who is in Bandol, France, telling her of the new life they must live and the 'new world' they must make:

> When you come back, I want you and Murry to live with us, or near us, in unanimity: not these separations. Let us all live together and create a new world. If it is too difficult in England, because here all is destruction and dying and corruption, let us go away to Florida: soon.[53]

Similarly, Lawrence wanted only 'people who really care, and who really want a new world, to subscribe' to *The Signature*.[54] This 'new world' would be brought about through a radical revolt against the past, emerging through a cyclical process of destruction and creation: 'We must let go of the old; when corruption is necessary, all must be given up to it; for then the creative process can and will begin again, a new dawn, a new world'.[55] This was the central idea around which Lawrence structured his allegorical philosophy in 'The Crown'.

Lawrence had the habit of working on more than one piece of writing at a time, each at a different stage of composition, so that there is a strong element of continuity across his philosophical works. In his 'Foreword' to *Sons and Lovers* (1913), Lawrence began to apply a religious dichotomy between 'Word' and 'Flesh' to his explication of personal conflicts between man and woman. In 'Study of Thomas Hardy', begun the following year, he worked out his conviction that conflict and the marriage of opposites was the structuring element in both sexual relationships and artistic creativity: from the Father ('Word') and Son ('Flesh') comes the Holy Spirit and the work of art. In 'The Crown', Lawrence restated this central dialectic, now imaged in the two beasts of the royal coat of arms, the unicorn ('Word') and the lion ('Flesh'), fighting unceasingly under a crown created out of the clash of their own opposition. By 1915, the horror of the war's stalemate had sharpened Lawrence's belief that destruction and creation were cyclical and seasonal: sometimes there can be no creation, victory or cessation, only chaos. In the third instalment of the essay published in *The Signature*, Lawrence begins to analyse the total disintegration that, he now sees, must precede any creation. Only when the previous consummation has completely disintegrated back to its original elements can the creative process begin again, Lawrence suggests. When people cling to the outwardly known, when they insist upon preserving old forms of society, relationship or value, there can be no creation; the only way forward must be to let go of the past completely; only then can a 'new world' of consummation and creation begin.

Lawrence believed that the war had come about because of a refusal to renounce the past and the old forms of society, and that this had created a rottenness and corruption at the heart of European civilisation. When the war ended, therefore, he did not rejoice. David Garnett recalled that Lawrence told a gathering of Bloomsbury's inner circle celebrating the armistice: 'the war isn't over. The hate and evil is greater now than ever [. . .] and will show itself in all sorts of ways which will be worse than war.'[56] There had not been the radical transformation in consciousness Lawrence had hoped for, and the same rottenness would therefore persist. The responsibility for this ultimately lay with the individual. In his 'Foreword' to *Women in Love* (1920), for example, Lawrence declares: 'We are now in a period of crisis. Every man who is acutely alive is acutely wrestling with his own soul. The people that can bring forth the new passion, the new idea, this people will endure.'[57]

Whilst Mansfield was consistently sceptical about Lawrence's plans to establish an actual island community of 'Rananim', she was clearly influenced by his idea of a permanent 'world' of 'pure reality', 'eternal spirit' and 'living truth' created in opposition to the war's disintegration and destruction. In 1918, for example, she writes to Ida Baker, contrasting 'this imperfect, present world' with 'the real unchanging world'.[58] Similarly, Mansfield tells Murry that she feels 'full of HATE – hate for this awkward hideous world': 'The world is *hideous* – & we are apart'.[59] To Morrell she notes that 'the War [. . .] has made me realise so deeply and finally the *corruption* of the world': 'the only possible life is remote – remote'.[60] Mansfield tells Morrell that they are both 'in the Same World': by contrast, 'one must hate humankind in the mass – hate them as passionately as one loves the few – the very few'.[61] And, writing to Morrell about her garden at Garsington, Mansfield declares:

> God – isn't it a joy really to have a world of one's own – into which all the unreal people never can come – even if the real ones tarry dreadfully – too – At any rate – its [*sic*] *there* – its [*sic*] *ready* – there are moments even now when all its [*sic*] thrilling beauty is almost discovered.[62]

Mansfield attempts to imagine a 'world' that is waiting to be discovered, a world divorced from 'the cruelty and corruptness of mankind'.[63] This would be a world of the 'very few', separate and remote from 'other people who are in the other world and never have known ours'.[64] Writing to Murry in 1920, for example, Mansfield celebrates 'how PURE artists are – how clean and faithful' and 'so remote from all this corruption': 'One can't afford to MIX with people. One must keep clear of all the worldly world. And we can do it.'[65]

As well as directing Mansfield's ideas about a 'world' apart, *The Signature* was also important in shaping her notion of a 'new word'. In his articles for the magazine, Murry developed a deeply personal response to the war that not infrequently spilled over into a self-pitying mode of address, as evidenced in the title for his contributions to *The Signature*, 'There Was a Little Man'. Mansfield later chided Murry for this writing style, criticising one of his 1917 reviews as 'indecent' and 'a "Signature" style of writing': 'I feel that you are going to uncover yourself and quiver'.[66] Yet Murry's articles were important in reiterating the same philosophical outlook as promoted in Lawrence's contributions. Both writers advocate a complete renunciation of the past, with Murry observing: 'the new freedom will not be as the old; it cannot be. The bitter knowledge of evil is in our blood.'[67] As in 'The Crown', the Bible is also a structuring element in 'There Was a Little Man'. If Christ 'said: I will die in this life that I may be free in the life to come, and you may be free in me', then Murry declares: 'I have a new word. In this life must life be justified.'[68]

This idea of a 'new word' became ever more central to Murry's writings after 1915. When Mansfield moved to the south of France after the failure of *The Signature*, Murry joined her, and it was here, in Bandol, that he wrote his first critical monograph, a book on Dostoevsky published in 1916 that established his reputation as a literary critic. Previously, Murry had collaborated with S. S. Koteliansky on a translation of Dostoevsky's journals; this process of translation refined Murry's opinions about the author. In his critical study, for instance, Murry observes: 'In *The Journal of an Author* and his letters Dostoevsky returned again and again to the definition of literary genius as the power which should bring "a new word" into literature'.[69] This was the distinguishing feature of Russian literature, Murry argued:

> In Russian literature alone can be heard the trumpet-note of a new word: other writers of other nations do no more than play about the feet of the giants who are Tolstoi and Dostoevsky, for even though the world knows it not, an epoch of the human mind came to an end in them. In them humanity stood on the brink of the revelation of a great secret.[70]

As his biographer has noted, Murry was less concerned with Dostoevsky as an author than 'as a seeker, who simply made use of the novel as a vehicle for his explorations'.[71] And what Dostoevsky's explorations revealed, Murry proclaimed, was the necessity of the 'dawn of a new consciousness': 'the sudden revelation of a new consciousness, when all eternity shall be gathered into a moment'.[72] Dostoevsky had pushed scepticism to its furthest limits, and had thereby found faith. For Murry, his novels were records of this struggle, a spiritual crisis from which a new dispensation, a new mode of consciousness might emerge; the power of Dostoevsky's novels was in his willingness to confront this crisis with honesty.

As David Goldie has observed, it was the 'intellectual honesty tempered in the fires of angst' that Murry perceived in the novels of Dostoevsky that he also found in the works of the French wartime writers.[73] For Murry, the war as described by Henri Barbusse, Jules Romains and, above all, Georges Duhamel represented a manifestation of the 'new consciousness' that he had recognised in the works of Dostoevsky: 'The strange and splendid honesty of soul which seemed once to be the prerogative of Russia alone is descending upon France also', he wrote.[74] Reviewing Duhamel's *Civilisation* in 1918, for example, Murry celebrated the work for illuminating the fact that 'what has been called the bankruptcy of civilisation is, more exactly, the failure of a mode of consciousness'.[75] Murry's reading of Duhamel shaped his idea that 'modern civilisation' is 'only a complex of material discoveries and nothing more. In other words, it is not a civilisation at all. It is a material condition which has usurped a spiritual title.'[76] Murry also became convinced that the responsibility for maintaining a 'spiritual' civilisation and inaugurating a new mode of consciousness lay with a select minority. Romain's poem *Europe*, for example, is described as 'the tormented cry of the European soul made articulate': this 'is the soul of civilisation itself', Murry writes, 'a soul maintained in life by the ideal faith of a handful of men'.[77] In an article written at the end of 1918, Murry echoes Mansfield's division between 'the very few' and 'humankind in the mass' when he contrasts the 'minority' with the 'majority'. Murry writes that, during the war:

> Imagination was a reed; if humanity leaned upon it, it broke under the weight of the majority. [. . .] The problem of the minority was to orientate themselves in a new world [. . .] a world which at the first sight seemed cold and alien and hostile, yet afterwards appeared to have at least the attraction that discoveries might be made in it and new lessons learned.[78]

The 'new consciousness' revealed in the writings of Duhamel, then, would provide a way for the minority to orientate themselves and make discoveries in the new post-war world.

Mansfield also shared this enthusiasm for the work of Duhamel. After reading *Civilisation*, she wrote to Murry to say that Duhamel 'is the most sympathetic frenchman [*sic*] I've ever read – I think he is really *great* [. . .] Its [*sic*] his *dignity* of *soul*.'[79] This assessment prefigures Murry's summary in *The Athenaeum* of the spiritual 'gospel' that Duhamel's work imparts:

> We are to cultivate our gardens, to spread the sails of the soul to every authentic air. Every satisfaction that is truly spiritual, whether knowledge, or art, or generosity, or sympathy, is a stage in our spiritual possession of the world.[80]

Figure 3.2 Katherine Mansfield and John Middleton Murry, in Menton, France (c. 1920)

Duhamel even becomes part of the imaginative world of 'the Heron' that Mansfield and Murry created for each other, with Mansfield describing how 'OUR world and the world of Duhamel is there and waits for us to give a sign'.[81] In describing 'the Beauty of the human soul', moreover, she implores Murry: 'Dont [*sic*] let us *ever* forget – You & I know it – Duhamel knows it – There will be others – we will build an alter'.[82] Again, therefore, the 'new world' ('OUR world') is something to be both created and discovered. This was the '*critical point of view*' that the work of Duhamel imparted, shaping the language of Mansfield's reviews.[83]

Editorially, *The Athenaeum* was moulded by the belief, derived in part from Duhamel, that it was a moral necessity to restore 'civilisation' from spiritual disintegration. For the first issues of the periodical under his editorship, for example, Murry secured for serialisation Paul Valéry's 'La Crise de l'esprit', translated as 'The Spiritual Crisis'. Alluding to the First World War, Valéry writes that an 'extraordinary terror has run through the spiritual marrow of Europe' and that 'the whole spectrum of intellectual light has displayed its incompatible colours, illuminating with a strange, contradictory gleam the agony of the European soul'.[84] Throughout his own contributions to the periodical, Murry continually echoed this idea of a 'spiritual crisis'. For instance, he observed that the 'most marked characteristic of the present age is a continual disintegration of the consciousness; more or less deliberately in every province of man's spiritual life the reins are being thrown on to the horse's neck'.[85] Like most of his generation, Murry saw the First World War as the decisive event in generating this moral and spiritual confusion:

> One does not need sharp eyes to discern the symptoms of 'war-coarsening' everywhere. The spiritual fibre of the world has been roughened and abraded. The common consciousness of civilization, the sense of distinction between right and wrong, is being worn away.[86]

For Murry, like Valéry, 'the war has been the dividing line between one epoch of the spirit and another'.[87] After the deluge, the task of the writer, artist and intellectual must be to restore the 'common consciousness of civilization' and the 'spiritual fibre of the world'.[88] In his first leader as editor of *The Athenaeum*, Murry called for the creation of a new 'aristocracy of the spirit' able to 'defend the truth' and 'the universality of the ideal'.[89] In other words, *The Athenaeum* under Murry's editorship was founded upon a call to a minority of artists and intellectuals to oppose the disintegration of the 'worldly world' and corruption of 'humankind in the mass' in order to defend a higher world of 'spirit' and 'truth'.

This was exactly the philosophy upon which *The Signature* had been founded in 1915. Indeed, whilst Murry accepted only one of Lawrence's three submissions to *The Athenaeum*, this submission demonstrates a line of continuity from *The Signature*. Written under the pseudonym Grantorto, 'Whistling of Birds' adopts the same allegorical mode of writing as used by Lawrence in 'The Crown' to describe the same cyclical, seasonal process of destruction and creation. The piece opens with an image of 'innumerable' bird corpses, torn apart by 'invisible beasts of prey' and 'held for many weeks' by the frost of winter.[90] Then, 'quite suddenly', spring arrives and birds begin to sing: 'It was almost a pain to realize, so swiftly, the new world'.[91] Out of the destruction of the war, Lawrence suggests, a 'new world' of creation can come into being. By 1919–20, this idea of the 'new world' had gained common currency, as is demonstrated by a prominent advertisement printed in *The Athenaeum* for a series of school textbooks titled 'The New World' that declares: 'the Old World has died. The New World is not created. There is no hush of

Figure 3.3 'The New World' advertisement in *The Athenaeum*

perfection in the cool of the evening: instead – to man is given infinite possibilities' (Figure 3.3).

Mansfield's reviews in *The Athenaeum* clearly respond to these contexts. In one review, for instance, she echoes Lawrence's language of seasonal change and animalistic awakening to describe the conflict of the First World War: 'We are still very dazed, very dumb and stiff after the four years' winter sleep; the winter has lasted too long; our sleep has been like death. We are dazed creatures, "lizards of convalescence," creeping back into the sun.'[92] In particular, though, Mansfield's reviews intersect in significant ways with Murry's writings in *The Athenaeum*, reflecting the assertion made throughout her letters that 'our minds *cross*. You are feeling the war again just as I am – and just at the same *time*.'[93] In particular, Mansfield's reviews echo Murry's emphasis on 'truth' and 'honesty', expressing the belief that the war was a 'test' that must be applied to fiction.[94] It was this philosophy that shaped Mansfield's perception of the editorial role she and Murry must play in *The Athenaeum*, in which they must 'stand for something' and 'be honest':

> The change has *come*. Nothing *is* the same. I positively feel one has no right to run a paper without preaching a gospel [. . .] I want to make an

> appeal to all our generation who do believe that the war has changed everything to come forward and lets [*sic*] start a crusade.[95]

Writing at the beginning of 1921, for example, Mansfield states: 'I believe the only way to *live* as artists under these new conditions in art and life is to put everything to the test for ourselves [. . .] if artists were really thorough & honest they would save the world'.[96]

These ideas provided the motivating impulse behind Mansfield's much-quoted criticism of Woolf's second novel *Night and Day*, in the review titled 'A Ship Comes into the Harbour'. In an article written in 1916, Murry had stated: 'We stand before the need of new artists and the fact of a new world'.[97] It is in these terms that Mansfield's review should be read; it was motivated not by personal or professional jealousy towards Woolf, but by a firmly held belief that fiction should register the impact of the war and that writers must look to create new forms able to express this profound change in consciousness. Mansfield writes:

> There is at the present day no form of writing which is more eagerly, more widely discussed than the novel. What is its fate to be? We are told on excellent authority that it is dying; and on equally good authority that only now it begins to live. [. . .] But in all this division and confusion it would seem that opinion is united in declaring this to be an age of experiment. If the novel dies it will be to give way to some new form of expression; if it lives it must accept the fact of a new world.[98]

The problem with Woolf's novel, Mansfield argues, is that it neither embodies a 'new form of expression' (a new word) nor accepts 'the fact of a new world'. In the case of the former, Mansfield argues that *Night and Day* is 'a novel in the tradition of the English novel': with its conventional marriage plot, it might almost be considered 'Miss Austen up-to-date', 'extremely cultivated, distinguished and brilliant, but above all – deliberate'.[99] It is not the 'new word'. Moreover, considering 'the fact of a new world', Mansfield argues that Woolf's novel emerges from the 1914–18 conflict entirely unscathed. Using the extended metaphor of the ship, she imagines the 'strange sight' of the novel 'sailing into port serene and resolute on a deliberate wind. The strangeness lies in her aloofness, her air of quiet perfection, her lack of any sign that she has made a perilous voyage – the absence of any scars.'[100] The use of personal pronouns to describe the novel/ship has the unfortunate effect of drawing an implicit connection between the author and her work. With some justification, Woolf took the criticism personally, writing: 'A decorous elderly dullard she describes me; Jane Austen up to date'.[101] Subsequently, this review has been interpreted through the personal terms of a literary rivalry between Mansfield and Woolf.

However, it is Woolf's apparent refusal to 'accept the fact of a new world' that is the focus of Mansfield's criticism. Writing to Murry about *Night and Day*, she states:

> My private opinion is that it is a lie in the soul. The war has never been, that is what its [*sic*] message is. I don't want G. forbid mobilisation and the violation of Belgium – but the novel can't just leave the war out. There *must* have been a change of heart. It is really fearful to me the 'settling down' of human beings. I feel in the *profoundest* sense that nothing can ever be the same that as artists we are traitors if we feel otherwise: we have to take it into account and find new expressions new moulds for our new thoughts & feelings.[102]

The phrase 'a lie in the soul' was one taken from Murry's own critical writings. As early as February 1914, Murry had written that François Villon 'was a great poet, because he had not the lie in the soul'.[103] Murry developed this idea during the war, noting the 'splendid honesty of soul' evident in the work of the French wartime writers, 'young men of letters whom [*sic*] before the war we knew were not unlike their similars in England, have now with a common impulse of the spirit passed beyond them into another world. In them the war has cauterized the lie in the soul.'[104] When Murry responded to Mansfield's letter about Woolf's novel, he wrote:

> So few people have felt the war; and for us who have, the work of those who have not – if it pretends to be true at all – must sound a lie. And we're not arbitrary in requiring the truth from them. The War *is* Life; not a strange aberration of Life, but a revelation of it. It is a test we must apply; it must be allowed for in any truth that is to touch us.[105]

A common vocabulary emerges here in the writings of Mansfield and Murry: the war is a 'test' that must be applied to literature, which should always aspire towards 'truth'.

Throughout her reviews, Mansfield continually asserts that the task of the author is 'to keep faith with Truth' and that 'the novel which is not an attempt at nothing short of Truth is doomed':

> To be fobbed off, at the last, with something which we feel to be less true than the author knew it to be, challenges the importance of the whole art of writing, and instead of enlarging the bounds of our experience, it leaves them where they are.[106]

A writer such as H. M. Tomlinson impresses Mansfield because he 'has no need to exaggerate or heighten his effects. One is content to believe that what he tells you happened to him and it was the important thing; it was the spiritual truth which was revealed.'[107] This search for 'spiritual truth' is contextualised against the war in Mansfield's reviews:

> To say that the war has changed our attitude to life is not a very useful thing to say, neither is it wholly true. But what it has done is to fix for ever in our minds the distinction between what is a fashion and what is permanent. In spite of all the nonsense that is admired and the rubbish that is extolled we do perceive a striving after something nearer the truth, something more deeply true among a few writers to-day.[108]

It is this critical emphasis on permanence that reflects the notion of a 'new world' promoted since the days of *The Signature*: a higher world of 'pure reality', 'eternal spirit' and 'living truth' opposed to the contingent 'worldly world' of 'disintegration'.

This opposition is reflected in the contrast between *The Athenaeum* and the newspaper press that Mansfield establishes in her letters. In 1918, Mansfield writes that the newspaper press is an 'appalling abyss of vulgarity'.[109] After the war, she writes to Morrell:

> [W]hy is the world so ugly – so corrupt and *stupid*. When I heard the drunks passing the house on Monday night, singing the good old pre-war drunken rubbish, I felt cold with horror. THEY are not changed – & then the loathsome press about Germany's cry for food [. . .] How horrid they are *not* to – why don't they fly at each other kiss & cry & share everything.[110]

In 1920, likewise, Mansfield describes the press as 'sordid; theres [*sic*] no other word for it'.[111] Lawrence also articulated his revulsion towards the press in his novel of 1923, *Kangaroo*, describing 'the genuine debasement' and 'unspeakable baseness of the press and the public voice, the reign of that bloated ignominy, *John Bull*'.[112] As Goldie has argued, such revulsion reflects the post-war cultural climate in which Murry's editorship of *The Athenaeum* was begun, a climate in which many commentators were arguing 'that the written word, in all its forms, had not come out of the war entirely untarnished; that, in fact, the written word, like the truth it purported to convey, had become one of the prime casualties of total war'.[113] Newspaper slogans and reductive distortions of events during wartime had unsettled public trust in the press. The demand for the 'truth' of a 'new word' in literature, repeatedly articulated in Mansfield's reviews for *The Athenaeum*, was a response to these historical contexts of print journalism during and immediately after the war.

The revulsion shown by Mansfield towards the press was coupled with her highly negative attitude towards contemporary literary criticism. In 1918, she writes 'oh! how *ignorant* these reviewers are' and notes 'how shockingly ill the novels are reviewed'.[114] In particular, Mansfield opposed *The Athenaeum* to what she believed was 'the *disgraceful* dishonesty' and 'filthy scandal' of the reviews in *The Times Literary Supplement*.[115] This view reflected the terms of a continued debate within *The Athenaeum* about the state of contemporary literary criticism. In an article titled 'Critical Interest', for instance, Murry writes: 'In the phrase "critical interest," as we use it, the emphasis is upon the adjective, for in our own opinion the present age is in danger of become definitely uncritical'.[116] Mansfield echoed this idea in her own reviews, imploring Dorothy Easton, for example, 'in these uncritical days, to treat herself with the utmost severity'.[117] Eliot, likewise, unequivocally declares in *The Athenaeum* that 'modern criticism is degenerate' and 'the amount of good literary criticism in English is negligible'.[118] Similarly, Frank Swinnerton argues that the convention of reviewing is 'too well-established' and produces 'stumbling criticism'.[119] Like the reaction to the 'vulgarity' of the press at large, these opinions in *The Athenaeum* about contemporary literary criticism were shaped in response to the war. In an unsigned article, for instance, A. de Sélincourt observed: 'We have bitter need at the present time for a reconsideration of critical principles; for a non-partisan criticism to disperse the miasma of name-worship and of chaotic emotionalism, which are the part-legacy of the war'.[120]

Under Murry's editorship, *The Athenaeum* looked to counter the 'debasement' of the 'word' within the press at large and, specifically, the 'dishonesty' of other literary journals; contributors to the periodical did this by promoting critical principles of permanence, such as 'truth', 'value' and 'standards'. If Murry argued that the 'most marked characteristic of the present age is a continual disintegration', then the rehabilitation of 'immutable standards' in literary criticism would provide constancy and integrity.[121] Mansfield clearly subscribed to this idea, invoking a post-war *Zeitgeist* to describe the unprecedented difficulties faced by the literary critic: 'the spirit of the age is against us; it is an uneasy, disintegrating, experimental spirit'.[122] In *The Athenaeum*, Murry declared that 'a standard should be once more created and applied' and that 'the first essential is to apply the corrective of disinterested criticism to that capacity for self-deception which seems to have become infinite under the stress of war'.[123] Only then, Murry argued, could an 'intellectual renascence' begin.[124] Moreover, in dialogue with an essay by Eliot, and highlighting synergies with Eliot's ideas at this time, Murry wrote an article for *The Times Literary Supplement* in which he argued that the 'function of true criticism is to establish a definite hierarchy among the great artists of the past, as well as to test the production of the present'.[125]

The Athenaeum promoted the idea that a rehabilitated 'criticism' would pave the way for a 'renascence' of literary innovation. Indeed, Murry understood the widespread interest in 'the present condition of literary criticism' as 'symptomatic of a general hesitancy and expectation' in the contemporary 'world of letters', in which everything is 'up in the air, volatile and uncrystallised': before the war, he writes, 'one had a tolerable certainty that the new star, if the new star was to appear, would burst upon our vision in the shape of a novel'; '[t]o-day we feel it might be anything [. . .] it has no predetermined form'.[126] As such, 'if the *lusus naturae*, the writer of genius, were to appear, there ought to be a person or an organization capable of recognizing him, however unexpected': in other words, there ought to be critics who are receptive to the 'new' and unforeseen.[127] Similarly, Mansfield observes that the 'new word' will be of indeterminate form, most likely 'in prose' but 'a great deal shorter than a novel' and 'neither a short story, nor a sketch, nor an impression, nor a tale'.[128] Elsewhere, moreover, Mansfield echoes the language used by Murry when she writes: 'We are told also that we are on the eve of a literary renascence. True, no star has been seen in the sky, but the roads are thronged with shepherds. This is the moment of attention.'[129] Mansfield viewed her critical writings within this context: she considered her work as a reviewer to be part of a vital post-war project of rehabilitating critical standards, a project that would help to shepherd writers into creating the 'new word'.

Throughout her reviews for *The Athenaeum*, Mansfield imagines what the 'new word' might look like by contrasting it with what she terms the 'pastime novel'. Again reflecting the distinction between a select 'minority' and the public 'majority', she writes: 'Reading, for the great majority – for the reading public – is not a passion but a pastime, and writing, for the vast number of modern authors, is a pastime and not a passion'.[130] *Hope Trueblood* by Patience Worth is 'almost too good an example of the pastime novel'.[131] Similarly, *The Ancient Allan* by

Rider Haggard is described as a 'variety of the pastime novel'.[132] What defines the 'pastime novel' is the want of 'truth'. Mansfield writes: 'It is not as though the pastime novel were out to tell the truth and nothing but the truth'.[133] Elsewhere, she observes that 'a long acquaintance with pastime novels' has shown her that 'so many books' are 'not concerned with anything more serious than to amuse, or, perhaps it were truer to say, to distract' the reader: 'By far the greatest number of them aim at nothing more positive than a kind of mental knitting – the mind of the reader is grown so familiar with the pattern that the least possible effort is demanded of it'.[134] Importantly, Mansfield contrasts the novel of 'distraction' and 'entertainment' with the novel of discovery and exploration: 'the great writers of the past have not been "entertainers". They have been seekers, explorers, thinkers. It has been their aim to reveal a little of the mystery of life.'[135]

This distinction between the plot-driven 'pastime novel' and the undiscovered medium of a 'new word' was echoed in *The Athenaeum* by J. W. N. Sullivan, a prolific contributor to the periodical and, together with Aldous Huxley, an assistant editor to Murry. Sullivan argues that literature must possess 'broad, robust qualities [. . .] if it is to be regarded by serious men as anything more than a pastime': 'literature which no longer gives adequate expression to the soul of man ranks with the other amusements with which we stuff our leisure hours'.[136] As well as echoing Mansfield's idea of the 'pastime novel' here, Sullivan also employs geographical metaphors of exploration to describe the new possibilities before the artist. In an article titled 'Dissolving Views', for instance, he argues that it was possible, before the war, 'with the sense of being fairly accurate, [to] give the latitude and longitude of everything on our map'; in 'the intervening years we have watched the old picture becoming more and more blurred and the new one gradually taking shape'.[137] Given that certainties of morality, religion and nationality have dissolved, Sullivan argues, 'the work now being done in the arts is chiefly valuable in its negative aspect' only:

> The universe must be discovered over again. If art is to survive it must show itself worthy to rank with science; it must be as adequate, in its own way, as is science. To do that, it must become, to an unprecedented degree, profound and comprehensive, for it is living in a world which is unprecedentedly wide and deep. What the new world will be like we do not know, but it is already apparent that it will be a bigger thing altogether than the pre-war world.[138]

In this 'new world', the artist 'must consult the compass, find out where he is and very earnestly and sincerely try to discover where he wants to go'.[139] What Sullivan's articles show is that the language of geographical 'exploration' and 'discovery' in *The Athenaeum* reflected the contemporary idea of a 'new world': a world in which the artist must try to discover direction without reverting to forms that are 'only too definite and circumscribed'.[140]

Similarly, Mansfield's reviews consistently use geographical metaphors of exploration and discovery in order to formulate a critical response to contemporary writing and suggest new directions for writers hoping to make their work adequate to a new post-war world. For instance, she celebrates the feeling of excitement and anticipation before exploration, when we long 'to put ourselves to the test, to lose ourselves in other countries, other lives, to give what we have in exchange for what we want, and thus to acquire strange unfamiliar treasure'.[141] Linking this feeling to the novel form, she writes:

> There must be the same setting out upon a voyage of discovery (but through unknown seas instead of charted waters), the same difficulties and dangers must be encountered, and there must be an ever-increasing sense of the greatness of the adventure and an ever more passionate desire to possess and explore the mysterious country.[142]

Indeed, the metaphor of the sea voyage is constant throughout Mansfield's critical writings, as is demonstrated in the review of *Night and Day*, in which the 'harbour' signifies safety, caution and a refusal to embrace adventure. Elsewhere, Mansfield writes that 'part of [the] "appeal"' of 'the sweetly pretty novel' is that 'you are never out of sight of the happy ending from the very first page': 'Your faith is tried, but not unduly tried; the boat may rock a little and a dash or two of spray come over, but you are never out of harbour – never so much as turned towards the open sea'.[143] Similarly, Mansfield observes of Frank Swinnerton's novel *September*: 'What has happened to Marion, to Nigel, Cherry and Howard? Nothing. They have weathered the storm, and dawn finds them back again in the same harbour from which they put out – none the worse or the better for their mock voyage.'[144] Writing to Morrell about her review of Joseph Hergesheimer's *Java Head*, likewise, Mansfield notes in exasperation: 'one always seems to arrive at the same conclusion – nothing goes deep enough – the *risk* has not been taken – Whenever the crisis is reached they decide to wait until the sea is calmer.'[145] In Mansfield's reviews, the harbour provides a visual image for forms that are too definite and circumscribed; by contrast, the open sea signifies the 'risk' of exploration.

Throughout her reviews, Mansfield also tends to equate an author's 'mind' with an image of landscape. In her very first review in *The Athenaeum*, for example, she describes *The Tunnel* as indicative of 'the clear, shadowless country' of Dorothy Richardson's 'mind'.[146] Similarly, she summarises *The Arrow of Gold* as an 'example of Mr Conrad in search of himself, Mr Conrad, a pioneer, surveying the rich untravelled forest landscape of his mind': 'When we think of his fine economy of expression, his spare use of gesture, his power of conveying the mystery of another's being' evident in his earlier novels, Mansfield writes, 'we are amazed to think of the effort it has cost him to clear that wild luxurious country and to build thereupon his dignified stronghold'.[147] Instead, the courageous author must be at 'great pains to discover a path that is less trodden than the familiar, popular route'.[148] There emerges in Mansfield's critical writings, as such, a distinction between the safe, cultivated landscape and 'wildness'. In her review of Edith Wharton's *The Age of Innocence*, for example, Mansfield entreats the author to depict 'a little wildness, a dark place or two in the soul'.[149] Mansfield develops this idea in a notebook extract that echoes the language of her review of *Night and Day*, which also references the 'cultivated' mind of the author:

> [The] cultivated mind doesn't really attract me. I admire it [. . .] but it leaves me cold. After all, the adventure is over. There is now nothing to do but to trim & to lop and to keep back – all faintly depressing labours. No, no the mind I love must have wild places [. . .] *real* hiding places, not artificial ones – not gazebos and mazes. And I have never yet met the cultivated mind that has not had its shrubberies. I loathe & detest shrubberies.[150]

Reviewing E. M. Forster's short story collection *The Story of the Siren*, likewise, Mansfield asks: 'How is it that the writer is content to do less than explore his own delectable country?'[151] Forster is too careful, so that his prose resembles the cultivated shrubbery; he is too reluctant to 'commit himself wholly', so that there 'is a certain leisureliness' about his style: 'By letting himself be borne along, by welcoming any number of diversions, he can still appear to be a stranger, a wanderer, within the boundaries of his own country, and so escape from any declaration of allegiance'.[152] Again, then, Mansfield contrasts leisurely writing confined to 'boundaries' (the 'pastime') with committed, wild 'exploration'. The metaphor of the mind as a 'country' or 'landscape' was a common one among Mansfield's contemporaries. In 1922, for example, Murry published a collection of essays titled *Countries of the Mind*. In Mansfield's reviews, this metaphor was employed to convey the idea that writers should be adventurous and take risks by exploring new forms of expression.

Mansfield's emphasis on exploration throughout her reviews often provides a way for her to contrast staid English literature with invigorating foreign influences. Mansfield praises Knut Hamsun's *Growth of the Soil*, for example, as 'one of those few novels in which we seem to escape from ourselves and to take an invisible part. We suddenly find to our joy that [. . .] the author's country is ours.'[153] Considering the novels of Louis Couperus, Mansfield evokes the Low Countries of the author's birth when she observes:

> There is an angle from which we seem to see them as the strangest landscapes, small, low-lying country swept continually by immense storms of wind and rain, with dark menacing clouds for ever pulling over and casting a weighty shadow that lifts and drifts away only to fall again.[154]

Reviewing a novel by the Japanese author Futabatei Shimei, likewise, Mansfield writes: 'after a long rolling on the heavy seas of our modern novels the critic feels as though he had stepped into a blue paper boat and was sailing among islands whose flowery branches overhang the water'.[155] Mansfield believed that 'the new novel' would perhaps be 'something brought from a far country, something never dreamed of, something new, marvellous, dazzling – changing the whole of life'.[156] In this preference for foreign literature, Mansfield responds to Sullivan's notion that a literature of the 'new world' must be 'profound and comprehensive, for it is living in a world which is unprecedently wide and deep'.

This preference is reflected in the comparisons Mansfield consistently makes between contemporary English writing and Russian literature. Reviewing Swinnerton's *September*, for instance, Mansfield asks: 'what do we mean exactly by that word "expression"? Can we afford to leave it out of a page, of a paragraph – after Tchehov?'[157] In particular, Russian literature and culture more broadly were discussed in *The Athenaeum* with a view to fostering greater internationalism; this was seen as a pressing need following the international conflagration of the First World War and also Russia's isolationism following the 1917 revolution. In an article titled 'True Internationalism', for instance, Murry observed:

> As, day by day, it becomes more evident that a political internationalism will be for many years to come a vain mirage, the need to foster intellectual internationalism grows more urgent. If we cannot at this stage

> of our spiritual development love our rival nations, let us at least try to understand them.[158]

Translations from Russian made by Koteliansky were integral to this project. In addition to those he produced in collaboration with Mansfield, translations by Koteliansky published in *The Athenaeum* included three stories by Anton Chekhov ('At the Cemetery', 'At the Post-Office' and 'A Moscow Hamlet'), an authorised translation of Leo Shestov's philosophy ('The Russian Spirit' and 'Chapters from a Book') and the preface to the first catalogue of the 'World Literature' book series by Maxim Gorky, 'Literature and Present-Day Russia'. Murry provided an editorial note to the translation of Gorky's preface that referenced the Russian Revolution, describing the essay as 'a literary document of the first importance, appearing as it does at a time when the necessity of resuming intellectual relations with Russia is felt to be increasingly urgent'.[159] Murry writes that Gorky showed how the 'domain of literary creation is the International of the spirit' and that literature is 'the all-seeing eye of the world, whose glance penetrates into the deepest recesses of the human spirit'.[160] The emphasis on Russian literature throughout *The Athenaeum*, as such, served to underline this idea of a spiritual internationalism.

It was in this context that Mansfield produced co-translations of writings by Chekhov with Koteliansky for publication in *The Athenaeum*. From April to October 1919, the two writers contributed thirteen sets of translations of Chekhov's letters to *The Athenaeum*, with one to four letters in each; and in April 1920, they contributed extracts from Chekhov's diaries. In July 1919, considering publishing these translations in book form, Mansfield wrote to Koteliansky, describing Chekhov's work by again using the metaphor of the sea voyage: 'here is this treasure – at the wharf only not unloaded'.[161] Significantly, when writing about the letters, Mansfield links Chekhov's writings to a 'new world' of discovery:

> Wonderful they are. The last one – the one to Souverin about the duty of the artist to *put* the 'question' – not to solve it but so to put it that one is completely satisfied seems to me one of the most valuable things I have ever read. It opens – it discovers rather, a new world.[162]

And, writing to Murry in October 1919, Mansfield notes: 'We could not, knowing what we know belong to others who know not. If I can only *convey* this difference this vision of the world as we see it: Tchekhov saw it, too, and so I think did Keats.'[163] The 'new world' is again envisaged as a world apart, a world of the minority, waiting to be discovered.

In her reviews for *The Athenaeum*, Mansfield consistently asks of each author: 'were there not mysterious moments when you felt that naught save a new world could contain your creations?'[164] The concepts of a 'new world' and 'new word' continually intersect throughout Mansfield's critical writings: metaphors of geographical exploration and discovery figure the belief that writers must seek to break the boundaries of 'definite and circumscribed' literary forms in order to express new thoughts and feelings. As has been examined in this section of the chapter, such metaphors simultaneously reflect a contemporary intellectual response to the 'spiritual crisis' of the First World War. By postulating the idea of a 'new world' waiting to be discovered, contributors to *The Athenaeum* looked to counter the 'disintegration' and 'corruption' of the 'worldly world' and 'humankind in the mass': the idea of a 'world' apart provided a metaphor for postulating a post-war project of spiritual rejuvenation among a select, aristocratic minority of the 'very few' that extended beyond national boundaries. As a metaphor for the undiscovered 'new word' of truth and honesty, in particular, the concept of the 'new world' was formulated in direct response to a perceived 'debasement' of the 'word' throughout the newspaper press and among other literary journals during and immediately following the war. This is highlighted in a letter Mansfield wrote to Murry in June 1918:

> You will not always be a 'failure' even where the world is concerned, because we'll change the world. Fancy believing that & feeling as I do – all this hatred and contempt for human beings – all this desire to cut absolutely off from them. And of course I dont [*sic*] mean that well [*sic*] change the Daily Mirror world – but A world – OUR world and the world of Duhamel is there and waits for us to give a sign. I believe that, profoundly. [. . .] Bogey, my whole soul waits for the time when you and I shall be withdrawn from everybody – when we shall go into our own undiscovered darling country and dwell therein.[165]

First articulated in the famous notebook entries Mansfield made in Bandol in 1916, the idea of an 'undiscovered country' not only echoed a spatial vocabulary of empire, therefore, but also intersected with a contemporary cultural discourse of post-war rehabilitation. Positioned within this context, the recurring metaphors in Mansfield's reviews of turning towards the open sea or exploring the wild landscape beyond the well trodden path gesture towards the idea that contemporary literature must develop new forms of expression if it is to be adequate to the new modes of experience in a post-war world.

Between two worlds

In Virginia Woolf's *The Years*, the last novel she published in her lifetime, the chapter for the year 1917 opens with a description of a 'very cold' and dark 'winter's night, so silent that the air seemed frozen': 'No light shone, save when a searchlight rayed round the sky'.[166] As the characters gather at the house of Renny and Maggie for dinner, the wail of an air-raid siren in the street outside forces them all to take shelter in the coal cellar. After the planes pass overhead and the danger moves on, they all raise a toast: '"Here's to the New World!" they all cried, raising their glasses, and clinking them together'.[167] Later, Eleanor sits by the fire thinking '[a]bout the new world' and asks Nicholas: 'how can we improve ourselves [. . .] live more naturally . . . better. . . . How can we?'[168] Nicholas, a Polish-American émigré, struggles to find the right words in English to express himself, responding to Eleanor:

> 'It is only a question,' he said – he stopped. He drew himself close to her – 'of learning. The soul. . . .' Again he stopped.
>
> 'Yes – the soul?' she prompted him.
>
> 'The soul – the whole being,' he explained. He hollowed his hands as if to enclose a circle. 'It wishes to expand; to adventure; to form – new combinations?'
>
> 'Yes, yes,' she said, as if to assure him that his words were right.
>
> 'Whereas now,' – he drew himself together; put his feet together; he looked like an old lady who is afraid of mice – 'this is how we live, screwed up into one hard little, tight little – knot?'[169]

Looking back to the war years in London, Woolf has her characters express the same ideas of a 'spiritual crisis' before the coming of a 'new world' articulated across *The Signature* and *The Athenaeum*. Like Lawrence in 'Whistling of Birds', for example, she chooses to set her narrative in the cold of winter, the seasonal frost figuring the 'old world' from which the 'new world' might spring. And, significantly, Woolf has her characters describe this 'new world' through the same language of spiritual expansion and 'adventure' used by Mansfield and other contributors to *The Athenaeum* in the immediate post-war years.

Virginia Woolf made eighteen contributions to *The Athenaeum* in the period of its rejuvenation under Murry's editorship, with her husband Leonard making twenty-five; both were therefore important, central names in what Woolf herself identified as 'the most brilliant list of contributors on record'. As highlighted in the example from *The Years* given above, the idea of a 'new world' developed in the pages of *The Signature* and *The Athenaeum* clearly registered in Woolf's fiction, and it also influenced ideas expressed in her literary reviews and essays about the 'new combinations' of modernist 'form'. In this section of the chapter, I examine the ways in which the notion of being between the decaying 'old world' and a 'new world' yet to emerge shaped ideas of literary innovation in the critical writings produced by both Woolf and Mansfield in the years 1919–20. Taken together, these ideas develop the principles of literary impressionism, which, as Jesse Matz has observed, occupies a middle ground between various oppositions. Matz argues that this 'in-betweenness is essential', as impressionism 'promises *mediation*': between object and subject, exterior world and inner life, materialism and spiritualism, intellect and emotion, ideas and sensations, or surface appearances and deep knowledge.[170] For Woolf and Mansfield, these oppositions mapped onto that of the 'old' and 'new' worlds: in this scheme, the task of the modern writer was to find new modes of expression able to envisage or articulate an emergent 'new world'.

The week following the publication of the first issue of *The Athenaeum* under Murry's editorship, Woolf's seminal essay 'Modern Novels' was printed in *The Times Literary Supplement*. Later substantially revised under the title 'Modern Fiction' for inclusion in *The Common Reader* (1923), this essay outlines distinctions that have come to define how we understand literary modernism. Contrasting 'modern fiction' with the 'old', Woolf begins by stating that her quarrel is not with the 'classics' (Fielding, Thackeray, Austen), but with the 'materialists' (Wells, Bennett, Galsworthy).[171] Each of these Edwardian novelists, she writes, has been too concerned with 'the solidity of his fabric' and 'more often misses than secures the thing we seek': 'Whether we call it life or spirit, truth or reality, this, the essential thing, has moved off, or on, and refuses to be contained any longer in such ill-fitting vestments'.[172] 'Modern Novels' is Woolf's manifesto for a new kind of fiction; it is her rallying cry for a new literary form that would be adequate to the task of representing the 'essential thing'. In this essay, Woolf famously states that the task of the modern writer is to record the myriad 'impressions' that fall upon the surface of the mind like 'an incessant shower of innumerable atoms, composing in their sum what we might venture to call life itself'.[173] A writer who goes some way to achieving this, Woolf argues, is James Joyce. In contrast to the 'materialists' of the Edwardian period, Joyce is the pre-eminent example of a modern writer who is 'spiritual', because he is 'concerned at all costs to reveal the flickerings of that innermost flame which flashes its myriad message through the brain'.[174] However, Joyce's writing is so 'centred in a self' that it never 'reaches out or embraces or comprehends what is outside and beyond'.[175] This is an important distinction. For Woolf, modern fiction must look to mediate between the external world and the inner self; it must look to find a middle ground between lifeless realism and disconnected solipsism, communicating personal experience at a level that is universally comprehensible; only then can fiction capture the 'essential thing'.

Woolf ends 'Modern Novels' by noting that the writers to date who have successfully mediated between the external and internal realms are the Russian writers of the nineteenth century, and particularly Anton Chekhov. The essential quality of Russian literature, Woolf suggests, is something between 'matter' and 'spirit': it is its 'heart'.[176] These works, filtering through to a British readership for the first time in translation, convey 'sympathy for the sufferings of others, love towards them'.[177] Unlike Joyce, Woolf argues, the Russian writers reach 'outside and beyond' the self and thus achieve a degree of universality in their work; she observes, for instance, that the 'Russian mind' is 'comprehensive and compassionate'.[178] These word choices in Woolf's essay, of 'heart', 'love' and 'compassionate' 'sympathy', underscore an implicit emphasis on emotion, feeling and sensibility as that which can mediate between the internal and external, the personal and universal. Moreover, Woolf further highlights her resistance to the 'solidity' of plot-driven Edwardian fiction by praising the 'inconclusiveness' of Russian literature, observing that such works give 'the sense that there is no answer, that if honestly examined life presents question after question which must be left to sound on and on'.[179] The work of Chekhov, in particular, 'leaves us with the suggestion that the strange chords he has struck sound on and on' and that 'there is perhaps no answer to the questions which [he] raises'.[180]

On reading 'Modern Novels' in April 1919, Mansfield immediately wrote to Woolf to relate her enthusiasm for the essay. What's more, Mansfield surely had this essay in mind when she wrote to Woolf again the following month, describing the translation of a letter by Chekhov that she had made with Koteliansky that was about to be printed in *The Athenaeum*. Echoing Woolf's emphasis on the unresolved 'question' of Russian literature, Mansfield writes:

> Tchekhov has a very interesting letter published in next week's A . . . what the writer does is not so much to *solve* the question but to *put* the

> question. There must be the question put. That seems to me a very nice dividing line between the true & the false writer – Come & talk it over with me.[181]

Throughout their letters and diaries, Mansfield and Woolf continually refer to the importance of their 'talk' with each other. After one of their first meetings together, for example, Mansfield wrote to Woolf: 'It was good to have time to talk to you. We have got the same job, Virginia & it is really very curious & thrilling that we should both, quite apart from each other, be after so very nearly the same thing.'[182] Throughout the autumn and winter of 1918, Mansfield and Woolf met weekly. Whilst these visits became irregular in 1919 and 1920, interrupted by Mansfield's worsening health, Woolf records in her diary in June 1920 that they had '2 hours priceless talk – priceless in the sense that to no one else can I talk in the same disembodied way about writing' and considers this 'exalted talk' and 'intercourse' as 'more fundamental than many better established ones': 'I can talk straight out to her'.[183] Talking to Mansfield, Woolf experiences 'the queerest sense of echo coming back to me from her mind the second after I've spoken'.[184] Likewise, in December 1920, Mansfield writes to Woolf: 'I think of you often – very often. I long to talk to you [. . .] You are the only woman with whom I long to talk *work*. There will never be another.'[185] And after Mansfield's death in 1923, it is this 'exalted talk' that Woolf misses: 'there are things about writing I think of & want to tell Katherine'.[186]

Through the critical writings that they produced at this time, I argue in this chapter, Mansfield and Woolf established a dialogue in print, each echoing the terms of debate and conceptual ideas advanced in the literary reviews written by the other. This dialogue and 'talk' exemplifies the 'conversational model for modernism' that Suzanne Churchill and Adam McKible suggest early twentieth-century periodicals looked to enact.[187] Indeed, Woolf often used conversation as a formal device for her essays, as in 'A Talk About Memoirs' (1920), 'Mr Conrad: A Conversation' (1923) and 'Bryon & Mr Briggs' (drafted in 1922), in which characters from her own novels talk about literature. In Woolf's 'How It Strikes a Contemporary' (1923), the idea of the talking voice and 'random chatter' dominates.[188] And in 'On Being Ill' (1926), Woolf envisions heaven as a place of conversation and gossip between writers and readers. As Hermione Lee has observed, these thematic strands of open conversation and 'random chatter' highlight Woolf's wider aims for her essays and reviews. Woolf disclaimed the kind of literary 'authority' that she associated with the (usually male) forms of literary criticism that set out to dictate and delineate: as Lee writes, Woolf's essays are instead conversational in tone and open-ended in form, resisting 'definitiveness, closure and opinionated certainties', and are thus 'closely connected to her recommendations for a democratic literary community'.[189] In other words, Woolf's essays deliberately opened up a space for dialogue, and Mansfield responded to this. After Woolf wrote a review of Dorothy Richardson's novel *The Tunnel*, for instance, she records in her diary visiting Mansfield: 'At once she flung down her pen & plunged, as if we'd been parted for 10 minutes, into the question of Dorothy Richardson; & so on with the greatest freedom & animation on both sides'.[190] Two weeks later, Mansfield's own review of *The Tunnel* appeared in *The Athenaeum*, echoing Woolf's emphasis on the novel's 'surface' impressions by arguing that it was lacking in those 'large pauses in which we creep away into our caves of contemplation' and each thing that happens in the mind is 'judged' and given 'its appointed place in the whole scheme'.[191] Even in the absence of specific instances such as these, whereby a diary entry or letter helps us to trace particular correlations between an actual conversation and the reviews, we can measure the impact of Mansfield's 'talk' with Woolf through the remarkably similar language choices made by each writer in their critical works. Deploying a shared vocabulary of empathetic 'emotion' and deep 'feeling', the critical writings produced by Mansfield and Woolf at this time highlight the degree to which their professional relationship was based upon what Woolf herself termed a 'common certain understanding'.[192]

Throughout her contributions to *The Athenaeum*, for instance, Mansfield continually employs 'emotion' as a critical standard for evaluating literature, arguing that '[w]ithout emotion writing is dead' and that 'emotion is essential to a work of art; it is that which makes a work of art a unity'.[193] Using the language of 'adventure' in her review of Joseph Conrad's *The Rescue*, for example, she states that the 'feeling that we are not so much reading a story of adventure as living in and through it' arises 'from the quality of the emotion in which the book is steeped'.[194] Likewise, Woolf identifies books with the 'shock of emotion' that they produce.[195] In a notebook entry made under the heading 'Misc. Reading', for example, Woolf observes: 'One grades one's feelings'.[196] This emphasis on 'emotion' and 'feeling' can be seen in relation to the idea of 'significant form' advanced by Clive Bell. Whilst the Bloomsbury group had no specific manifesto, as Andrew McNeillie observes, Bell's

Art (1914) has been claimed by many as having served 'as a platform for the group cause'.[197] In this book, Bell states that '[t]he starting-point for all systems of aesthetics must be the personal experience of a peculiar emotion' and then asks 'What quality is shared by all objects that provoke our aesthetic emotions?'[198] In answer to this question, he outlines the notion of 'significant form', arguing that it is 'lines and colours combined in a particular way, certain forms and relations of forms, [that] stir our aesthetic emotions'.[199] In their critical writings, Mansfield and Woolf can be seen to respond to this idea of 'aesthetic emotions'. For Woolf, however, it is emotion that creates form, rather than form that elicits emotion. In an article written in 1922, for instance, she responds to Percy Lubbock's argument in *The Craft of Fiction* by stating that the 'book itself' is not 'form which you see, but emotion which you feel': 'we feel with singular satisfaction, and since all our feelings are in keeping, they form a whole which remains in our minds as the book itself'.[200] This clearly parallels Mansfield's assertion that it is emotion 'which makes a work of art a unity'. This privileging of 'emotion' distinguishes Mansfield and Woolf's critical writings from the entirely formalist approach adopted by Bell. Whereas Bell states that it is 'significant form' that stirs 'aesthetic emotions', Mansfield and Woolf argue that it is 'emotion' that creates form, making the book a 'unity' or 'whole'.

With both Mansfield and Woolf writing for *The Athenaeum*, their shared emphasis on 'emotion' can also be contextualised against other contributions to this periodical. In his own articles for *The Athenaeum*, for example, Murry consistently argues that 'reading is, essentially, a process of enlarging our experience by the direct absorption of emotion'; that literature 'is rooted in emotion, and that it grows by the mastery of emotion, and that its significance finally depends upon the quality and comprehensiveness of the emotion'.[201] In his essay 'Hamlet and His Problems', which was first published in *The Athenaeum* in September 1919, moreover, T. S. Eliot famously argues that the 'only way of expressing emotion in the form of art is by finding an "objective correlative" [. . .] a set of objects, a situation, a chain of events which shall be the formula of that *particular* emotion'.[202] Murry later illustrated this concept in his book *The Problem of Style* (1922) by distinguishing between the author who pursues the 'active ideal of art' and 'the matter-of-fact vision of the professional accumulator of details': 'For in the latter case, the detail, having been the cause of no emotion in the writer, can awaken none in the reader'.[203] Mansfield responds to this distinction in her own critical writings, arguing that when an author's method is simply to amass observations 'we feel that no one observation is nearer the truth than another'.[204] This clearly echoes Woolf's argument in 'Modern Novels' that 'truth' can no longer be contained in the 'ill-fitting vestments' of an outdated form of literary realism focused almost exclusively on recording the material details of the external world.

Indeed, the idea of 'emotion' shaped the response to the so-called 'materialists' in Mansfield and Woolf's critical writings. When they reviewed a reissue of George Moore's 1894 novel *Esther Waters*, for example, both emphasised 'emotion' in contrast to the 'object'. Mansfield argues that Moore's novel presents 'a world of objects accurately recorded' but 'it has no emotion' and, therefore, 'who cares?'[205] Again emphasising the idea of 'unity' when discussing 'emotion', Mansfield writes:

> To contemplate the object, to let it make its own impression – which is Mr Moore's way in 'Esther Waters' – is not enough. There must be an initial emotion felt by the writer, and all that he sees is saturated in that emotional quality. It alone can give incidence and sequence, character and background, a close and intimate unity.[206]

This assessment is directly echoed in Woolf's review:

> Vivid, truthful, so lightly and yet so firmly constructed as it is, what then prevents us from talking of immortality and greatness? In one word, the quality of the emotion. [. . .] The conception springs from no deep original source, and the execution has that sort of evenness which we see in the work of a highly sensitive student copying on to his canvas the picture of some great master.[207]

Writing in May and June 1919 respectively, Woolf and Mansfield both reiterated the argument of 'Modern Novels' when they reviewed Joseph Hergesheimer's *Java Head*, devoting considerable space to detailing the novel's plot, for example, and thereby foregrounding that aspect of contemporary writing that they were both trying to counter in their own fiction. When critiquing Hergesheimer for his extensive descriptions of clothing, Woolf also echoes 'Modern Novels' by celebrating the 'heart': 'It is very difficult to write beautifully about the heart. When Mr Hergesheimer has to describe not what people wear but what they feel, he shows his lack of ease or of interest.'[208] In her own review, likewise, Mansfield calls attention to Hergesheimer's focus on the materiality of clothing, arguing that it 'is not enough to be comforted with colours, to finger bright shawls [. . .] our curiosity is roused as to what lies beneath these strange rich surfaces. Mr Hergesheimer leaves us wondering and unsatisfied.'[209] For both Mansfield and Woolf, therefore, the object must be related to that which is below the surface; it must become the formula for a particular 'emotion' that springs from a 'deep original source'.

In the critical writings produced by Mansfield and Woolf at this time, a constellation of interrelated words and concepts forms around this idea of deep 'emotion'. In one review, for example, Mansfield states: '*revelation* comes from that *emotional reaction* which the artist felt and was impelled to communicate' (my emphasis).[210] To be taken seriously, authors must make this 'serious attempt at revelation'.[211] For example, a novel such as R. O. Prowse's *A Gift of the Dusk*, which narrates the life of a consumptive exiled to a retreat in the Swiss mountains, affects Mansfield because it 'is not only a record of suffering' but is 'a revelation'.[212] When reviewing fictions about the First World War, in particular, it is the revelation of a personal, 'spiritual truth' that is the essential thing for Mansfield, 'a revelation of [the author's] inner self which would perhaps never have been revealed in times less terrible and strange'.[213] In their correspondence with each other, Mansfield and Murry highlight the importance of this idea of 'revelation' in the post-war context. Murry writes, for instance: 'The War *is* Life; not a strange aberration of Life, but a revelation of it. It is a test we must apply; it must be allowed for in any truth that is to touch us.'[214] As examined in the previous section of this chapter, Mansfield also argued that the modern writer must attempt to find a new form through which to communicate the 'revelation' of new emotions following the war.

In an article published in *The Athenaeum* in November 1919, Murry borrows the title of one of Thomas Hardy's poetry collections, *Moments of Vision*, to clarify what is meant by this contemporary idea of 'revelation':

> The word 'revelation' is fertile in false suggestion; the creative act of power which we seek to elucidate is an act of plenary apprehension, by which one manifestation, one form of life, one experience is seen in its rigorous relation to all other and to all possible manifestations, forms, and experiences. [. . .] In a 'moment of vision' the poet recognises in a single separate incident of life, life's essential quality. The uniqueness of the whole, the infinite multiplicity and variety of its elements, are manifested and apprehended in a part.[215]

In this article, Murry both echoes Woolf's emphasis in 'Modern Novels' on the 'essential thing' and anticipates her later idea of 'moments of being', which Hermione Lee has observed was developed out of an essay on Hardy that Woolf published in 1928, in which she also borrowed the title *Moments of Vision* to describe the 'sudden quickening of power' in a novel when 'a single scene breaks off from the rest'.[216] In the essay 'A Sketch of the Past', written in 1939, Woolf distinguishes 'moments of being' from the 'cotton wool of daily life': each of these moments, she writes, is like a violent 'shock' of recognition that 'is or will become a *revelation* of some order; it is a token of some real thing behind appearances' (my emphasis).[217] For both Murry and Woolf, then, the idea of 'revelation' was connected with perception or 'vision' and the notion of a privileged 'moment'.

When Mansfield uses a specific vocabulary in her reviews, therefore, we can see how these word choices register a set of interrelated concepts also advanced by her contemporaries. Reiterating the idea of a 'sudden quickening', for instance, Mansfield tells us that we must ask of each book: 'Has it *quickened* our perception, or increased our mysterious response to Life? Do we feel that we have partaken of the author's *vision* – that something has been *revealed* that we are the richer for having seen?' (my emphasis).[218] Similarly, she praises Conrad's 'peculiar responsive sensitiveness to the significance of everything, down to the slightest detail that has a place in his *vision*': 'in this heightened, *quickened* state of awareness we are made conscious of his passionate insistence upon the importance of extracting from the *moment* every drop of life that it contains' (my emphasis).[219] In letters and notebook entries, likewise, Mansfield elaborates on this notion of a revelatory 'moment of vision'. In a letter to Ottoline Morrell composed in July 1918, for instance, she anticipates Woolf's idea of the 'moment of being', later conceptualised as 'a token of some real thing behind appearances', when she writes:

> My secret belief – the innermost 'credo' by which I live is that *although* Life is loathsomely ugly and people are terribly often vile and cruel and base, nevertheless there is something at the back of it all – which if only I were great enough to understand would make *everything* everything indescribably beautiful. One just has glimpses, divine warnings – signs – [220]

Likewise, in a notebook entry pointedly given the title 'The Glimpse' when it was published posthumously by Murry, Mansfield develops this idea of a revelatory 'moment':

> The waves, as I drove home this afternoon, and the high foam, how it was suspended in the air before it fell. . . . What is it that happens in that

> moment of suspension? It is timeless. In that moment (what *do* I mean?) the whole life of the soul is contained. One is flung up – out of life – one is 'held', and then, – down, bright, broken, glittering on to the rocks, tossed back, part of the ebb and flow.[221]

This idea of experiencing a privileged 'moment' or glimpsing a 'timeless' truth shapes the language of Mansfield's reviews. Assessing Vita Sackville-West's novel *Heritage*, for example, she argues that 'the form of the novel' is lost without 'central points of significance': 'the gradual unfolding in growing, gaining light' must 'be followed by one blazing moment'; without this 'blazing moment', Mansfield asks, 'how are we to appreciate the importance of one "spiritual event" rather than another?'[222] And what impresses Mansfield about Woolf's short story 'Kew Gardens' is precisely the 'blazing moment' of illumination and revelation that is presented to the reader: 'for a moment the secret life is half-revealed [. . .] we believe these things are all [the author's] concern until suddenly with a gesture she shows us the flower-bed, growing, expanding in the heat and light, filling a whole world'.[223] As such, it is possible to trace in Mansfield's writings a genealogy of ideas through which Woolf would later go on to develop the celebrated concept of the 'moment of being'.

Importantly, the passage from Murry's article on Hardy quoted above highlights how this shared vocabulary of the 'moment', 'vision' and 'revelation' was also employed to signal the belief that literature should connect the subject and object, the self and other, the part and whole, the particular and universal; that each 'creative act' should look to be a manifestation of all life. In August 1920, Woolf records a conversation in her diary in which Mansfield told her: 'one ought to merge into things'.[224] We see this articulated further in Mansfield's famous letter to Dorothy Brett about the 'moment' of merging between subject and object: 'There follows the moment when you are *more* duck, *more* apple or *more* Natasha than any of these objects could ever possibly be, and so you *create* them anew'.[225] In their reviews, both Mansfield and Woolf emphasise this idea of merging self and other in order to move beyond the particular. As in Woolf's 'Modern Novels', both writers argue that literature should be 'comprehensive and compassionate', reaching out and embracing 'what is outside and beyond'. As such, Mansfield and Woolf consistently advocated the idea that 'modern fiction' should seek to blur the lines between the inner ego and outer world. In 1920, for example, Mansfield writes: 'The word that haunts me is egocentric'.[226]

Looking to move beyond the ego in her own fiction, Mansfield sought to rise 'above all pain, and all infirmity – rising above everything'.[227] As such, she defined her 'philosophy' at this time as 'the defeat of the personal':

> People today are simply cursed by what I call the *personal*. . . . What is happening to ME. Look at ME. This is what has been done to ME. Its [*sic*] just as though you tried to run and all the while an enormous black serpent fastened on to you.[228]

As Lee notes, Woolf also 'wanted her criticism to express deep feeling, but not to be personal'.[229] Right from the beginning of her essay-writing career, in 1905, Woolf set herself against what she termed 'the unclothed egoism' of many of the essayists of her time.[230] The critical writings by Mansfield and Woolf highlight a sustained attempt to negotiate a position between personal 'emotion' and the world beyond. Throughout their essays and literary reviews, both writers are seeking to find a language and vocabulary by which to celebrate 'emotion' and 'feeling' yet resist 'unclothed egoism', praising those books that successfully relate personal experience at a level that is comprehensive and universal. As Woolf observes in a notebook entry, for example: 'The better books universalise/disinfect personality. Simply they are dealing with important feelings.'[231]

This resistance to the 'egocentric' shaped how Mansfield and Woolf responded to the so-called 'stream of consciousness' technique and the contemporary vogue for fiction influenced by psychoanalysis. In her first review for *The Athenaeum*, for instance, Mansfield criticises Dorothy Richardson for 'registering every single thing that happens in the clear, shadowless country of her mind': 'There is Miss Richardson, holding out her mind, as it were, and there is Life hurling objects into it as fast as she can throw'.[232] In a later review of Richardson's novel *Interim*, titled 'Dragonflies', Mansfield argues that the habit of 'registering every single thing' in the novel blocks the possibility of any one object or event being imbued with the 'importance' that she elsewhere associates with the 'blazing moment': 'everything being of equal importance to her, it is impossible that everything should not be of equal unimportance'.[233] In her review of *The Tunnel*, likewise, Woolf argues that reality exists 'beneath the surface': like Mansfield's image of a dragonfly '[d]arting through life, quivering, hovering' and skimming the water,[234] Woolf argues that Richardson is too content to focus on surface impressions and that she fails to penetrate any deeper: 'sensations, impressions, ideas and emotions glance off her, unrelated and unquestioned, without shedding quite as much light as we had hoped into the hidden depths'.[235] Instead,

Woolf argues, the writer 'should make us feel ourselves seated at the centre of another mind' and 'we should perceive in the helter-skelter of flying fragments some unity, significance, or design'.[236] Again, therefore, Mansfield and Woolf both promote the idea that the inner ego should be connected to the outer world, and that particular 'emotions' and 'sensations' of the inner life should be communicated at a level that is immediately comprehensible to others; only then can the work of art become a 'unity' of importance or significance.

Richardson's novels were first described as presenting a 'stream of consciousness' by May Sinclair in 1918, who borrowed the term from philosopher and psychologist William James. Famously, this was a term that Richardson herself didn't favour, but the work of the so-called 'stream of consciousness' novelists revealed a pressing problem for the modern author and critic: how to relate the insights of psychology and psychoanalysis to fiction? In 'Modern Novels', for instance, Woolf states: 'The tendency of the moderns and part of their perplexity is no doubt that they find their interest more and more in [the] dark region of psychology'.[237] Likewise, in an article titled 'Is There a New Generation?' published in *The Athenaeum*, Murry observed:

> The 'modern' is too fond of thinking that he has shown up life. What he shows up is not life at all. He is typified by the novelist who pathetically believes that psycho-analysis has added a cubit to his stature, whereas he staggers like a pygmy under the burden.[238]

Mansfield critiqued Sinclair for staggering under this burden, writing: 'she has allowed her love of writing to suffer the eclipse of psycho-analysis'.[239] Elsewhere, Mansfield expresses exasperation at the recurring 'character in modern English fiction [. . .] who from childhood up has suffered from what our psycho-analytical skimmings have taught us to call the sex-complex'.[240] Again, therefore, the focus of Mansfield's critique is on the failed attempt to access hidden depths, with English fiction never getting beyond superficial 'skimmings'. Similarly, when Woolf reviewed J. D. Beresford's *An Imperfect Mother* under the title 'Freudian Fiction' in *The Times Literary Supplement*, she critiqued the novel for being 'strictly in accordance with the new psychology', observing that 'all the characters have become cases' and, in becoming so, 'they have ceased to be individuals':

> We must protest that we do not wish to debar Mr Beresford from making use of any key that seems to him to fit the human mind. Our complaint

> is rather that in *An Imperfect Mother* the new key is a patent key that opens every door. It simplifies rather than complicates, detracts rather than enriches. The door swings open briskly enough, but the apartment to which we are admitted is a bare little room with no outlook whatever.[241]

When she reviewed this novel in *The Athenaeum*, Mansfield employed a very similar spatial metaphor to Woolf in order to highlight its deficiencies. Beresford and R. H. Bretherton, turning 'from the vague outlines and spaces of the open country, have chosen to build their new novels in what might be called the Garden City of literature', a 'desirable site' lately 'discovered by the psychoanalysts' in which 'the houses are still scattered and few, but there is no doubt as to its dawning popularity with the novelists'.[242] However, Mansfield argues, Beresford 'brings nothing from the vasty deep' and reveals only the 'essential emptiness' of the psychoanalytical novel: 'The house is not furnished at all; nobody lives there'.[243]

Mansfield's and Woolf's criticism of those novelists following the 'new psychology' reflects their wider argument that modern literature must not attempt to answer a question, but simply pose it: characters must not be made into 'cases' and human experience must not be explained away; intellect and reason must always be combined with 'emotion' and 'imagination'. Where Mansfield criticises Frank Swinnerton for leaving 'expression' out of his novel *September*, for example, Woolf also describes his 'lucid rather than [. . .] beautiful mind, intellectual in its scope, rather than imaginative'.[244] Moreover, positioning the 'intellect' and 'vision' in a dialectical relation in an article published in December 1919, Woolf writes: 'The greatest poets, having both the visionary imagination and the intellectual imagination, deal with both sides of life; in the lesser poets either the one kind of imagination or the other predominates'.[245] Likewise, Mansfield writes in one of her reviews:

> [W]hat is the use, to your artist at any rate, of thought that is not the outcome of feeling? You must feel before you can think; you must think before you can express your-self. It is not enough to feel and write; or to think and write. True expression is the outcome of them both, yet a third thing, and separate.[246]

In other words, both Mansfield and Woolf argued that literature must seek to mediate between 'vision' and 'feeling' (intuition) and 'intellect' and 'thought' (reason), producing a third, separate thing out of this dialectic: only then might the author approximate, in the words of Woolf's

'Modern Novels', 'what we might venture to call life itself'. In a review of a novel by Louis Couperus, for example, Mansfield asks:

> What is it then that differentiates these living characters from the book-bound creatures of even our brilliant modern English writers? Is it not that the former are seen ever, and always in relation to life – not to a part of life, not to a set of society, but to the bounding horizon, life, and the latter are seen in relation to an intellectual idea of life? In this second case life is made to fit them; something is abstracted – something quite unessential – that they wouldn't in the least know what to do with . . . and they are set in motion. But life cannot be made to 'fit' anybody.[247]

For Mansfield and Woolf, the writer staggering under the burden of psychoanalysis presumes to explain that which cannot be explained, fitting people to a theory of life that diminishes rather than enhances lived experience. This idea was in part derived from Chekhov. In letters translated by Mansfield for publication in *The Athenaeum*, for example, Chekhov writes that it is 'not the business of a psychological writer to understand that which he does not understand' or to 'pretend that he understands that which nobody understands'; instead, the writer must simply be 'an impartial witness': 'For writers, particularly for writers who are artists, it is high time to confess [. . .] that you can't understand anything in this world'.[248] As such, rather than try to answer the question, the artist can only pose it; and rather than attempt to explain life, the artist must learn to accept it. In her review praising Couperus, for instance, Mansfield concludes: 'It is only by accepting life as M. Couperus accepts it that the novelist is free – through his characters – to question it profoundly'.[249]

Throughout her letters and diaries at this time, Mansfield argued that one must learn to accept life and 'learn to submit': 'Its [*sic*] only by risking losing yourself – giving yourself up to Life – that you can ever find out the answer'.[250] This submission meant merging the self with the other, as Mansfield made clear on several occasions: 'when I am writing of "another" I want to lose myself in the soul of the other that I am not'; the artist 'must accept Life, he must submit, give himself so utterly to Life that no personal quâ personal self remains'; one 'must learn, one must practise, to *forget* oneself'.[251] Through this 'act of surrender' one will be able 'to lose oneself more utterly, to love more deeply, to feel oneself part of life, – not separate' and will thereby 'pass from personal love to greater love'.[252] As such, the submission of the 'personal' self would lead to a more universal comprehension and compassion: 'This is the moment which, after all, we live for, – the moment of direct feeling when we are most ourselves and least personal'.[253]

Like Woolf in 'Modern Novels', therefore, Mansfield postulates 'love' and 'direct feeling' as that which can mediate between self and other, subject and object, part and whole. Like Woolf, too, Mansfield derived this idea from her reading of Chekhov, a writer praised across *The Athenaeum* at this time. In his articles for the periodical, for instance, Murry argues that Chekhov is not an 'intellectualist' who seeks to explain human experience or to answer life's great problems; instead, he is a writer 'driven to art by the excess of his humanity' and his work maintains 'sensibility at its most sensitive, and experience at its most comprehensive'.[254] This comprehensiveness and universality is key: for Murry, the 'great writer' is one who can refine 'emotional experience' into 'a system of emotional conviction' and thereby apprehend 'the quality of life as a whole' and 'make the particular a symbol of the universal'.[255] Mansfield and Woolf promoted very similar ideas when reviewing Chekhov's work. Appraising Constance Garnett's translation of Chekhov's *The Bishop and Other Stories*, for example, Woolf writes of his story 'The Steppe': 'Without metaphor, the feelings of his characters are related to something more important and far more remote than personal success or happiness'.[256] Corresponding with Koteliansky about 'The Steppe', likewise, Mansfield writes: 'One feels about this story not that it *becomes* immortal – it always was'.[257] In this way, both writers place emphasis on how Chekhov's story moves beyond the particular, relating personal 'feelings' at a level that is universal or timeless; as made clear in 'Modern Novels', Chekhov's work conveys a comprehensive vision of 'love' and 'sympathy' that exceeds personal interest and egoism. In her review of a production of *The Cherry Orchard* published in July 1920, furthermore, Woolf writes: 'I do not know how better to describe the sensation at the end of *The Cherry Orchard*, than by saying that it sends one into the street feeling like a piano played upon at last, not in the middle only but all over the keyboard and with the lid left open so that the sound goes on'.[258] And in her own review of this production for *The Athenaeum*, Mansfield describes how all 'that comes under the author's spell is bathed, is steeped and saturated in an emotional atmosphere'.[259] For both Mansfield and Woolf, then, the work of Chekhov exemplified the qualities of emotion, sensation, compassion and universality on which 'modern fiction' should be based.

Mansfield's attempts to convey 'feeling' and 'compassion' in her own fiction were sometimes critiqued by her contemporaries for slipping into excessive displays of personal emotion or 'sentimentalism'. When Beatrice Hastings reviewed Mansfield's first short story collection for *The New Age* in 1911, for example, she accused the younger writer of exhibiting a 'lachrymose sentimentality' that obscured an otherwise 'amusing and refreshing' gift for observational satire.[260] This denigration of Mansfield's 'sentimentality' served to place her beyond the pale of an emerging modernist culture of aesthetic impersonality and 'classicism' then being developed within the pages of *The New Age* by the likes of T. E. Hulme and Ezra Pound. Undoubtedly motivated in part by professional jealousy, Woolf also occasionally accused Mansfield's writing of being 'sentimental'. On reading 'Bliss', for example, she dismissed the story as 'so hard, & so shallow, & so sentimental'.[261] Similarly, writing to Jacques Raverat in 1923, Woolf explained that she didn't like Mansfield's writing because as soon as she tried to 'put thoughts, or feelings, or subtleties of any kind into her characters' she became either 'hard' or 'sentimental'.[262] Arguably, Mansfield's posthumous reputation has also suffered under this charge of being too 'sentimental'. As Meghan Marie Hammond has argued, however, modernism can be understood not only as the turn towards abstraction and a concomitant break with 'empathy', figured by the likes of Hulme and Pound, but also as a reinvestment in the idea of 'fellow feeling'. Hammond points to a number of modernist writers of the late nineteenth and early twentieth centuries, including Mansfield and Woolf, who promoted 'sympathetic imagination' or 'empathy' as integral to the modernist project, advancing the idea of 'feeling with' or 'feeling oneself into' the other. Whilst Hammond points to the ways in which Mansfield and Woolf depict these empathetic acts with a certain ambivalence, noting the 'psychological violence' often involved in the merging between self and other in Woolf's political writings and late novels, in particular, the notion that modernist writing should aim to overcome the barriers between different subjective entities through 'compassion' or 'emotion' runs directly counter to a version of modernism based upon the distancing techniques of abstraction and radical interiority.[263]

In the essays and reviews written in 1919–20, both Mansfield and Woolf emphasised the ideas of deep emotion and fellow feeling as essential to the coming 'new word' of modern fiction. Reading these critical writings, a common vocabulary emerges around the concept of 'emotion' that suggests the extent to which Woolf's writings 'talk' to Mansfield's, and vice versa. In particular, both writers employ 'emotion' as a critical standard against which to evaluate works by the so-called 'materialists' and those contemporary novelists influenced by the 'new psychology'. Moreover, it is the concept of 'fellow feeling' that shapes Mansfield and Woolf's shared idea that modern fiction should aim to reach 'outside and beyond' by mediating between the self and other. On occasions, Mansfield's writings even pre-empt some of Woolf's later, more celebrated ideas, such as the concept of a revelatory 'moment of being'. Indeed, after her death in 1923, Mansfield's writings continued to speak to Woolf. When she read Mansfield's posthumously published journals, for instance, Mansfield's observation that writing should come from 'deep feeling' provoked Woolf to ask: 'Am I writing *The Hours* [*Mrs Dalloway*] from deep emotion? [. . .] Have I the power of conveying the true reality? Or do I write essays about myself?'[264] As Lee observes, '[t]his passage, so often quoted, where [Woolf] asks herself the crucial questions of her writing life, [came] directly out of her argument with Katherine'.[265] As this chapter has examined, each woman's work provoked the other into questioning how the modern writer might produce fiction from the 'deep original source' of emotion whilst avoiding the trap of personal sentimentality, thus conveying the 'essential thing' or 'true reality' that is universal. Throughout their contemporaneous critical writings, then, Mansfield and Woolf can be seen to enact a dialogue in print, formulating remarkably similar ideas that help us to place 'emotion' at the heart of literary modernism.

Conclusion

In October 1920, Mansfield wrote a letter to Murry in which she reiterated the concept of a separate, remote 'world' of a select few, a 'mysterious' world waiting to be discovered:

> I return to [Walter] DelaMare's [*sic*] letter. I long to hear of your time with him. Its [*sic*] very queer; he haunts me here – not a persistent or substantial ghost but as one who shares my (our) joy in the *silent world*. Joy is not the word: I only used it because it conveys a stillness – a remoteness – because there is a faraway sound in it. [. . .] Isn't it possible that if one yielded there is a whole world into which one is received? It is so near and yet I am conscious that I hold back from giving myself up to it. What is this something mysterious that waits – that beckons?[266]

Murry, like other periodical editors at the time, often commissioned his contributors to write favourable reviews of books by his close associates. Remarkably, for instance, Woolf reviewed for *The Athenaeum* two books of poetry by Murry and Eliot that she herself had printed at the Hogarth Press. In December 1920, then, Mansfield wrote to Murry, saying: 'If DeLaMare [*sic*] would do my book – Id [*sic*] rather him than anyone'.[267]

When Walter de la Mare anonymously reviewed Mansfield's *Bliss and Other Stories* for *The Athenaeum* in January 1921, he employed her own critical vocabulary of literary impressionism to describe the merits of the story collection. Like Mansfield, for instance, he uses metaphors of 'intrepid' exploration to describe the 'spirit' and 'truth' of the book:

> Without fear, without favour, though not without predilection, she accepts, explores, makes herself at home in the chosen phase of reality. Her consciousness is as clear, it is only *apparently* as indiscriminating, as a looking-glass. The spirit that surveys its field is delicate yet intrepid, fastidiously frank. To her very finger-tips she is in love with beauty, and securely so because her love springs out of her devotion to truth.[268]

Recalling Mansfield's emphasis on 'vision' and perception, de la Mare writes that the book offers 'glimpses' into the life of each character and that Mansfield's 'vision casts far its beams, illuminates a naughty world; and we may be content merely to scrutinize the world in its light'.[269] Like Mansfield, de la Mare suggests that works of modern fiction should make their readers feel that they are positioned at the centre of another mind: to 'any true observer', he argues, the most 'precious' thing about reading *Bliss* 'is the experience of watching [another] conscience in deliberation behind the eyes'.[270] This experience, he writes, 'is one of the rarest of lessons, the most secret of joys'.[271] In this way, de la Mare echoes the concept advanced throughout Mansfield's reviews of the 'secret life' of the self: for instance, he writes that for each of Mansfield's 'meek' and 'cheated' characters, people who must endure the 'vile' world and the 'human abuse of it', 'heaven is out of sight, deep, illimitable, within themselves'.[272] In accordance with this emphasis on the inner life, de la Mare also highlights the importance of the 'emotional' reaction to the 'object' and the fusion between imagination and intellect. Whilst Mansfield's 'pitch of mind is invariably emotional', he writes, her writing method also 'captivates the intelligence': 'minute strokes disclose the method of this writer, and prove that her imaginative gaze is fixed on the object'.[273] Whilst 'Mansfield's personality, whatever its disguises, haunts her work', therefore, de la Mare also celebrates 'the discipline and self-sacrifice' of her prose, the 'acceptance of life' that proves she is 'an artist'.[274] This echoes Mansfield's 'philosophy' of the 'defeat of the personal' and the submission of the self. Finally, de la Mare writes that

Mansfield's characters are 'engrossed in every conceivable manifestation of the depicted problem, Life; whose answer – to go on with – is merely its indefatigable insistence on itself, its defiant momentum'.[275] Like Mansfield, then, de la Mare argues that the task of the author is to pose questions, not to answer them. Describing the 'world of this book' as 'lovely and significant', for instance, de la Mare writes: 'If perhaps we ask, Significant of what? Miss Mansfield does not answer, outright'.[276] Addressed to *The Athenaeum*'s readership, who had come to know Mansfield over the last two years as 'K.M.' the critic, de la Mare's review employs Mansfield's own critical vocabulary in order to designate *Bliss*, only Mansfield's second published short story collection, as 'a kind of divination' that 'justifies or validates her criticism'.[277] In this way, we can see how Mansfield's reviews for *The Athenaeum* conditioned the public reception and interpretation of her own creative work.

Reviewers of *Bliss* were quick to note that the characters presented by Mansfield were on the whole unsympathetic and even 'horrible'. An anonymous reviewer in *The Times Literary Supplement*, for example, described the collection as 'fourteen different sorts of unhappiness or horror', summarising its central characters: 'Some of them are horrible; all of them are dismal'.[278] Writing in *The Dial*, likewise, Malcolm Cowley observed that '*Bliss* is not at all a likeable book [. . .] the disagreeable people far outnumber the sympathetic'.[279] And Jasper Pendlewaite, writing in *The Saturday Westminster Gazette*, noted that the stories are 'nearly all cruel'.[280] For these reviewers, though, the 'cruel' presentation of such 'dismal' characters made Mansfield's achievement all the more remarkable. Appraising 'Je ne parle pas français' after its initial publication as a limited edition in early 1920, for example, Murry's assistant editor, J. W. N. Sullivan, contributed a review to *The Athenaeum* in which he observed that the 'illusion of reality' in the story 'is so complete that it is, in truth, a new experience that we are being called upon to live through. We see everything through the eyes of the young French "literary" man and *procurer* Raoul Duquette': as such, the 'story may be regarded as an exposition of this man's world' and every episode 'assumes the perspective which belongs to it in this new world'.[281] Sullivan here echoes the idea reiterated across Mansfield's reviews that the truly new literary work would immerse the reader in a 'new world' adequate to 'new experience'. Similarly, in *The Times Literary Supplement* review of Mansfield's collection, which was published directly alongside a review of Murry's book *Aspects of Literature* and an advertisement for Lawrence's novel

The Lost Girl, the anonymous reviewer echoes Mansfield's language of geographical exploration and adventure when observing that her book 'sends the reader's imagination voyaging into invisible distances of suggestion'.[282] Like Sullivan, the reviewer concedes that the characters presented may not be likeable, but that the success of the book hinges on the way in which the reader is immersed in a new 'world':

> In the end, what we enjoy is getting into Miss Mansfield's world – whether we may 'like' that world when we get into it, or not. The short story of commerce seems clumsily to report, where it pretends to create. Miss Mansfield, with the air of dispassionately reporting, is making all the while her own world. In other words, she is an artist in fiction.[283]

This distinction between the 'artist' and the writer of 'commerce' recalls Mansfield's own distinction between the 'artist' and the 'popular' writer as well as the idea that she derived from Chekhov, that what the 'true' writer does 'is not so much to *solve* the question but to *put* the question'. *The Times Literary Supplement* reviewer, for instance, observes that 'all moral judgment, even all emotion' is left to the reader of Mansfield's collection: 'Right and wrong, pity and blame, she seems to say to us, are your affair. Mine is only to put the case to you.'[284]

Indeed, the anonymous reviewer in *The Times Literary Supplement* explicitly notes this debt to Russian literature, writing that 'Miss Mansfield's stories might be likened to Tchehov's'.[285] Sullivan also observes that both 'Dostoevsky and Tchehov can be found amongst her ancestors'.[286] And Cowley writes that the 'form' of Mansfield's stories 'carries her, in most of her work, to about the same stage as Chekhov': 'like him, she has come to a point where she writes most of her stories around a situation instead of around a plot'.[287] From this observation of Mansfield's debt to the Russians, both Cowley and the reviewer in *The Times Literary Supplement* emphasise the 'form' of each story. The anonymous reviewer writes that Mansfield has produced 'work which is at once precise and suggestive' and shaped by 'exactness of definition': 'The plan of the whole, moreover, is in each case calculated with a pure sense of proportion' and, 'from the first to the last' sentence, 'the "real" point', the 'essential' thing 'is never overlooked'.[288] Likewise, Cowley emphasises Mansfield's precision, observing that 'not a word is wasted', and describes the sense of proportion and completeness given by each story: 'her best descriptions are final and perfect; one must fight back the temptation to quote whole pages of them'.[289] Focusing on 'Je ne parle pas français', he writes that 'the story appears as handled with a sense of form both strong and delicate' and describes the 'new form' of Mansfield's work:

> In one part of the story Raoul Duquette speaks of discussing the modern novel. For him this discussion was equivalent to stating 'the need of a new form, or the reason why our young men appeared to be just missing it.' Katherine Mansfield has got hold of that new and necessary form.[290]

The recurring motif in Mansfield's diaries, letters and critical writings, that a 'new form' was needed to express 'our new thoughts & feelings' in a post-war world, is taken up here by Cowley to designate *Bliss* a resounding success.

For Cowley, the 'new form' of Mansfield's stories is equivalent to 'the suppleness and some of the abstractedness of music'.[291] For other reviewers, Mansfield's prose resembles poetry. Reviewing *The Garden Party and Other Stories* when it was published in 1922, Rebecca West discusses the 'beauty' of 'Miss Mansfield's poetic temperament': 'Most of her tales are laid in the glowing setting of the sub-tropics', West writes, and the 'mind takes pleasure in merely moving in such an atmosphere, apart from the meanings it may find there. That is where the writer who is a poet like Miss Mansfield scores over a writer who is not a poet.'[292] As such, reviewers picked up on Mansfield's stated aim in her journals, to produce 'a kind of special prose' 'trembling on the brink of poetry'. Reviewing the same story collection for *The Freeman*, for instance, Conrad Aiken writes that 'Miss Mansfield goes to the short story as the lyric poet goes to poetry – Miss Mansfield's short story is, in essence, an essentially "subjective" thing, far more subjective than one is accustomed to expect a short story to be'.[293] Whilst finding fault with this method, viewing each character in the collection as 'so many projections of Miss Mansfield's mind and personality', Aiken concedes that the 'short story created in this manner approaches the poetic in proportion as its theme is largely and emotionally significant'.[294] Moreover, Aiken's review, titled 'The Short Story as Colour', points to the painterly qualities of Mansfield's prose. Pendlewaite similarly writes that the stories are 'clever pegs on which the fine cloths of Miss Mansfield's visual memories hang shimmering with colour and design'.[295] And the reviewer for *The Times Literary Supplement* notes: 'Every touch in these stories shows the author's sensitiveness to the beauty of sound, colour, scent': each story is 'enjoyable because of the beauty, sensuous or spiritual, which Miss Mansfield sets to glow in the stuff of her tale'.[296]

Across *The Athenaeum*, as this chapter has examined, contributors looked to recuperate the 'spiritual' in response to the disintegration and 'crisis' of the First World War. The 'spiritual' beauty identified by the anonymous reviewer of *Bliss* associated Mansfield's prose with this post-war cultural project. The reviewer notes that this beauty is registered as a result of the author's acute 'sensitiveness', a word also employed by Pendlewaite, who writes that Mansfield's stories are 'records of the life of an over-sensitive mind' which 'enjoys beauty to the same exquisite point as it endures pain'.[297] On reading Mansfield's posthumously published journals in 1927, likewise, Virginia Woolf wrote a review for the *New York Herald Tribune* titled 'A Terribly Sensitive Mind'. In this review, Woolf writes:

> It is not the quality of her writing or the degree of her fame that interest us in her diary, but the spectacle of a mind – a terribly sensitive mind – receiving one after another the haphazard impressions of eight years of life.[298]

Mansfield here exemplifies the modern writer identified by Woolf in 'Modern Novels' who successfully records myriad 'impressions' as they fall upon the surface of the mind like 'an incessant shower of innumerable atoms, composing in their sum what we might venture to call life itself'. Woolf here also reiterates the vocabulary used by both writers in their critical writings during the immediate post-war years, describing how Mansfield's journals offer 'glimpses' in which 'the moment itself suddenly put[s] on significance'.[299]

The language that Mansfield used in her reviews shaped the way in which contemporaries received her creative work, therefore. In dialogue with Woolf and other contributors to *The Athenaeum*, Mansfield's reviews positioned formal experimentation and artistic 'newness' as a precondition for post-war cultural and 'spiritual' rejuvenation. Mansfield's idea of a 'new world' removed from the corruption and disintegration of the 'worldly world' not only provided a spatial metaphor that was in part overlaid with colonial connotations of reaching and exploring an 'undiscovered country', but also enabled her to envision a space of affiliation between a select minority of writers, artists and intellectuals that she described to Murry as 'OUR world' and 'the *silent world*'. Moreover, this idea of a 'new world' waiting to be discovered informed the way in which Mansfield communicated her sense of a 'new word' yet to be realised, a 'new form' of literary innovation which would defy the staid conventions of 'popular' fiction and the traditions of the realist novel, as well as counter the spiritual disintegration resulting from the war. In this way, Mansfield's reviews anticipated the more striking experimentalism of the 1920s and helped to condition the critical response to her own work, with reviewers of *Bliss* and *The Garden Party* hailing her as 'the story-writing genius' who 'has got hold of that new and necessary form'.[300]

Notes

1. Clare Hanson, 'Introduction', in Clare Hanson (ed.), *The Critical Writings of Katherine Mansfield* (London: Macmillan, 1987), p. 136.
2. Katherine Mansfield, *The Katherine Mansfield Notebooks, Complete Edition, Volume II*, ed. Margaret Scott (Minneapolis: University of Minnesota Press, 2002), pp. 32–3.
3. Katherine Mansfield, *The Collected Letters of Katherine Mansfield, Volume II: 1918–1919*, ed. Vincent O'Sullivan and Margaret Scott (Oxford: Clarendon Press, 1987), p. 275.
4. Ibid., p. 343.
5. Katherine Mansfield, *The Collected Letters of Katherine Mansfield, Volume III: 1919–1920*, ed. Vincent O'Sullivan and Margaret Scott (Oxford: Clarendon Press, 1993), p. 262.
6. Katherine Mansfield, *The Collected Letters of Katherine Mansfield, Volume IV: 1920–1921*, ed. Vincent O'Sullivan and Margaret Scott (Oxford: Clarendon Press, 1996), p. 19.
7. Ibid., p. 317.
8. Angela Smith, *Katherine Mansfield: A Literary Life* (Basingstoke: Palgrave, 2000), p. 123.
9. Mansfield, *The Katherine Mansfield Notebooks, Volume II*, p. 32.
10. See Leslie A. Marchand, *The Athenaeum: A Mirror of Victorian Culture* (Chapel Hill: University of North Carolina, 1940).
11. Mansfield, *The Collected Letters of Katherine Mansfield, Volume II*, p. 303.
12. Michael H. Whitworth, 'Enemies of Cant: *The Athenaeum* (1919–21) and *The Adelphi* (1923–48)', in Peter Brooker and Andrew Thacker (eds), *The Oxford Critical and Cultural History of Modernist Magazines, Volume I: Britain and Ireland, 1880–1955* (Oxford: Oxford University Press, 2009), p. 366.
13. Virginia Woolf, *The Diary of Virginia Woolf, Volume I*, ed. Anne Olivier Bell (London: Hogarth Press, 1977), p. 260.
14. Quoted by Michael Holroyd, *Lytton Strachey: A Critical Biography, Volume II* (London: Heinemann, 1968), pp. 351–2.
15. David Goldie, *A Critical Difference: T. S. Eliot and John Middleton Murry in English Literary Criticism, 1919–1928* (Oxford: Clarendon Press, 1998), p. 14.
16. Oscar Wellens, '"The Brief and Brilliant Life of *The Athenaeum* under Mr Middleton Murry" (T. S. Eliot)', *Neophilologus*, 85 (2001), p. 138.
17. Quoted in F. A. Lea, *The Life of John Middleton Murry* (London: Methuen, 1959), p. 83.

18. T. S. Eliot, *The Sacred Wood: Essays on Poetry and Criticism* (London: Methuen, 1920), p. viii; quoted in Whitworth, 'Enemies of Cant', p. 366.
19. John Middleton Murry, *The Letters of John Middleton Murry to Katherine Mansfield*, ed. Cherry A. Hankin (London: Constable, 1983), p. 185.
20. Ibid., pp. 280, 210.
21. Anon. [Katherine Mansfield], 'Three Women Novelists', *Athenaeum*, 4640 (4 April 1919), p. 140.
22. Angela Smith, 'GUTS – Katherine Mansfield as a Reviewer', *Katherine Mansfield Studies*, 1 (2009), p. 9.
23. K.M. [Katherine Mansfield], 'The Public School Mixture', *Athenaeum*, 4646 (16 May 1919), p. 335.
24. Mansfield, *The Collected Letters of Katherine Mansfield, Volume III*, p. 48.
25. Murry, *The Letters of John Middleton Murry to Katherine Mansfield*, p. 194.
26. Mansfield, *The Collected Letters of Katherine Mansfield, Volume III*, p. 104.
27. K.M. [Katherine Mansfield], 'Fishing as a Fine Art', *Athenaeum*, 4717 (24 September 1920), p. 407; K.M. [Katherine Mansfield], 'A Plea for Less Entertainment', *Athenaeum*, 4669 (24 October 1919), p. 1067.
28. Marysa Demoor, *Their Fair Share: Women, Power and Criticism in the* Athenaeum, *from Millicent Garrett Fawcett to Katherine Mansfield, 1870–1920* (Aldershot: Ashgate, 2000), p. 145.
29. Wellens, '"The Brief and Brilliant Life of *The Athenaeum* under Mr Middleton Murry" (T. S. Eliot)', p. 142.
30. Jenny McDonnell, *Katherine Mansfield and the Modernist Marketplace: At the Mercy of the Public* (Basingstoke: Palgrave Macmillan, 2010), p. 117.
31. David Dowling, 'Katherine Mansfield's Criticism: "There Must Be the Question Put"', *Journal of New Zealand Literature*, 6 (1988), pp. 158–60.
32. McDonnell, *Katherine Mansfield and the Modernist Marketplace*, pp. 116–17.
33. Mansfield, *The Collected Letters of Katherine Mansfield, Volume III*, pp. 21, 46.
34. Ibid., p. 79.
35. Ibid., p. 84; Mansfield, *The Collected Letters of Katherine Mansfield, Volume II*, p. 344.
36. Mansfield, *The Collected Letters of Katherine Mansfield, Volume III*, p. 104; Mansfield, *The Collected Letters of Katherine Mansfield, Volume IV*, p. 74.
37. Mansfield, *The Collected Letters of Katherine Mansfield, Volume IV*, pp. 17, 8.
38. Ibid., p. 20.
39. Mansfield, *The Collected Letters of Katherine Mansfield, Volume III*, pp. 73–4.
40. Mansfield, *The Collected Letters of Katherine Mansfield, Volume IV*, p. 68.
41. Mansfield, *The Katherine Mansfield Notebooks, Volume II*, pp. 176–7.
42. Mansfield, *The Collected Letters of Katherine Mansfield, Volume III*, p. 31.
43. J. D. Beresford, '"Between Two Worlds"', *Adelphi*, 10.1 (April 1935), p. 13.
44. Matthew Arnold, 'Stanzas from the Grande Chartreuse', in *The Poems of Matthew Arnold*, ed. Miriam Allott (London: Longman, 1979), p. 305.
45. Suzanne W. Churchill and Adam McKible, 'Introduction', in Suzanne W. Churchill and Adam McKible (eds), *Little Magazines and Modernism: New Approaches* (Aldershot: Ashgate, 2007), p. 12.
46. D. H. Lawrence, *The Letters of D. H. Lawrence, Volume II*, ed. George J. Zytaruk and James T. Boulton (Cambridge: Cambridge University Press, 1982), p. 394.
47. Ibid., p. 411.
48. Figures estimated from S. S. Kotelianksy's papers in the British Library.

49. Saralyn R. Daly, *Katherine Mansfield*, rev. edn (Oxford: Maxwell Macmillan, 1994), p. 46.
50. Peter Brooker, 'Harmony, Discord, and Difference: *Rhythm* (1911–13), *The Blue Review* (1913), and *The Signature* (1915)', in Peter Brooker and Andrew Thacker (eds), *The Oxford Critical and Cultural History of Modernist Magazines, Volume I: Britain and Ireland, 1880–1955* (Oxford: Oxford University Press, 2009), p. 323.
51. Lawrence, *The Letters of D. H. Lawrence, Volume II*, p. 386.
52. Katherine Mansfield, *The Collected Letters of Katherine Mansfield, Volume I: 1903–1917*, ed. Vincent O'Sullivan and Margaret Scott (Oxford: Clarendon Press, 1984), pp. 218–19.
53. Lawrence, *The Letters of D. H. Lawrence, Volume II*, p. 482.
54. Ibid., p. 387.
55. Quoted in Mark Kinkead-Weekes, *D. H. Lawrence: Triumph to Exile, 1912–1922* (Cambridge: Cambridge University Press, 1996), p. 271.
56. David Garnett, *The Flowers of the Forest* (London: Chatto and Windus, 1955), pp. 190–1.
57. D. H. Lawrence, 'Foreword', *Women in Love*, ed. David Farmer, Lindeth Vasey and John Worthen ([1920] London: Penguin, 1995), p. 486.
58. Mansfield, *The Collected Letters of Katherine Mansfield, Volume II*, p. 262.
59. Ibid., pp. 48, 138.
60. Ibid., p. 86.
61. Ibid., pp. 352, 339.
62. Ibid., p. 293.
63. Ibid., p. 256.
64. Mansfield, *The Collected Letters of Katherine Mansfield, Volume III*, p. 15.
65. Ibid., p. 255.
66. Mansfield, *The Collected Letters of Katherine Mansfield, Volume I*, pp. 317–18.
67. John Middleton Murry, 'There Was a Little Man', *Signature*, 3 (1 November 1915), p. 21.
68. Ibid., pp. 22–3.
69. John Middleton Murry, *Fyodor Dostoevsky: A Critical Study* (London: Martin Secker, 1916), p. 116.
70. Ibid., p. 263.
71. Lea, *The Life of John Middleton Murry*, p. 49.
72. Murry, *Fyodor Dostoevsky*, p. 241.
73. Goldie, *A Critical Difference*, p. 32.
74. John Middleton Murry, 'The Discovery of Pain', *Times Literary Supplement*, 803 (7 June 1917), p. 270.
75. John Middleton Murry, 'The Great Hallucination', *Times Literary Supplement*, 856 (13 June 1918), p. 274.
76. John Middleton Murry, 'The Nature of Civilization' (4 January 1919), in *The Evolution of an Intellectual* (London: Cobden-Sanderson, 1920), p. 173.
77. John Middleton Murry, 'The Poet of the War', *Athenaeum*, 4647 (23 May 1919), p. 376.
78. John Middleton Murry, 'The Defeat of Imagination' (28 December 1918), in *The Evolution of an Intellectual*, pp. 164–5.
79. Mansfield, *The Collected Letters of Katherine Mansfield, Volume II*, p. 209.
80. John Middleton Murry, 'The Gospel of M. Duhamel', *Athenaeum*, 4641 (11 April 1919), p. 185.
81. Mansfield, *The Collected Letters of Katherine Mansfield, Volume II*, p. 227.

82. Ibid., p. 244.
83. Mansfield, *The Collected Letters of Katherine Mansfield, Volume III*, p. 119.
84. Paul Valéry, 'The Spiritual Crisis', *Athenaeum*, 4641 (11 April 1919), pp. 182–3.
85. J. M. M. [John Middleton Murry], 'Poetry and Criticism', *Athenaeum*, 4691 (26 March 1920), p. 409.
86. Anon. [John Middleton Murry], 'Notes and Comments', *Athenaeum*, 4723 (5 November 1920), p. 607.
87. Anon. [John Middleton Murry], 'The New Imperative', *Athenaeum*, 4641 (11 April 1919), p. 165.
88. Ibid.
89. Anon. [John Middleton Murry], 'Prologue', *Athenaeum*, 4640 (4 April 1919), pp. 130–1.
90. Grantorto [D. H. Lawrence], 'Whistling of Birds', *Athenaeum*, 4641 (11 April 1919), p. 167.
91. Ibid.
92. Anon. [Katherine Mansfield], 'Two Novels of Worth', *Athenaeum*, 4641 (11 April 1919), p. 173.
93. Mansfield, *The Collected Letters of Katherine Mansfield, Volume II*, p. 62.
94. Ibid., p. 107.
95. Mansfield, *The Collected Letters of Katherine Mansfield, Volume III*, p. 81; Mansfield, *The Collected Letters of Katherine Mansfield, Volume IV*, p. 82.
96. Mansfield, *The Collected Letters of Katherine Mansfield, Volume IV*, p. 173.
97. John Middleton Murry, 'The Sign Seekers' (October 1916), in *The Evolution of an Intellectual*, p. 8.
98. K.M. [Katherine Mansfield], 'A Ship Comes into the Harbour', *Athenaeum*, 4673 (21 November 1919), p. 1227.
99. Ibid.
100. Ibid.
101. Woolf, *The Diary of Virginia Woolf, Volume I*, p. 314.
102. Mansfield, *The Collected Letters of Katherine Mansfield, Volume III*, p. 82.
103. John Middleton Murry, 'François Villon', *Times Literary Supplement*, 630 (12 February 1914), p. 70.
104. Murry, 'The Discovery of Pain', p. 270.
105. Murry, *The Letters of John Middleton Murry to Katherine Mansfield*, p. 211.
106. K.M. [Katherine Mansfield], 'Old Writers and New', *Athenaeum*, 4725 (19 November 1920), p. 695; K.M. [Katherine Mansfield], 'New Season's Novels', *Athenaeum*, 4718 (1 October 1920), p. 439.
107. K.M. [Katherine Mansfield], 'A Citizen of the Sea', *Athenaeum*, 4642 (18 April 1919), p. 205.
108. K.M. [Katherine Mansfield], 'A Dull Monster', *Athenaeum*, 4716 (17 September 1920), p. 376.
109. Mansfield, *The Collected Letters of Katherine Mansfield, Volume II*, pp. 46, 123.
110. Ibid., p. 291.
111. Mansfield, *The Collected Letters of Katherine Mansfield, Volume IV*, p. 116.
112. D. H. Lawrence, *Kangaroo* ([1923] London: Heinemann, 1955), p. 220.
113. Goldie, *A Critical Difference*, p. 18.
114. Mansfield, *The Collected Letters of Katherine Mansfield, Volume II*, pp. 88, 124.
115. Mansfield, *The Collected Letters of Katherine Mansfield, Volume III*, pp. 80–1; Mansfield, *The Collected Letters of Katherine Mansfield, Volume IV*, p. 73.

116. M. [John Middleton Murry], 'Critical Interest', *Athenaeum*, 4686 (20 February 1920), p. 233.
117. K.M. [Katherine Mansfield], 'Wanted, a New Word', *Athenaeum*, 4704 (25 June 1920), p. 832.
118. T. S. Eliot, 'The Perfect Critic', *Athenaeum*, 4706 (9 July 1920), p. 40; T. S. E. [Eliot], 'Criticism in England', *Athenaeum*, 4650 (13 June 1919), p. 456.
119. Frank Swinnerton, 'The Difficulties of Criticism', *Athenaeum*, 4699 (21 May 1920), p. 662.
120. Anon. [A. de Sélincourt], 'Common-Sense Criticism', *Athenaeum*, 4704 (25 June 1920), p. 827.
121. M. [John Middleton Murry], 'The False Dawn', *Athenaeum*, 4680 (9 January 1920), p. 37.
122. K.M. [Katherine Mansfield], 'A Backward Glance', *Athenaeum*, 4658 (8 August 1919), p. 720.
123. Murry, 'Poetry and Criticism', p. 408; 'The False Dawn', p. 38.
124. Murry, 'The False Dawn', p. 38.
125. John Middleton Murry, 'The Function of Criticism', *Times Literary Supplement*, 956 (13 May 1920), p. 290.
126. Murry, 'The Function of Criticism', p. 289.
127. Ibid.
128. Mansfield, 'Wanted, a New Word', p. 831.
129. K.M. [Katherine Mansfield], 'A Woman's Books', *Athenaeum*, 4698 (14 May 1920), p. 639.
130. Mansfield, 'Three Women Novelists', p. 140.
131. Ibid.
132. K.M. [Katherine Mansfield], 'Mystery and Adventure', *Athenaeum*, 4687 (27 February 1920), p. 274.
133. K.M. [Katherine Mansfield], 'Entertainment – and Otherwise', *Athenaeum*, 4719 (8 October 1920), p. 472.
134. K.M. [Katherine Mansfield], 'On the Road', *Athenaeum*, 4690 (19 March 1920), p. 369.
135. K.M. [Katherine Mansfield], 'The New Infancy', *Athenaeum*, 4651 (20 June 1919), p. 494.
136. Anon. [J. W. N. Sullivan], 'Science and Literature', *Athenaeum*, 4650 (13 June 1919), p. 464.
137. S. [J. W. N. Sullivan], 'Dissolving Views', *Athenaeum*, 4677 (19 December 1919), p. 1361.
138. Ibid.
139. Ibid., p. 1362.
140. Ibid., p. 1361.
141. K.M. [Katherine Mansfield], 'A Hymn to Youth', *Athenaeum*, 4707 (16 July 1920), p. 78.
142. K.M. [Katherine Mansfield], 'A Novel Without a Crisis', *Athenaeum*, 4648 (30 May 1919), p. 399.
143. K.M. [Katherine Mansfield], 'Anodyne', *Athenaeum*, 4656 (20 July 1919), p. 654.
144. K.M. [Katherine Mansfield], 'Portraits and Passions', *Athenaeum*, 4667 (10 October 1919), p. 1002.
145. Mansfield, *The Collected Letters of Katherine Mansfield, Volume II*, p. 326.
146. Mansfield, 'Three Women Novelists', p. 140.
147. Mansfield, 'A Backward Glance', p. 720.

148. K.M. [Katherine Mansfield], 'Two Novels', *Athenaeum*, 4700 (28 May 1920), p. 702.
149. K.M. [Katherine Mansfield], 'Family Portraits', *Athenaeum*, 4728 (10 December 1920), p. 811.
150. Mansfield, *The Katherine Mansfield Notebooks, Volume II*, p. 163.
151. K.M. [Katherine Mansfield], 'Throw Them Overboard!', *Athenaeum*, 4711 (13 August 1920), p. 209.
152. Ibid.
153. K.M. [Katherine Mansfield], 'A Norwegian Novel', *Athenaeum*, 4702 (11 June 1920), p. 767.
154. K.M. [Katherine Mansfield], 'The Books of the Small Souls', *Athenaeum*, 4703 (18 June 1920), pp. 798–9.
155. K.M. [Katherine Mansfield], 'A Japanese Novel', *Athenaeum*, 4699 (21 May 1920), p. 671.
156. Mansfield, 'New Season's Novels', p. 439.
157. Mansfield, 'Portraits and Passions', p. 1002.
158. Anon. [John Middleton Murry], 'True Internationalism', *Athenaeum*, 4716 (17 September 1920), p. 365.
159. Anon. [John Middleton Murry], 'Editorial Note', *Athenaeum*, 4701 (4 June 1920), p. 748.
160. Maxim Gorky, 'Literature and Present-Day Russia (II.)', *Athenaeum*, 4702 (11 June 1920), p. 781; Maxim Gorky, 'Literature and Present-Day Russia', *Athenaeum*, 4701 (4 June 1920), p. 748.
161. Mansfield, *The Collected Letters of Katherine Mansfield, Volume II*, p. 341.
162. Ibid., p. 324.
163. Mansfield, *The Collected Letters of Katherine Mansfield, Volume III*, p. 47.
164. Mansfield, 'New Season's Novels', p. 439.
165. Mansfield, *The Collected Letters of Katherine Mansfield, Volume II*, p. 227.
166. Virginia Woolf, *The Years* ([1937] London: Vintage, 2004), p. 244.
167. Ibid., p. 256.
168. Ibid., pp. 258–9.
169. Ibid., p. 259.
170. Jesse Matz, *Literary Impressionism and Modernist Aesthetics* (Cambridge: Cambridge University Press, 2001), pp. 16–17.
171. Virginia Woolf, 'Modern Novels', in *The Essays of Virginia Woolf, Volume III: 1919–1924*, ed. Andrew McNeillie (London: Hogarth Press, 1988), pp. 30–2.
172. Ibid., pp. 32–3.
173. Ibid.
174. Ibid., p. 34.
175. Ibid.
176. Ibid., p. 35.
177. Ibid.
178. Ibid., p. 36.
179. Ibid.
180. Ibid., p. 35.
181. Katherine Mansfield, *The Collected Letters of Katherine Mansfield, Volume V: 1922–1923*, ed. Vincent O'Sullivan and Margaret Scott (Oxford: Clarendon Press, 2008), p. 320.
182. Mansfield, *The Collected Letters of Katherine Mansfield, Volume I*, p. 327.
183. Virginia Woolf, *The Diary of Virginia Woolf, Volume II*, ed. Anne Olivier Bell (Harmondsworth: Penguin, 1981), pp. 45–6.

184. Ibid., p. 61.
185. Mansfield, *The Collected Letters of Katherine Mansfield, Volume IV*, p. 154.
186. Woolf, *The Diary of Virginia Woolf, Volume II*, p. 227.
187. Churchill and McKible, 'Introduction', p. 12.
188. Virginia Woolf, 'How It Strikes a Contemporary', in *The Essays of Virginia Woolf, Volume III*, p. 354.
189. Hermione Lee, 'Virginia Woolf's Essays', in Susan Sellers (ed.), *The Cambridge Companion to Virginia Woolf*, 2nd edn (Cambridge: Cambridge University Press, 2010), p. 93.
190. Woolf, *The Diary of Virginia Woolf, Volume I*, p. 257.
191. Virginia Woolf, 'The Tunnel', in *The Essays of Virginia Woolf, Volume III*, p. 11; Mansfield, 'Three Women Novelists', p. 140.
192. Woolf, *The Diary of Virginia Woolf, Volume II*, p. 45.
193. K.M. [Katherine Mansfield], 'Esther Waters Revisited', *Athenaeum*, 4710 (6 August 1920), p. 176.
194. K.M. [Katherine Mansfield], 'Mr Conrad's New Novel', *Athenaeum*, 4705 (2 July 1920), p. 15.
195. Virginia Woolf, 'Mr Byron & Mr Briggs', in *The Essays of Virginia Woolf, Volume III*, p. 487.
196. Quoted in Hermione Lee, *Virginia Woolf*, 2nd ed. (London: Vintage, 1997), p. 410.
197. Andrew McNeillie, 'Bloomsbury', in Susan Sellers (ed.), *The Cambridge Companion to Virginia Woolf*, 2nd edn (Cambridge: Cambridge University Press, 2010), p. 3.
198. Clive Bell, *Art* (London: Chatto and Windus, 1914), pp. 6, 8.
199. Ibid., p. 8.
200. Virginia Woolf, 'On Re-reading Novels', in *The Essays of Virginia Woolf, Volume III*, p. 340.
201. J.M.M. [John Middleton Murry], 'On Reading', *Athenaeum*, 4712 (20 August 1920), p. 235; J.M.M. [John Middleton Murry], 'The Condition of English Poetry', *Athenaeum*, 4675 (5 December 1919), pp. 1284–5.
202. T.S.E. [T. S. Eliot], 'Hamlet and His Problems', *Athenaeum*, 4665 (26 September 1919), p. 941.
203. John Middleton Murry, *The Problem of Style* (London: Oxford University Press, 1922), p. 100.
204. K.M. [Katherine Mansfield], 'Observation Only', *Athenaeum*, 4720 (15 October 1920), p. 520.
205. Mansfield, 'Esther Waters Revisited', p. 176.
206. Ibid.
207. Virginia Woolf, 'A Born Writer', in *The Essays of Virginia Woolf, Volume III*, p. 251.
208. Virginia Woolf, 'Java Head', in *The Essays of Virginia Woolf, Volume III*, p. 49.
209. K.M. [Katherine Mansfield], 'Glancing Light', *Athenaeum*, 4650 (13 June 1919), p. 463.
210. Mansfield, 'Esther Waters Revisited', p. 176.
211. K.M. [Katherine Mansfield], 'Letters', *Athenaeum*, 4715 (10 September 1920), p. 332.
212. K.M. [Katherine Mansfield], 'The Silence Is Broken', *Athenaeum*, 4722 (29 October 1920), p. 584.
213. Mansfield, 'A Citizen of the Sea', p. 205; K.M. [Katherine Mansfield], 'Portrait of a Little Lady', *Athenaeum*, 4643 (25 April 1919), p. 237.
214. Murry, *The Letters of John Middleton Murry to Katherine Mansfield*, p. 211.

215. J.M.M. [John Middleton Murry], 'The Poetry of Mr Hardy', *Athenaeum*, 4671 (7 November 1919), p. 1148.
216. Hermione Lee, 'Introduction', in Virginia Woolf, *Moments of Being: Autobiographical Writings*, ed. Jeanne Schulkind (London: Pimlico, 2002), p. vii.
217. Virginia Woolf, 'A Sketch of the Past', in *Moments of Being: Autobiographical Writings*, ed. Jeanne Schulkind (London: Pimlico, 2002), p. 85.
218. K.M. [Katherine Mansfield], 'A Model Story', *Athenaeum*, 4701 (4 June 1920), p. 736.
219. Mansfield, 'Mr Conrad's New Novel', p. 15.
220. Mansfield, *The Collected Letters of Katherine Mansfield, Volume II*, p. 254.
221. Katherine Mansfield, *Journal of Katherine Mansfield: Definitive Edition*, ed. John Middleton Murry (London: Constable, 1954), pp. 202–3.
222. Mansfield, 'A Novel Without a Crisis', p. 399.
223. K.M. [Katherine Mansfield], 'A Short Story', *Athenaeum*, 4650 (13 June 1919), p. 459.
224. Woolf, *The Diary of Virginia Woolf, Volume II*, pp. 61–2.
225. Mansfield, *The Collected Letters of Katherine Mansfield, Volume I*, p. 330.
226. Mansfield, *Journal of Katherine Mansfield*, p. 212.
227. Ibid.
228. Ibid., p. 195; Mansfield, *The Collected Letters of Katherine Mansfield, Volume III*, p. 196.
229. Lee, 'Virginia Woolf's Essays', p. 104.
230. Virginia Woolf, 'The Decay of Essay-Writing', in *The Essays of Virginia Woolf, Volume I, 1904–1912*, ed. Andrew McNeillie (London: Hogarth Press, 1986), p. 27.
231. Quoted in Lee, *Virginia Woolf*, p. 410.
232. Mansfield, 'Three Women Novelists', p. 141.
233. K.M. [Katherine Mansfield], 'Dragonflies', *Athenaeum*, 4680 (9 January 1920), p. 48.
234. Ibid.
235. Woolf, 'The Tunnel', pp. 10–11.
236. Ibid., p. 11.
237. Woolf, 'Modern Novels', p. 35.
238. Anon. [John Middleton Murry], 'Is There a New Generation?', *Athenaeum*, 4703 (18 June 1920), p. 789.
239. K.M. [Katherine Mansfield], 'Ask No Questions', *Athenaeum*, 4721 (22 October 1920), p. 552.
240. K.M. [Katherine Mansfield], 'The "Sex Complex"', *Athenaeum*, 4661 (29 August 1919), p. 816.
241. Virginia Woolf, 'Freudian Fiction', in *The Essays of Virginia Woolf, Volume III*, pp. 196–7.
242. K.M. [Katherine Mansfield], 'Two Modern Novels', *Athenaeum*, 4693 (9 April 1920), p. 479.
243. Ibid.
244. Virginia Woolf, 'September', in *The Essays of Virginia Woolf, Volume III*, p. 104.
245. Virginia Woolf, 'The Intellectual Imagination', in *The Essays of Virginia Woolf, Volume III*, p. 134.
246. K.M. [Katherine Mansfield], 'Looking On', *Athenaeum*, 4700 (28 May 1920), p. 703.
247. K.M. [Katherine Mansfield], 'A Foreign Novel', *Athenaeum*, 4709 (30 July 1920), p. 144.

248. Anton Chekhov, 'Letters of Anton Tchehov II', *Athenaeum*, 4642 (18 April 1919), p. 216; 'Letters of Anton Tchehov III', *Athenaeum*, 4643 (25 April 1919), p. 249.
249. Mansfield, 'A Foreign Novel', p. 1336.
250. Mansfield, *The Collected Letters of Katherine Mansfield, Volume IV*, p. 180; Mansfield, *The Collected Letters of Katherine Mansfield, Volume III*, p. 196.
251. Mansfield, *The Collected Letters of Katherine Mansfield, Volume IV*, pp. 180–1; Mansfield, *Journal of Katherine Mansfield*, p. 269.
252. Mansfield, *The Collected Letters of Katherine Mansfield, IV Four*, p. 105; Mansfield, *Journal of Katherine Mansfield*, pp. 228–9.
253. Mansfield, *Journal of Katherine Mansfield*, p. 205.
254. John Middleton Murry, 'More Notes on Tchehov', *Athenaeum*, 4732 (7 January 1921), p. 12.
255. Murry, *The Problem of Style*, pp. 92–3.
256. Virginia Woolf, 'The Russian Background', in *The Essays of Virginia Woolf, Volume III*, p. 85.
257. Mansfield, *The Collected Letters of Katherine Mansfield, Volume II*, p. 353.
258. Virginia Woolf, 'The Cherry Orchard', in *The Essays of Virginia Woolf, Volume III*, p. 248.
259. Anon. [Katherine Mansfield], 'The Cherry Orchard', *Athenaeum*, 4707 (16 July 1920), p. 91. The marked files for *The Athenaeum* list Murry as the author of this piece, but the review is usually attributed to Mansfield.
260. Anon. [Beatrice Hastings], 'In a German Pension', *New Age*, 10.8 (21 December 1911), p. 188.
261. Virginia Woolf, *The Letters of Virginia Woolf, Volume II*, ed. Nigel Nicolson (London: Hogarth Press, 1976), p. 514.
262. Virginia Woolf, *The Letters of Virginia Woolf, Volume III*, ed. Nigel Nicolson (London: Hogarth Press, 1977), p. 59.
263. Meghan Marie Hammond, *Empathy and the Psychology of Literary Modernism* (Edinburgh: Edinburgh University Press, 2014), p. 153.
264. Woolf, *The Diary of Virginia Woolf, Volume II*, p. 248.
265. Lee, *Virginia Woolf*, p. 399.
266. Mansfield, *The Collected Letters of Katherine Mansfield, Volume IV*, p. 75.
267. Ibid., p. 133.
268. Anon. [Walter de la Mare], 'Prelude', *Athenaeum*, 4734 (21 January 1921), p. 67. The marked files for *The Athenaeum* clearly attribute authorship of this review to de la Mare.
269. Ibid.
270. Ibid.
271. Ibid.
272. Ibid.
273. Ibid.
274. Ibid.
275. Ibid.
276. Ibid.
277. Ibid.
278. Anon., 'Miss Mansfield's Stories', *Times Literary Supplement*, 987 (16 December 1920), p. 855.
279. Malcolm Cowley, '"Page Dr Blum": *Bliss*', *Dial*, 71 (September 1921), p. 365.
280. Jasper Pendlewaite, 'The Two Magics', *Saturday Westminster Gazette*, 8579 (1 January 1921), p. 16.

281. J.W.N.S. [Sullivan], 'The Story-Writing Genius', *Athenaeum*, 4692 (2 April 1920), p. 447.
282. Anon., 'Miss Mansfield's Stories', p. 855.
283. Ibid.
284. Ibid.
285. Ibid.
286. J.W.N.S. [Sullivan], 'The Story-Writing Genius', p. 447.
287. Cowley, '"Page Dr Blum"', p. 365.
288. Anon., 'Miss Mansfield's Stories', p. 855.
289. Cowley, '"Page Dr Blum"', p. 365.
290. Ibid.
291. Ibid.
292. Rebecca West, 'The Garden Party', *New Statesman*, 18 (18 March 1922), p. 678.
293. Conrad Aiken, 'The Short Story as Colour', *Freeman*, 5 (21 June 1922), p. 357.
294. Ibid.
295. Pendlewaite, 'The Two Magics', p. 16.
296. Anon., 'Miss Mansfield's Stories', p. 855.
297. Pendlewaite, 'The Two Magics', p. 16.
298. Virginia Woolf, 'A Terribly Sensitive Mind', *New York Herald Tribune*, 125 (18 September 1927), p. 716.
299. Ibid.
300. J.W.N.S. [Sullivan], 'The Story-Writing Genius'; Cowley, '"Page Dr Blum"', p. 365.

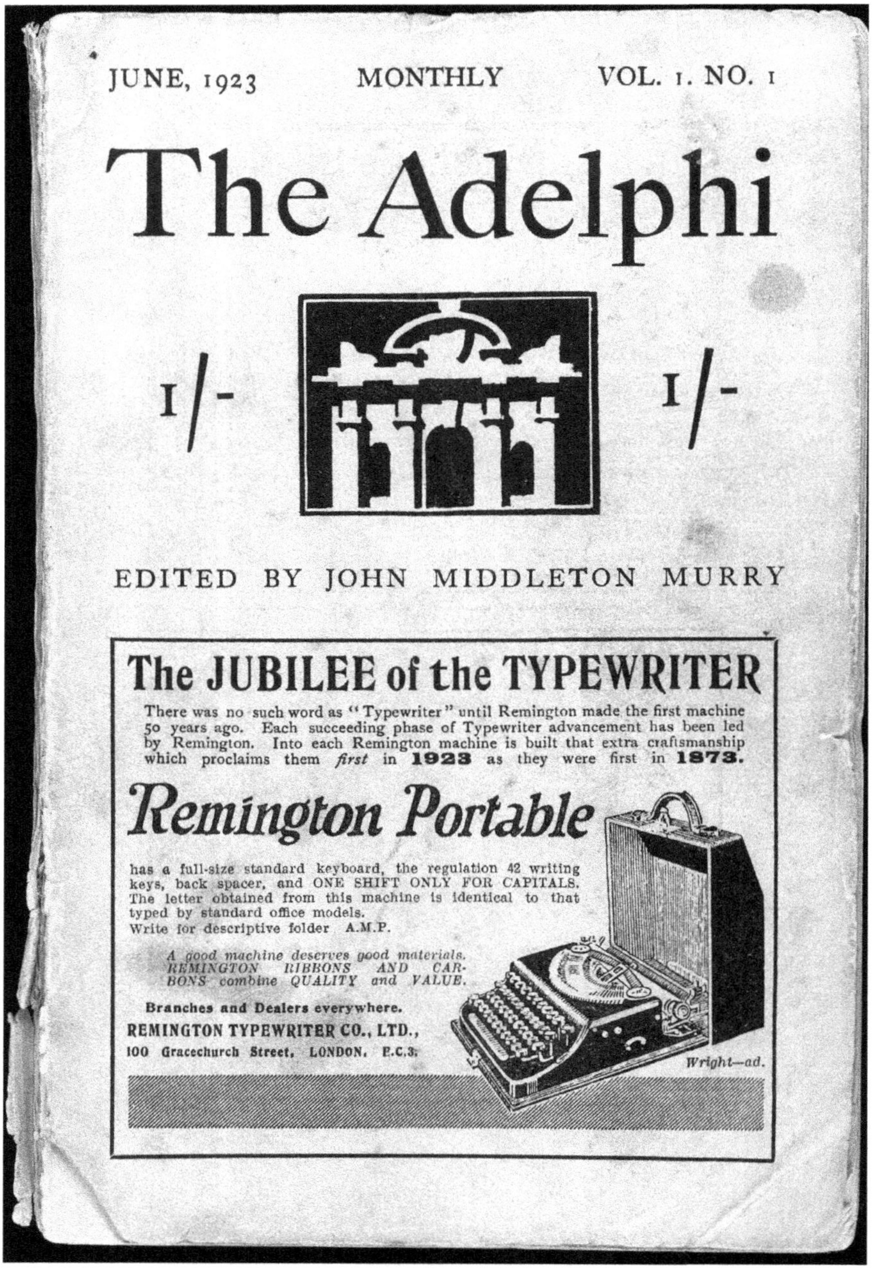

Figure 4.1 *The Adelphi*

Chapter 4

The Adelphi: Katherine Mansfield's Afterlives

On 9 January 1923, Katherine Mansfield died at the Institute for the Harmonious Development of Man near Fontainebleau, established by the mystic philosopher G. I. Gurdjieff, at the age of just thirty-four. In his letter of condolence to Murry, D. H. Lawrence was uncharacteristically generous, suggesting that '[p]erhaps it is good for Katharine [*sic*] not to have seen the next phase': 'It has been a savage enough pilgrimage these last four years. Perhaps K. has taken the only way for her. We keep faith – I always feel death only strengthens that, the faith between those who have it.'[1] In the same letter, Lawrence also told Murry that he would ask his publisher to send his latest work, *Fantasia of the Unconscious*, which he wished Mansfield could have read: 'She'll know though', he wrote. 'The dead don't die. They look on and help.'[2]

This was a defining moment for Murry. In February 1923, he retreated to the solitude of a cottage in the forest of Twyford in Sussex, where he read *Fantasia of the Unconscious* as he came to terms with his grief. It was here, inspired by Lawrence's descriptions of primary pre-mental consciousness, that Murry underwent a profound mystical experience that he later described as 'the one entirely revolutionary happening' in his life.[3] This experience seemed to confirm Murry in the belief that the 'dead don't die' but instead 'look on and help'. In July 1923, he recounted these events:

> Not many months ago I lost someone whom it was impossible for me to lose – the only person on this earth who understood me or whom I understood. This impossible thing happened. Katherine Mansfield died. For a fortnight I lived in a dream. [. . .]
>
> I began to be aware that there was something I must do. At first it was simply that I must go away. Then it hardened and became clearer: I must *be* alone. Not merely have loneliness thrust on me by the high gods, as it

> had been, but achieve and perfect it in myself and by myself. And then, knowing this, I was terribly afraid. [. . .]
>
> Then in the dark, in the dead, still house, I sat at the table facing the fire. I sat there motionless for hours, while I tried to face the truth that I was alone. [. . .] At last I had the sensation that I *was* in my hands and feet, that where they ended I also ended, as at a frontier of my being, and beyond that frontier stretched out the vast immensities, of space, of the universe, of the illimitable something that was other than I. Where I ended, it began – other, strange, terrible, menacing. It did not know me, would never acknowledge me, denied me utterly. Yet out upon this, from the fragile rampart of my own body, I found the courage to peer, to glance, at last to gaze steadily. And I became aware of myself as a little island against whose slender shores a cold, dark, boundless ocean lapped devouring. [. . .]
>
> What happened then? [. . .] [A] moment came when the darkness of that ocean changed to light, the cold to warmth; when it swept in one great wave over the shores and frontiers of my self; when it bathed me and I was renewed; when the room was filled with a presence, and I knew I was not alone – that I never could be alone any more, that the universe beyond held no menace, for I was part of it[.][4]

Six years later, in a book titled *God: Being an Introduction to the Science of Metabiology*, Murry offered this clarification regarding the warm 'presence' felt in the Sussex cottage:

> One point which I clearly remember, was passed over deliberately in my account of the experience. Where I say that 'the room was filled with a presence,' the 'presence' was definitely connected with the person of Katherine Mansfield. [. . .] The 'presence' of Katherine Mansfield was of the same order as the 'presence' which filled the room and me. In so far as the 'presence' was connected with her it had a moral quality, or a moral effect: I was immediately and deeply convinced that 'all was well with her.'[5]

As Sydney Janet Kaplan has observed, this incident became 'central' in Murry's personal and professional development: 'He quickly discovered that it could serve the purpose of explaining his new direction as a writer – and most significantly, as an editor'.[6] Religion and the spiritual life became major themes in Murry's work. Furthermore, as the passages above indicate, he felt emboldened by his reading of *Fantasia of the Unconscious* and his deeply felt experience in the Sussex cottage to discard all pretence of impersonality in his writing. Personal experience now became the basis for Murry's work, and his article 'Relevancy', published in *The Nation and the Athenaeum* in April 1923 and written in a style highly reminiscent of Lawrence's prose, signals this change.

Within a week of writing this article, moreover, Murry had abruptly resigned all his regular literary work and resolved himself to launching a new magazine, the venture with which his name would principally be associated from then on: *The Adelphi*.

Initially, there was talk of Murry taking over *The New Age* from Orage. Now a devoted follower of Gurdjieff, Orage was keen to sell the periodical to Murry on very generous terms. In the second week of April 1923, Murry made another pilgrimage to Fontainebleau to negotiate the sale. Later, after Orage's death in 1934, Murry claimed that Orage had 'begged of me to take over the "New Age" from him, and I was sorely tempted'.[7] Consulting Koteliansky and Sullivan, however, Murry was persuaded that it was better to start something new. For the magazine's title, Sullivan suggested the name of the building in which the men had worked together on *The Athenaeum*, Adelphi Terrace.[8] Out of the £400 given by Vivian Locke Ellis for the purpose of launching the magazine, Murry spent £250 on preliminary advertising, among which was a promotional flyer for the new magazine that confidently proclaimed:

> The standard by which the contents of *The Adelphi* will be decided is 'significance for life'. [. . .] We are bored to death by modern dilettantism. We are sick of 'Art'. Inspired by no living purpose it has brought us nowhere. If modern literature is to be anything better than a pastime for railway journeys or a parlour game for effete intellectuals, it must be built upon some active conviction. [. . .] *The Adelphi* will not be a high-brow magazine. It aims at being comprehensive and interesting to as many people as possible. But it will not be written down to suit the needs of an imaginary audience of the semi-educated and half-witted.[9]

When the first issue of *The Adelphi* was published, the total exclusion of literary reviews underlined Murry's divergence from the 'high-brow' *Athenaeum*, which had been concerned with shoring up cultural 'standards' after the war. As F. A. Lea has suggested, the promotional flyer for *The Adelphi* 'is at least as eloquent of Murry's revulsion from [elitist] Bloomsbury as of any more positive belief'.[10] In particular, the founding of *The Adelphi* can be considered a response to the periodical edited by T. S. Eliot from 1922, *The Criterion*, and it was in these two publications that Murry and Eliot conducted the extended debate between their respective positions of romanticism and classicism over the following years.

In the first issue of his new magazine, Murry attempted 'to justify *The Adelphi*, to write boldly, to unfurl and wave a flag'.[11] '*The Adelphi* is nothing if it is not an act', he wrote:

> It is not a business proposition, or a literary enterprise, or a nice little book in a pretty yellow cover; it is primarily and essentially an assertion of a faith that may be held in a thousand different ways, of a faith that life is important, and that more life should be man's chief endeavour [. . .] a common conviction that man must be true to his own experience.[12]

When it came to it, however, the awkwardness of such a faith, manifold and essentially indefinable, made Murry nervous; after publication of the first issue, he was gripped with worry that he would be misunderstood or simply dismissed as 'a crank'.[13] Yet the preliminary and widespread advertising campaign proved incredibly and unexpectedly successful. The voice of Koteliansky, who had been appointed 'business manager' of the magazine, as he had before with *The Signature*, 'seemed to explode over the telephone' when he rang Murry to tell him: 'It's gone with a *bang*'.[14] The first issue sold out within a week and had to be reprinted three more times over the next fortnight to meet demand. Rather than the 5,000 copies that Murry had initially anticipated, the first issue sold at least 18,000 copies.[15] By contrast, the first issue of *The Criterion* sold just 600 copies. *The Adelphi* was a sensational success; no literary monthly had touched such a figure before. The second issue sold 12,000, and over the next six months there was a steady decline to the more reasonable circulation of between 5,000 and 6,000 copies. Nevertheless, the conservative estimate of an average circulation of 4,200 copies per month in the years 1923–7 highlights the fact that *The Adelphi* was one of the most significant independent journals of inter-war Britain. This success proved to be enduring. After undergoing a title change to *The New Adelphi* in 1927, when it appeared as a quarterly, the magazine reverted to a monthly publication from October 1930, the point at which Murry handed over the editorial reins to Max Plowman and Richard Rees. The magazine survived the Second World War and Murry continued to be a guiding force behind the venture, contributing articles professing his pacifism and returning for a brief period as editor before the journal ceased publication in 1955.

From the very beginning, however, the success of *The Adelphi* was attended by notable derision within the 'high-brow' circles of literary London. To Desmond MacCarthy, writing under the pseudonym Affable Hawk in his regular review section of *The New Statesman*, Murry's first editorial was composed by 'one who has suddenly become ashamed of being "a high-brow" without becoming anything else'; MacCarthy argued that Murry was in danger of throwing away 'his fine gifts as a literary connoisseur' in favour of becoming a dubious 'moral prophet'.[16] This was followed by another article in *The New Statesman*, by Raymond Mortimer in July 1923, denigrating *The Adelphi* for its 'romanticism'. Virginia Woolf signalled the mood of Bloomsbury when she recorded in her diary a conversation with her husband and MacCarthy in which they discussed their deep unease about Murry's willingness to act like 'a revivalist preacher' in writing frankly and publicly about his own spiritual crises and personal 'revelations' following Mansfield's death.[17] And yet, it was precisely this willingness to be forthright and open that attracted so many readers to Murry's magazine. Like *The New Age* before it, as observed by John Carswell, *The Adelphi* had a significant impact outside London, and especially in the Methodist and Nonconformist communities in the north of England, 'where its vaguely religious and cultural message, mixed with modernity, struck home for those with a chapel childhood and an adolescence of doubt mingled with regret'.[18] To these readers, Murry's unashamed foregrounding of his own spiritual experience and his rhetoric of cultural democratisation were immensely appealing. Whilst *The Adelphi* may have been anathema to the literary elite of London, therefore, it proved incredibly popular more widely; and the central place afforded to Lawrence, the pre-eminent 'regional' modernist of his day, was integral to this appeal.

In the first instance, *The Adelphi* was established as an organ for Lawrence's work. The early issues of the magazine serialised chapters from *Fantasia of the Unconscious*, as well as some of Lawrence's poems and the travelogues written in New Mexico. In particular, Lawrence's writings helped to add weight to Murry's otherwise vague editorial philosophy; Lawrence promoted an individualist concept of religious experience that chimed well with Murry's ambiguous 'faith in life'. In his most controversial article for *The Adelphi* (in which he labelled Jesus a 'failure'), for example, Lawrence argued that 'man is responsible to God alone' and 'must carry forward the banner of life'.[19] Elsewhere, he argued that 'the wholeness of our being' could be found in the 'Holy Ghost within us' and that '[e]very man must live as far as he can by his own soul's conscience. To submit the conscience to a creed, or an idea, or a tradition, or even an impulse, is our ruin.'[20] Echoing Murry's own desire to 'be alone' in February 1923, Lawrence wrote:

> [T]o be alone with one's own soul! This, and the joy of it, is the real goal of love. My own soul and myself. Not my ego, my conceit of myself. But my very soul. To be at one in my own self. Not to be questing any more.

> Not to be yearning, seeking, hoping, desiring, aspiring. But to pause and be alone.[21]

These ideas provided the philosophical basis for *The Adelphi*. Murry now renounced the idea that had once been so central to the editorial project of *Rhythm*, of 'questing' in the name of 'Art'. As he wrote in the fifth issue of *The Adelphi*, 'I follow Mr D. H. Lawrence into rebellion, and carry my small flag in the shadow of his sombre-splendid banner'.[22]

By his own account, Murry established *The Adelphi* both as a vehicle for Lawrence's ideas and as a journal that would later become Lawrence's own. The idea was to 'prepare a place' for Lawrence when he eventually returned to England from New Mexico: 'I neither desired, nor intended, to remain editor of it. I was, in my own eyes, simply *locum tenens*, literally lieutenant, for Lawrence; and I waited eagerly for his coming.'[23] This is highlighted in the first number of *The Adelphi*, when Murry writes that 'I am only a *locum tenens* for a better man'.[24] However, Lawrence was far from enthusiastic about *The Adelphi*. Rather than encouraging him to return to England, it appeared that the magazine in fact strengthened his resolve to stay in New Mexico. On receiving the first number, for example, he wrote to Koteliansky that he was 'badly disappointed' with the magazine, which seemed 'so weak, apologetic, knock-kneed, with really nothing to justify its existence'.[25] 'Is this the best possible in England?' he asked with exasperation.[26] In February 1924, he wrote to Murry: 'Your articles in the *Adelphi* always annoy me [. . .] Can't you focus yourself outside yourself? Not forever focussed on yourself, ad nauseam?'[27] Later that year, Lawrence further berated Murry, viciously responding to what he characterised as the 'little yellow cry from your liver' (a reference to the colour of the magazine's cover):

> Why in the name of hell didn't you rouse up a bit, last January, and put a bit of gunpowder in your stuff and fire a shot or two. But you preferred to be soft, and go on stirring your own finger in your own vitals [. . .] Spunk is what one wants, not introspective sentiment. The last is your vice. You rot your manhood to the roots, with it.[28]

By contrast, Lawrence was relieved to find that *The Criterion* had some 'guts'.[29] By early 1926, he completely severed his ties with *The Adelphi*: 'I can't go between the yellow covers of the *Adelphi* without taking on a tinge of yellow which is all right in itself, but not my colour for me'.[30] After this, whilst Murry continued to publish his writings, Lawrence exhibited no sense of personal commitment to *The Adelphi* and certainly had no intention of returning to England to become its editor.

A significant contributing factor to Lawrence's objection to *The Adelphi* was Murry's tireless publication of Mansfield's literary remains. 'Murry's *Adelphi* came', Lawrence wrote to his US publisher, Thomas Seltzer, in mid-June 1923: 'How feeble it is! Oh God, am I going back to Europe to that? [. . .] I don't feel like supporting the knock-kneed *Adelphi*, Katharine [*sic*] Mansfield's ugly bits.'[31] Murry probably succeeded in alienating Lawrence further when, in the third issue of the magazine, published in August, he paid this dubious compliment: 'Mr Lawrence [. . .] is become, since Katherine Mansfield's death, incomparably the most important English writer of his generation'.[32] Lawrence showed his frustration with what he perceived to be this inflated judgement of Mansfield's talents when he wrote thanking Murry for a copy of *The Dove's Nest and Other Stories* in October: 'Poor Katharine [*sic*], she is delicate and touching. – But not *Great*! Why say great?'[33] And, sending the book to a friend in New York, Lawrence made clear: 'I think it's a downright cheek to ask the public to buy that waste-paper basket'.[34] Whilst *The Adelphi* may have been founded in the first instance as a vehicle for Lawrence's ideas, the centrality of Mansfield's image and writings suggests a different editorial impulse: as Michael Whitworth has observed, 'early readers may not have perceived the magazine so simply' and may 'have taken it to be as much inspired by Katherine Mansfield as by Lawrence'.[35] Indeed, the frontispiece to the first issue of the magazine was a photograph of Mansfield, which seemed to indicate that she was the divining spirit behind the new venture. As well as publishing Mansfield's 'The Samuel Josephs' in the first issue, Murry also promised his readers that from the next issue 'we shall begin to publish Katherine Mansfield's "Journal"'.[36] From then until as late as August 1924, not a single issue of *The Adelphi* appeared without including something by Mansfield.

As Galya Diment has observed, what may have helped persuade Murry to begin the magazine was not only the idea that it could function as a vehicle for the serialisation of Lawrence's *Fantasia of the Unconscious* but also the idea 'that the initial issues of *The Adelphi* could honour Mansfield's memory'.[37] Indeed, in later accounts to his friends, Koteliansky liked to justify the project 'as a gesture of posthumous tribute to Katherine Mansfield'.[38] *The Adelphi* was established as an act of memorialisation and tribute to Mansfield, then; it became the most important forum for the posthumous publication of her writings, to such an extent that – even though she was dead – she could be considered to be one of the magazine's most prolific contributors. Whilst Murry was by far the most frequent contributor to *The Adelphi* in the period from 1923 to 1927, as Whitworth notes, he was followed in frequency first by Mansfield and then by Lawrence.[39] These posthumous works by Mansfield included previously unpublished short stories, poems, drawings sketched in her letters to Murry, co-translations made with Koteliansky, unfinished fragments of stories and, most controversially of all, extracts from her journals and notebooks, which were serialised in instalments and often prefaced with Murry's own self-conscious and self-serving 'introductions'.

Murry's idea that the magazine could function as an act of memorialisation to Mansfield is signalled in the issue for January 1924, which commemorates the anniversary of her death with an opening poem by Murry, titled 'In Memory of Katherine Mansfield'. In his introduction to *The Dove's Nest*, published the previous year, Murry had developed the theme of 'purity' at the expense of other qualities that had endeared Mansfield to others; in his poem, he continued to develop this theme and to cultivate also the idea of Mansfield as childlike. Murry describes Mansfield as 'a perfect thing' and 'a child withouten stain' (*sic*): 'And so she wandered, looking upon the world / Wildered as one who knew not where to love, / Save in the shining dreams of memory curled / About her child heart'.[40] Subsequently, *The Adelphi* continued to advance the idea of Mansfield as a writer of the 'child heart'. Of the twenty-one poems and nine short stories by Mansfield that Murry published in his first period as editor of the magazine, between 1923 and 1930, most were devoted to the theme of childhood, including: 'The Samuel Josephs' (an extract from the beginning of 'Prelude'), the six 'Poems of Childhood' published in August 1923, 'The Little Girl' (first published in *Rhythm* in 1912), 'A Suburban Fairy Tale' (in which a little boy turns into a sparrow), 'Something Childish but Very Natural' (serialised in two parts), 'See-Saw' (in which a boy and girl play make-believe) and 'Three Children' (three unfinished stories about childhood, written in 1921–2). Not one of the short stories by Mansfield that appeared in *The Adelphi* exhibited her savage wit, irreverence or proficiency for merciless parody. Instead, the magazine promoted the notion of her authorial innocence.

In her contributions to *The New Age*, Mansfield had consistently challenged the idealisation of female 'purity' and the conformity to rigid gender stereotypes, but the emphasis in *The Adelphi* on Mansfield's innocence served to silence her feminist politics. Murry now fostered an image of Mansfield as religious, saintly and pure of soul. In the second issue of the magazine, for example, he published Mansfield's elegiac poem 'To L.H.B. (1894–1915)', in which she imagines the ghostly visitation of her dead brother:

> Last night for the first time since you were dead
> I walked with you, my brother, in a dream. [. . .]
> By the remembered stream my brother stands
> Waiting for me with berries in his hands.
> 'These are my body. Sister, take and eat.'[41]

The poem functions in this issue of *The Adelphi* as an inter-textual echo of Murry's editorial in which he describes Mansfield's 'presence' in the Sussex cottage. As such, the poem aligns Mansfield's pseudo-religious experience with Murry's own, serving as a literary precedent that legitimises his mystical awakening. Published after this poem in *The Adelphi* are a series of journal extracts by Mansfield that all focus on her renewed commitment to writing following her brother's death. Among these extracts is a passage in which Mansfield imagines seeing her dead brother:

> [L]ast evening he called me while I sat down by the fire. At last I obeyed and came upstairs. I stayed in the dark and waited. [. . .] [W]hen I leaned out of the window I seemed to see my brother dotted all over the field – now on his back, now on his face, now huddled up, now half-pressed into the earth. Wherever I looked, there he lay. I felt that God showed him to me like that for some express purpose, and I knelt down by the bed. But I could not pray. I had done no work. I was not in an active state of grace.[42]

Again, the shared detail of sitting by the fire before seeing or feeling the 'presence' of a dead loved one links the writings by Mansfield published in this issue of *The Adelphi* with Murry's description, in the opening editorial, of his experience in the Sussex cottage. In another journal extract selected by Murry for publication in the magazine, Mansfield begins by imploring her brother to 'Awake, awake! my little boy': 'I want to write down the fact that not only am I not afraid of death – I welcome the idea of death. I believe in immortality because he is not here, and I long to join him.'[43] Consistently employing the trope of immortality and the spectral return, Mansfield's writings about her brother published in *The Adelphi* supported spiritual notions of a communion between the living and the dead.

In his article 'Lost Secrets', for example, Murry declares that '[t]o hold the great opposites together, in our minds and in our souls, as of equal truth and equal potency, to stand fast by *all* our knowledge, however contradictory it may seem – is the road to victory':

> Of all the great oppositions, the opposition between life and death is the one that sits closest to us; moreover, it includes the others, because all that we may be and therefore all that we may know, depends upon our attitude to this. If men could overcome death, not by falsely representing it as life, but by accepting it for what it is – 'Death is life's high meed' – their inheritance in life would be changed.[44]

Murry argues that 'we [. . .] must begin with death. We have to know death in order to know life.'[45] This focus is demonstrated in *The Adelphi* when Murry imagines the conversation he would have had with William Archer, a reader of the magazine who had written a letter to Murry before he died; in this article, Murry literally imagines himself communing with the dead.[46] This imagined conversation illuminates the 'profound and ineradicable belief' that Murry had arrived at, that elements of personality are immortal; that there is 'a core of living reality' that can be glimpsed in 'strange inward tremors of the human being [that] can be ascribed only to something which we at once are and are not'.[47] In an article in the October 1926 issue, likewise, he writes: 'Life, spelled with a capital, is life *and* death. That Life goes on; that Life we have to serve; that is the Life we touch through the contemplation and acceptance of death.'[48] There then follows an extract by Mansfield titled 'Evening', in which she reflects upon her conversations with her brother before his death. In this way, Mansfield's selected posthumous writings in *The Adelphi* served to advance Murry's quasi-religious idea of spiritual immortality.

Throughout the 1920s and 1930s, *The Adelphi* continued to emphasise Mansfield's 'religious' and 'spiritual' qualities. When Murry published Mansfield's journal in book form in 1927, H. M. Tomlinson wrote a review of the book for *The Adelphi*, in which he praised Mansfield's 'beauty' and purity, and described her 'clear soul' and 'clear spirit': 'No saint ever more ruthlessly handled his body, to let it know its place, than K.M. did her mind'; '[r]eligion for her was the practice of her art. It was her testimony. It had to be genuine.'[49] Just under a fortnight following Mansfield's death, Tomlinson had previously written in *The Nation and the Athenaeum* that Mansfield 'was hardly corporeal' and possessed a beauty that was 'unearthly'; that she occupied a 'place above good and evil' and had the 'power' of 'divination which is supposed to belong to those not quite of this world'; in short, that she 'stood between this world and the next'.[50] As one of the founding 'brothers' of *The Adelphi* (together with his brother Philip Tomlinson, Murry, Koteliansky and Sullivan), Tomlinson's notion of Mansfield as an 'unearthly' spiritual presence mediating 'between this world and the next' was reiterated across the magazine. Reviewing the biography of Mansfield by Ruth Mantz and Murry published in 1932, for instance, J. P. Hogan also described Mansfield as a 'unique and lovely spirit': 'Katherine Mansfield *was*. She did not seek to formulate life and joy and pain and God and art; she experienced them' and her 'life, indeed, dramatises the supremacy of an artistic imagination which sees God in all things.'[51]

This emphasis on 'experiencing' God echoed ideas across *The Adelphi* that were formulated in the debate between Murry and Eliot delineating the opposition between romanticism and classicism. In *The Adelphi*, Murry consistently promoted the idea of 'the interdependence of literature and religion'.[52] In this, he took his cue from Lawrence, who wrote in *The Adelphi*: 'get a glimpse of this new relation of men and women to the great God of the End, who is the father, not the Son, of all our beginnings: and you get a glimpse of the new literature'.[53] Just as Sullivan's essay in the first issue of the magazine, 'On Being Oneself', empowered readers to follow their own individual predilections and tastes rather than defer to an approved, official canon of literature, then, *The Adelphi* advanced an individualist concept of religion, in which faith was arrived at through personal experience rather than the doctrines of the established Church. Murry argued that 'the man who believes in God does not need a Church'; that whilst 'a man needs both authority and tradition [. . .] it is best for him to find them out for himself'; and that God 'cannot, in the ordinary sense of the word, be *known*, but only experienced'.[54] As David Goldie has observed, 'Murry's adoption of an extreme individualist position, and his attempt to subsume the study of literature into a broader, religiously informed "criticism of life"' prompted Eliot to 'drop his earlier reticence and engage in the polemic in which his, and the *Criterion*'s, principles would become articulated'.[55] In his editorial for *The Criterion* in the month following the first issue of *The Adelphi*, for instance, Eliot defined 'The Function of a Literary Review' by directly responding to Murry's editorial, denouncing the 'insidious catchword: "life"'.[56] Whereas Murry promoted the idea of 'inner voice' as the basis for literary criticism and religious experience, Eliot became a champion of external authority and tradition.[57] Spurred on by this debate, the two writers provoked each other into adopting the increasingly polarised positions of romanticism and classicism. Called upon to define his beliefs in 1924, for example, Murry described them as 'romantic through and through: in politics it is a tradition of individualism, in religion of protestantism, and in literature of romanticism'.[58] This was diametrically opposed to Eliot's pronouncement four years later that he was 'classicist in literature, royalist in politics, and anglo-catholic in religion'.[59] In *The Adelphi*, Murry incorporated Mansfield's writings into this debate, idealising her as a 'unique and lovely spirit' who had experienced God on her own terms.

Notably, Murry also connected romanticism with an English national tradition in *The Adelphi*. In the piece he composed in response to Mortimer's article in *The New Statesman*, for example, Murry happily accepted the term 'romanticism' to describe himself and his magazine, but offered this clarification:

> In England there never has been any classicism worth talking about: we have had classics, but no classicism. And all our classics are romantic. That is to say, the *decorum* the great English writers naturally observe is one that they fetch out of the depths in themselves. It is not imposed by tradition or authority.[60]

The previous month, as already noted, he had written that Lawrence had 'become, since Katherine Mansfield's death, incomparably the most important *English* writer of his generation' (my emphasis). Clearly, then, both Lawrence and Mansfield belonged to the 'English' tradition that Murry was outlining in his expositions of romanticism at this time. Murry argued that there is 'a tradition in English life and English literature' that 'is not formulated or formulable' but 'is something you have to sense by intuition, if you are to know it at all'.[61] English writers 'inherit no rules from their forebears: they inherit only this: a sense that in the last resort they must depend upon the inner voice' and 'dig deep' in their 'pursuit of self-knowledge'.[62] 'Romanticism is the discovery and discrimination of inward reality' and 'individualism – which is only another name for Romanticism – is in our British bones':

> Romanticism, as I have tried to describe it, is itself the English tradition: it is national, and it is the secret source of our own peculiar vitality. In England it is the classicist who is the interloper and the alien.[63]

Murry was clearly taking aim at the expatriate 'interloper' from Missouri, T. S. Eliot. Yet, by associating Mansfield with the 'English tradition',

Murry was also carrying out an incredible feat of rewriting biographical fact. Whilst he didn't shy away from making reference to Mansfield's New Zealand origins, and included writings in *The Adelphi* that made this clear, Murry attempted to present her 'alien' colonial identity as tangential to her more binding association, as he perceived it, with an English national tradition of individualist romanticism, felt inwardly and inherited through intuition.

Linking romanticism and Englishness ever more unequivocally, Murry began to see England as nothing less than the saviour of world culture. In December 1923, he wrote: 'the fact that the soul of England is an *anima naturaliter romantic* points to the likelihood that England has a great part to play in the immediate future of mankind':

> [I]t is part of my creed that England has a mission; because I believe that the real continuity of the Western consciousness is preserved in her alone. [. . .] England is still living, still organically evolving. And she has no need of the restraining influences of a classicism that has no root in the English soul.[64]

Given that the 'compass by which we may steer across the uncharted ocean of the future [. . .] is a true individualism' that belongs to England alone, Murry argued, 'England will yet show the way out of the confusion that has fallen upon the West'.[65] This increasingly national viewpoint is further highlighted in an article titled 'Patriotism *Is* Enough', in which Murry reflects upon what 'troubled' him when reading the work of an unnamed Indian poet:

> What troubled me, I concluded, was a constant hiatus that I felt between the language and the thought, between the expression and the experience. The poet was using English words to convey what English words never could convey. It was not that other English words than those he used would have done the work better: on the contrary, his diction was surprisingly felicitous. The truth was that no English words could possibly convey what he wanted them to convey, and no doubt supposed that they did convey.[66]

Only the native Englishman can access the subtleties of the English language and intuit a way into the unformulated English literary tradition, Murry argues. Reading these poems, he concludes that 'there is an abyss' between 'the Indian poet's consciousness and mine': 'I have been brought up against a racial otherness', he writes, and 'it repels me'.[67] This is a far cry from the celebration in *Rhythm* of diversity and difference as cultural rejuvenators. Instead, with reprehensible racism, Murry writes of the Indian poet as being 'backboneless' like 'the snake'.[68] As Kaplan has argued, Murry's increasingly solipsistic nationalism is indicative of 'the same kind of withdrawal from cosmopolitan modernism to a localised, England-centred "shrinking island" that Jed Esty discerns in the writings of the later Woolf and Eliot'.[69] Indeed, the 'shrinking island' was a metaphor that Murry himself used to describe his mystical experience in the Sussex cottage in 1923: 'I became aware of myself as a little island against whose slender shores a cold, dark, boundless ocean lapped devouring'. The turn inwards of personal introspection by which Murry defined romanticism and outlined the tenets of *The Adelphi*, then, was symptomatic of his more profound withdrawal from 'the world without': from the avant-garde cosmopolitanism of *Rhythm*, or the internationalism of *The Athenaeum*, to England-centred nationalism.[70] As Kaplan suggests, this nationalism is also indicative of Murry's break with 'modernist' literature.

Identifying his magazine in opposition to the intellectuals of Bloomsbury, Murry argued that 'classicism' was characterised by the 'absolute scepticism' of the following writers:

> Mr Lytton Strachey, Mrs Virginia Woolf, Mr Aldous Huxley, Mr David Garnett, and Mr T. S. Eliot. Mr Strachey, Mr Garnett, and Mr Huxley do indeed belong together, though there are signs of incipient *malaise* in Mr Huxley: but Mrs Virginia Woolf and Mr Eliot are of another kind. They are serious, while the others are cynical, 'classicists'.[71]

Regarding *Mrs Dalloway* and *The Waste Land*, Murry makes a naive and short-sighted prediction: 'Fifty, ten years hence no one will take the trouble (no small one) to read either of these works'.[72] Similarly, in November 1923, Murry wrote an article in which he stated that Proust and Joyce 'are nothing. Landmarks, perhaps, to tell me twice again that the intellectual consciousness is utterly *kaput*'.[73] Murry reiterated this opinion three years later, in September 1926, when he compared Proust and Joyce with Lawrence and Forster: 'purposeless knowing' and 'purposeless being' is what 'finds expression in Proust and Joyce', he writes, whereas 'Mr Lawrence and Mr Forster stand together because they are in their different ways acutely aware of this condition'.[74] Associating Mansfield with the anti-traditional tradition of romanticism, therefore, Murry was arguably responsible for placing her outside the developing canon of modernist literature that took shape throughout the 1920s and '30s that encompassed Woolf, Eliot and Joyce. By implicitly designating her as a romantic, moreover, Murry placed Mansfield's writings within an explicitly English national tradition, eliding reference to her troubled, ambiguous colonial status. Placed within this tradition, Mansfield's writings were also associated with English Nonconformist religion, with Murry's saintly idealisation of her as innocent and 'pure' serving to erase Mansfield's sexual past, queer identity and radical gender politics.

Critics have long recognised how Murry's editing of Mansfield's journals and letters in book form presented a partial picture of the author that fostered what Jeffrey Meyers and Ruth Mantz have respectively termed the 'cult of Mansfield' and the 'Mansfield myth'.[75] What has not been recognised in enough detail, however, is how the 'Mansfield myth' advanced by Murry – of the sentimentalised and ghostly 'child' of purity – owed much to the periodical contexts in which it was first formulated. Christopher Bains has suggested that mid-twentieth-century magazines sought to shape and re-enunciate 'not only a genealogy of modernism but also its mythology'.[76] *The Adelphi* epitomises this trend, used by Murry as a forum in which to 'fix' Mansfield's posthumous reputation and elide those aspects of her life and work that did not fit his saintly idealisation of her. In particular, the posthumous publication of writings by Mansfield in *The Adelphi* erased and smoothed over those aspects of ambiguity and radical subversion in her work analysed in the previous chapters of this book: of Mansfield the feminist, who eschewed gender stereotypes of feminine 'purity' and 'saintliness' in *The New Age*; of Mansfield the (post)colonial writer, at 'home' neither in the centre nor at the periphery, who negotiated a position for her work between England and New Zealand in *Rhythm*; and of Mansfield the modernist, whose critical writings in *The Athenaeum* indubitably helped to shape the literary innovations of the early 1920s.

Importantly, *The Adelphi* also fostered an image of Mansfield as an isolated genius, more in touch with the 'spiritual' world than with the earthly realm of her contemporaries; a 'child withouten stain' rather than a jobbing author deeply embedded in the material contexts in which she had produced the majority of her work. In returning to these contexts, this book has looked to challenge the Mansfield hagiography initiated by Murry and sustained by many subsequent critics. Situating her work within constellations of contemporary texts and ideas, *Katherine Mansfield and Periodical Culture* has sought to read Mansfield's writings not in isolation, but as conditioned by and constituted through networks of association.

Notes

1. D. H. Lawrence, *The Letters of D. H. Lawrence, Volume IV*, ed. Warren Roberts, James T. Boulton and Elizabeth Mansfield (Cambridge: Cambridge University Press, 1987), p. 375.
2. Ibid.
3. Quoted in F. A. Lea, *The Life of John Middleton Murry* (London: Methuen, 1959), p. 102.
4. John Middleton Murry, 'A Month After', *Adelphi*, 1.2 (July 1923), pp. 94–5.
5. John Middleton Murry, *God: Being an Introduction to the Science of Metabiology* (London: Cape, 1929), pp. 37–8.
6. Sydney Janet Kaplan, *Circulating Genius: John Middleton Murry, Katherine Mansfield and D. H. Lawrence* (Edinburgh: Edinburgh University Press, 2010), p. 170.
7. J. [John] Middleton Murry, 'Obituary Letters to the Editor', *New English Weekly* (15 November 1934), pp. 114–15.
8. It was only later that the meaning of 'Adelphi' as 'Brothers' would gain significance.
9. Quoted in Lea, *The Life of John Middleton Murry*, pp. 106–7.
10. Ibid., p. 106.
11. John Middleton Murry, 'The Cause Of It All', *Adelphi*, 1.1 (June 1923), p. 4.
12. Ibid., p. 8.
13. Lea, *The Life of John Middleton Murry*, p. 108.
14. Murry, 'A Month After', p. 90.
15. Figures from Michael H. Whitworth, 'Enemies of Cant: *The Athenaeum* (1919–21) and *The Adelphi* (1923–48)', in Peter Brooker and Andrew Thacker (eds), *The Oxford Critical and Cultural History of Modernist Magazines, Volume I: Britain and Ireland, 1880–1955* (Oxford: Oxford University Press, 2009), p. 379.
16. Affable Hawk [Desmond MacCarthy], 'Books in General', *New Statesman*, 21 (9 June 1923), p. 270.
17. Virginia Woolf, *The Diary of Virginia Woolf, Volume II*, ed. Anne Olivier Bell (Harmondsworth: Penguin, 1981), pp. 252–3.
18. John Carswell, *Lives and Letters: A. R. Orage, Beatrice Hastings, Katherine Mansfield, John Middleton Murry, S. S. Koteliansky, 1906–1957* (London: Faber, 1978), p. 199.
19. D. H. Lawrence, 'Education and Sex', *Adelphi*, 1.2 (July 1923), p. 135.
20. D. H. Lawrence, 'On Love and Marriage', *Adelphi*, 1.4 (September 1923), p. 308.
21. Ibid., p. 311.
22. John Middleton Murry, 'On Waiting', *Adelphi*, 1.5 (October 1923), p. 364.
23. Quoted in Whitworth, 'Enemies of Cant', p. 376.
24. Murry, 'The Cause Of It All', p. 9.
25. Lawrence, *The Letters of D. H. Lawrence, Volume IV*, p. 462.
26. Ibid.
27. Ibid., p. 572.
28. D. H. Lawrence, *The Letters of D. H. Lawrence, Volume V*, ed. James T. Boulton and Lindeth Vasey (Cambridge: Cambridge University Press, 1989), p. 170.
29. Ibid., p. 181.
30. Ibid., p. 385.
31. Lawrence, *The Letters of D. H. Lawrence, Volume IV*, p. 458.
32. John Middleton Murry, 'Religion and Faith', *Adelphi*, 1.3 (August 1923), p. 183.
33. Lawrence, *The Letters of D. H. Lawrence, Volume IV*, p. 521.

34. Ibid., p. 503.
35. Whitworth, 'Enemies of Cant', pp. 376–7.
36. Murry, 'The Cause Of It All', p. 11.
37. Galya Diment, *A Russian Jew of Bloomsbury: The Life and Times of Samuel Koteliansky* (London: McGill-Queen's University Press, 2011), p. 143.
38. Ibid.
39. Whitworth, 'Enemies of Cant', p. 384.
40. John Middleton Murry, 'In Memory of Katherine Mansfield', *Adelphi*, 1.8 (January 1924), pp. 663–5.
41. Katherine Mansfield, 'To L.H.B. (1894–1915)', *Adelphi*, 1.2 (July 1923), p. 136.
42. Katherine Mansfield, 'Extracts from a Journal', *Adelphi*, 1.2 (July 1923), pp. 142–3.
43. Ibid., p. 138.
44. John Middleton Murry, 'Lost Secrets', *Adelphi*, 2.4 (September 1924), p. 285.
45. Ibid., p. 286.
46. John Middleton Murry, 'William Archer and the Survival of Personality', *Adelphi*, 2.10 (March 1925), p. 806.
47. John Middleton Murry, 'Personality and Immortality', *Adelphi*, 2.12 (May 1925), p. 953.
48. John Middleton Murry, 'The Second Religiousness', *Adelphi*, 4.4 (October 1926), p. 209.
49. H. M. Tomlinson, 'Katherine Mansfield', *New Adelphi*, 1.1 (September 1927), pp. 94–6.
50. H. M. Tomlinson, 'Katherine Mansfield', *Nation and the Athenaeum*, 32 (20 January 1923), p. 609.
51. J. P. Hogan, 'The Life of Katherine Mansfield', *Adelphi*, 7.3 (December 1932), p. 232.
52. John Middleton Murry, 'On Fear; and On Romanticism', *Adelphi*, 1.4 (September 1923), p. 276.
53. D. H. Lawrence, 'The Proper Study', *Adelphi*, 1.7 (December 1923), p. 589.
54. John Middleton Murry, 'Religion and Christianity', *Adelphi*, 1.8 (January 1924), p. 670; John Middleton Murry, 'Quo Warranto?', *Adelphi*, 2.3 (August 1924), p. 190; John Middleton Murry, 'The "Classical" Revival (II.)', *Adelphi*, 3.10 (March 1926), p. 653.
55. David Goldie, *A Critical Difference: T. S. Eliot and John Middleton Murry in English Literary Criticism, 1919–1928* (Oxford: Clarendon Press, 1998), pp. 95–6.
56. T. S. Eliot, 'The Function of a Literary Review', *Criterion*, 1.4 (July 1923), p. 421.
57. Murry, 'On Fear; and On Romanticism', p. 275.
58. John Middleton Murry, 'In Defence of the "Adelphi"', *Spectator*, 5003 (17 May 1924), p. 785.
59. T. S. Eliot, *For Lancelot Andrewes: Essays on Style and Order* (London: Faber and Gwyer, 1928), p. 7.
60. Murry, 'On Fear; and On Romanticism', pp. 274–5.
61. Ibid., p. 275.
62. Ibid.
63. Ibid., pp. 275–6.
64. John Middleton Murry, 'More About Romanticism', *Adelphi*, 1.7 (December 1923), p. 565.
65. John Middleton Murry, 'A Divagation on Politics', *Adelphi*, 3.1 (June 1925), p. 11.
66. John Middleton Murry, 'Patriotism *Is* Enough', *Adelphi*, 4.5 (November 1926), p. 271.
67. Ibid., pp. 272–3.

68. Ibid., p. 272.
69. Kaplan, *Circulating Genius*, p. 210.
70. John Middleton Murry, 'Two Worlds', *Adelphi*, 1.10 (March 1924), p. 859.
71. John Middleton Murry, 'The "Classical" Revival', *Adelphi*, 3.9 (February 1926), p. 589.
72. Ibid., p. 590.
73. The Journeyman [John Middleton Murry], 'Novels and Thought-Adventures', *Adelphi*, 1.6 (November 1923), p. 536.
74. Anon. [John Middleton Murry], 'Lemonade?', *Adelphi*, 4.3 (September 1926), pp. 144–6.
75. Jeffrey Meyers, 'Murry's Cult of Mansfield', *Journal of Modern Literature*, 7.1 (February 1979), pp. 15–38; Ruth Mantz, 'Fifty Years After', *Adam International Review*, 370 (1973), pp. 117–27.
76. Christopher Bains, 'Critics Abroad: The Early Years of *The Paris Review* (1953-65)', in Peter Brooker and Andrew Thacker (eds), *The Oxford Critical and Cultural History of Modernist Magazines, Volume II: North America 1894–1960* (Oxford: Oxford University Press, 2012), p. 760.

Conclusion

In one of the translations that Mansfield produced with Koteliansky for publication in *The Athenaeum*, Anton Chekhov notes: 'The thought that I am writing for a weighty magazine, and that my little thing will be looked upon more seriously than it deserves, keeps on jerking my elbow, as the devil did the monk'.[1] Whether writing for an established and 'weighty' literary journal such as *The Athenaeum*, an avant-garde little magazine such as *Rhythm*, or a periodical positioned somewhere between, such as *The New Age*, Mansfield's periodical contributions consistently bear out this observation that print contexts indelibly shape what a writer produces; that a writer's elbow will always feel the pull and the tug of the publication to which they are contributing. *Katherine Mansfield and Periodical Culture* has sought to demonstrate the extent to which Mansfield's writings are laden with meanings that will always remain hidden to the reader who isolates the text from the original print contexts of publication. In the relational model of creation sustained by periodicals and magazines, all contributions have the potential to condition the meanings of other contributions. Reading Mansfield's writings within these contexts therefore enables us to situate her work more resolutely as historically embedded within particular political, aesthetic and social debates, and as produced through networks of association with other writers and artists.

This approach to Mansfield's work positions her as an important female figure in the history of early twentieth-century periodical culture. Over recent years, the burgeoning field of feminist periodical studies has led to increasing attention being paid to the significant, formative role played by women writers and editors in the emergence of literary modernism.[2] *Katherine Mansfield and Periodical Culture* enlarges this field of enquiry, highlighting the ways in which Mansfield's periodical contributions responded to the suffrage movement and articles about feminism in *The New Age*, for instance, and presented a gendered critique of other contributions to *Rhythm*. Similarly, this book highlights the crucial editorial role performed by Beatrice Hastings at *The New Age*, as well as Mansfield's own significance as an editor of *Rhythm* and *The Blue Review*. Whilst Mansfield did not occupy an official position on the editorial staff of *The Athenaeum*, moreover, her letters from 1919–20 demonstrate her major contribution to the running of the periodical and illuminate the extent to which her ideas informed the editorial direction and philosophy of the paper.

Focusing on Mansfield's career in the years before the publication of her most successful short story collections, *Bliss* (1920) and *The Garden Party* (1922), also helps to challenge the misconception of Mansfield as a writer of limited generic interest. Mansfield was not a writer who restricted herself to the short story form; her periodical contributions reveal the incredible diversity of genres that she employed throughout her writing career, including the fictionalised travelogue, aphorisms, the dialogue for one voice, the satirical sketch, poems, 'parodic' and co-translations, the editorial essay and the literary review. This broad focus helps to reorient attention away from Mansfield's later, more celebrated stories, allowing us to consider the extent to which her development as a writer was intrinsically conditioned by her engagement and experimentation with a number of literary forms employed in response to specific periodical contexts in the decade 1910–20.

Perhaps most significantly, returning to the periodicals and magazines in which Mansfield published enables us to reposition her more decisively as a colonial-metropolitan modernist, writing both within and against the London literary establishment. This adds another dimension to the recent re-evaluation of Mansfield as a colonial, proto-postcolonial presence within the history of British modernism. As I have argued throughout this book, the mediating spaces of metropolitan periodical culture provided one of the primary sites in which Mansfield could speak both of and as the 'outsider': by evoking 'other' places throughout her periodical contributions, Mansfield consistently generated moments of intercultural contact and transnational exchange that served either to undermine the idea of a homogenous and integrated 'imagined community' of the nation or gesture towards 'imagined worlds'. Whether focusing on Germany and France in *The New Age*, eastern Europe and New Zealand in *Rhythm* or the 'new world' of an 'undiscovered', 'hidden country' in *The Athenaeum*, Mansfield's writings consistently demonstrate how twentieth-century periodicals and magazines facilitated imagined mobility, enabling the production and contestation of different geographical imaginaries.

In this way, the case study of Mansfield allows us to trace convergences between the material, textual space of the periodical form and global, transnational spatial imaginaries. As this book has demonstrated, these convergences were constituted by the dialogic oscillation in periodicals and magazines between identification and difference, or conversation and conflict. In *The New Age*, for example, Mansfield identified her work with articles of feminist political analysis by Beatrice Hastings, another colonial 'outsider' in London, as a way of challenging and subverting the dominant contemporary public discourse linking motherhood and nationalism, or conventional gender roles and imperialism. Furthermore, both Mansfield and Hastings subverted the political and social consensus of the metropolis by adopting fragment forms, such as the aphoristic and elliptical, and by formulating alternative modes of identification, as demonstrated by their shared enthusiasm for contemporary French literature and culture. In this way, both writers challenged ideas of linguistic integrity and national superiority advanced by other contributors to *The New Age*.

When Mansfield began contributing to *Rhythm*, conversely, she quickly became integrated into its cosmopolitan and avant-garde community of writers and artists who shared her experience of an exile that had been self-imposed, in the interests of cultivating individual artistic identity. However, it was precisely this experience of exile from a colonised country that made it difficult for Mansfield to wholeheartedly subscribe to the discourse of spatial conquest and geographical expansion upon which ideas of modernist, metropolitan affiliation had been constituted in *Rhythm*, and her contributions enact a highly ambiguous, ambivalent negotiation of this discourse. In this way, Mansfield's writings served to unsettle and complicate articulations of 'community' in the magazine, which were premised upon a spatial-temporal opposition between the metropolitan centre of modernity and the 'wild' peripheries tamed by the 'neo-barbarian' artist-pioneers; dissolving rigid centre/periphery binaries, Mansfield's contributions promote a far more hybridised art of intercultural contact and transnational, translational exchange, as exemplified by her 'parodic translations'.

In contrast to this attempt by Mansfield to articulate difference from within the imagined 'community' of *Rhythm*, her contributions to *The*

Athenaeum served to promote a sense of unified affiliation across the periodical. Along with other contributors, such as Murry, Lawrence and Sullivan, Mansfield employed tropes of geographical 'discovery' throughout her contributions to *The Athenaeum* in order to evoke a 'hidden country' of spiritual rejuvenation and artistic innovation. Mansfield can be seen here unsettling the centre/periphery hierarchy by reclaiming the colonial 'new world' as an enabling space of cultural transformation. This idea of an 'undiscovered country' of the mind also provided a vocabulary through which Mansfield could identify with other contributors to the periodical as well as contest the outer 'worldly world' and official mind of post-war public consensus. The 'imagined world' formulated within *The Athenaeum* was international in scope, in particular incorporating Russian and French literature, and was opposed to the jingoist nationalism of the mainstream press. This implicit critique of nationalism aligns Mansfield's expressions of affiliation in *The Athenaeum* with the same impulse of resistance to ideas of nation and empire that had motivated her earlier contributions to *The New Age* and *Rhythm*.

In the first instance, it has been the aim of this book to use print media as the lens through which to offer new interpretations of Mansfield's work that might augment our understanding of her development as a writer as well as her position within networks of association. However, I have also sought to use the single-author case study of Mansfield to gesture towards ways in which the field of modernist studies more widely might develop the language and conceptual tools with which to examine, describe and contextualise early twentieth-century print media, making use of the analytical perspectives offered by postcolonial theory and transnational literary studies. In particular, Mansfield's writings demonstrate how those who were located on the fringes of metropolitan culture or occupied an ambivalent relation to the literary establishment could use the mediating spaces of print to contest dominant ideologies and spatial imaginaries, play with different authorial identities, make subversive interventions within established discursive contexts, and articulate fantasies of global movement. As such, Mansfield's work prompts us to think about the possible points of intersection between our study of transnational, global modernisms and our analysis of the periodicals and magazines in which modernist texts first circulated.

Notes

1. Anton Chekhov, 'Letters of Anton Tchehov III', *Athenaeum*, 4643 (25 April 1919), p. 249.
2. See Jayne E. Marek, *Women Editing Modernism: 'Little' Magazines and Literary History* (Kentucky: University Press of Kentucky, 1995); Barbara Green, 'The Feminist Periodical Press: Women, Periodical Studies, and Modernity', *Literature Compass*, 6.1 (2009), pp. 191–205; Barbara Green, 'Recovering Feminist Criticism: Modern Women Writers and Feminist Periodical Studies', *Literature Compass*, 10.1 (2013), pp. 53–60; Manushag N. Powell, 'We Other Periodicalists, or, Why Periodical Studies?', *Tulsa Studies in Women's Literature*, 30.2 (fall 2011), pp. 441–50.

Appendix I

Katherine Mansfield's Periodical Contributions

The genre of each item is indicated at the end of the reference. Each item is signed 'Katherine Mansfield' unless otherwise stated at the beginning of the reference in brackets. Posthumous publications are not included in this appendix, and any information about disputed authorship is given in the notes.

[Kathleen Beauchamp] 'Enna Blake', *High School Reporter* (1898), pp. 21–2: fiction

[Kathleen Beauchamp] 'A Happy Christmas Eve', *High School Reporter* (1899), pp. 3–4: fiction

[Kathleen M. Beauchamp] 'His Little Friend', *New Zealand Graphic and Ladies' Journal*, 25.15 (13 October 1900), pp. 710–11: fiction

[Cousin Kathleen], *New Zealand Graphic and Ladies' Journal*, 25.20 (17 November 1900), p. 950: letter

[Kathleen Beauchamp], *New Zealand Graphic and Ladies' Journal*, 26.23 (8 June 1901), p. 1098: letter

[Kathleen Beauchamp] 'The Pine-Tree, The Sparrows, and You and I', *Queen's College Magazine* (1903), pp. 74–6: fiction

[Kathleen Beauchamp] 'Die Einsame', *Queen's College Magazine* (March 1904), pp. 126–31: fiction

[Kathleen M. Beauchamp] 'Your Birthday', *Queen's College Magazine* (December 1904), pp. 203–5: fiction

[K. M. Beauchamp] 'One Day', *Queen's College Magazine* (July 1905), pp. 294–5: fiction

[K. M. Beauchamp] 'About Pat', *Queen's College Magazine* (December 1905), pp. 344–7: fiction

[K. Mansfield] 'Vignettes', *Native Companion*, 2.3 (1 October 1907), pp. 129–32: fiction

[K. Mansfield] 'Silhouettes', *Native Companion*, 2.4 (1 November 1907), p. 229: fiction

[K. Mansfield] 'In a Café', *Native Companion*, 2.5 (2 December 1907), pp. 265–9: fiction

[Julian Mark] 'In the Botanical Gardens', *Native Companion*, 2.5 (2 December 1907), pp. 285–6: fiction

[Kathleen Beauchamp] 'The Lonesome Child', *Dominion*, 1.217 (6 June 1908), p. 11: poetry

[K. Mansfield] 'Study: The Death of a Rose', *Triad* (1 July 1908), p. 35: fiction

[Unsigned] 'Almost a Tragedy: The Cars on Lambton Quay', *Dominion* (23 December 1908), p. 11: fiction

[K. Mansfield] 'The Education of Audrey', *Evening Post* (30 January 1909), p. 12: fiction

[K. M. Beauchamp] 'A Day in Bed', *Lone Hand*, 5.1 (1 October 1909), p. 636: poetry

[K. Mansfield], 'November', *Daily News* (3 November 1909): poetry
[K. Mansfield] 'The Pillar Box', *Pall Mall Magazine*, 45.202 (February 1910), p. 300: poetry
[Katharine Mansfield] 'Bavarian Babies: The Child-Who-Was-Tired', *New Age*, 6.17 (24 February 1910), pp. 396–8: fiction
[K. Mansfield] 'Mary', *Idler*, 36.90 (March 1910), pp. 661–5: fiction
[Katharine Mansfield] 'Germans at Meat', *New Age*, 6.18 (3 March 1910), pp. 419–20: fiction
[Katharine Mansfield] 'The Baron', *New Age*, 6.19 (10 March 1910), p. 444: fiction
[Katharine Mansfield] 'The Luft Bad', *New Age*, 6.21 (24 March 1910), p. 493: fiction
'Loneliness', *New Age*, 7.4 (26 May 1910), p. 83: poetry
[Katharina Mansfield] 'At "Lehmann's"', *New Age*, 7.10 (7 July 1910), pp. 225–7: fiction
'Frau Brechenmacher Attends a Wedding', *New Age*, 7.12 (21 July 1910), pp. 273–5: fiction
'The Sister of the Baroness', *New Age*, 7.14 (4 August 1910), pp. 323–4: fiction
'A Paper Chase', *New Age*, 7.15 (11 August 1910), pp. 354–5: letter to the editor
'Frau Fischer', *New Age*, 7.16 (18 August 1910), pp. 366–8: fiction
'North American Chiefs', *New Age*, 7.17 (25 August 1910), p. 407: letter to the editor
[Katherina Mansfield] 'A Fairy Story', *Open Window*, 1.3 (December 1910), pp. 162–76: fiction
'Pamieci Stanislawa Wyspianskiego' (translation of 'To Stanislaw Wyspianski'), *Gazieta poniedzialkowa, Dodatek literacki Swiatecznyo Numer*, 36 (26 December 1910), p. 10: poetry
'A Birthday', *New Age*, 9.3 (18 May 1911), pp. 61–3: fiction
[K.M. and B.H.] 'A P.S.A.', *New Age*, 9.4 (25 May 1911), p. 95: letter to the editor [co-authored with Beatrice Hastings]
'The Modern Soul', *New Age*, 9.8 (22 June 1911), pp. 183–6: fiction
'The Festival of the Coronation (With Apologies to Theocritus)', *New Age*, 9.9 (29 June 1911), p. 196: dialogue
[Unsigned] 'The Breidenbach Family in England', *New Age*, 9.16 (17 August 1911), p. 371: fiction[1]
'The Journey to Bruges', *New Age*, 9.17 (24 August 1911), pp. 401–2: fiction
'Being a Truthful Adventure', *New Age*, 9.19 (7 September 1911), pp. 450–2: fiction
'Along the Gray's Inn Road', *New Age*, 9.23 (5 October 1911), p. 551: letter to the editor
'Love Cycle', *New Age*, 9.25 (19 October 1911), p. 586: poetry
[Mouche] 'The Mating of Gwendolyn', *New Age*, 10.1 (2 November 1911), pp. 14–15: fiction[2]
'A Marriage of Passion', *New Age*, 10.19 (7 March 1912), pp. 447–8: fiction
'Pastiche: At the Club', *New Age*, 10.19 (7 March 1912), pp. 449–50: pastiche
'The Woman at the Store', *Rhythm*, 4 (spring 1912), pp. 7–24: fiction
[Boris Petrovsky] 'Very Early Spring', *Rhythm*, 4 (spring 1912), p. 30: poetry
[Boris Petrovsky] 'The Awakening River', *Rhythm*, 4 (spring 1912), p. 30: poetry
'The Sea Child', *Rhythm*, 5 (June 1912), p. 1: poetry
'The Meaning of Rhythm', *Rhythm*, 5 (June 1912), pp. 18–20: non-fiction [co-authored with John Middleton Murry]
'*Moods, Songs and Doggerls* by John Galsworthy', *Rhythm*, 5 (June 1912), p. 35: review
'Pastiche: Puzzle: Find the Book', *New Age*, 11.7 (13 June 1912), p. 165: pastiche
'Seriousness in Art', *Rhythm*, 6 (July 1912), pp. 46, 49: non-fiction [co-authored with John Middleton Murry]
[K.M.] '*The Triumph of Pan* by Victor Neuberg', *Rhythm*, 6 (July 1912), p. 70: review

[K.M.] '*The Green Fields* by Kenneth Hare', *Rhythm*, 6 (July 1912), p. 71: review
'Pastiche: Green Goggles', *New Age*, 11.10 (4 July 1912), p. 237: pastiche
'Tales of a Courtyard', *Rhythm*, 7 (August 1912), pp. 99–105: fiction
[The Two Tigers] 'Jack & Jill Attend the Theatre', *Rhythm*, 7 (August 1912), pp. 120–1: dialogue [co-authored with John Middleton Murry]
[K.M.] '*Elsie Lindter* by Karin Michaelis', *Rhythm*, 7 (August 1912), p. 122: review
[Mouche] 'A Flirtation', *New Age*, 11.14 (1 August 1912), pp. 326–8: fiction[3]
[Boris Petrovsky] 'The Earth-Child in the Grass', *Rhythm*, 8 (September 1912), p. 125: poetry
[Lili Heron] 'How Pearl Button Was Kidnapped', *Rhythm*, 8 (September 1912), pp. 136–9: fiction
'Spring in a Dream', *Rhythm*, 8 (September 1912), pp. 161–5: fiction
[K.M.] '*Confession of a Fool* by August Strindberg', *Rhythm*, 8 (September 1912), pp. 181–2: review
[Unsigned] '*The Happy Family*', *Saturday Westminster Gazette*, 40.6029 (21 September 1912), p. 12: review
'New Dresses', *Rhythm*, 9 (October 1912), pp. 189–201: fiction
[Lili Heron] 'The Little Girl', *Rhythm*, 9 (October 1912), pp. 218–21: fiction
[The Tiger] 'Sunday Lunch', *Rhythm*, 9 (October 1912), pp. 223–5: fiction
[K.M.] '*An Anthology of Modern Bohemian Poetry* by P. Selver', *Rhythm*, 9 (October 1912), p. 235: review
[Boris Petrovsky] 'To God the Father', *Rhythm*, 10 (November 1912), p. 237: poetry
'The House', *Hearth and Home*, 44.1124 (28 November 1912), pp. 233–4: fiction
'The Opal Dream Cave', *Rhythm*, 11 (December 1912), p. 306: poetry
'Sea', *Rhythm*, 11 (December 1912), p. 307: poetry
'Old Cockatoo Curl', *T.P.'s Weekly* (27 December 1912), pp. 46, 48, 50: fiction [co-authored with John Middleton Murry]
'Ole Underwood', *Rhythm*, 12 (January 1913), pp. 334–7: fiction
[Boris Petrovsky] 'Jangling Memory', *Rhythm*, 12 (January 1913), p. 337: poetry
[Unsigned] 'Virginia's Journal. January', *Rhythm*, 12 (January 1913), pp. 360–2: fiction
'Floryan Nachdenklich', *Saturday Westminster Gazette*, 41.6129 (18 January 1913), p. 7: poetry[4]
'Sea Song', *Rhythm*, 14 (March 1913), pp. 453–4: poetry
[Boris Petrovsky] 'There Was a Child Once', *Rhythm*, 14 (March 1913), p. 471: poetry
'Epilogue: Pension Seguin', *Blue Review*, 1 (May 1913), pp. 37–42: fiction
'Millie', *Blue Review*, 2 (June 1913), pp. 82–7: fiction
'Epilogue: II', *Blue Review*, 2 (June 1913), pp. 103–9: fiction
'Epilogue: III Bains Turcs', *Blue Review* (July 1913), pp. 181–5: fiction
[Unsigned] 'Lu of the Ranges', *Saturday Westminster Gazette*, 42.6282 (19 July 1913), p. 12: review
[Mouche] 'The Wild Rabbit: A Fantasy of the Future', *New Age*, 13.15 (7 August 1913), pp. 427–8: fiction[5]
[Matilda Berry] 'Autumns: I', *Signature*, 1 (4 October 1915), pp. 15–18: fiction
[Matilda Berry] 'Autumns: II', *Signature*, 1 (4 October 1915), pp. 18–23: fiction
[Matilda Berry] 'The Little Governess', *Signature*, 2 (18 October 1915), pp. 11–18: fiction
'Old Tar', *Saturday Westminster Gazette* (25 October 1913), p. 9: fiction
[Matilda Berry] 'The Little Governess: Part II', *Signature*, 3 (1 November 1915), pp. 11–18: fiction
'Stay-Laces', *New Age*, 18.1 (4 November 1915), pp. 14–15: dialogue

'Pastiche: Alors, Je Pars; Living Alone; E. M. Forster; Beware of the Rain!; L. M.'s Way; Cephalus', *New Age*, 20.25 (19 April 1917), p. 595: pastiche
'Two Tuppenny Ones, Please', *New Age*, 21.1 (3 May 1917), pp. 13–14: dialogue
'Late at Night', *New Age*, 21.2 (10 May 1917), p. 38: monologue
'The Black Cap', *New Age*, 21.3 (17 May 1917), pp. 62–3: dialogue
'In Confidence', *New Age*, 21.4 (24 May 1917), pp. 88–9: dialogue
'The Common Round', *New Age*, 21.5 (31 May 1917), pp. 113–15: dialogue[6]
'A Pic-Nic', *New Age*, 21.6 (7 June 1917), pp. 136–8: dialogue
'Mr Reginald Peacock's Day', *New Age*, 21.7 (14 June 1917), pp. 158–61: fiction
'M. Seguin's Goat', *New Age*, 21.19 (6 September 1917), pp. 411–12: translation[7]
'An Album Leaf', *New Age*, 21.21 (20 September 1917), pp. 450–2: fiction[8]
'A Dill Pickle', *New Age*, 21.23 (4 October 1917), pp. 489–91: fiction
'Pastiche: Miss Elizabeth Smith', *New Age*, 22.7 (13 December 1917), p. 138: pastiche
[Unsigned] 'Paris Through an Attic', *Times Literary Supplement*, 851 (9 May 1918), p. 220: review
[Unsigned] 'A Frenchman's Englishman', *Times Literary Supplement*, 855 (6 June 1918), p. 261: review
[Unsigned] 'Pour Toi, Patrie', *Times Literary Supplement*, 859 (4 July 1918), p. 312: review
'Bliss', *English Review*, 27.2 (August 1918), pp. 108–19: fiction
'Carnation', *Nation*, 23.23 (7 September 1918), pp. 595–6: fiction
[Unsigned] 'Three Women Novelists', *Athenaeum*, 4640 (4 April 1919), pp. 140–1: review
[Unsigned] 'Letters of Anton Tchehov', *Athenaeum*, 4640 (4 April 1919), pp. 148–9: translation [collaboration with S. S. Koteliansky]
[Unsigned] 'Two Novels of Worth', *Athenaeum*, 4641 (11 April 1919), pp. 173–4: review
[Elizabeth Stanley] 'Fairy Tale', *Athenaeum*, 4642 (18 April 1919), p. 199: poetry
[K.M.] 'A Citizen of the Sea', *Athenaeum*, 4642 (18 April 1919), p. 205: review
[Unsigned] 'Letters of Anton Tchehov II', *Athenaeum*, 4642 (18 April 1919), pp. 213–16: translation [collaboration with S. S. Koteliansky]
[Elizabeth Stanley] 'Covering Wings', *Athenaeum*, 4643 (25 April 1919), p. 233: poetry
[Elizabeth Stanley] 'Firelight', *Athenaeum*, 4643 (25 April 1919), p. 233: poetry
[K.M.] 'Portrait of a Little Lady', *Athenaeum*, 4643 (25 April 1919), pp. 237–8: review
'Letters of Anton Tchehov III', *Athenaeum*, 4643 (25 April 1919), p. 249: translation [collaboration with S. S. Koteliansky]
'Perambulations', *Athenaeum*, 4644 (2 May 1919), pp. 264–5: fiction
[K.M.] 'A Victorian Jungle', *Athenaeum*, 4644 (2 May 1919), p. 272: review
'Letters of Anton Tchehov IV', *Athenaeum*, 4644 (2 May 1919), p. 282: translation [collaboration with S. S. Koteliansky]
[K.M.] 'Inarticulations', *Athenaeum*, 4645 (9 May 1919), p. 302: review
[K.M.] 'The Public School Mixture', *Athenaeum*, 4646 (16 May 1919), p. 335: review
[unsigned] 'Out and About', *Athenaeum*, 4646 (16 May 1919), p. 336: review
[Elizabeth Stanley] 'Sorrowing Love', *Athenaeum*, 4647 (23 May 1919), p. 366: poetry
[K.M.] 'A Bouquet', *Athenaeum*, 4647 (23 May 1919), p. 366: review
'Letters of Anton Tchehov V', *Athenaeum*, 4647 (23 May 1919), p. 378: translation [collaboration with S. S. Koteliansky]
[K.M.] 'A Novel Without a Crisis', *Athenaeum*, 4648 (30 May 1919), p. 399: review
[K.M.] 'A Child and Her Note-Book', *Athenaeum*, 4648 (30 May 1919), p. 400: review
[K.M.] 'An Exoticist', *Athenaeum*, 4649 (6 June 1919), p. 430: review
'Letters of Anton Tchehov VI', *Athenaeum*, 4649 (6 June 1919), pp. 441–2: translation [collaboration with S. S. Koteliansky]
[K.M.] 'A Short Story', *Athenaeum*, 4650 (13 June 1919), p. 459: review

[K.M.] 'Glancing Light', *Athenaeum*, 4650 (13 June 1919), p. 463: review
[Unsigned] 'The Dean', *Athenaeum*, 4650 (13 June 1919), p. 477: review
[K.M.] 'The New Infancy', *Athenaeum*, 4651 (20 June 1919), p. 494: review
[Unsigned] 'The Caravan Man', *Athenaeum*, 4651 (20 June 1919), p. 511: review
[K.M.] 'Flourisheth in Strange Places', *Athenaeum*, 4652 (27 June 1919), p. 526: review
'Letters of Anton Tchehov VII', *Athenaeum*, 4652 (27 June 1919), p. 538: translation [collaboration with S. S. Koteliansky]
[Elizabeth Stanley] 'A Little Girl's Prayer', *Athenaeum*, 4653 (4 July 1919), p. 552: poetry
[K.M.] 'Uncomfortable Words', *Athenaeum*, 4653 (4 July 1919), p. 556: review
[K.M.] 'The Great Simplicity', *Athenaeum*, 4654 (11 July 1919), p. 591: review
'Letters of Anton Tchehov VIII', *Athenaeum*, 4654 (11 July 1919), p. 602: translation [collaboration with S. S. Koteliansky]
[K.M.] 'A Novel of Suspense', *Athenaeum*, 4655 (18 July 1919), p. 662: review
[Unsigned] 'A Sailor's Home', *Athenaeum*, 4655 (18 July 1919), p. 639: review
[K.M.] 'Anodyne', *Athenaeum*, 4656 (25 July 1919), p. 654: review
'Letters of Anton Tchehov IX', *Athenaeum*, 4656 (25 July 1919), p. 667: translation [collaboration with S. S. Koteliansky]
[K.M.] 'A "Poser"', *Athenaeum*, 4657 (1 August 1919), p. 687: review
[K.M.] 'A Backward Glance', *Athenaeum*, 4658 (8 August 1919), p. 720: review
'Letters of Anton Tchehov X', *Athenaeum*, 4658 (8 August 1919), pp. 731–2: translation [collaboration with S. S. Koteliansky]
[K.M.] 'Mr Walpole in the Nursery', *Athenaeum*, 4659 (15 August 1919), p. 752: review
[Elizabeth Stanley] 'Secret Flowers', *Athenaeum*, 4660 (22 August 1919), p. 776: poetry
[K.M.] 'Sans Merci', *Athenaeum*, 4660 (22 August 1919), pp. 782–3: review
[K.M.] 'Hand Made', *Athenaeum*, 4661 (29 August 1919), p. 815: review
[K.M.] 'The "Sex Complex"', *Athenaeum*, 4661 (29 August 1919), p. 816: review
[K.M.] 'Mr De Morgan's Last Book', *Athenaeum*, 4662 (5 September 1919), p. 846: review
'Letters of Anton Tchehov XI', *Athenaeum*, 4662 (5 September 1919), p. 858: translation [collaboration with S. S. Koteliansky]
[K.M.] 'A Landscape with Portraits', *Athenaeum*, 4663 (12 September 1919), p. 881: review
[K.M.] 'Lions and Lambs', *Athenaeum*, 4664 (19 September 1919), p. 915: review
[K.M.] 'Dea Ex Machina', *Athenaeum*, 4665 (26 September 1919), p. 948: review
[K.M.] 'Sensitiveness', *Athenaeum*, 4666 (3 October 1919), pp. 976–7: review
[K.M.] 'Portraits and Passions', *Athenaeum*, 4667 (10 October 1919), p. 1002: review
[K.M.] 'Humour and Heaviness', *Athenaeum*, 4668 (17 October 1919), p. 1035: review
[K.M.] 'A Plea for Less Entertainment', *Athenaeum*, 4669 (24 October 1919), p. 1067: review
'Letters of Anton Tchehov XII', *Athenaeum*, 4669 (24 October 1919), pp. 1078–9: translation [collaboration with S. S. Koteliansky]
[K.M.] 'A Standstill', *Athenaeum*, 4670 (31 October 1919), p. 1123: review
'Letters of Anton Tchehov XIII', *Athenaeum*, 4670 (31 October 1919), p. 1135: translation [collaboration with S. S. Koteliansky]
'The Pictures', *Art and Letters*, 2.4 (autumn 1919), pp. 153–6, 159–62: fiction[9]
[K.M.] 'Three Approaches', *Athenaeum*, 4671 (7 November 1919), p. 1153: review
[K.M.] 'A "Real" Book and an Unreal One', *Athenaeum*, 4672 (14 November 1919), p. 1187: review
[K.M.] 'A Ship Comes into the Harbour', *Athenaeum*, 4673 (21 November 1919), p. 1227: review

[K.M.] 'Some Aspects of Dostoyevsky', *Athenaeum*, 4674 (28 November 1919), p. 1256: review

[K.M.] 'Control and Enthusiasm', *Athenaeum*, 4674 (28 November 1919), p. 1259: review

[K.M.] 'A Revival', *Athenaeum*, 4675 (5 December 1919), pp. 1289–90: review

[K.M.] 'A Foreign Novel', *Athenaeum*, 4676 (12 December 1919), p. 1336: review

[K.M.] 'A Post-War and a Victorian Novel', *Athenaeum*, 4677 (19 December 1919), p. 1371: review

[K.M.] 'A Collection of Short Stories', *Athenaeum*, 4678 (26 December 1919), p. 1399: review

[K.M.] 'The Plain and the Adorned', *Athenaeum*, 4679 (2 January 1920), p. 15: review

[Elizabeth Stanley] 'Old-Fashioned Widow's Song', *Athenaeum*, 4680 (9 January 1920), p. 42: poetry

[K.M.] 'Dragonflies', *Athenaeum*, 4680 (9 January 1920), p. 48: review

[K.M.] 'Words – Words – Words', *Athenaeum*, 4681 (16 January 1920), p. 79: review

[K.M.] 'The Stale and the Fresh', *Athenaeum*, 4681 (16 January 1920), p. 79: review

[Elizabeth Stanley] 'A Sunset', *Athenaeum*, 4682 (23 January 1920), p. 103: poetry

[Unsigned] 'Anton Tchehov Biographical Note (1860–1887)', *Athenaeum*, 4682 (23 January 1920), p. 124: non-fiction [collaboration with S. S. Koteliansky]

[K.M.] 'Amusement', *Athenaeum*, 4683 (30 January 1920), p. 143: review

[K.M.] 'Portrait of a Child', *Athenaeum*, 4683 (30 January 1920), pp. 143–4: review

[K.M.] 'The Easy Path', *Athenaeum*, 4684 (6 February 1920), p. 179: review

[K.M.] 'Promise', *Athenaeum*, 4684 (6 February 1920), p. 179: review

[Unsigned] 'Anton Tchehov, Biographical Note (1860–1887)' (Part II), *Athenaeum*, 4684 (6 February 1920), p. 191: non-fiction [collaboration with S. S. Koteliansky]

[K.M.] 'Simplicity', *Athenaeum*, 4685 (13 February 1920), p. 211: review

[K.M.] 'Orchestra and Solo', *Athenaeum*, 4686 (20 February 1920), p. 241: review

[Unsigned] 'The Wider Way', *Athenaeum*, 4686 (20 February 1920), p. 258: review

[K.M.] 'Mystery and Adventure', *Athenaeum*, 4687 (27 February 1920), p. 274: review

[K.M.] 'A Party', *Athenaeum*, 4687 (27 February 1920), p. 274: review

[K.M.] 'On the Road', *Athenaeum*, 4690 (19 March 1920), p. 369: review

[K.M.] '"My True Love Hath my Heart"', *Athenaeum*, 4691 (26 March 1920), pp. 415–16: review

[K.M.] 'Short Stories', *Athenaeum*, 4692 (2 April 1920), p. 446: review

'The Diary of Anton Tchehov', *Athenaeum*, 4692 (2 April 1920), pp. 460–1: translation [collaboration with S. S. Koteliansky]

[K.M.] 'Two Modern Novels', *Athenaeum*, 4693 (9 April 1920), p. 479: review

[K.M.] 'Butterflies', *Athenaeum*, 4694 (16 April 1920), p. 511: review

[K.M.] 'Kensingtonia', *Athenaeum*, 4695 (23 April 1920), p. 543: review

[K.M.] 'Alms', *Athenaeum*, 4696 (30 April 1920), p. 573: review

[K.M.] 'Mrs Humphrey Ward's Last Novel', *Athenaeum*, 4697 (7 May 1920), p. 606: review

[K.M.] 'Pressed Flowers', *Athenaeum*, 4697 (7 May 1920), p. 606: review

[K.M.] 'Mr Mackenzie's Treat', *Athenaeum*, 4698 (14 May 1920), p. 639: review

[K.M.] 'A Woman's Books', *Athenaeum*, 4698 (14 May 1920), p. 639: review

[Unsigned] 'A Tragic Comedienne', *Nation*, 27.7 (15 May 1920), pp. 228–30: review

[K.M.] 'A Japanese Novel', *Athenaeum*, 4699 (21 May 1920), p. 671: review

[K.M.] 'An Enigma', *Athenaeum*, 4699 (21 May 1920), p. 671: review

[K.M.] 'Two Novels', *Athenaeum*, 4700 (28 May 1920), p. 702: review

[K.M.] 'Looking On', *Athenaeum*, 4700 (28 May 1920), pp. 702–3: review

'The Man Without a Temperament', *Art and Letters*, 3.2 (spring 1920), pp. 10–14, 17–22, 25: fiction
[K.M.] 'A Model Story', *Athenaeum*, 4701 (4 June 1920), p. 736: review
[K.M.] 'A Spring to Catch Woodcocks', *Athenaeum*, 4701 (4 June 1920), p. 736: review
'Revelations', *Athenaeum*, 4702 (11 June 1920), pp. 759–9: fiction
[K.M.] 'A Norwegian Novel', *Athenaeum*, 4702 (11 June 1920), p. 767: review
[K.M.] 'Echoes', *Athenaeum*, 4702 (11 June 1920), p. 767: review
[K.M.] 'The Books of the Small Souls', *Athenaeum*, 4703 (18 June 1920), pp. 798–9: review
[K.M.] 'A Prize Novel', *Athenaeum*, 4704 (25 June 1920), p. 831: review
[K.M.] 'Wanted, a New Word', *Athenaeum*, 4704 (25 June 1920), pp. 831–2: review
[Unsigned] 'The Stars in Their Courses', *Athenaeum*, 4705 (2 July 1920), p. 5: non-fiction leader
[K.M.] 'Mr Conrad's New Novel', *Athenaeum*, 4705 (2 July 1920), p. 15: review
'The Escape', *Athenaeum*, 4706 (9 July 1920), pp. 38–9: fiction
[K.M.] 'First Novels', *Athenaeum*, 4706 (9 July 1920), p. 49: review
[K.M.] 'The Old and the New Hand', *Athenaeum*, 4707 (16 July 1920), p. 78: review
[K.M.] 'A Hymn to Youth', *Athenaeum*, 4707 (16 July 1920), p. 78: review
[Unsigned] 'The Cherry Orchard', *Athenaeum*, 4707 (16 July 1920), p. 91: review[10]
[K.M.] 'Rather a Give-away', *Athenaeum*, 4708 (23 July 1920), p. 111: review
[K.M.] 'The Luxurious Style', *Athenaeum*, 4708 (23 July 1920), pp. 111–12: review
[K.M.] 'Hypertrophy', *Athenaeum*, 4709 (30 July 1920), p. 144: review
[K.M.] 'A Foreign Novel', *Athenaeum*, 4709 (30 July 1920), p. 144: review
'Bank Holiday', *Athenaeum*, 4710 (6 August 1920), pp. 166–7: fiction
[K.M.] 'Esther Waters Revisited', *Athenaeum*, 4710 (6 August 1920), p. 176: review
'A Holiday Novel', *Athenaeum*, 4711 (13 August 1920), p. 209: review
[K.M.] 'Throw Them Overboard!', *Athenaeum*, 4711 (13 August 1920), pp. 209–10: review
[M.] 'Degrees of Reality', *Athenaeum*, 4711 (13 August 1920), p. 220: review[11]
[Unsigned] 'Stop Press Biography', *Athenaeum*, 4712 (20 August 1920), p. 229: non-fiction leader
[K.M.] 'Deader than the Dodo', *Athenaeum*, 4712 (20 August 1920), p. 241: review
[K.M.] 'Victorian Elegance', *Athenaeum*, 4712 (20 August 1920), pp. 241–2: review
[Unsigned] 'The Critics' New Year', *Athenaeum*, 4713 (27 August 1920), p. 261: non-fiction leader
'The Wind Blows', *Athenaeum*, 4713 (27 August 1920), pp. 262–3: fiction[12]
[K.M.] 'Hearts are Trumps', *Athenaeum*, 4713 (27 August 1920), p. 272: review
[K.M.] 'A Witty Sentimentalist', *Athenaeum*, 4713 (27 August 1920), p. 272: review
[K.M.] 'Sussex, All Too Sussex', *Athenaeum*, 4714 (3 September 1920), p. 304: review
[K.M.] 'Savoir-Faire', *Athenaeum*, 4714 (3 September 1920), p. 304: review
[K.M.] 'Letters', *Athenaeum*, 4715 (10 September 1920), p. 332: review
[K.M.] 'An Imagined Judas', *Athenaeum*, 4715 (10 September 1920), p. 332: review
[K.M.] 'A Dull Monster', *Athenaeum*, 4716 (17 September 1920), p. 376: review
[K.M.] 'The Case of Mr Newte', *Athenaeum*, 4717 (24 September 1920), p. 407: review
[K.M.] 'Fishing as a Fine Art', *Athenaeum*, 4717 (24 September 1920), p. 407: review
'Sun and Moon', *Athenaeum*, 4718 (1 October 1920), pp. 430–2: fiction
[K.M.] 'New Season's Novels', *Athenaeum*, 4718 (1 October 1920), p. 439: review
[K.M.] 'Entertainment – and Otherwise', *Athenaeum*, 4719 (8 October 1920), p. 472: review
[K.M.] 'Observation Only', *Athenaeum*, 4720 (15 October 1920), pp. 519–20: review

[K.M.] 'Some New Thing', *Athenaeum*, 4720 (15 October 1920), p. 520: review
[K. M.] 'Ask No Questions', *Athenaeum*, 4721 (22 October 1920), pp. 552–3: review
'The Young Girl', *Athenaeum*, 4722 (29 October 1920), pp. 575–7: fiction
[K.M.] 'The Silence Is Broken', *Athenaeum*, 4722 (29 October 1920), p. 584: review
[K.M.] 'A Batch of Five', *Athenaeum*, 4723 (5 November 1920), pp. 616–17: review
[K.M.] '"The Magic Door"', *Athenaeum*, 4724 (12 November 1920), pp. 652–3: review
[K.M.] 'Old Writers and New', *Athenaeum*, 4725 (19 November 1920), pp. 694–5: review
'Miss Brill', *Athenaeum*, 4726 (26 November 1920), pp. 722–3: fiction
[K.M.] 'A Set of Four', *Athenaeum*, 4726 (26 November1920), pp. 728–9: review
[K.M.] 'Friends and Foes', *Athenaeum*, 4727 (3 December 1920), pp. 758–9: review
[K.M.] 'Two Novels', *Athenaeum*, 4727 (3 December 1920), p. 760: review
[K.M.] 'Family Portraits', *Athenaeum*, 4728 (10 December 1920), pp. 810–11: review
[M.] 'The Decay of Mr D. H. Lawrence', *Athenaeum*, 4729 (17 December 1920), p. 836: review[13]
'The Lady's Maid', *Athenaeum*, 4730 (24 December 1920), pp. 858–9: fiction
'The Stranger', *London Mercury*, 3.15 (January 1921), pp. 259–68: fiction
[J.M.M.] 'More Notes on Tchehov', *Athenaeum*, 4732 (7 January 1921), pp. 11–12: review[14]
'Life of Ma Parker', *Nation and the Athenaeum*, 28.22 (26 February 1921), pp. 742–3: fiction
'The Singing Lesson: A Story', *Sphere* (23 April 1921), p. 96: fiction
'The Daughters of the Late Colonel', *London Mercury*, 4.19 (May 1921), pp. 15–30: fiction
'Sixpence', *Sphere* (6 August 1921), p. 144: fiction
[J. Middleton Murry] 'The Nostalgia of Mr D. H. Lawrence', *Nation and the Athenaeum*, 29.20 (13 August 1921), pp. 713–14: review[15]
'Mr and Mrs Dove', *Sphere* (13 August 1921), pp. 172–3: fiction
'An Ideal Family', *Sphere* (20 August 1921), pp. 196–7: fiction
'A Family Saga', *Daily News* (5 November 1921), p. 8: review
'Her First Ball', *Sphere* (28 November 1921), pp. 15, 25: fiction
'The Voyage', *Sphere* (24 December 1921), pp. 340–1: fiction
'Marriage à la Mode', *Sphere* (31 December 1921), pp. 364–5: fiction
'At the Bay', *London Mercury*, 5.27 (January 1922), pp. 239–65: fiction
'The Doll's House', *Nation and the Athenaeum*, 30.19 (4 February 1922), pp. 692–3: fiction
'The Garden-Party: Part I', *Saturday Westminster Gazette* (4 February 1922), pp. 9–10: fiction
'The Garden-Party: Part II', *Saturday Westminster Gazette* (11 February 1922), p. 10: fiction
'The Garden-Party: Part III', *Saturday Westminster Gazette* (18 February 1922), pp. 16–17: fiction
[Katharine Mansfield] 'Taking the Veil', *Sketch* (22 February 1922), p. 296: fiction
'The Fly', *Nation and the Athenaeum*, 30.25 (18 March 1922), pp. 896–7: fiction
'Honeymoon', *Nation and the Athenaeum*, 31.5 (29 April 1922), pp. 156–7: fiction
'A Cup of Tea', *Story-Teller* (May 1922), pp. 121–5: fiction
[J. Middleton Murry] 'Two Remarkable Novels', *Nation and the Athenaeum*, 31.20 (12 August 1922), pp. 655–6: review[16]

Notes

1. Disputed authorship. B. J. Kirkpatrick attributes the sketch to Mansfield, whereas Antony Alpers attributes it to Beatrice Hastings and C. E. Bechofer as a parody of Mansfield's 'Pension Sketches'.
2. Disputed authorship. The story is attributed to Mansfield by Kirkpatrick, as well as Clare Hanson and Andrew Gurr.
3. Disputed authorship. Both Kirkpatrick and Alpers have rejected the attribution of authorship to Mansfield.
4. Reprinted in *Dominion* (3 March 1913), p. 11.
5. Disputed authorship. Attributed to Mansfield by Alpers.
6. An early version of 'Pictures'.
7. Translation from the French of Alphonse Daudet.
8. Later published as 'Feuille d'Album'.
9. Initially composed in dialogue form as 'The Common Round' for *The New Age*. Later titled 'Pictures'.
10. The marked files for *The Athenaeum* list Murry as the author of this piece, but the review is usually attributed to Mansfield. Reprinted in *Adelphi*, 3.3 (August 1925), pp. 214–16.
11. Attributed to Mansfield by Kirkpatrick.
12. Revised version of 'Autumns II', first published in *The Signature*.
13. Usually attributed to Murry. However, the marked files of *The Athenaeum* record 'K.M.' as the reviewer.
14. Kirkpatrick argues that Mansfield wrote this review. However, the marked copies clearly attribute this to Murry.
15. As above.
16. As above.

Appendix II

Katherine Mansfield, 'A Little Episode' (1909)

(The one charm of the past is that it is past.
But women never know when the curtain has fallen.)
Lord Henry in 'Dorian Gray'

Yvonne moved slowly up the long, brilliantly lighted Concert Hall. She bowed slightly to several acquaintances, faintly conscious of the men's admiring glances and the women's air of eager familiarity.

Suddenly she felt a slight pull at her skirt, and, looking down, saw Mrs Mason, a stout, moustached woman in an aggressively décolleté dress, smiling and holding out her hand.

'Good evening, Mrs Mason,' said Yvonne, smiling also, and pressing the hand gently.

'Good evening, Lady Mandeville. . . . All alone? I hope that your husband's not seedy?'

'He's a little afraid that he's catching a cold in the head,' Yvonne replied, 'so thought it better to stay by the fire and nurse himself.'

'O very wise, very wise indeed,' said Mrs Mason, ruffling the lace on her bosom until she had all the appearance of a pigeon, 'sickness is so very prevalent just now.'

'Yes, wretchedly so,' answered Yvonne.

'My Ethel has had a frightful nosey cold and now it's gone to her chest with a horrid loose cough. Of course she makes a great fuss but I know the secret of all these things – good strong mustard plasters.'

'Is that so,' said Yvonne. She glanced at Mrs Mason's stout red arms and shivered slightly.

'I hope you're not catching anything,' continued Mrs Mason, 'you're looking a little puffy about the eyes, my dear.'

She turned to a small pale woman seated beside her, whose paleness was accentuated by a great cluster of scarlet geraniums and maidenhair fern which crept up her left shoulder. . . . 'May I introduce my friend Mrs Wood – '

'How do you do?' said Yvonne, and moved to her seat.

'What a distinguished looking woman,' said Mrs Wood, 'such grace, Amelia – she looks like a Du Maurier picture, doesn't she?'

'O yes, a dear little girl,' said Mrs Mason, fanning herself vigorously. 'I knew her husband before they were married – a very good, practical fellow. Don't you know about her?'

'No, nothing except that she is Lady Mandeville. Please tell me about her?'

'O, she is a niece of Dr and Mrs Parratt – you know – those nice, quiet, thoughtful Church of England people in Bellevue Avenue. This girl was the daughter of Oswald Parratt – a younger brother and a complete failure. They tried him in everything – and at last he left all his family – went to Paris and took to Art.'

Mrs Wood murmured a little exclamation – which might have been horror or pity or sympathy.

'Then,' said Mrs Mason, pulling up her long gloves, and carefully smoothing out the creases, 'he married some little obscure weed,' her voice was full of withering contempt, 'who died when this girl, Yvonne, was born. They say the Father never recovered from that – and the child was brought up helter-skelter in a dreadful way, until when she was seventeen her Father died. You remember Dr and Mrs Parratt were abroad at the time, so they rescued Yvonne – who hadn't a penny – and brought her to Manchester.'

'Just like them,' murmured Mrs Wood, softly.

'Yes. The child – at least she was half woman then – didn't even know the Catechism – had no clothes and smoked cigarettes. . . . It was a positive reformation. They changed her absolutely – and, as she was pretty, Geoffrey Mandeville fell in love with her and married her. Of course, as I told her, it was a mere fluke – the most wonderful good fortune. She, indeed, was perfectly dazed at the whole affair.'

'And has it been a success?'

'Turning out very well.'

'Have they any children?'

'No, not yet – but I should think they would, certainly – they can easily afford it, and Geoffrey is just that sort of man – good and earnest and very thorough. . . .'

Mrs Wood glanced curiously at Yvonne – she leant back in her chair, her pale delicate face in repose wore a strangely listless expression – her fair, shining hair was arranged in fashionable puffs and curls. She wore a long black velvet kimono coat and looked the very embodiment of elegant languor.

And the girl was thinking –

'I am a damned fool to come here – I can't think why I did, and it would have been so easy to get out of it. But it was too great a temptation. . . . I wonder if he'll be the same – I wonder if he'll notice me – I shall certainly not dream of going to see him afterwards. . . .'

A man came on to the platform to open the piano – Yvonne stirred slightly in her seat – and opened and shut her hands convulsively.

A moment later Jacques Saint Pierre was bowing before the audience.

She did not look up until he had seated himself at the piano – then – he had not changed – the same slim figure – the same profusion of black hair brushed straight back from his face – the pouting, eager mouth, the beautiful expressive Musician hands.

A sudden wave of colour flooded her face – as he began to play –

Recollections – exquisite bitter sweet memories began to flock past her – a motley, mad, fascinating troupe. She closed her eyes. . . . Back again in her Father's rooms – Jacques at the piano – Emil, half lying across the table – Jean by the fire – sketching them all. . . . She, sitting huddled up by her Father – his arm around her, cheek to cheek, heart to heart.

A thunderous, deafening burst of applause followed the Appassionata. The sharp, hard sound seemed to hurt her physically – seemed to fall upon her bruised, trembling soul – like brutal blows.

Seized by an ungovernable impulse she rose and swiftly passed out of the hall.

'Please direct me to the Artists' Room,' she said.

The man looked at her enquiringly.

'M. does not care to see –'

'I am a personal friend of M. Saint Pierre. It is by appointment.'

The man bowed. They passed down a narrow stone passage – through swing doors – 'second door to the right,' said the attendant and left her there.

Yvonne stood still a moment – she felt half suffocated – her heart seemed to be thudding – loudly and dully.

Then she suddenly ran forward and knocked at the door.

'Entrez,' said a voice.

She opened the door and stood, tremulous, tears trembling on her lashes, on the threshold.

Jacques was standing before a little fire – smoking a cigarette. He looked up, inquiringly – and then, seeing her – ran forward and took her two hands –

'Yvonne – Yvonne.'

'Jacques – Jacques.'

She was half laughing, half crying, inexpressibly, intoxicatingly beautiful . . . the little charming chrysalis of studio days had become this fascinating Society butterfly – and to her – this dear, affectionate boy had become ideal man – ideal musician – the symbol of all her happy life – her Paris days.

'O,' she said, impulsively – childishly. 'I have been so miserable –'

She felt she must tell him everything – confide in him – ask his advice – win his sympathy. She felt she must hear again that curious caressing tone of his voice . . . 'O Jacques.'

He drew forward a chair.

'Tenez,' he said, 'I must go and play again. Wait here – nobody will come near you. Here are some cigarettes and you must talk to me – afterwards –'

'O yes – yes,' she cried.

He left her, closing the door.

Yvonne took a cigarette – lit it with a shadowy smile on her face. Very faintly she could hear the sound of the piano. If only they could see her now – all those fat, stolid Philistines – that idiot husband.

When Jacques came back she looked like an adorable child caught mischief-making – the man caught his breath sharply. He was excited by the music – and his hands trembled perceptibly. He did not wish to hear a long, burdensome confession – he wanted to hold this woman and kiss her. Some tremendous passion seemed to be shaking him.

'Well, tell me everything,' he said, leaning against the mantelpiece and looking into the fire.

Yvonne got up and stood beside him. She spoke very rapidly – in a low, even voice.

'It's only this Jacques. When I came from Paris here, O, I really thought I should have died – Jacques, I longed to die. I cried every night – but they had me in hand – they tortured me with everything. It went on for weeks – and until at last I made up my mind that whatever happened – I should leave them. But I hadn't a penny – not even enough to pay postage stamps with – and no education – I couldn't teach – or sew – or anything. . . .'

She put her hand on his sleeve. 'They crushed all my ideals – all my hopes – they made me think of Paris – as Hell, the fools – and Father the Arch Fiend. Bon Dieu – I was friendless – homeless – helpless. Then Lord Mandeville came – and engaged himself to me – yes, that's the way to put it – and we've been married nine months.'

The man turned sharply – he was breathing hard.

'Ah! it is true,' said Yvonne. 'He thought he had never seen anyone so pale – and – think – here I am. I thought – once I married, I would be freer – but I'm *caged*. This great heavy brute who whistles "Little Mary" out of tune the whole day long – and who doesn't know a picture from a whisky advertisement. He's my husband – pity me,' she cried.

Like a child she looked at him and he suddenly caught her in his arms. She felt as though she had left the world altogether. He seemed to give her just that support she had been needing. Jacques bent down and whispered, 'Stay here until the Concert is over – and then I will walk home with you. Be a good girl and promise me.'

She assented – and he placed her back in the chair. She never moved again – never looked up – or stirred – until he stood before her in his long coat and soft hat. 'Come along,' he said.

Out in the cold lighted streets they began talking again. He had drawn her arm through his and kept pressing her hand. Each time he did so a tremor ran through her – it was as though she held her life in her hand – and he crushed it – so.

'Is there nowhere where we can talk?' he said. Yvonne thought a moment – then she suddenly laughed.

'Well, there's my house – it's a little gardener's cottage not far from the gate – hidden by trees, from the road and the house. There are just two rooms that I have furnished for myself – and Geoffrey has never been inside the door. We'll go there.'

It was almost disappointing. Yvonne could feel unhappy no longer – she could no longer realise what had made her so wretched. Nothing on earth seemed to matter – except that she was alive and loving, and tremendously excited.

'Jacques,' she said, 'you have all the air of the Great Life round you – you are making me feel again all the adorable irresponsibility of everything.'

He laughed shortly. It was making him half mad to walk thus – crushing her hand.

They passed through the wide iron gates.

Yvonne led the way – down an overgrown path – and into a little tree fringed space. There the house stood – a desolate place – she stooped down and groped for the key under the doormat.

'Enter,' she said, 'and give me some matches.'

They walked into a small square room. Yvonne lit four candles on the mantelpiece.

'How do you like it?' she said, joyously.

He looked round – here were all her Paris treasures – her Father's pictures – little odd familiar pieces of drapery – a charcoal sketch of himself at the piano and then he turned and looked at Yvonne. Her fair shining hair glowed in the candle light – her mouth was scarlet – her eyes, curiously bright. She was still wrapped in her long cloak.

Never before had Yvonne needed so much love in her life. Primitive woman she felt – with primitive impulses – primitive needs – all conventions – all scruples were thrown to the four winds.

Jacques flung off his coat. Then he came forward. She could not look at him – but stood – suddenly silent.

'Here,' he said, 'let me help you off with this,' and caught hold of her cloak.

'Thank you,' she murmured – suddenly and absurdly glad that her dress was beautiful. Then he caught hold of her – kissed her – roughly – repeatedly.

'Let me go,' she said, 'let me go,' yet lay passive in his arms.

'Yvonne – Yvonne – look at me.'

She put her arms round his neck, and held up her face.

'O, you are killing me,' she moaned.

Yvonne – dishevelled – flushed – entered the hall of her home.

Lord Mandeville came out of the library.

'Hallo, what's up – what's the matter?' he said. 'Have you had an accident? Where's the carriage?'

'I walked,' said Yvonne, 'and the wind has blown me about.'

'You've cut your lip, or something,' said Lord Mandeville, 'there's some blood on your chin.'

'It's nothing,' Yvonne answered.

She slowly mounted the stairs – then looked back over her shoulder. 'I'm going to bed.'

'O, alright, hurry up – I'm coming, too. Don't you want anything to eat?'

'No, thank you.'

When she reached her room she turned on all the lights. There was a large bright fire burning in the grate – the curtains were drawn and the room felt hot – stifling.

She ran to the glass – threw off her cloak and looked at herself, critically.

'O, I have lived – I have lived,' she cried. 'And I shall see Jacques tomorrow of course – something beautiful and stupendous is going to happen – I am alive again – at last!'

She threw off her clothes, hastily, brushed out her long hair, and then suddenly looked at the wide, empty bed. A feeling of intolerable disgust came over her. By Lord Mandeville's pillow she saw a large bottle of Eucalyptus and two clean handkerchiefs. From below in the hall she heard the sound of bolts being drawn – then the electric light switched off.

She sprang into bed – and suddenly, instinctively with a little childish gesture – she put one arm over her face – as though to hide something hideous and dreadful – as her husband's heavy, ponderous footsteps sounded on the stairs. . . .

About the same time, Jacques Saint Pierre sat in his rooms at the Hotel Manchester, writing a letter –

'To-night – think of it – I saw Yvonne – she is quite a little Society lady – and I assure you – no longer one of us. But she bores me – she has the inevitable feminine passion for trying to relight fires that have long since been ashes. Take care, little one, that you do not – like wise. I hear her husband is very wealthy – and – what they call here – a "howling bore".

Adieu – cherie – I shall be with you in two days – if I manage to avoid the charming Yvonne. There is the penalty, you see, for being so fascinating.

Jacques Saint Pierre.'

Appendix III

Katherine Mansfield, 'Bites from the Apple' (1911)

1. Repentance is the duster with which we sop up the spilt milk. It serves its estimable purpose but is nothing but a damp rag afterwards to be thrown into the soiled linen bag.
2. Love is the germ – passion the disease.
3. Take Regret as your mistress but never make her your wife. For she will hang about your neck and twine her arms around your body, and she is heavy to hold as the dead are heavy. Take Regret as your mistress but never make her your wife – for her body is salt to taste with the tears of a thousand lovers and her womb is barren.
4. If a man bore in mind the fact that when he chose his wife his wife also chose him, there would be less talk of the equality of the sexes and more realisation.
5. The average Englishwoman imagines that every Frenchman is a devil – with his horns only half concealed under an opera hat.
6. If you wish to live you must first attend your own funeral.
7. People are charmingly conservative. The story of the Garden of Eden is practically the only plot to fill and refill out West End theatres and the pages of our magazines. . . . Domestic felicity destroyed by a twentieth-century serpent in an embroidered shirt front and that dangerous little gift which Eve . . . hands to her husband.
8. Before confessing be perfectly certain that you do not wish to be forgiven.
9. I keep the God of my childhood hanging around my neck by a string, like a little camphor bag – an old-fashioned remedy for warding off infectious and dangerous complaints. Of course there is one disadvantage . . . when I wear evening dress . . . it is impossible. Most women do the same – that is why men find my sex so far more vulnerable when they are décolleté.
10. Enough for the Present – yet they say no woman is ever satisfied – yet she does not wish you to give her a Past.

11. Life's a game of cards – which mainly consists of shuffling.
12. It took a woman to realise the fact that the greatness of great men depends mainly upon the length of their hair.
13. Easy enough to strike a match – but it requires experience to keep a fire burning.
14. If you attempt to pull out the arrow with which Cupid has speared you, be certain that you shall find your heart impaled upon its point. If you let it remain be equally certain that Cupid will call around for it himself and manage the operation with far greater dexterity.
15. 'Patience' is a game only for one – if two people wish to play they invariably choose 'animal grab'.
16. A good figure costs a good figure and is seldom paid for with interest.
17. The man of the people has only one sole which he keeps under his feet . . . that is why it is so often contaminated with the mud on the road.
18. I find substance beautiful for the shadows it throws, just as I find reality bearable for the dreams it brings me.
19. 'Tis better far to count the cost than never to accost at all.
20. Defiance is the trumpet which we blow in the ears of the world. 'Ah,' cries the world, turning from us, 'how brazen.' But it does not hear the pitiful little attempts that we have made in the privacy of our own room before we were able to emit any sound at all.
21. Epigrams are the froth of life, blown into your face from the waves of the sea. But they leave a bitter taste in the mouth.
22. She wove her thoughts, her desire, her dreams into a long garment of strange colour. And when she had finished the shining length of it she wrapped herself in its folds and went, in the dawn, to the battlefield. And young men in the pride of their youth – women far older and stronger than she, were cut down. The girl stood silently watching. 'I have woven so strongly,' said she, 'that the sharp swords of Reality cannot pierce through my garment of Dreams.' So she smiled. . . . But in the full heat of the day she felt heavy and oppressed – the yellow sun beat down upon her. 'Oh,' she cried, 'I stifle – this heat – I am choking!' and she sought to loosen the heavy folds. But they clung around her, heavily, her arms, yea, even her head and breast, bound round in the shining fabric.

    'Alas!' she moaned, 'now is mine the more terrible tragedy. For I, too, must die, but never having known the fierce, splendid reality of being wounded.'
23. However frugal the meal that Life shows you, she always gives you your desert.
24. Those who eat greatly of the fruit of the Tree of Knowledge must expect to find themselves crucified on the bare branches.

25. One must envy Christ his crucifixion for few indeed of us are permitted at the close of day to cry 'It is finished'.

26. One thing keeps me from going into deep waters; I am so afraid of finding shallows there.

27. She gave him a rose and an old glove. He fell down on his knees and cried to her that he worshipped her – the ground she trod on – the image of her hand was sacred to him for Ever. She gave him a little book and a curl of her hair. He flung out his arms . . . did she feel his kisses tangled in the shining web of her curls. . . . His heart was bound to her Eternally by that little golden twist. She sent him a letter, and he, by devious lover's arts, found the place where her hand had rested as she signed her name, and he kissed it over and over, and slept with the letter under his pillow. Then she gave him her mouth and he swore Absolute Homage – darkness for him was light, the crooked straight – etc. etc. She gave him herself, and by and bye he pulled out his watch and said: Jove, time was getting on, and would she be at the Foodleum's dance on the 12th of next month? She started laughing, and the pitiful thing is that she cannot stop. The unsophisticated, seeing her face hidden, think that she is drying her tears, but we know better.

28. We are all of us in a gigantic maze – running round and round, but at last, sooner or later, we reach the gate – the station – and breathless, worn out, dishevelled, we fly through – it is locked and barred from us. Where are we now, we ask of the grinning janitor. He does not speak but points to the name on the board – it is Life's last, stupendously fiendish joke – it is her letter of introduction to her superior – Death – the name of the place is Eternity.

29. The sooner Eve meets the serpent the better – then she leaves the Garden of Eden and has the whole world before her.

30. Life's little flutter inevitably ends in 'broken wings.'

31. Dawn is a herald running with wind-tossed hair and rosy feet to cry that Night is fast approaching.

32. To be completely lost is to take the first step towards finding yourself.

33. Reality is only so strong a dream that it becomes a Nightmare.

34. Life is a tremendous game of 'Hide the Thimble', without the delicious, childish certainty that there is any thimble to be found.

35. If you must be a moth make the splendid sacrifice worthwhile. Do not revolve around a farthing dip, but, once having chosen your candle with all due consideration take care that you extinguish its flame at your own death. There is something hideously vulgar in the thought that the candle keeps on burning.

36. What so many people seem to forget is that you must have a Past before you can possibly have a Future.

37. I love chance and hate certainty – than the latter there is no more miserable prop to depend upon. Lean on it, and it is hard that it breaks – Chance is a supple thing that has the option of delicately yielding.

38. Turn in upon yourself for comfort and you are like a poor spider caught in the web of its own weaving.

39. If you have *once* known Love – if you have been chained by him – and he to you – then everything that grows springs as a sign and token from his grave. I walk in the fields and the buttercups are full of the young gold in his hair – these flowers – growing strongly scarlet are full of the passion of his red mouth – I put my arms round a tree and it is not strong and more lean than his young body. If you would find Peace in the silent places do not go to them as a lover with a sick heart to be cured but as a child, who, knowing nothing of Death finds but an infinitely sweet promise – a prophecy that is always just about to be fulfilled. Who finds Autumn – Spring in a dream – Winter – Summer in the enchanted sleep that is broken by a kiss.

40. There is the gift that we can do very well without – it is the Present that the Past persists in thrusting upon us.

41. Love is the Wine of Life – Marriage the non-alcoholic beverage.

42. Of course the game is worth a candle, but it is often better played without one.

43. Of course most people keep a skeleton in the cupboard. The trouble with the majority of women is that they will persist in shutting themselves up in that cupboard with that skeleton. . . .

44. Small wonder that a pillar box is such a channel for gossip – like a woman, it never shuts its mouth.

45. Love has grown blind through being kept so long in the dark.

46. The secret of remaining satisfied is to make it a rule to leave the table long before you have had enough.

47. In these days of social depravity we do not look *under* the bed before retiring, but *in* it.

48. Progressive women can never be popular – why Eve gave Adam the pip – what can you expect. However, generous soul! he did not keep it, but gave it her for seed – And wasn't she wild! She just raised Cain as far as she was Able (Abel.)

49. Love feeds upon itself – that is why it is so soon starved to Death.

50. The classic is that which is eternally modern – the modern that which can never be classic.

Select Bibliography

Alpers, Antony, *The Life of Katherine Mansfield*, rev. edn (Harmondsworth: Penguin, 1982).

Anderson, Benedict, *Imagined Communities: Reflections on the Origin and Spread of Nationalism*, rev. edn (London: Verso, 2006).

Antliff, Mark, *Inventing Bergson: Cultural Politics and the Parisian Avant-Garde* (Princeton: Princeton University Press, 1993).

Appadurai, Arjun, 'Disjuncture and Difference in the Global Cultural Economy', *Theory and Society*, 7 (1990), pp. 295–310.

Ardis, Ann L., 'Debating Feminism, Modernism, and Socialism: Beatrice Hastings' Voices in *The New Age*', in Bonnie Kime Scott (ed.), *Gender in Modernism: New Geographies, Complex Intersections* (Urbana: University of Illinois Press, 2007), pp. 160–85.

Ardis, Ann L., 'The Dialogics of Modernism(s) in *The New Age*', *Modernism/Modernity*, 14.3 (September 2007), pp. 407–34.

Ardis, Ann L., 'Staging the Public Sphere: Magazine Dialogism and the Prosthetics of Authorship at the Turn of the Twentieth Century', in Ann L. Ardis and Patrick Collier (eds), *Transatlantic Print Culture, 1880–1940: Emerging Media, Emerging Modernisms* (Basingstoke: Palgrave Macmillan, 2008), pp. 30–47.

Ardis, Ann L. and Patrick Collier (eds), *Transatlantic Print Culture, 1880–1940: Emerging Media, Emerging Modernisms* (Basingstoke: Palgrave Macmillan, 2008).

Arnold, Matthew, *The Poems of Matthew Arnold*, ed. Miriam Allott (London: Longman, 1979).

Bains, Christopher, 'Critics Abroad: The Early Years of *The Paris Review* (1953–65)', in Peter Brooker and Andrew Thacker (eds), *The Oxford Critical and Cultural History of Modernist Magazines, Volume II: North America 1894–1960* (Oxford: Oxford University Press, 2012), pp. 759–74.

Bell, Clive, *Art* (London: Chatto and Windus, 1914).

Bennett, Andrew, *Katherine Mansfield* (Tavistock: Northcote House, 2004).

Bhabha, Homi K., *The Location of Culture*, rev. edn (London: Routledge, 2004).

Binckes, Faith, 'Lines of Engagement: *Rhythm*, Reproduction, and the Textual Dialogues of Early Modernism', in Suzanne W. Churchill and Adam McKible (eds), *Little Magazines and Modernism: New Approaches* (Aldershot: Ashgate, 2007), pp. 21–34.

Binckes, Faith, *Modernism, Magazines, and the British Avant-Garde: Reading* Rhythm, *1910–1914* (Oxford: Oxford University Press, 2010).

Boehmer, Elleke, *Colonial and Postcolonial Literature: Migrant Metaphors*, 2nd edn (Oxford: Oxford University Press, 2005).

Boehmer, Elleke, 'Mansfield as Colonial Modernist: Difference Within', in Gerri Kimber and Janet Wilson (eds), *Celebrating Katherine Mansfield* (Basingstoke: Palgrave Macmillan, 2011), pp. 57–71.

Bornstein, George, *Material Modernism: The Politics of the Page* (Cambridge: Cambridge University Press, 2001).

Brooker, Peter, 'Harmony, Discord, and Difference: *Rhythm* (1911–13), *The Blue Review* (1913), and *The Signature* (1915)', in Peter Brooker and Andrew Thacker (eds), *The Oxford Critical and Cultural History of Modernist Magazines, Volume I: Britain and Ireland, 1880–1955* (Oxford: Oxford University Press, 2009), pp. 314–36.

Brooker, Peter and Andrew Thacker (eds), *The Oxford Critical and Cultural History of Modernist Magazines, Volume I: Britain and Ireland, 1880–1955* (Oxford: Oxford University Press, 2009).

Bru, Sascha, '"The Will to Style": The Dutch Contribution to the Avant-Garde. Leiden: *De Stijl* (1917–32), *Mécano* (1922–3); Amsterdam: *Wendingen* (1918–32), *i10* (1927–9); and Groningen: *The Next Call* (1923–6)', in Peter Brooker, Sascha Bru, Andrew Thacker and Christian Weikop (eds), *The Oxford Critical and Cultural History of Modernist Magazines, Volume III, Europa 1880–1940* (Oxford: Oxford University Press, 2013), pp. 293–312.

Bulson, Eric, *Little Magazine, World Form* (New York: Columbia University Press, 2016).

Carswell, John, *Lives and Letters: A. R. Orage, Beatrice Hastings, Katherine Mansfield, John Middleton Murry, S. S. Koteliansky, 1906–1957* (London: Faber, 1978).

Carter, David, *Almost Always Modern: Australian Print Cultures and Modernity* (Melbourne: Australian Scholarly Publishing, 2013).

Churchill, Suzanne W. and Adam McKible (eds), *Little Magazines and Modernism: New Approaches* (Aldershot: Ashgate, 2007).

Codell, Julie F. (ed.), *Imperial Co-Histories: National Identities and the British Colonial Press* (London: Associated University Presses, 2003).

Collier, Patrick, 'Imperial/Modernist Forms in the *Illustrated London News*', *Modernism/Modernity*, 19.3 (September 2012), pp. 487–514.

Connors, Linda E. and Mary Lou MacDonald, *National Identity in Great Britain and British North America, 1815–1851: The Role of Nineteenth-Century Periodicals* (Farnham: Ashgate, 2011).

Daly, Saralyn R., *Katherine Mansfield*, rev. edn (Oxford: Maxwell Macmillan, 1994).

Davin, Anna, 'Imperialism and Motherhood', *History Workshop*, 5 (spring 1978), pp. 9–63.

Davison, Claire, *Translation as Collaboration: Virginia Woolf, Katherine Mansfield and S. S. Koteliansky* (Edinburgh: Edinburgh University Press, 2014).

Davison, Claire, 'Introduction', in Claire Davison, Gerri Kimber and Todd Martin (eds), *Katherine Mansfield and Translation* (Edinburgh: Edinburgh University Press, 2015), pp. 1–11.

Delap, Lucy, 'Feminist and Anti-Feminist Encounters in Edwardian Britain', *Historical Research*, 78.201 (August 2005), pp. 377–99.

Demoor, Marysa, *Their Fair Share: Women, Power and Criticism in the* Athenaeum, *from Millicent Garrett Fawcett to Katherine Mansfield, 1870–1920* (Aldershot: Ashgate, 2000).

Diment, Galya, *A Russian Jew of Bloomsbury: The Life and Times of Samuel Koteliansky* (London: McGill-Queen's University Press, 2011).

Dowling, David, 'Katherine Mansfield's Criticism: "There Must Be the Question Put"', *Journal of New Zealand Literature*, 6 (1988), pp. 157–69.

Dunbar, Pamela, *Radical Mansfield: Double Discourse in Katherine Mansfield's Short Stories* (London: Macmillan, 1997).

Eliot, T. S., *The Sacred Wood: Essays on Poetry and Criticism* (London: Methuen, 1920).

Eliot, T. S., *For Lancelot Andrewes: Essays on Style and Order* (London: Faber and Gwyer, 1928).

Esty, Jed, *Unseasonable Youth: Modernism, Colonialism, and the Fiction of Development* (Oxford: Oxford University Press, 2012).

Fabian, Johannes, *Time and the Other: How Anthropology Makes Its Object* (New York: Columbia University Press, 1983).

Fernihough, Anne, 'Introduction', in Katherine Mansfield, *In a German Pension*, ed. Anne Fernihough (London: Penguin, 1999), pp. ix–xxix.

Fernihough, Anne, *Freewomen and Supermen: Edwardian Radicals and Literary Modernism* (Oxford: Oxford University Press, 2013).

Garner, Les, *Stepping Stones to Women's Liberty: Feminist Ideas in the Women's Suffrage Movement 1900–1918* (London: Heinemann, 1984).

Garnett, David, *The Flowers of the Forest* (London: Chatto and Windus, 1955).

Garrity, Jane, *Step-Daughters of England: British Women Modernists and the National Imaginary* (Manchester: Manchester University Press, 2003).

Garver, Lee, 'The Political Katherine Mansfield', *Modernism/Modernity*, 8.2 (April 2001), pp. 225–43.

Gasston, Aimee, 'Katherine Mansfield, Cannibal', in Janet Wilson, Gerri Kimber and Delia da Sousa Correa (eds), *Katherine Mansfield and the (Post)colonial* (Edinburgh: Edinburgh University Press, 2013), pp. 15–28.

Gelder, Ken and Rachel Weaver, 'Literary Journals and Literary Aesthetics in Early Post-Federation Australia', *JASAL: Journal of the Association for the Study of Australian Literature*, 14.5 (2014), p. 1.

Gillies, Mary Ann, 'Oceans Apart? Emily Carr and Katherine Mansfield's Encounters With Modernism', in Mary Ann Gillies, Helen Sword and Steven Yao (eds), *Pacific Rim Modernisms* (Toronto: University of Toronto Press, 2009), pp. 233–60.

Goldie, David, *A Critical Difference: T. S. Eliot and John Middleton Murry in English Literary Criticism, 1919–1928* (Oxford: Clarendon Press, 1998).

Gray, Stephen, *Free-Lancers and Literary Biography in South Africa* (Amsterdam: Rodopi, 1999).

Gray, Stephen, *Beatrice Hastings: A Literary Life* (London: Viking, 2004).

Green, Barbara, 'The Feminist Periodical Press: Women, Periodical Studies, and Modernity', *Literature Compass*, 6.1 (2009), pp. 191–205.

Green, Barbara, 'Recovering Feminist Criticism: Modern Women Writers and Feminist Periodical Studies', *Literature Compass*, 10.1 (2013), pp. 53–60.

Hammill, Faye and Mark Hussey, *Modernism's Print Cultures* (London: Bloomsbury, 2016).

Hammond, Meghan Marie, *Empathy and the Psychology of Literary Modernism* (Edinburgh: Edinburgh University Press, 2014).

Hanson, Clare (ed.), *The Critical Writings of Katherine Mansfield* (London: Macmillan, 1987).

Hanson, Clare and Andrew Gurr, *Katherine Mansfield* (Basingstoke: Macmillan, 1981).

Harrison, Andrew, 'Ambivalence, Language and the Uncanny in Katherine Mansfield's *In a German Pension*', in Delia da Sousa Correa, Gerri Kimber, Susan Reid and Gina Wisker (eds), *Katherine Mansfield and the Fantastic* (Edinburgh: Edinburgh University Press, 2012), pp. 51–62.

Harrison, Charles, Francis Frascina and Gill Perry (eds), *Primitivism, Cubism, Abstraction: The Early Twentieth Century* (London: Open University Press, 1994).
Hastings, Beatrice, *The Old 'New Age': Orage and Others* (London: Blue Moon Press, 1936).
Haycock, David Boyd, *A Crisis of Brilliance: Five Young British Artists and the Great War* (London: Old Street Publishing, 2009).
Holroyd, Michael, *Lytton Strachey: A Critical Biography, Volume II* (London: Heinemann, 1968).
Hulme, T. E., *Speculations: Essays on Humanism and the Philosophy of Art*, ed. Herbert Read (New York: Harcourt, 1924).
Huyssen, Andreas, *After the Great Divide: Modernism, Mass Culture, Postmodernism* (Bloomington: Indiana University Press, 1986).
Irvine, Dean, *Editing Modernity: Women and Little-Magazine Cultures in Canada, 1916–1956* (Toronto: University of Toronto Press, 2008).
Johannesson, Eric O., 'Vilhelm Ekelund: Modernism and the Aesthetics of the Aphorism', *Scandinavian Studies*, 56 (1984), pp. 213–34.
Johnson, Benjamin and Erika Jo Brown (eds), *Beatrice Hastings: On the Life and Work of a Lost Modern Master* (Warrensburg: Pleiades Press, 2016).
Kalliney, Peter, *Modernism in a Global Context* (London: Bloomsbury, 2016).
Kandinsky, Wassily, *The Art of Spiritual Harmony*, trans. Michael T. H. Sadler (London: Constable, 1914).
Kaplan, Sydney Janet, *Katherine Mansfield and the Origins of Modernist Fiction* (New York: Cornell University Press, 1991).
Kaplan, Sydney Janet, *Circulating Genius: John Middleton Murry, Katherine Mansfield and D. H. Lawrence* (Edinburgh: Edinburgh University Press, 2010).
Kascakova, Janka, 'Katherine Mansfield's "How Pearl Button Was Kidnapped"', *Explicator*, 72.2 (2014), pp. 118–21.
Kimber, Gerri, *Katherine Mansfield: The View from France* (Oxford: Peter Lang, 2008).
Kimber, Gerri, 'Mansfield, *Rhythm* and the Émigré Connection', in Janet Wilson, Gerri Kimber and Susan Reid (eds), *Katherine Mansfield and Literary Modernism* (London: Continuum, 2011), pp. 13–29.
Kimber, Gerri, 'Circles of Influence: Katherine Mansfield, S. S. Koteliansky and Russia', in Sarah Ailwood and Melinda Harvey (eds), *Katherine Mansfield and Literary Influence* (Edinburgh: Edinburgh University Press, 2015), pp. 78–90.
Kimber, Gerri, '"That Pole outside our door": Floryan Sobieniowski and Katherine Mansfield', in Janka Kascakova and Gerri Kimber (eds), *Katherine Mansfield and Continental Europe* (Basingstoke: Palgrave Macmillan, 2015), pp. 59–83.
Kimber, Gerri and Angela Smith (eds), *The Poetry and Critical Writings of Katherine Mansfield* (Edinburgh: Edinburgh University Press, 2014).
Kinkead-Weekes, Mark, *D. H. Lawrence: Triumph to Exile, 1912–1922* (Cambridge: Cambridge University Press, 1996).
Kirkpatrick, B. J., *A Bibliography of Katherine Mansfield* (Oxford: Clarendon, 1989).
Krebs, Paula, *Gender, Race, and the Writing of Empire: Public Discourse and the Boer War* (Cambridge: Cambridge University Press, 1999).
Krueger, Kate, *British Women Writers and the Short Story, 1850–1930: Reclaiming Social Space* (Basingstoke: Palgrave Macmillan, 2014).
Latham, Sean and Robert Scholes, 'The Changing Profession: The Rise of Periodical Studies', *PMLA*, 121.2 (March 2006), pp. 517–31.
Lawrence, D. H., *Kangaroo* ([1923] London: Heinemann, 1955).

Lawrence, D. H., *The Letters of D. H. Lawrence, Volume II*, ed. George J. Zytaruk and James T. Boulton (Cambridge: Cambridge University Press, 1982).

Lawrence, D. H., *The Letters of D. H. Lawrence, Volume IV*, ed. Warren Roberts, James T. Boulton and Elizabeth Mansfield (Cambridge: Cambridge University Press, 1987).

Lawrence, D. H., *The Letters of D. H. Lawrence, Volume V*, ed. James T. Boulton and Lindeth Vasey (Cambridge: Cambridge University Press, 1989).

Lawrence, D. H., *Women in Love*, ed. David Farmer, Lindeth Vasey and John Worthen ([1920] London: Penguin, 1995).

Lea, F. A., *The Life of John Middleton Murry* (London: Methuen, 1959).

Leddy, Thomas, 'Nietzsche on Unity of Style', *Historical Reflections/Réflexions Historiques*, 21.3 (fall 1995), pp. 553–67.

Lee, Hermione, *Virginia Woolf*, 2nd edn (London: Vintage, 1997).

Lee, Hermione, 'Virginia Woolf's Essays', in Susan Sellers (ed.), *The Cambridge Companion to Virginia Woolf*, 2nd edn (Cambridge: Cambridge University Press, 2010), pp. 89–106.

Lehan, Richard, 'Bergson and the Discourse of the Moderns', in Frederick Burwick and Paul Douglass (eds), *Crisis of Modernism* (Cambridge: Cambridge University Press, 1992), pp. 306–29.

Lloyd, David, *Nationalism and Minor Literature: James Clarence Mangan and the Emergence of Irish Cultural Nationalism* (London: University of California Press, 1987).

Maclean, Caroline, 'Russian Aesthetics in Britain: Kandinsky, Sadleir, and *Rhythm*', in Rebecca Beasley and Philip Ross Bullock (eds), *Russia in Britain, 1880–1940: From Melodrama to Modernism* (Oxford: Oxford University Press, 2013), pp. 145–61.

Maddison, Isobel, 'Mansfield's "Writing Game" and World War One', in Isobel Maddison and Alice Kelly (eds), *Katherine Mansfield and World War One* (Edinburgh: Edinburgh University Press, 2014), pp. 42–54.

Mairet, Philip, *A. R. Orage: A Memoir* (London: Dent, 1936).

Majumdar, Saikat, *Prose of the World: Modernism and the Banality of Empire* (New York: Columbia University Press, 2013).

Mansfield, Katherine, *Novels and Novelists*, ed. John Middleton Murry (London: Constable, 1930).

Mansfield, Katherine, *Poems by Katherine Mansfield*, ed. John Middleton Murry (London: Constable, 1930).

Mansfield, Katherine, *Journal of Katherine Mansfield: Definitive Edition*, ed. John Middleton Murry (London: Constable, 1954).

Mansfield, Katherine, *The Collected Letters of Katherine Mansfield, Volume I: 1903–1917*, ed. Vincent O'Sullivan and Margaret Scott (Oxford: Clarendon Press, 1984).

Mansfield, Katherine, *The Collected Letters of Katherine Mansfield, Volume II: 1918–1919*, ed. Vincent O'Sullivan and Margaret Scott (Oxford: Clarendon Press, 1987).

Mansfield, Katherine, *The Collected Letters of Katherine Mansfield, Volume III: 1919–1920*, ed. Vincent O'Sullivan and Margaret Scott (Oxford: Clarendon Press, 1993).

Mansfield, Katherine, *The Collected Letters of Katherine Mansfield, Volume IV: 1920–1921*, ed. Vincent O'Sullivan and Margaret Scott (Oxford: Clarendon Press, 1996).

Mansfield, Katherine, *The Katherine Mansfield Notebooks, Complete Edition*, 2 vols, ed. Margaret Scott (Minneapolis: University of Minnesota Press, 2002).

Mansfield, Katherine, *The Collected Letters of Katherine Mansfield, Volume V: 1922–1923*, ed. Vincent O'Sullivan and Margaret Scott (Oxford: Clarendon Press, 2008).

Mansfield, Katherine, *The Collected Fiction of Katherine Mansfield, 1898–1915*, ed. Gerri Kimber and Vincent O'Sullivan (Edinburgh: Edinburgh University Press, 2012).

Mansfield, Katherine, *The Collected Fiction of Katherine Mansfield, 1916–1922*, ed. Gerri Kimber and Vincent O'Sullivan (Edinburgh: Edinburgh University Press, 2012).

Mansfield, Katherine, *The Poetry and Critical Writings of Katherine Mansfield*, ed. Gerri Kimber and Angela Smith (Edinburgh: Edinburgh University Press, 2014).

Mantz, Ruth, 'Fifty Years After', *Adam International Review*, 370 (1973), pp. 117–27.

Mao, Douglas and Rebecca L. Walkowitz, 'The New Modernist Studies', *PMLA*, 123.3 (May 2008), pp. 737–48.

Marchand, Leslie A., *The Athenaeum: A Mirror of Victorian Culture* (Chapel Hill: University of North Carolina Press, 1940).

Marek, Jayne E., *Women Editing Modernism: 'Little' Magazines and Literary History* (Kentucky: University Press of Kentucky, 1995).

Martin, Todd, 'Constructing Jealousy, Exacting Revenge: Katherine Mansfield's "Poison" and Robert Browning's "My Last Duchess"', in *Re-forming World Literature: Katherine Mansfield and the Modernist Short Story*, ed. Gerri Kimber and Janet Wilson (Stuttgart: Ibidem Press, 2018), pp. 185–208.

Matz, Jesse, *Literary Impressionism and Modernist Aesthetics* (Cambridge: Cambridge University Press, 2001).

McClintock, Anne, *Imperial Leather: Race, Gender and Sexuality in the Colonial Contest* (New York: Routledge, 1995).

McDonnell, Jenny, '"Wanted, a New Word": Katherine Mansfield and the *Athenaeum*', *Modernism/Modernity*, 16.4 (November 2009), pp. 727–42.

McDonnell, Jenny, *Katherine Mansfield and the Modernist Marketplace: At the Mercy of the Public* (Basingstoke: Palgrave Macmillan, 2010).

McGann, Jerome, *The Textual Condition* (Princeton: Princeton University Press, 1991).

McKible, Adam, *The Space and Place of Modernism: The Russian Revolution, Little Magazines, and New York* (London: Routledge, 2002).

McNeil, Helen, 'Vortex Marsden: A Little Magazine and the Making of Modernity', in Kate Campbell (ed.), *Journalism, Literature and Modernity: From Hazlitt to Modernism* (Edinburgh: Edinburgh University Press, 2000), pp. 141–69.

McNeillie, Andrew, 'Bloomsbury', in Susan Sellers (ed.), *The Cambridge Companion to Virginia Woolf*, 2nd edn (Cambridge: Cambridge University Press, 2010), pp. 1–28.

Meyers, Jeffrey, 'Katherine Mansfield's "To Stanislaw Wyspianski"', *Modern Fiction Studies*, 24.3 (autumn 1978), pp. 337–40.

Meyers, Jeffrey, 'Murry's Cult of Mansfield', *Journal of Modern Literature*, 7.1 (February 1979), pp. 15–38.

Meyers, Jeffrey, *Katherine Mansfield: A Darker View* (New York: Cooper Square Press, 2002).

Meyers, Jeffrey, *Modigliani: A Life* (London: Duckworth Overlook, 2008).

Mikoś, Michael J., *Polish Literature from 1864 to 1918: Realism and Young Poland* (Bloomington: Slavica, 2006).

Milburn, Diane, *The Deutschlandbild of A. R. Orage and the New Age Circle* (Frankfurt: Peter Lang, 1996).

Mills, Carol, *The Native Companion: Complete Indexes to Text, Illustrators, Book Notices and Subjects and Brief Bibliographies and an Introduction* (Canberra: Mulini Press, 1999).

Moretti, Franco, *The Way of the World: The Bildungsroman in European Culture* (London: Verso, 1987).

Morrisson, Mark S., *The Public Face of Modernism: Little Magazines, Audiences and Reception, 1905–1920* (Madison: University of Wisconsin Press, 2001).

Mourant, Chris, '"A Little Episode": The Forgotten Typescripts of Katherine Mansfield, 1908–11', in Janet Wilson, Gerri Kimber and Delia da Sousa Correa (eds), *Katherine Mansfield and the (Post)colonial* (Edinburgh: Edinburgh University Press, 2013), pp. 154–66.

Murry, John Middleton, *Fyodor Dostoevsky: A Critical Study* (London: Martin Secker, 1916).

Murry, John Middleton, *The Evolution of an Intellectual* (London: Cobden-Sanderson, 1920).

Murry, John Middleton, *The Problem of Style* (London: Oxford University Press, 1922).

Murry, John Middleton, *God: Being an Introduction to the Science of Metabiology* (London: Cape, 1929).

Murry, John Middleton, *Between Two Worlds: An Autobiography* (London: Jonathan Cape, 1935).

Murry, John Middleton, 'Coming to London', in John Lehmann (ed.), *Coming to London* (London: Phoenix House, 1957), pp. 105–6.

Murry, John Middleton, *The Letters of John Middleton Murry to Katherine Mansfield*, ed. Cherry A. Hankin (London: Constable, 1983).

Nash, Catherine, 'Remapping the Body/Land: Cartographies of Identity, Gender, and Landscape in Ireland', in Alison Blunt and Gillian Rose (eds), *Writing Women and Space: Colonial and Postcolonial Geographies* (New York: Guildford Press, 1994), pp. 227–50.

Nathanson, Carol A., 'Anne Estelle Rice: Theodore Dreiser's "Ellen Adams Wrynn"', *Women's Art Journal*, 13.2 (autumn 1992/winter 1993), pp. 3–11.

Nathanson, Carol A., *The Expressive Fauvism of Anne Estelle Rice* (New York: Hollis Taggert Galleries, 1997).

Nietzsche, Friedrich, *Aphorisms on Love and Hate*, trans. Marion Faber and Stephen Lehmann ([1878] London: Penguin, 2015).

Orage, A. R., *Friedrich Nietzsche, the Dionysian Spirit of the Age* (Edinburgh: T. N. Foulis, 1906).

Orage, A. R., *Nietzsche in Outline and Aphorism* (Edinburgh: T. N. Foulis, 1907).

O'Sullivan, Vincent and Margaret Scott, 'Introduction', in Katherine Mansfield, *The Collected Letters of Katherine Mansfield, Volume I: 1903–1917*, ed. Vincent O'Sullivan and Margaret Scott (Oxford: Clarendon Press, 1984), pp. vii–xvii.

Peppis, Paul, *Literature, Politics, and the English Avant-Garde: Nation and Empire, 1901–1918* (Cambridge: Cambridge University Press, 2000).

Potter, Simon J., *News and the British World: The Emergence of an Imperial Press System* (Oxford: Oxford University Press, 2003).

Powell, Manushag N., 'We Other Periodicalists, or, Why Periodical Studies?', *Tulsa Studies in Women's Literature*, 30.2 (fall 2011), pp. 441–50.

Rainey, Lawrence, *Institutions of Modernism: Literary Elites and Public Culture* (New Haven: Yale University Press, 1999).

Rice, Anne Estelle, 'Memories of Katherine Mansfield', *Adam International Review*, 300 (1965), pp. 76–85.

Rogers, Gayle, *Modernism and the New Spain: Britain, Cosmopolitan Europe, and Literary History* (Oxford: Oxford University Press, 2012).

Rose, Gillian, *Feminism and Geography: The Limits of Geographical Knowledge* (Minneapolis: University of Minneapolis Press, 1993).

Said, Edward, *Beginnings: Intention and Method* (New York: Columbia University Press, 1975).

Scholes, Robert, 'Model Artists in Paris', in *Paradoxy of Modernism* (New Haven: Yale University Press, 2006), pp. 221–56.

Scott, Bonnie Kime (ed.), *Gender in Modernism: New Geographies, Complex Intersections* (Urbana: University of Illinois Press, 2007).

Sellers, Susan (ed.), *The Cambridge Companion to Virginia Woolf*, 2nd edn (Cambridge: Cambridge University Press, 2010).

Selver, Paul (ed.), *An Anthology of Modern Bohemian Poetry* (London: Henry J. Drane, 1912).

Seshagiri, Urmila, *Race and the Modernist Imagination* (Ithaca: Cornell University Press, 2010).

Shattock, Joanne and Michael Wolff (eds), *The Victorian Periodical Press: Samplings and Soundings* (Leicester: Leicester University Press, 1982).

Sinnema, Peter, *Dynamics of the Pictured Page: Representing the Nation in the* Illustrated London News (Aldershot: Ashgate, 1998).

Smith, Angela, *Katherine Mansfield: A Literary Life* (Basingstoke: Palgrave, 2000).

Smith, Angela, 'Fauvism and Cultural Nationalism', *Interventions: International Journal of Postcolonial Studies*, 4.1 (June 2002), pp. 35–52.

Smith, Angela, 'Katherine Mansfield and *Rhythm*', *Journal of New Zealand Literature*, 21 (2003), pp. 102–21.

Smith, Angela, 'GUTS – Katherine Mansfield as a Reviewer', *Katherine Mansfield Studies*, 1 (2009), pp. 3–18.

Smith, Angela, 'J. D. Fergusson's Painting *Rhythm*', *Katherine Mansfield Studies*, 2 (2010), pp. 184–7.

Smith, Angela, '"As fastidious as though I wrote with acid": Katherine Mansfield, J. D. Fergusson and the *Rhythm* Group in Paris', *Katherine Mansfield Studies*, 3 (2011), pp. 4–20.

Snaith, Anna, *Modernist Voyages: Colonial Women Writers in London, 1890–1945* (Cambridge: Cambridge University Press, 2014).

Snyder, Carey, 'Katherine Mansfield and the *New Age* School of Satire', *Journal of Modern Periodical Studies*, 1.2 (2010), pp. 125–58.

Snyder, Carey, 'Katherine Mansfield, *Rhythm*, and Metropolitan Primitivism', *Journal of Modern Periodical Studies*, 5.2 (2014), pp. 139–60.

Stafford, Jane and Mark Williams, 'Katherine Mansfield: A Modernist in Maoriland', in *Maoriland: New Zealand Literature 1872–1914* (Wellington: Victoria University Press, 2007), pp. 142–70.

Stern, J. P., *Lichtenberg: A Doctrine of Shattered Occasions* (Bloomington: Indiana University Press, 1959).

Stone, Jean E., *Katherine Mansfield: Publications in Australia, 1907–09* (Sydney: Wentworth Books, 1977).

Tearle, Oliver, *T. E. Hulme and Modernism* (London: Bloomsbury, 2013).

Thacker, Andrew, 'Modern Tastes in *Rhythm*: The Visual and Verbal Culture of Advertisements in Modernist Magazines', *Katherine Mansfield Studies*, 2 (2010), pp. 4–19.

Thatcher, David, *Nietzsche in England, 1890–1914: The Growth of a Reputation* (Toronto: University of Toronto Press, 1970).

Tina, Beatrice [Beatrice Hastings], *Woman's Worst Enemy: Woman* (London: New Age Press, 1909).

Tomalin, Claire, *Katherine Mansfield: A Secret Life* (London: Viking, 1987).

Wellens, Oscar, '"The Brief and Brilliant Life of *The Athenaeum* under Mr Middleton Murry" (T. S. Eliot)', *Neophilologus*, 85 (2001), pp. 137–52.

Wevers, Lydia, 'The Short Story' in Terry Sturm (ed.), *The Oxford History of New Zealand Literature in English* (Oxford: Oxford University Press, 1991), pp. 245–320.

White, Eric B., *Transatlantic Avant-Gardes: Little Magazines and Localist Modernism* (Edinburgh: Edinburgh University Press, 2013).

Whitworth, Michael H., 'Enemies of Cant: *The Athenaeum* (1919–21) and *The Adelphi* (1923–48)', in Peter Brooker and Andrew Thacker (eds), *The Oxford Critical and Cultural History of Modernist Magazines, Volume I: Britain and Ireland, 1880–1955* (Oxford: Oxford University Press, 2009), pp. 364–88.

Williams, Mark, 'Mansfield in Maoriland: Biculturalism, Agency and Misreading', in Howard J. Booth and Nigel Rigby (eds), *Modernism and Empire* (Manchester: Manchester University Press, 2000), pp. 249–74.

Wilson, Janet, '"Where is Katherine?" Longing and (Un)belonging in the Works of Katherine Mansfield', in Gerri Kimber and Janet Wilson (eds), *Celebrating Katherine Mansfield* (Basingstoke: Palgrave Macmillan, 2011), pp. 175–88.

Wilson, Janet, 'Mansfield as (Post)colonial-Modernist: Rewriting the Contract with Death', in Janet Wilson, Gerri Kimber and Delia da Sousa Correa (eds), *Katherine Mansfield and the (Post)colonial* (Edinburgh: Edinburgh University Press, 2013), pp. 29–44.

Wilson, Janet, Gerri Kimber and Delia da Sousa Correa (eds), *Katherine Mansfield and the (Post)colonial* (Edinburgh: Edinburgh University Press, 2013).

Woods, Joanna, *Katerina: The Russian World of Katherine Mansfield* (Auckland: Penguin, 2001).

Woolf, Virginia, *The Letters of Virginia Woolf, Volume II*, ed. Nigel Nicolson (London: Hogarth Press, 1976).

Woolf, Virginia, *The Letters of Virginia Woolf, Volume III*, ed. Nigel Nicolson (London: Hogarth Press, 1977).

Woolf, Virginia, *The Diary of Virginia Woolf, Volume I*, ed. Anne Olivier Bell (London: Hogarth Press, 1977).

Woolf, Virginia, *The Diary of Virginia Woolf, Volume II*, ed. Anne Olivier Bell (Harmondsworth: Penguin, 1981).

Woolf, Virginia, *The Essays of Virginia Woolf, Volume I: 1904–1912*, ed. Andrew McNeillie (London: Hogarth Press, 1986).

Woolf, Virginia, *The Essays of Virginia Woolf, Volume III, 1919–1924*, ed. Andrew McNeillie (London: Hogarth Press, 1988).

Woolf, Virginia, *Moments of Being: Autobiographical Writings*, ed. Jeanne Schulkind (London: Pimlico, 2002).

Woolf, Virginia, *The Years* ([1937] London: Vintage, 2004).

Young, Iris Marion, 'The Scaling of Bodies and the Politics of Identity', in Linda McDowell and Joanne Sharp (eds), *Space, Gender, Knowledge: Feminist Readings* (London: Arnold, 1997), pp. 218–31.

Youngs, Tim (ed.), *The Cambridge Introduction to Travel Writing* (Cambridge: Cambridge University Press, 2013).

Yska, Redmer, *A Strange Beautiful Excitement: Katherine Mansfield's Wellington, 1888–1903* (Dunedin: Otago University Press, 2017).

Index

CPSIA information can be obtained
at www.ICGtesting.com
Printed in the USA
JSHW030346041120
9291JS00002B/39

9 781474 439466